DAILY LIFE DURING

THE
HOLOCAUST

Recent Titles in
The Greenwood Press "Daily Life Through History" Series

The New Testament
James W. Ermatinger

The Hellenistic Age: From Alexander to Cleopatra
James Allan Evans

Imperial Russia
Greta Bucher

The Greenwood Encyclopedia of Daily Life in America, Four Volumes
Randall M. Miller, general editor

Civilians in Wartime Twentieth-Century Europe
Nicholas Atkin, editor

Ancient Egyptians, Second Edition
Bob Brier and Hoyt Hobbs

Civilians in Wartime Latin America: From the Wars of Independence
to the Central American Civil Wars
Pedro Santoni, editor

Science and Technology in Modern European Life
Guillaume de Syon

Cooking in Europe, 1650–1850
Ivan P. Day

Victorian England, Second Edition
Sally Mitchell

The Ancient Greeks, Second Edition
Robert Garland

Chaucer's England, Second Edition
Jeffrey L. Forgeng and Will McLean

DAILY LIFE DURING

THE
HOLOCAUST

Second Edition

EVE NUSSBAUM SOUMERAI
AND CAROL D. SCHULZ

The Greenwood Press "Daily Life Through History" Series

GREENWOOD PRESS
Westport, Connecticut • London

Library of Congress Cataloging-in-Publication Data

Soumerai, Eve Nussbaum.
  Daily life during the Holocaust / Eve Nussbaum
Soumerai and Carol D. Schulz. — 2nd ed.
      p. cm. — (The Greenwood Press Daily life through history series,
ISSN 1080–4749)
   Includes bibliographical references and index.
   ISBN 978–0–313–35308–6 (alk. paper)
   1. Jews—Persecutions—Europe—History—20th century.   2. Holocaust,
Jewish (1939–1945)—Personal narratives.   I. Schulz, Carol D., 1948–   II. Title.
   D804.195.S68   2009
   940.53'18092—dc22   2008056017

British Library Cataloguing in Publication Data is available.

Library of Congress Catalog Card Number: 2008056017
ISBN: 978–0–313–35308–6
ISSN: 1080–4749

First published in 2009

Greenwood Press, 88 Post Road West, Westport, CT 06881
An imprint of Greenwood Publishing Group, Inc.
www.greenwood.com

Printed in the United States of America

The paper used in this book complies with the
Permanent Paper Standard issued by the National
Information Standards Organization (Z39.48–1984).

10 9 8 7 6 5 4 3 2 1

*To my father Berthold Nussbaum,
my mother Frieda Nussbaum,
and my brother Norbert Nussbaum*

Frieda (1899–1945) and Berthold (1889–?) Nussbaum, summer of 1934, last holiday in Swiendemünde, on the Baltic Sea in Germany.

Last photo of Norbert Nussbaum (1927–1945), taken in April 1939 in Berlin.

CONTENTS

PREFACE TO THE SECOND EDITION

It is now the twenty-first century. You can conduct a search on the Internet for "child soldier," "modern day slavery," "recent news of genocide," and within seconds find dozens of Web sites to click on. Many of you will be surprised, even shocked. At the end of World War II, the discovery of the scope of the inhumanity of the Holocaust gave birth to the refrain "never again." But in many cases this outrage has been short lived. Some deny that the Holocaust ever occurred. Others refuse to recognize that new atrocities continue daily.

Throughout the second half of the twentieth century and into the twenty-first, slavery, torture, and genocide have continued, in most cases with little effective intervention from anyone. In some countries, such as Sudan, the behavior of the perpetrators is much like that of the Nazis: national armies, intelligence agencies, and government leaders directly participate in attacks on innocent people. In other nations, involuntary servitude has continued without interference, for centuries, hidden within a violent, abusive subculture, where the buying and selling of people isn't even outlawed. Like the Final Solution, committing genocide has become a way of life for some, and seeking refuge in foreign lands an imperative for others.

Thus, for the second edition of *Daily Life During the Holocaust,* we add our voices to the small but growing outcry against these abuses. The newest chapters include anecdotal accounts about real victims of post-Holocaust atrocities, many reported in their own words. If we expect others to help them, we need to make our readers aware of what is happening.

We also detail the means by which these events are carried out, and cite examples of individual efforts to give aid and comfort. Ironically, the growth of the global economy, with its high-tech communication and transportation systems, rather than improving the lives of those most vulnerable, has made their exploitation easier than ever. But technology can be used for good as well as evil. It has enabled us to learn more about our global village and to pass that knowledge on. We hope that the inclusion of a list of human rights organizations and Web sites will inspire readers to get involved.

Lastly, for those of you who work with young people, we have added an appendix with ideas for projects that can unite communities, inspire students, and increase their desire to help others. In his book *Teacher and Child*, the famed child psychologist Haim Ginott, himself a survivor, shares his thoughts about the Holocaust with teachers. He tells them that education is not enough.

> My eyes saw what no man should witness:
> Gas chambers built by LEARNED engineers
> Children poisoned by EDUCATED physicians
> Infants killed by TRAINED nurses
> Women and babies shot and burned by HIGH SCHOOL and COLLEGE
>   graduates.
> So I am suspicious of education.
> My request is: Help your students become human. Your efforts must never
>   produce learned monsters, skilled psychopaths, educated Eichmanns.
> Reading, writing, and arithmetic are important only if they serve to make
>   our children more humane. (317)

We concur wholeheartedly.

The Authors

PREFACE

Daily Life During the Holocaust recalls a period unlike any other in history. Mass murder, torture, and incredible suffering have occurred throughout history but never before has an entire state apparatus carefully planned, enthusiastically endorsed, and willingly participated in the deaths of millions of Jews and others deemed unworthy of life.

In 1942, to commemorate this feat for posterity, Adolf Hitler ordered the creation of a Central Jewish Museum in Prague to display thousands of Jewish artifacts—Torah scrolls, Kiddush cups, violins, pianos, wedding rings—of the soon-to-be "Extinct Race." Jewish curators, wearing their yellow stars of David, worked day and night to sort and label the items arriving daily from occupied lands even as they themselves were being regularly dispatched to their deaths in the concentration camps.

Had the museum opened, the exhibition would have included the scrapbook of one Walter Bernhard, an SS (*Schutzstaffel*) officer, titled "Memories from Auschwitz." The scrapbook contained 260 photographs, documenting in meticulous detail the process by which countless numbers of innocent men, women, and children were put to death.

Detailed consideration has been given to Adolf Hitler and the National Socialist Party's rise to power, demonstrating the horrifying consequences of a government with no checks and balances. In total control of every aspect of life, the Nazi government operated with terror, brutality, and violence, making it both feared and respected by the German people.

To portray this dark world, we turned to the journals, diaries, photos, poetry, and personal testimonies of those who survived and those who did not, along with the documents of the unrelenting officials in charge of this process of annihilation.

The accounts of the day-to-day life of the victims, victimizers, and bystanders enable the reader to become an eyewitness to the Holocaust and to begin to understand what really happened, not only in terms of geography, dates, and statistics, but in authentic human terms as well.

In addition to the victims, victimizers, and bystanders, there were the rescuers. They were few in number, but accounts of their refusal to hurt others or look the other way amaze us. Their willingness to risk their lives to save their fellow human beings fills us with awe. We learn that goodness does exist and has many faces.

It leaves us with the questions of where we fit in this fragile universe and what we are prepared to risk for others.

ACKNOWLEDGMENTS

The authors wish to thank the following survivors who provided authentic details of the events they witnessed: Nettie Allweiss, Ivan A. Backer, Dr. Leon Chameides, Rena Ferber Finder, Berthold Gaster, Ernest Gelb, Henry Klein, Joseph Korzenik, Rabbi Philip Lazowski, Lorelei Lewis, Hannah S., Fred S., Mrs. Arthur Seaman, Bernice Sobotka, Mark Sobotka, Robert Wagemann, and Yakov.

We also wish to thank Dr. Jochen Heller, who in Munich in 1946 volunteered his schoolboy copy of *Für Meinen Lebensweg* "so that children may learn from our [Germany's] experiences"; Emily M. Birch, our patient editor, whose sincere support and encouragement enabled us to write this book; and Leslie Swift, of the U.S. Holocaust Memorial Museum's Photo Archives, who was always at the other end of the phone to accommodate our many and diverse requests.

And, last but not least, we thank the many individuals whose efforts supplied us with much of our information. In writing this book, we feel we have become members of a community dedicated to making this world a kinder and more understanding place.

COAUTHOR'S NOTE

Nearly thirty years ago, I read William Styron's novel *Sophie's Choice,* a heart-rending tale about a young, Catholic mother forced to endure torture and humiliation at Auschwitz. Sophie's story, which remained in my thoughts for weeks, generated many questions: What did husbands say to their wives the night before they were to report for deportation? How did children watch their mothers die? What did mothers say to their children on the journey to the concentration camps? Who made the decision to charge passengers so much per ticket, half price for children, with a special rate for groups? Did they sit around a table drinking coffee and eating refreshments while they argued over costs plus profits? Did anyone care that they were talking about transporting people to their deaths?

In my search for answers, I went to those who, like the fictitious Sophie, had lived in Europe during those dreadful years from 1933 to 1945. The first person I met was Eve Nussbaum Soumerai, whose life was spared when her courageous, loving father and mother found the strength of will to send their little girl to safety, far from home, knowing they might never see her again.

Working with Eve, now a grandmother as spunky and as brave as she was when she crossed the English Channel at the age of twelve, has enriched my life immeasurably. Through the pages of this book, you will meet her and dozens of other eyewitnesses to those terrible years. From their stories, and from the memos, reports, journals, diaries, news articles, and testimonies included in this book, you will discover the consequences of the countless decisions made by millions of individuals, Jews and Christians, Nazis and resistance fighters, collaborators and rescuers. Woven together, their actions made history. For example:

- Without volunteers to serve in the SS, there might have been no deportations to concentration camps.
- Without pesticide companies who chose to sell Zyklon B to the government, there might have been no gas chambers.
- Without men like Oscar Schindler, who chose to risk their lives for others, there might have been no survivors.
- Without courageous ghetto dwellers, who continued to record events despite the prohibition against doing so, we might never have learned what became of the Jews.

In the grand scope of things, it is easy to overlook the importance of these choices. Yet, in reality, this is how history happens. More than anything else, this is the message of the Holocaust. Individual people do matter, and their choices, for good or for evil, determine the course of the future.

Carol D. Schulz

PROLOGUE

Some memories stay with you for a lifetime.

The way Adolf Hitler, the new chancellor, shouted *"Juden"* from our Blaupunkt radio in the middle of our living room and made everybody nervous. It was early spring 1933, and we were living in Berlin. I was seven years old and attended the Bochumerstrasse Elementary School, on the other side of the river Spree. I remember skipping to school sucking one of Oma's (grandmother's) fruit bonbons, clutching the straps of my school backpack and making one of my wish-resolutions: I'd invite Herr Hitler over to our house for supper. I even planned the menu, my mother's favorite, a slow-simmering pot roast with dumplings and red cabbage. Everybody loved it and so would Hitler. And then he would see that *Juden* were all right—just like other people. Thinking was equal to doing, and I felt very proud that particular day.

This mood didn't last. I lost my best friend. My father lost his job. Things got worse and worse. Wish-resolutions turned into prayers, but they didn't seem to work either.

The very worst occurred on November 9, 1938. We were dismissed early from our Jewish school in the Grunewald and told to rush home. Strange things were happening. I noticed, while looking out of the window of the train taking us home, that the fancy Fassanenstrasse synagogue was burning. Flames and smoke were shooting into the sky, and nobody seemed to be doing anything. Police and firemen just stood there—watching. I was twelve years old and felt some of that familiar icy fear welling up inside of me. I had to do something to calm myself.

I opened the poetry book laying on my lap, took a pencil out of my school bag, and wrote on the first page, *Tante Lilo's synagogue brennt und die Leute stehen einfach herum. Warum lieber Gott, warum?* (Aunt Lilo's synagogue is burning and people just stand there. Why dear God, why?) One of Goethe's lines, *Edel sei der Mensch hilfreich und gut* (Man should be noble, helpful and good), happened to grace that page.

Goethe was my mother's favorite poet. When she was sad, which was more and more often, she recited lines from one of his poems that she had learned as a child:

> Calm is over the hills
> In the tree tops
> You can hardly feel a breeze
> The birds are hushed in the woods
> Just wait, you too will have peace

And then she would add her own words:

> Peace, *lieber Gott* [dear Lord], peace.

My father, my best friend, reminded me regularly to do happy things, no matter how difficult and sad the circumstances might be, while Opa (grandfather), the proud German and guardian of our Jewish heritage, was fond of telling us bits and pieces of ancient wisdom necessary to live the good life. One of his favorites was "Life is like a scale, on one side are the good deeds, on the other the bad ones which include the don't care attitudes, and what you *mein Kind* [my child] do—tilts the scale one way or the other."

These then were my gifts—my inheritance.

Eve Nussbaum Soumerai

TIMELINE

1933

January 30   Adolf Hitler becomes chancellor of Germany.

February 27   Terror begins. The Reichstag (Germany's parliament) is set on fire, and the Communists are blamed.

March 20   Dachau, the first concentration camp, is established.

March 27   The Enabling Act suspends individual civil liberties and freedom of the press, speech, and assembly, giving Hitler absolute power.

April 1–21   Official persecution of the Jews begins. Jewish shops and businesses are boycotted. The first anti-Jewish decree barring Jews from entering the civil service and from obeying religious dietary laws is passed.

May 10   Books, including those by Jewish authors and others holding democratic ideas and ideals, are burned in bonfires throughout Germany. Jewish professors are expelled from universities.

Fall   Jews are barred from practicing their professions, including doctors, dentists, artists, and musicians.

Winter   Hitler usurps all remaining power and holds total control.

1934

June 30–July 1   Blood purge of the SA (*Sturmabteilung,* or "Brownshirts") and other so-called undesirables occurs.

August 2   President Paul von Hindenburg dies. Title of president is abolished. Hitler becomes Reich chancellor and the fuehrer of Germany.

1935

September 15   Nuremberg Race Laws, announced at the annual Nazi Party rally, deprive Jews of citizenship and forbid marriage between Jews and non-Jews.

1936

July 12   First German Rom (Gypsies) are arrested and deported to Dachau concentration camp.

Summer   Olympic Games take place in Berlin. Anti-Jewish signs are removed and anti-Jewish activities are temporarily halted.

1937

July 16   Buchenwald concentration camp opens.

1938

March 13   *Anschluss:* Austria is annexed by Germany; all German anti-Semitic decrees immediately apply in Austria.

July 6–15   Representatives from thirty-two countries convene at Evian, France, to discuss refugee policies. Most of the representatives go to great lengths to explain their country's inability to help the Jews.

August 1   Adolf Eichmann sets up his office in Vienna.

October 28   Thousands of Polish Jews living in Germany are expelled to a no-man's-land between Germany and Poland.

November 9–10   On Kristallnacht ("night of the broken glass"), synagogues are burned throughout Germany and Austria. Jewish businesses are destroyed, and thousands of Jews are arrested and sent to concentration camps.

November 12   All Jewish retail businesses must be transferred to Aryan owners.

December 2–3   All Gypsies must register with the German police.

1939

January 30	Hitler's address to the Reichstag states that if Jewry plots another world war, European Jews will be exterminated.
March 15	German troops invade Czechoslovakia.
May–June	Ship St. Louis, carrying 936 Jewish passengers, is forced to return to Europe; neither Cuba nor the United States will permit entry, even though each passenger has a landing permit for Cuba and visas to the United States.
September 1	Germany invades Poland.
September 3	World War II begins.
September 6	Adam Czerniakow begins to keep his diary in Warsaw.
September 27	Reinhard Heydrich establishes Jewish councils (Judenräte) in German-occupied Poland. Adam Czerniakow becomes president of the Judenrat of the Warsaw ghetto.
October	Hitler personally extends the euthanasia program to include Jews (and backdates his decision to September 1, so that it appears to be a wartime measure).

1940

April	French Foreign Legion is sent to labor camps in North Africa.
April 9	Germany invades and occupies Denmark and southern Norway.
May 7	Lodz ghetto is sealed: approximately 165,000 inhabitants are forced to live in 1.6 square miles.
May 10	Germany invades Holland, Belgium, and France.
May 20	Concentration camp is established at Auschwitz.
June 22	France surrenders to Germany.
August 8	Air war against Britain begins.
October 12	Warsaw ghetto is established.
November 16	Warsaw ghetto is sealed: almost 500,000 persons, or thirty percent of the city's total population, are crammed within its walls. Some 5,000 Austrian Jews are deported from Vienna to Poland to the Kiecle and Lublin ghettos.

1941

January–March	Jews are expelled from the countryside outside Warsaw. Thousands of skilled workers from Upper Silesia in Poland

	are rounded up and sent to Germany to work in mines, in metallurgy factories, and in textile plants.
April 6	Yugoslavia and Greece are invaded; 145,000 Jews are taken to concentration camps; 3,000 Yugoslavian Jews are shot.
May 5	Some 1,000 foreign-born Jews in Paris are arrested.
June 22	German troops invade the Soviet Union. The Einsatzgruppen (mobile killing squads) begin their mass murder of Jews, Gypsies, and Polish leaders in occupied areas of the Soviet Union.
September 23	Nazis test gas chambers at Auschwitz. Victims include Polish and Soviet prisoners of war.
September 28–29	Almost 34,000 Jews are murdered by the Einsatzgruppen at Babi Yar in the Ukraine.
October 31	More than thirty Jewish communities in Yugoslavia are exterminated.
October– November	The first groups of German and Austrian Jews are deported to the ghettos in the east. (By March 1942 most of the Jews in Berlin have been rounded up—street by street—and deported to the east, including Eve Soumerai's entire family.)
November	Chelmno, the first death camp, is built in occupied Poland. Belgium's Jews are sent to Warsaw.
December 3	Jews still remaining in Germany are told to establish special "W" accounts to finance the transports to the death camps.
December 7	Japan attacks Pearl Harbor.
December 8	Full operations, including gassing, begin at the Chelmno extermination camp.
December 11	Germany declares war on the United States.
1942	
January–July	Jewish resistance groups organize in the Vilna, Kovno, and Warsaw ghettos.
January 20	Wannsee Conference: Heydrich invites high-level Nazi functionaries to lunch to discuss the "Final Solution" and to acquaint them with programs already in operation in the Soviet Union and at Chelmno.
March 1	Gas exterminations begin at Sobibor in eastern Poland; by October 1943, 250,000 have been murdered.

April 1942– **June 1943**	Some 434,000 Jews from Galicia, in Poland, are sent to their deaths.
Summer–Winter	Deportations are carried out from Holland, Poland, France, Belgium, Norway, Germany, and Greece. A Jewish partisan movement organizes in the forests near Lublin, Poland.
July 16–17	There are 4,051 Parisian children seized and sent to Auschwitz.
July 22	Treblinka death camp in Poland begins operations. Irmfried Eberl, a doctor whose training began in the euthanasia program, becomes commandant of the killing center. (Approximately 300,000 Jews from the Warsaw ghetto alone are transported to Treblinka during a six-week period that summer.)
July 22– September 1942	Deportations begin from the Warsaw ghetto; most of the 250,000 who travel in freight cars are sent to Treblinka.
July 23	Adam Czerniakow cannot cope with the unfolding tragedy and commits suicide in the Warsaw ghetto. His last words, in the ninth book of his diary: "The SS want me to kill children with my own hands."
July 28	Jewish Combat Organization formed in the Warsaw ghetto.
July–October	Jan Karski visits ghettos and meets with Jewish leaders, then relates his findings to the Allies.
August	One hundred factories open in Lodz. The Jews hope their usefulness will keep them alive.
November 26	Norway's Jews are shipped to Auschwitz; 900 evade roundup and flee to safety in Sweden.
1943	
January 18	Mass deportations of Jews in the Warsaw ghetto resume.
February 2	Germans surrender at Stalingrad.
Spring	Inmates in Auschwitz-Birkenau are forced to build four crematoriums; 46,000 victims from Salonika, Greece, arrive.
April 19– Early June	German attempt to liquidate 70,000 Warsaw ghetto inhabitants meets full-scale resistance.
May 15–June 15	There are 434,351 Hungarian Jews on 147 trains taken to Auschwitz; 400,000 are gassed.
June	Heinrich Himmler orders the liquidation of all ghettos

August 2	Inmates revolt at Treblinka.
October	Ninety percent of the Jews in Denmark escape to Sweden on fishing boats.
October 14	Armed revolt takes place at Sobibor.

1944

January	U.S. government creates the War Refugee Board and seeks international help to protect Hungarian Jews. Raoul Wallenberg, a Swede, is chosen to lead the effort.
March 19–May 15	Germany occupies Hungary. The Red Army repels German forces.
May 16	Allies refuse a German offer to free 1 million Jews in exchange for ten thousand trucks.
June 6	Allied invasion of Normandy begins.
July 9	Raoul Wallenberg arrives in Budapest.
July 20	German officers' attempt to assassinate Hitler fails.
July 24	Russians liberate Majdanek (Poland) extermination camp.
August 2	Germans destroy the Gypsy camp at Auschwitz; approximately 3,000 are gassed.
November	Last Jews are deported from Theresienstadt, a work camp, to Auschwitz.

1945

January 16	Russians bomb Auschwitz.
January 19	Auschwitz is evacuated and forced death marches begin.
January 27	Soviet troops enter Auschwitz.
April	Americans liberate Buchenwald, Dachau, and other concentration camps.
April 12	British troops enter Bergen-Belsen, near Hamburg.
April 30	Hitler commits suicide in his bunker in Berlin.
May 5	Americans liberate Mauthausen, near Linz, Austria.
May 7	Germany surrenders: the one-thousand-year Reich ends.
August 5	Japan surrenders, ending World War II.
November 20	War crimes trials begin in Nuremberg, Germany, and end on October 6, 1946.

1

MAN'S INHUMANITY TO MAN: A SHORT HISTORICAL BACKGROUND

The Scottish poet Robert Burns (1759–1796), who was passionate about freedom and respect for humankind, wrote, "Man's Inhumanity to Man, makes countless thousands mourn" ("Man Was Made to Mourn," Stanza 7, 1786). Throughout history, countless thousands continue to mourn as a result of pain, torture, and loss of life inflicted upon them or those near and dear to them—innocent men, women, and children. In spite of the teachings of Moses, Jesus, Buddha, and Mohammed, perpetrators and victims of pain and suffering have been found among all peoples, all nations, all religions, and all races. Yet, we must also note the poets, journalists, statesmen, and ordinary people, who, in many voices and often at great risk to themselves, elect to speak out against the inhumanity they see, in the hope that in time parents might raise their children in peace.

Time has not been on the side of progress toward humanity. The twentieth century has witnessed unparalleled progress in science and technology and the glorification of human freedom and equality; it also gave birth to the Holocaust—an event of unspeakable atrocities and death—aided by those very achievements of science and technology designed to improve life. In order to gain some perspective and understanding of the enormity of this event, some of the earlier examples of man's inhumanity, which have occurred throughout the ages, will be examined.

ANCIENT GREECE

As early as the fifth century B.C., the banished Greek historian Thucydides, forced to spend twenty years in exile, wrote *A History of the Peloponnesian*

War (431–404 B.C.), a war he experienced firsthand. He lamented the devastation of the cities, the great loss of life, and the war's resulting refugees. He described the young Athenians, setting sail as gaily as though they were going on a picnic, only to suffer incredible hardships and "die like flies" as prisoners in the quarries near Syracuse (Books VI, VII). Through his writing he hoped to add "clear understanding" of the events because he believed that "evil deeds" not only unleash enormous suffering but also brutalize those who practice those deeds, while at the same time destroying the values underlying their civilization. When, after his exile, he returned to Athens, he was assassinated by those opposed to his ideas.

The Greek comic poet Aristophanes used satire to voice his opposition to the Peloponnesian War. In *The Peace*, the hero, a simple peasant, fattens an enormous beetle on which he flies to heaven to seek an end to hostilities. In *Lysistrata*, Aristophanes suggests that the women of Greece unite and refuse sexual relations with their husbands until the men bring an end to the war.

A historian concerned more with suffering than with chronicling endless battles and a comic poet suggesting that wives refuse sexual relations with their husbands to end the wars were among those who early on chose to use their talents to alleviate rather than simply record the needless suffering they witnessed.

THE MIDDLE AGES

The launching of the Crusades in 1096 by European Christians unleashed four centuries of persecutions of those considered to be infidels. In the beginning, undisciplined hordes of peasants and pilgrims, led by nobles, knights, and monks, set out to reclaim the Holy Land from the Moslem infidels. On the way, the crusaders massacred other infidels, among them Jews who refused conversion. The idea of converting to the one "true" religion gained more and more unwilling adherents among the infidels as time went on, because most of them preferred a safe life to the precarious position of an infidel. As noted in Eve Soumerai and Stuart S. Sellinger's *Man's Inhumanity to Man*, tortures used to persuade the unwilling "took the form of logging, burning, the rack or solitary imprisonment in the dark and narrow dungeons. The feet of the accused might be slowly roasted over burning coals, or he might be bound over a triangular frame, and have his arms and legs pulled by cords wound on a windlass" (Soumerai and Sellinger 1982, 5).

In 1099, the proud Crusaders conquered Jerusalem. So much blood was shed, we are told, that the Crusaders' horses were knee deep in the blood of Jews and Muslims. The Jews who remained were gathered into a synagogue and burned alive. All non-Christians were banned from living in Jerusalem, and their holy sites came under the Crusaders' control.

AMERICA'S SAD LEGACIES

Native Americans

American settlers building a new nation held conflicting views about the natives they encountered in the New World. Some thought them to be not quite human, whereas others Americans believed them to be "noble savages" in dire need of conversion to Christianity. In the beginning, the natives controlled the balance of power and the settlers were obliged to negotiate a series of treaties. However, as time went on, the settlers grew in number and the natives blocked the way of the new nation's manifest destiny. Treaties were broken and brutal battles ensued between the settlers and the natives. Not only did the settlers fight with superior weapons, but they also used other means of destruction such as the deliberate spreading of smallpox through gifts of infected blankets. Natives were also forcibly removed from their fertile native lands to reservations in barren regions where the living conditions were substandard. Because hunting of the buffalo was no longer allowed, many of the natives died of malnutrition as well as other diseases. Despair was widespread.

Toward the end of the nineteenth century, a revivalist cult known as the Ghost Dance religion began to spread among the tribes, including members of the Sioux. It promised that "ghosts" of their dead would return to help them overcome their misery, provided they perform the ritual dance. To whites, and especially the U.S. Army, the Ghost Dance was symbolic of native resistance. A fierce battle ensued between the Sioux and the U.S. Army at Wounded Knee Creek in South Dakota on December 29, 1890.

Black Elk, a member of the Sioux tribe, who was considered a holy man by many, felt personal responsibility to record the tragedy on behalf of his people. He considered the earth "a world of darkness and many shadows" and favored the Other World, "where the spirit, beauty and truth reign eternal." He lamented the loss of life and the suppression of his peoples' culture at "The Butchering at Wounded Knee": "When I look back now from this high hill of my old age, I can still see the butchered women and children lying heaped and scattered all along the crooked gulch as plain as I saw them with eyes still young. . . . A people's dream died there. . . . There is no center any longer and the sacred tree is dead" (Momaday 1976, 38, 48).

Slavery

Many civilizations have climbed to power and glory on the backs of slaves. In many societies, slavery has been a vital part of economic life. The slave trade in America began when Africans landed at Jamestown, Virginia, in 1619 and were sold for life as indentured servants. The slave trade became commercially important when the tobacco culture became profitable. Enslavement of the native population was briefly considered, but there were too many disadvantages, including their ability to escape easily. Furthermore, some of the tribes had been helpful to the settlers, especially in the beginning.

By 1857 the Supreme Court, in the Dred Scott case, declared that a Negro whose ancestors were sold as slaves was not entitled to the rights of a federal citizen. Racism began to evolve in the South. "All slaves are black; slaves are degraded and contemptible; therefore all blacks are degraded and contemptible and should be kept in a state of slavery. This assumption took on a life of its own [including] the horror of miscegenation" (Elkins 1963, 61).

Many voices throughout the country, however, were raised against the inhumanity of slavery and racism, including that of Thomas Jefferson, even though he himself was a slave owner. He unsuccessfully proposed condemning the slave trade in the original draft of the Declaration of Independence in 1776.

Japanese American Relocations

By 1860 there were some 4 million slaves in a total Southern population of 12 million. By that time, slavery was as much due to the ideology of white supremacy as economic considerations.

At the height of the Civil War, in 1862, President Abraham Lincoln's Emancipation Proclamation fused the cause of the Union with that of human liberty by abolishing slavery in the belligerent states in an effort to end the fighting. No one was freed, however, until 1865, when the Thirteenth Amendment to the Constitution was passed by Congress.

Another sad chapter in American history occurred during World War II. Wartime fears led the U.S. government to remove by force 110,000 Japanese—two-thirds of them U.S. citizens—to relocation centers where many were confined for as long as two years and some even longer, though they had broken no laws. "Military necessity" was the reason given by the government, which even the Supreme Court hesitated to challenge. One of the few voices raised in dissent was that of Supreme Court Justice Robert H. Jackson who, in his dissenting opinion in the case of *Korematsu v. United States* (December 1944), objected to confining American citizens in "concentration camps" and depriving them of their freedom simply because of their race. He warned of the danger of such a decision; when a judicial opinion rationalizes such an order, the Court for all time validates the principle of racial discrimination.

Ironically, more than 30,000 Japanese Americans served, many with distinction, in the U.S. armed forces during the war. Although we were at war with Japan, we were also at war with Germany, but no German Americans were ever deprived of their freedom.

During the bicentennial celebration held in 1976, President Gerald Ford formally apologized to Japanese Americans for their internment. Four years later, the Commission on Wartime Relocation and Internment of Civilians began an investigation that culminated in the passage of the Civil Liberties Act of 1988, which included a fund for educating the public about the internment experience.

Why did this happen? Among the various reasons given are anti-Japanese prejudice and anti-immigrant hysteria, particularly in California, which was, at that time, experiencing economic difficulties.

ARMENIAN GENOCIDE: PROLOGUE TO THE HOLOCAUST

Inhumanity, as we have seen, is as old as history itself. Thousands mourn and continue to mourn as a result of war, the takeover of lands, religious persecutions, ethnic hatreds, racism, slavery, and political or military "necessity." In the twentieth century, however, in spite of progress and enlightenment, it became necessary to invent a new term: *genocide*, meaning "the extermination of an entire people." The word, coined in 1944, stands for the premeditated, total destruction of a national or ethnic group by depriving all members of life itself. Genocide combines all of the previously discussed forms of inhumanity with a new notion. Perpetrators were now saying: *You* members of an inferior race have no right to live among *us* members of the pure and superior race. We will therefore systematically and scientifically create a death machine to cause your extermination and that of your children.

Armenians were the first people subjected to genocide. The Armenians, who had settled originally around Lake Van (eastern Turkey) hundreds of years earlier, were among the first people of the region to adopt Christianity. They lived in relative peace within the largely Muslim Ottoman (Turkish) empire but were considered alien by the dominant group. During World War I, however, the Ittihat Party (Union and Progress Party), known as the Young Turks, determined to revive a single Turkish empire "for Turks only" and decided to free the fatherland of the accursed Armenian race.

What was done to the Armenians was beyond belief. Henry Morgenthau, the American ambassador to Turkey, noted in his diary that he was told that members of the Union and Progress Committee held nightly meetings to discuss in detail new methods of inflicting pain. They researched various methods employed during the Spanish Inquisition and adopted all the suggestions found there. They also added some variations: "In some cases gendarmes would nail hands and feet of prisoners to pieces of wood—evidently in imitation of the Crucifixion, and then, while the sufferer writhed in agony, they would cry: 'Now let your Christ come and help you!'" (Morgenthau 1918, 306).

One day, Interior Minister Talaat asked Ambassador Morgenthau, "Why are you so interested in the Armenians, anyway? You are a Jew; these people are Christians. We are treating the Jews all right. Why can't you let us do with these Christians as we please?" (1918, 333–34).

Henry Morgenthau's inability to stop the destruction of the Armenians made his stay in Turkey untenable, and he decided to return to the United States, write his story, and help in the reelection of President Woodrow Wilson. The dedication in his book, which explains his reasons, also suggests America's possible role as a beacon of freedom for the world.

To Woodrow Wilson

the exponent in America of the enlightened public opinion of the world, which has decreed that the rights of small nations shall be respected and that such crimes as are described in this book shall never again darken the pages of history. (Morgenthau 1918, Dedication)

No one heeded Ambassador Morgenthau's pleas; no one in a position to initiate policy took notice. One undistinguished Austrian corporal, who had served in World War I, did take notice of this event, and less than ten years later, he, Adolf Hitler, initiated similar policies. On August 22, 1939, in Germany, now chancellor and fuehrer, Hitler said in a speech prior to his invasion of Poland:

I have given orders to my Death Units to exterminate without pity men, women and children belonging to the Polish-speaking race. It is only in this manner that we can acquire the vital territory we need. After all, who remembers today, the exterminations of the Armenians? (From reports received by the Associated Press Bureau Chief in Berlin, Louis Lochner)

DEFINING ANTI-SEMITISM

Anti-Semitism is a term used to refer to the hostile attitude of non-Jews toward the Jewish people. Although the term itself is fairly new, the hatred of Jews is possibly as old as Jewish history itself, about four thousand years. In the twentieth century, anti-Semitism, a key ingredient in the Holocaust, resulted in the unimaginable suffering of millions of Jews. Millions died in the gas chambers; millions more were shot to death, worked to death, or died of disease as a result of mass starvation. Approximately 6 million Jews ended their lives in the crematoria or in mass graves, frequently dug with their own hands.

Before the beginning of Jewish history, people worshipped a multiplicity of gods. They believed that these gods controlled natural occurrences, human events in the life cycle, and tribal or community life. Some believed that these gods warred with one another to prove which were the strongest, and some of the worshippers fought as well. Most people, however, acknowledged and tolerated the existence of a different god, or gods, in the cultures of the other societies around them.

Then, according to the Bible, Abraham, the first Hebrew patriarch, began to espouse a new idea: There is only one God, who is omnipotent and omniscient, just and merciful.

No other nation at that time had denied the gods of its neighbors. This one Hebrew God, the creator of the universe and of humankind, demanded of Abraham that he organize his people and keep God's covenant to spread among all the people of the world the knowledge of the one true God and to formalize the ritual and ethical requirements of his law. In return, God promised that the Hebrew (Jewish) people would be a blessing to all mankind and a "light unto the nations."

Many Jewish practices offended the values of those around them. "The Jews regard it as crime to kill any newborn infant," wrote the Roman historian Tacitus. The Romans, and earlier the Greeks, believed in killing mentally and physically handicapped infants because they served no useful purpose. Greek and Roman leaders even accused the Jews of slaughtering and eating non-Jews in religious rituals.

SPREAD OF CHRISTIANITY

Monotheism, the notion of one God, was later espoused by Christians, as well as Muslims, and the Judeo-Christian tradition became an integral part of Western civilization. The Jewish "gift" of ethical monotheism, however, neither pleased the worshippers of the many gods nor endeared the Jews to those who integrated ethical monotheism into their own religions, because the Jews would convert neither to Christianity nor to Islam. Massive anti-Jewish resentment resulted.

Furthermore, various customs of the Jews also set them apart. The laws regarding food preparation and consumption made sharing meals with non-Jews impossible. Special requirements for prayer and the observance of holy days, festivals, and the weekly Sabbath, as well as their strict laws against intermarriage, also separated Jews from their neighbors. These customs were interpreted by non-Jews as Jewish hostility to others, not simply the Jewish desire to obey the dictates of their own religion.

For whatever reasons—anger, fear, jealousy, envy, or hurt feelings—anti-Semitism developed. Those who abandoned their Jewish practices were accepted by the non-Jewish community, but those who did not were persecuted.

By the fourth century, Christianity had spread throughout the Roman Empire, and, although Christianity was considered the "daughter" of Judaism, Christian hostility to the Jews had spread as well. Because they refused to accept their fellow Jew Jesus as the "son of God," Jews were regarded as a threat to the power of the Church fathers. If the Jews rejected Jesus as the Messiah, they reasoned, so might others.

Even so, the numbers of those who joined the Church grew. Catholicism preached that Jewish laws were unnecessary as long as people had faith. Thus Catholicism became an easier route to salvation than Judaism. In a world filled with hardship and pain, this was a welcome development for pagans, but a growing Catholic population made life for the Jewish people even more precarious and miserable. The Jews were not just accused of rejecting Jesus's preachings, but were often accused of murdering "God" himself, an idea that caused the torture and death of Jews for the next two thousand years.

ANTI-SEMITISM GROWS IN THE MIDDLE AGES

During the Middle Ages, if life for the average European peasant (90% of the population) was, as Thomas Hobbes later wrote, "solitary, poor, nasty, brutish and short," life for the Jews was almost unbearable. Forbidden to own property, to farm even as serfs, to join guilds and work as craftsmen or merchants, or to deal in new products of any kind, Jews were reduced to a handful of occupations: selling used goods, safeguarding the money of traveling merchants, working for each other as teachers or butchers, and raising a few animals for food.

Despite the myth that the Jews were wealthy, as a group they were extremely poor. In one thousand years, from A.D. 500 to 1500, only a handful became even modestly comfortable. Barred from living in the countryside as serfs or freemen, they lived within the walled cities and towns, confined to ghettos, a "dwarfed, walled-off collection of alleys and creaking ancient buildings, its ugliness and loneliness in marked contrast to the warmth and charm" of its surroundings (Sachar 1977, 25). After nightfall on Sundays and on Christian holidays, the gates of the ghettos were locked by city officials to prevent anyone from leaving.

As late as the nineteenth century, one ghetto was described by an Italian writer as "a formless heap of hovels and dirty cottages, ill-kept, in which a population of nearly four thousand souls vegetates, when half that number could with difficulty live there. The conglomeration of human beings, wretched for the most part, render this hideous dwelling place nauseous and deadly" (Sachar 1977, 30).

Inside the ghetto, the Jews continued to practice their religious customs, to study the Torah, to run their own schools and hospitals, and to try to support themselves. Bad drinking water and little room to exercise caused most children to look drawn and sallow. Fires were frequent, and sanitary facilities were nonexistent. Plagues and epidemics were common. The Jews of Prussia were strictly limited in the number of children they were allowed, and restrictions were also placed on who could marry. In Hamburg, Jews were forbidden to worship in numbers greater than ten, to walk past church grounds during a service, or to appear in public on any occasion at which crowds of people assembled (Sachar 1977, 30).

Even when traveling from one region to the next, allowed for business purposes only, Jews were subjected to so-called head taxes not levied on the general population: "The duties levied by the customs officials of Mainz, for example, were classified under the following headings: Honey, Hops, Wood, Jews, Chalk, Cheese, Charcoal" (Sachar 1977, 28).

Once European political leaders had exhausted the resources of the Jewish communities through taxes and mandatory loans, the Jews were expelled from their homelands: from England in 1290, France in 1306, Germany in the fourteenth century, and Spain in 1492 during the time of the Inquisition. They were not allowed to return to England until the mid-seventeenth century, nor could they go back to France until the time of the French Revolution. Most Jews migrated to Poland, and their descendants remained there until the Holocaust.

In addition to the political attacks on the Jews, the Church of the Middle Ages carried out a continual campaign against the Jewish community, basing their persecution on a whole set of fabricated accusations.

Between the twelfth and the twentieth centuries, Jews and often entire Jewish communities were put on trial on over 150 occasions for engaging in ritual murder. In almost every instance Jews were tortured and put to death . . . despite the nonexistence of any supporting evidence except for confessions extracted under torture. (Sachar 1977, 98)

Jewish physicians were constantly accused of killing their patients. In his letters, Martin Luther wrote, "They know all that is known about medicine in Germany, they can give poison to a man of which he will die in an hour, or in 10 or 20 years" (Sachar 1977, 96).

Jews were repeatedly blamed for, and subsequently murdered for, other imaginary plots against Christians. Although they were the first religious community to outlaw human sacrifice and were forbidden by their own faith to consume even animal blood (the laws of *Kashrut* require that animals be slaughtered following specially designed humanitarian methods and that the meat be soaked in salt before cooking to remove all traces of blood), the Jews were routinely accused of drinking the blood of their fellow humans.

During the fourteenth century, Jews were even blamed for the existence and spread of the Black Plague, despite the fact that they, too, perished in large numbers. In September 1348, in Switzerland, Jews were tortured to confess to their spreading of the Plague; then all those over the age of seven were murdered. The orphans were baptized and raised as Christians. Throughout Europe, even as recently as the nineteenth century, whole communities of Jews were burned alive for supposedly "torturing the host," the wafer used during the mass (Prager and Telushkin 1983, 102).

THE NINETEENTH AND TWENTIETH CENTURIES

In the years leading up to World War II, life for Jews in Europe varied dramatically from region to region. The lingering presence of anti-Semitism was negligible in such Western European countries as France and Great Britain, and even in Austria and Germany, at the time of World

War I. In Poland, Russia, and other Eastern European countries, people vacillated between tolerating Jews and subjecting them to violent pogroms, or organized massacres.

By the early twentieth century, most Western European and German Jews had successfully assimilated into society, without having to convert to Christianity. Over the centuries, Jews had gradually gained most of the rights enjoyed by the Christians. Although most countries still maintained quota systems that limited Jewish participation (including the United States), Jews were allowed to attend universities, hold local offices, travel freely, own businesses, and serve in the military. In Germany, as in France, Italy, and England, there was a rising, educated middle class into which the Jews could fit comfortably.

On the other hand, the typical Eastern European Jew fared quite differently. In Germany there was a rising middle class comprising both Jews and non-Jews; in Eastern Europe, there was no significant middle class for either group. Therefore, city-dwelling Jews had no group within which to assimilate. When compared with their fellow Polish countrymen, most Polish Jews were better educated, looked different (especially their hairstyles), dressed differently, and often spoke a different language. Even more significant is the fact that their religion was much more important to the Jews of Poland, Romania, and Russia than to the Jews of Germany and France. Participation in the social, economic, and political life of their country was much less important to these more pious Jews.

Thus, Jews were found mostly in villages, towns, and cities living surrounded by, but apart from, Christians. Few Jewish boys were allowed to attend universities, and when they did go, it was usually to schools in Western Europe or even in the United States. By 1936, in Poland, for example, there was an unofficial *numerus clausus* (quota) against Jewish students, and by 1937 "ghetto benches" had been established at all Polish universities. The left side of the classroom was set aside for Jewish students—a policy that was implemented by "clubbing Jewish classmates, wrecking lecture halls, insulting and hooting down liberal professors" (Korzenik 1980).

Joseph Korzenik, a Holocaust survivor who grew up in Poland, recalls vividly his impression of these laws: "It was a mocking, ridiculing way of segregating the student within a learning facility . . . this was extremely cruel." In addition, "signs, like graffiti, on sidewalks, on fences, on the walls of houses, saying 'Jew get out,' 'Jew go to Palestine,' 'Jew you are not wanted,' appeared often" (1980).

Just before the rise of Nazism, Franz Kafka, a world-famous author and philosopher, and a Jewish-German resident of Czechoslovakia, wrote to his friend Milena:

I've spent all afternoon in the streets, wallowing in the Jew-baiting. *"Prasive plemeno"*—"Filthy rabble" I heard someone call the Jews the other day. Isn't it the natural thing to leave the place where one is hated so much? . . . The heroism which consists of staying on in spite of all is that of cockroaches which also can't be exterminated from the bathroom. (Spann 1976, 21)

The image of the cockroach reappeared later in his most famous work, *The Metamorphosis,* in which extreme alienation was a major theme. Hated by the Czechs for being an intellectual German and for being Jewish, Kafka experienced a great deal more anti-Semitism than the Jews in Germany before the Nazi era.

Although the Communist Party did not, for the most part, subject Jews in the Soviet Union to the pogroms common under the tsars, popular anti-Semitism still existed, especially in the Ukraine. In addition, as were members of other religious groups, Jews were forbidden by the Communists to practice religious customs of any kind.

Eastern European Jews who wished to become full citizens, "Poles" or "Russians" rather than "Polish Jews" or "Russian Jews," had to convert to Christianity and separate themselves from their families, their friends, their culture, and their histories. The only way to escape persecution and still remain Jewish was to emigrate, which many Jews did during the three centuries prior to the Holocaust. Not everyone, however, had the desire to leave home and family; the health to survive the journey; and the money needed to pay for the bureaucratic red tape, the cost of the trip, and the establishment of a new life elsewhere far from home.

THE ROLE OF ANTI-SEMITISM: AS OTHERS SAW THEM

In 1912, the Reverend A. E. Patton, a Protestant minister who visited Ellis Island wrote:

> For a real American to visit Ellis Island, and there look upon the Jewish hordes, ignorant of all true patriotism, filthy, vermin infested . . . too lazy to enter into real labor, too cowardly to face frontier life, too lazy to work as every American farmer has to work, too filthy to adopt ideals of cleanliness from the start, too bigoted to surrender any racial traditions or to absorb any true Americanism, for a real American to see those items of a filthy, greedy, never patriotic stream flowing in to pollute, all that has made America good as she is-is to waken in his thoughtful mind desires to check and lessen this source of pollution.

Source: Dorothy and Thomas Hoobler, *The Jewish American Family Album* (New York: Oxford University Press, 1995), 73.

THE ROLE OF ANTI-SEMITISM IN THE HOLOCAUST

By 1932, seventy-five percent of the Polish people were still uneducated peasant farmers, who had been "weaned on anti-Jewish folk legends" (Sacher 1977, 356) by their government and their Church. In fact, it would not have been at all surprising for the Holocaust to have begun in Poland. Most of the concentration camps and all of the death camps were situated not in Western Europe, not even in Germany, but in Poland, where the Nazi government expected the population to be far less sensitive to their presence.

The Holocaust, however, began in Germany, and although it was not caused by Christianity (Hitler and his followers were decidedly anti-Christian in their beliefs and philosophy), sixteen hundred years of Christian anti-Semitism made the Holocaust possible. Its tremendous success in creating a world without Jews was directly related to the manner in which the Christian population had historically viewed their Jewish compatriots.

In one significant way, Nazism and historical anti-Semitism differed. Although the Church, both Catholic and Protestant, had often encouraged hatred of the Jews, once a Jew converted and was no longer a Jew, the persecution stopped. To the Nazis, however, a Jew was a Jew no matter what. Medieval European rulers had forced the Jews to convert or to leave their lands; Nazi rulers called for the extermination of all Jews in all lands. In Germany, and most of Eastern Europe, nearly ninety percent of the Jews perished. In the countries of Western Europe fewer than fifty percent were murdered. In some countries the Christian population found a way to save most of their Jews (Hilberg 1967, 670).

Hitler had once complained to a friend, Hermann Rauschning, that it was the Jews who brought their "tyrannical God," and "his life-denying Ten Commandments" (Telushkin 2001, 373) into the world. Only if he murdered every Jew in the world, Hitler believed, would he fully eliminate the idea of one God and His one moral imperative.

WORKS CITED

Elkins, Stanley M. *Slavery.* New York: Universal Library, 1963.

Halsall, Paul, ed. *Modern History Sourcebook: Thomas Hobbes: Leviathan, Chapters 13-14, 1651.* http://www.fordham.edu/halsall/mod/hobbes-lev13.html.

Hilberg, Raul. *The Destruction of the European Jews.* Chicago: Quadrangle Books, 1967.

Korzenik, Joseph. Interview by Carol Schulz, West Hartford, Connecticut, July 15, 1980.

Momaday, Scott N. *American Indian Authors.* New York: Houghton-Mifflin, 1976.

Morgenthau, Henry. *Ambassador Morgenthau's Story.* New York: Doubleday, Page, 1918.

Prager, Dennis, and Joseph Telushkin. *Why the Jews? The Reasons for Anti-Semitism.* New York: Simon and Schuster, 1983.

Sachar, Howard Morley. *The Course of Modern Jewish History.* New York: Dell, 1977.

Schulz, Carol D., and Eve Soumerai. *Human Rights: The Struggle for Freedom, Dignity and Equality.* Hartford, Conn.: State Department of Education, 1987.

Soumerai, Eve, and Stuart S. Sellinger. *Man's Inhumanity to Man.* Hartford, Conn.: Department of Education, 1982.

Spann, Meno. *Franz Kafka.* Boston: Twayne Publishers, 1976.

Telushkin, Rabbi Joseph. *Jewish Literacy: The Most Important Things to Know about the Jewish Religion, Its People, and Its History.* New York: HarperCollins, 2001.

2

SETTING THE NATIONAL SOCIALIST (NAZI) STAGE

At noon on January 30, 1933, German President Paul von Hindenburg, acting within constitutional jurisdiction, chose Adolf Hitler, the leader of the National Socialist Party, to serve as chancellor (prime minister) of a coalition government. Reichstag (parliament) elections were called for March.

The German Jewish community was well aware of Hitler's hatred of Jews, yet many continued to believe that their future was with and in Germany. Eve Soumerai, author and survivor, recalls her family's reactions on the evening of that fateful day:

We, the entire family including Opa and Oma [grandfather and grandmother], were sitting at the table eating supper and listening to music on the radio when suddenly the program was interrupted for an important announcement: Adolf Hitler had become chancellor of Germany. His strident voice rang out over the airways promising the German people pride and jobs. My father's fist landed on the table and broke a plate, while out of the Blaupunkt radio with the pretty twinkling lights came what seemed like thousands of voices shouting, "Heil Hitler, Heil Hitler." Along with the shouts there were marching feet, the sound of drums, and according to the announcer, thousands of torches lighting up the night sky. He added that nothing like this had ever been seen before in the streets of Berlin, not even during the time of the emperor. Opa assured us that nothing terrible would happen, "I have faith in my fellow Germans," and he went on to count off the names of our many good German friends. There were so many, he lost count. "And remember, we live in the country of Goethe, Schiller and Beethoven—the most civilized country in all of Europe," he declared with absolute conviction. (Soumerai 1996)

HITLER'S EARLY INFLUENCES

Hitler's book *Mein Kampf,* published in 1925 and widely circulated, is filled to the brim with passages reviling Jews, whom he described as "jelly-like slime" in one's hand and impossible to get rid of. "Their unclean dress and their generally unheroic appearance" made him sick to his stomach. Their activities in "certain fields" he compared to an abscess, which, "if you cut even cautiously, you find like a maggot in a rotten body, often dazzled by the sudden light—*ein Juedlein* [a kike]" (Hitler 1943, 57). *Rassenreinheit* (purity of the race) was his answer to the problem. In a chapter entitled "Bastardized Peoples," Hitler wrote, "The lost purity of the blood destroys inner happiness forever and plunges man into the abyss for all time" (1943, 327).

In achieving his aims, Hitler wasted no time. Within a year he had solidified his power as dictator of all Germany, had eliminated all opposition, and had begun to put in place the machinery of death and destruction designed to eliminate the "blood-Jews and tyrants over peoples" (326), which was necessary to elevate the master race to its proper place in history.

In 1913, when he was twenty-four years old, Hitler emigrated from Vienna, Austria, to Munich, Germany. He had failed in his dreams of becoming either a painter or an architect. He had no family, no job, and no place he could call home. When war broke out in the summer of 1914, he seized the opportunity to find a place to belong and petitioned King Ludwig III of Bavaria to grant him permission to volunteer in a Bavarian regiment. When his wish was granted, he noted in *Mein Kampf:* "I sank down on my knees and thanked Heaven out of the fullness of my heart" (63).

He was different from the other soldiers. They would ask for leaves to visit their families and passed the time by complaining about trench warfare, their wet feet, the bitter cold, the rotting bodies around them, and the generally terrible conditions in which they had to serve. Hitler, instead, would sit in the corner of the mess in deep contemplation. His comrades noted that suddenly "he would leap up, run about excitedly and say that in spite of our big guns, victory would be denied us, for the invisible foes—the Jews and the Marxists . . . were the source of all evil" (Shirer 1960, 30–31).

HITLER'S LOVE OF RICHARD WAGNER'S MUSIC

In *The Rise and the Fall of the Third Reich,* William Shirer (1960, 101–2) describes how Hitler worshipped the composer Richard Wagner. "Whoever wants to understand National Socialist Germany must know Wagner," Hitler said. Both shared a fanatical hatred for the Jews. Wagner was convinced that the Jews were out to dominate the world with their money, whereas the Germans' special gifts made them "ennoblers of the world." Hitler was inspired by Wagner's four-part opera, *The Ring of the Niebelung,* based on the world of German antiquity: an old tale of gods, dwarfs, giants, dragons, loves and hates, murder, magic, and mysteries. This opera of an irrational, heroic, mystic world culminates with the *Goetterdaemmerung*—"the twilight of the gods." The great finale ends in flames and floods sent by the gods, while the music storms to a great climax ending in redemption when the ring is returned. Hitler not only took Wagner's music with him into the bunker, but in his final moments on April 30, 1945, declared that Germany, too, must go up in flames. This has been called his "scorched earth policy." He believed that eventually Germany would also be redeemed.

Source: William L. Shirer, *The Rise and the Fall of the Third Reich* (New York: Simon and Schuster, 1960).

THE AFTERMATH OF WORLD WAR I

Four years later, at 7 A.M. on November 8, 1918, World War I ended. General Erich Ludendorff, the leader of the High Command, had summoned the political leaders and demanded that they ask immediately for an armistice, and on November 11, 1918, the Armistice was signed and all hostilities ended. Almost 2 million Germans had died.

The German people, totally unprepared for this turn of events, looked for scapegoats—referred to as November criminals—to blame for their defeat and humiliation. The newly formed democratic government, which on June 28, 1919, was in the unfortunate position of having to sign the severely punitive Treaty of Versailles, fit perfectly into the scapegoat category. Many historians believe that the reasons for this development can be traced to some of the clauses contained in the Treaty of Versailles, particularly Article 231, the "war guilt" clause, which insisted that Germany and her allies accept sole responsibility for the war.

The German population was outraged by this charge, which helped lay the groundwork for Hitler's rise to power. Also difficult to accept for the defeated Germans was Article 233, which required Germany to pay for all damages done to the civilian populations of the Allied governments (including such items as French widows' pensions). This article, perceived as unfair, undermined Germany's ability to recuperate. By 1921 the amount owed to the Allies came to 35 billion dollars in gold, which severely crippled the German economy.

The military clause of the Treaty of Versailles also played into Hitler's hands. It forced Germany to reduce its military to a small volunteer force, but, worse, it was followed by the idealistic and unnecessary statement that "Germany's disarmament would be followed by general disarmament." Hitler seized on this clause and declared that the nonfulfillment of this unrealistic wish on the part of the framers of the treaty justified his own armament.

INFLATION AND ECONOMIC DISASTER

Germany experienced a devastating inflation as a result of the reparations imposed by the Allies. Because the government was too timid to levy taxes on the population, it created money to pay the huge bill. By the end of 1923, printing presses were turning out currency at top speed. In 1919 the mark had stood at 8.9 to the dollar, but by the end of 1923, the mark stood at 25 billion to the dollar. Extremely hard hit were members of the middle classes who saw their life savings disappear. To the working classes, inflation meant much lower and unpredictable wages aggravated by the fact that the inflation had wiped out the reserves of the independent trade unions, making payments of benefits to their members impossible and undermining the power of the unions that had played such a significant role in the German democratic process.

When world-famous pianist Artur Schnabel gave a concert, he received his fee in a suitcase full of bills. He had to ask someone to help him carry the suitcase. On the way, they passed a delicatessen and to "relieve the helper," Schnabel decided to lighten the suitcase by spending half of the banknotes on a few sausages. The next day he could not buy even one sausage for the rest of the bills (Friedrich 1972, 124).

The hero of Erich Maria Remarque's novel *Three Comrades* (1937) describes the general working conditions: "In 1923 I was advertising chief of a rubber factory. I had a monthly salary of 200 billion marks. We were paid twice a day and then everybody had an hour's leave so that he could rush to the stores and buy something before the next quotation on the dollar came out, at which time the money would lose half its value" (quoted in Craig 1966, 626).

People looked for solutions. Theo Hupfauer, a young German student who joined the Nazi Party in 1930, recalls the chaotic times: "German citizens were impoverished from one day to the next. A bread roll cost as much as 20 million marks. Mailing a letter cost 100 million. A quart of milk cost 300 million. Those who didn't own furniture or material possessions [to trade] were poorly off" (Steinhoff, Pechel, and Showalter 1994, xxvi).

Yet, even though people faced economic disaster, they remained stoic and went about their daily business, as noted by the Russian novelist Ilya Ehrenburg in his book *Memoirs* in 1921:

Coming from Brussels, well nourished and serene, I saw Berlin. The Germans were living as though they were at a railway station, no one knowing what would happen the next day. Newspaper men were shouting, "Latest edition! Preparation for a putsch in Munich and Communist demonstration in Saxony." People read their paper silently and went to work. . . . It seemed as though everything was about to collapse, but factory chimneys went on smoking, bank clerks neatly wrote astronomical figures, prostitutes painstakingly made up their faces. (quoted in Koonz 1987, 37)

Germany became dependent on loans from the United States and on international goodwill. Between 1924 and 1929, American companies including Ford, Chrysler, and Eastman Kodak assisted Germany in what was considered to be one of the most spectacular recoveries in the world's economic history.

"DECADENCE" IN DAILY LIFE

Ehrenburg also commented on the misery and decadence all around him in Berlin, where he rented a room in a boardinghouse. Clothing stores featured pink and blue dickeys as substitutes for shirts; cakes were baked from frostbitten potatoes; and cigars bearing Havana labels were made out of cabbage leaves steeped in nicotine.

Ehrenburg was invited to visit an interesting nightspot:

We traveled by underground . . . and finally found ourselves in a respectable flat. On the wall hung portraits of members of the family in officers' uniform and a painting of a sunset. We were given champagne—lemonade laced with spirits. Then the host's two daughters appeared—naked—and began to dance. One of them talked [about] Dostoyevsky's novels. The mother hopefully eyed the foreign guests: perhaps they would be tempted by her daughters and would pay: in dollars of course. (quoted in Friedrich 1972, 82)

Most Germans deplored this sort of decadence and listened attentively when, in a few years, would-be leader Adolf Hitler denounced it and vowed to bring morality back to Germany.

THE STOCK MARKET CRASH

On Wednesday, October 23, 1929, the stock market in New York City suddenly collapsed with immediate consequences in the United States as well as throughout Europe. Markets disappeared, factory workers and executives alike lost their jobs, and many committed suicide. The United States entered the worst economic depression in its history and demanded immediate payment from Germany on its short-term loans.

As in the United States, massive German unemployment was the result: 1.5 million people in 1929 and over 6 million by 1933 were unemployed. Bread lines stretched for blocks in every city of the land. Eve's grandmother often talked about the difficult times and what she and her neighbors did to augment their food supply.

People grew radishes and potatoes in their flower boxes and tried to get permission to keep a chicken on their balcony. A chicken lasted a family all week. First "she" walked through the soup. Ah, heavenly broth. Then "she" was chopped up with bread and served on dandelion leaves gathered in the Tiergarten. Then more soup consisting of all the remains boiled together. You ate very slowly, bite by bite—savoring, and pausing after every bite. (Soumerai 1996)

HITLER BECOMES A POLITICIAN

The depression challenged democratic institutions: Could they survive such severe economic crises? In the United States and Great Britain, they not only survived but were actually strengthened, which was not the case in Germany, which was a very fragile democracy at best. Hitler, who had returned from the war as a corporal, realized that the upheaval provided him with a golden opportunity to become a politician. He did not waste any time responding to the misery around him. First and foremost he blamed the young and inexperienced Weimar Republic, including the Jews and Communists (the Communist Party had gained many converts among working people who hoped it would enable them to put food in their mouths and a roof over their heads), and labeled them all November criminals.

Hitler chose a small, insignificant political group called the German Workers Party from which to launch his revolution. It was there that he met stocky, bull-necked, scarfaced Captain Ernst Roehm who, like Hitler, possessed a burning hatred for the democratic republic—those November criminals. Roehm, Hitler's earliest and closest associate, the only person to address the fuehrer in the familiar form of *du* ("thou"), would go on to head the SA (*Sturmabteilung*, or "Brownshirts"). Hitler, who became the party's spokesman, discovered his charismatic powers as an orator when he addressed his first mass rally on February 24, 1920.

There was a hail of shouts, there were violent clashes in the hall, a handful of the most faithful war comrades and other supporters battled with the disturbers Communists and Socialists and only little by little were we able to restore order.... I was able to go on speaking.... When after nearly four hours the hall began to empty, I knew that now the principles of the movement which could no longer be forgotten were moving out among the German people. (Hitler 1943, 8–10)

In the summer of 1920, Hitler added the words *National Socialist* to the name of the German Workers Party: *National* to signify patriotism and pride and to encompass all German people, and *Socialist Workers* to signify support, jobs, and solidarity. Hitler's enemies, by using the first two syllables of *National*, adopted the name Nazis.

CONSOLIDATION OF POWER

Hitler was aware that the masses needed slogans. *"Ein Reich, Ein Volk, Ein Fuehrer"* (One government, one people, one leader) was one of the many slogans ceaselessly hammered into the people's heads over the radio, in the streets, at meetings, and in the newspapers. Flags, banners, insignia, drums, and music became symbols designed to win the abiding faith and loyalty of the masses. Random, calculated acts of violence added another ingredient—injecting healthy doses of fear into the populace while also demonstrating power over those destined for exclusion and death.

Hitler, the frustrated artist, designed the symbol, the banner that would unite and energize the masses. After many attempts, he chose red, white, and black because they were the colors of the old imperial flag for which he had fought. He arranged them in a new setting and added the swastika in the white center. The swastika, or hooked cross, according to ancient Teutonic myths, was the fiery implement that had swirled round and round to create the primeval life-giving substance at the beginning of time. Hitler was proud of his genius: "In red we see the social idea of the movement, in white the nationalist idea, in the swastika the mission of the struggle for the Aryan man" (quoted in Shirer 1960, 44).

NATIONAL REVOLUTION

It also helped Hitler's cause that the German people loved order, believed in obedience, and longed for one man, a leader, a fuehrer, who would lead them out of their misery. As early as 1907, poet Stefan George had expressed the national longing for this one man who, no matter what his origins, would rise up and implement the desired change through some "deed."

> The man! The deed! Thus pine both people and High Council.
> Do not expect one who dined at your tables!
> Perhaps one who sat for years among you murderers
> Slept in your cells, will rise and do the deed. (quoted in Haffner 1979, 16)

The deed Hitler planned was a national revolution: to right the wrongs and punish the November criminals, the Communists, and the Jews. Hitler believed that only he had the power to change Germany's destiny and bring about an end to the Jews.

On November 8, 1923, Hitler and his early followers tried to start the revolution in an aborted putsch (coup) in a Munich beer hall. It earned him a stay at Landsberg prison where he was treated as an honored guest, with a room of his own and a splendid view. He asked permission to have his faithful comrade Rudolf Hoess visit regularly. During these visits he dictated to Hoess his future plans of blood and terror. The result was his book *Mein Kampf*, which was published in 1925. At the time, it was considered a failure. People either laughed at it or ignored it. According to historian Lothar Kahn, the internationally famous German Jewish writer Lion Feuchtwanger claimed that the book contained 139,900 mistakes in 140,000 words. As Hitler's power gradually increased, however, the book along with its message became a best seller, rivaling in sales only the Bible.

UNEMPLOYMENT AND UNREST AMONG THE PEOPLE

As unemployment increased, so did unrest. One young German student, Theo Hupfauer, was ready and willing to fight for change.

The radicalization of politics got worse after 1928 as unemployment increased. That meant that the competition between parties became increasingly fierce. In the end there were no longer political assemblies in one hall or another, but parades like military maneuvers, and large scale street fights. All the young men were involved. That was when I joined the Nazi party, in 1930. To me, the old line conservative parties were too tame, too "establishment." They were for old men who had lost their fire, but not for a young man ready and willing to do something! In 1931, I joined the SS. (Steinhoff, Pechel, and Showalter 1994, xxvi)

People were desperately looking for order. Hitler's close associate Albert Speer describes his mother joining the Nazi Party: "It must have been during these months [1931] that my mother saw an SA parade in the streets in Heidelberg. The sight of discipline in a time of chaos, the impression of energy in a time of universal hopelessness, seems to have won her over also. At any rate without ever having heard a speech or read a pamphlet, she joined the party" (Speer 1970, 47).

On November 6, 1932, after three years of a bread-and-butter crisis that affected nearly every German family in one way or another, elections took place. During the election campaign, the atmosphere was charged. Millions were unemployed and had nowhere to live. "Food before rent" was the Communist slogan. Hitler's National Socialist slogans were transmitted over the state-run radio, day after day: "Fourteen years ago Germany was stabbed in the back; now we will have a strong Germany; we will not pay reparations; we will repudiate the Versailles Treaty; stamp out corruption; bring the money barons to heel, especially the Jews" (Soumerai 1980).

The two parties on the left, the Communists and the Social Democrats, were in direct competition with the National Socialists for votes. When the votes were in, the Nazis continued to be the largest party in the Reichstag, even though they had lost thirty-four seats, reducing them to 196 deputies. The Communists had gained eleven seats, and their numbers had increased to 100 deputies. There was an ebb and flow in the other parties. Some thought the great Nazi tide was ebbing. Hitler was unable to secure the necessary workable majority, but neither could anyone else. Some thought civil war was a possibility. There was talk of a general strike, should Hitler be inaugurated.

On January 29, 1933, in fact, a thousand workers crowded into the Lustgarten in the center of Berlin to demonstrate their opposition to making Hitler chancellor. Hitler turned to the army for support and promised to restore the country to its place in the sun. He cast a spell over the aged President Hindenburg and promised to observe the Weimar Constitution and to solve the economic crisis and end the prolonged misery.

Shortly before noon, on January 30, 1933, though he looked on Hitler with considerable disdain, President Hindenburg officially anointed him chancellor. When the swearing-in ceremony was over, President Hindenburg spoke, as though he were dismissing the troops, "And now, gentle-men, forward with God" (Toland 1976, 289–90). The Third Reich was born. It would last a thousand years, boasted Hitler. It lasted twelve years, four months, and eight days and caused not "countless thousands," using Rob-ert Burns's words, but countless millions upon millions, to mourn.

On that fateful day, January 30, Hitler promised Hindenburg to uphold the Weimar Constitution and accept a coalition government. There was, therefore, little alarm. The very next day, the *New York Times* echoed many other editorials when it pointed out that there were only two Nazis, Her-mann Goering and Wilhelm Frick, out of a possible twenty in Hitler's cab-inet and concluded that "the composition of the government leaves Herr Hitler no scope for the gratifications of his dictatorial ambitions." Besides, most observers argued, the conservative President Hindenburg would use his constitutional powers and vast prestige to curtail any excesses. Few seemed to realize that Goering, in charge of the Prussian police, had free rein to add not only thousands of Nazis to the force but also help the National Socialist revolution in many sundry ways.

OPPOSING GERMAN COMMUNISTS

On February 24, 1933, Goering's police raided the Communist head-quarters in Berlin, the Karl Liebknecht House, searching for evidence of an alleged revolutionary plot. They said they found "documents" proving that the Communists were planning to burn down government buildings, museums, mansions, and essential plants. The actual documents were never published, but the Prussian government vouched for their authen-ticity, which was sufficient to assuage any doubt (Shirer 1960, 195). In view of these "findings," Goering urged the police to make use of firearms and show no mercy to those "hostile to the State." Given Hitler's aim to destroy the opposition, it was a good beginning but hardly a full-scale war. Hitler needed something more dramatic.

REICHSTAG FIRE: COMMUNIST CONSPIRACY

Three days later, on February 27, 1933, that something more dramatic occurred, frightening an already nervous public. The Reichstag (parlia-ment) building in Berlin was devastated by a fire that spread so quickly that arson was indicated. When Hitler noticed the red sky above Berlin's largest park, the Tiergarten, he shouted, "It's the Communists!" and set off with Joseph Goebbels for the scene of the fire. He vowed to crush the Communist perpetrators: "this murderous pest with an iron fist" (Shirer 1960, 298–99). Whether the Nazis merely exploited the incident or actually caused it is not known. What is known is that a young, demented Dutch Communist, Marinus van der Lubbe, who had arrived in Germany a week earlier under the impression that great things were about to happen and that he wanted to do his part, was accused of being the "murderous pest." He became the visible evidence, proof of the Red menace. He was tried, condemned, and beheaded.

The setting of the fire appeared to be a Communist takeover and gave Hitler the excuse to visit President Hindenburg the very next day to persuade him that, in view of these events, it was necessary to invoke Article 48 of the Weimar Constitution, an emergency measure enabling the president to dissolve parliament and suspend civil liberties including freedom of the press, speech, and assembly "for the protection of the people and the state." Article 48 also enabled those in charge to impose death sentences on individuals who "seriously disturb the peace." These emergency measures, which were never rescinded, became the legal basis not only for absolute power but also for the establishment of the concentration camps (Shirer 1960, 294). Hitler, in fact, utilized the democratic foundations of the Weimar Republic to achieve his totalitarian regime, which almost immediately ensured absolute obedience.

HITLER GAINS RESPECTABILITY

Hitler, the expert on mixed messages, dressed in the dark suit befitting the position of chancellor, took to the airwaves. He promised to return to the old virtues of the past, thus reassuring possible critics. After all, Hitler did look and sound civilized. In a four-hour speech, he had not ranted or even attacked the Jews. In return, even the Jewish National Union threw their support toward the new government and agreed with his ban on restricting the entry of eastern "peddler Jews" into Germany (Shirer 1960, 304). After all, people argued, the choice was between a Brown (Nazi) or a Red (Communist) Germany with strings to Moscow, and most preferred the Brown homegrown variety.

But while the fuehrer spoke his soothing words, his Brownshirts were active in the streets. They broke up Communist and Social Democrat rallies and beat their members on the street or in basements. In the beginning, although some people thought the Brownshirts' behavior was a bit excessive, they did not blame the fuehrer personally; in the view of many people, he was moving Germany forward, and some of those excesses were to be expected.

THE NAZIFICATION PROCESS

It took six months to effect the total Nazification of Germany. Hitler started the process by refusing to answer questions from members of the Catholic Center Party because, he claimed, previous negotiations with them had failed and only new elections would solve the impasse. President Hindenburg was persuaded to dissolve parliament and schedule new elections for March 5.

In the meantime, Hitler courted the industrialists and managed to win their approval as well as financial support by promising to put the Communists and organized labor in their appropriate place. "Private enterprise," he said, "cannot be maintained in the age of democracy . . . unless the people have a sound idea of authority and personality . . . to be introduced more or less with an iron fist" (Shirer 1960, 189–90).

WORKS CITED

Craig, Gordon A. *Europe Since 1815.* New York: Holt, Rinehart and Winston, 1966.

Ehrenburg, Ilya. *Memoirs.* London: MacGibbon and Kee, 1963.

Friedrich, Otto. *Before the Deluge.* New York: Harper and Row, 1972.

Haffner, Sebastian. *The Meaning of Hitler.* New York: Macmillan, 1979.

Hitler, Adolf. *Mein Kampf.* Boston: Houghton Mifflin, 1943.

"Hitler Made Chancellor of Germany but Coalition Cabinet Limits Power; Centrists Hold Balance in Reichstag." *The New York Times,* January 31, 1933.

Koonz, Claudia. *Mothers in the Fatherland.* New York: St. Martin's Press, 1987.

Soumerai, Eve. Interview by Carol Schulz, West Hartford, Connecticut, July 2, 1980.

———. Unpublished memoir, 1996.

Speer, Albert. *Inside the Third Reich.* New York: Avon, 1970.

Steinhoff, Johannes, Peter Pechel, and Dennis Showalter. *Voices from the Third Reich.* New York: DaCapo Press, 1994.

Toland, John. *Adolf Hitler.* New York: Doubleday, 1976.

3

THE TOTAL NAZIFICATION OF GERMANY

THE ENABLING ACT

On March 5, 1933, when the results of the very last democratic German election were in, the National Socialists, in spite of their tactics of terror and intimidation, received only 43.9 percent of the votes cast. Hitler was forced to rely on some of his Nationalist allies to supply him the bare majority in the Reichstag—to carry on the day-to-day business of government. He was still short of the two-thirds majority needed to govern without opposition to his planned program of blood and terror.

What happened next was vintage Hitler. On March 23 he requested that the parliament pass the Enabling Act: the constitutional law for "Removing the Distress of People and Reich," which would confer on Hitler's party exclusive legislative powers for four years. In other words, he suggested that all the other parties in the parliament take a four-year vacation and leave the governing to him. Obtaining the two-thirds majority necessary for passage was not difficult. President Paul von Hindenburg had signed the decree for the "Protection of the People" the day after the Reichstag fire. Hitler, therefore, was able to remove from the Reichstag and arrest as many of the opposition deputies as necessary to obtain the two-thirds majority needed to pass the act. On the day of the vote, eighty-one Communist members of the Reichstag and some "dangerous" Social Democrats were noticeably absent and unable to cast their votes (Shirer 1960, 196). When the results of the vote were announced, there were 441 votes in favor of the act and 84 (all the Social Democrats not in jail or in exile) against it. The one-party totalitarian state had been achieved. Following the victory announcement, the Nazi deputies rose in unison to stomp, cheer, and sing Germany's new national anthem, the Horst Wessel song:

> Raise high the flags! Stand rank on rank together.
> Storm troopers march with steady, quiet tread. . . .

The Enabling Act had dealt the death blow to Germany's fragile experiment with democracy. Parliament, its members handpicked by the Nazi Party, functioned as cheerleaders for Hitler's program. There were to be no more elections. In the street, the so-called rowdies were in charge of carefully orchestrated incidents for all to behold, ensuring that all marched to the Nazi drummer. Eve Soumerai describes an incident when a good friend disappeared in the summer of that year:

Our family lived in the sort of neighborhood where people were friendly and knew each other. Some were particularly fond of children; one of those was Hubi whose real name was Herr Eugen Huber-Schmidt. He was a glazier who fixed windows, and lived in a basement apartment with his little brown and white Dachshund named Mimi who had long velvety ears which my friend Adelheid and I loved to touch. As soon as we came into sight she'd wag her tail and bark a greeting. Hubi had endless patience and let Mimi lead him wherever she wished. She would take endless time smelling around trees and other dogs' behinds, which Hubi called one of those fun smells giving dogs a little *Vergnugen* (pleasure). Hubi carried little bits of putty in his pocket, which, along with bonbons (sweets), he generously dispensed to us. We'd work the putty at school. It helped us bear those boring lessons when we had to wait our turn to read one sentence. The sweets had soft centers and we tried to make them last all morning long.

One day Hubi did not appear on the street, which was strange because he always walked Mimi several times a day. The next day we called on him but found his shop and apartment closed and locked. We asked one of his neighbors. She looked worried, glanced over her shoulder, and whispered that the Brownshirts had beaten him up and taken him away. You could tell she was really upset. What happened to Mimi, Adelheid asked. I couldn't speak. I felt that icy fear. At first she didn't want to tell but Adelheid kept asking. "Well," she finally said, "Mimi had barked and whimpered something awful. One of the men beat her." Her husband had taken the little dog away. And that was that. Adelheid was silent and sad. I managed to ask, "Why Hubi? What did he do?" She said, "Didn't you know he was a Communist?" "What's a Communist?," I asked. But she left and didn't answer. Adelheid didn't know either. I had heard that word somewhere but couldn't remember where. Adelheid said, "What could be so bad that anyone would do this to Hubi, and Mimi too? All Mimi did was bark." Adelheid and I felt so close that day. (Soumerai 1996)

DACHAU CONCENTRATION CAMP

On March 20, 1933, just eleven days after becoming Munich's chief of police, Heinrich Himmler, one of Hitler's earliest followers, announced at a press conference that arrangements had been completed for setting up the first concentration camp on the grounds of a former gunpowder factory at Dachau, near Munich. Its purpose was to take known opponents of the new regime into "protective custody" for causing unrest. On April 11, the SS (*Schutzstaffel,* or blackshirted security police) took over control. The SS, which was independent of the ruling bureaucracy, had its own courts, its own press, and even its own military, known as the Waffen-SS. Those imprisoned at Dachau lost all civil and legal rights and were left completely defenseless. Many were brutally beaten as well as tortured before being sent home. Others were killed outright. Their families were told that they had suffered heart attacks, but the families could collect their ashes for a set fee. Dachau became the model for the concentration camps to come and served as a training ground for commandants and personnel for the death camps of the future. In Dachau the theories of National Socialism were tested and turned into the gruesome realities of the Holocaust.

SUPPORT FROM CITIZENS

Active support for the Nazi doctrines increased daily. Lydia Gottschewski, a tireless organizer for women's organizations, praised Hitler and his racist doctrines. In her newsletter for leaders in 1933, she exhorted readers to banish pity from their hearts when it came to Jews:

Often, much too often, one hears . . . , "I find the fight against the Jews too severe. It does not seem right that the good Jews must suffer on account of their race" . . . and so it goes. Sentimental gush that the other person is also a human being and feels and senses like ourselves . . . [*der* Fuehrer] has an inconceivably deep knowledge of final things. . . . We National Socialist women . . . should thank God that the movement exists and exert ourselves with words and deeds. . . . Did not our entire people do penance for years for the sins of individuals? And who were those sinners? For the most part, Jews! The Jew . . . is a subtle poison since he destroys what is necessary to our life. If we are to be healed as a people . . . and conquer a place in the world that is our due, then we must free ourselves ruthlessly from that parasite. . . . (cited in Koonz 1987, 152–53)

JEWISH REACTIONS

Eve described the first time she felt excluded—how this led to her first lie and the eventual breakdown and loss of her best friend:

Adelheid was still my very best friend. Our mothers were best friends too and had known each other from before we were born. One day in the early summer of 1933, on the way home from school, we decided to swing like monkeys along the wrought-iron fence which lined our street when Adelheid asked me the question which changed everything. "They are having a picnic in the Tiergarten on Sunday afternoon, why don't you come? It's so much fun. They are going to play Polkas. We'll dance along. And they are going to have 'Wurstchen' [hot dogs] and ice cream."

At the supper table, I asked about the picnic. "What picnic?," asked Papi [my father]. "Just a picnic, I don't know," but apparently Mutti [my mother] knew. "There are posters everywhere. It's a Brownshirt induction," she said. They were the ones who had taken Hubi and Mimi. I understood and felt that icy fear again.

"You can't go," said Papi rather brusquely. Something rather unusual for him.

"Why not?," I asked. We weren't Communists.

"Because we are Jewish."

"What that's got to do with it?"

"We celebrate Hannukah," volunteered Bibi [my brother]. That is one stupid reason I thought and said so, which ended the conversation. Mutti looked ashen and Papi left the table.

On the way to school the next morning, Adelheid asked what I was going to wear to the picnic. That's when I told her that first big lie. I was sorry I couldn't come because my Oma [grandmother] had planned a family reunion. Our friendship had suffered its first tiny crack. It would take another two years before the crack was a big divide and she had become my bitter enemy. By that time she had become a staunch and happy member of the Nazi Youth. Dressed up in that spiffy-looking uniform, she would stare at me when we met in the street and whistle a Nazi anthem. A few months later came the spitting and, finally, she and her friends would wait for me, chase me, and beat me up. (Soumerai 1996)

THE FAMILY OF ANNE FRANK

A few Jews and intellectuals saw the writing on the wall and began to make arrangements to leave Germany. Among those was Otto Frank, a Frankfurt businessman, who sought a safe haven in Amsterdam, Holland, for his wife, Edith, and his daughters, Margot and Anne. For a few years the family built their new life in hospitable Amsterdam. Anne and Margot attended Dutch schools, learned Dutch, and were content. In March 1934, Edith Frank wrote to a friend in Germany, "Since December we have a small flat here in Amsterdam. . . . Anne is a little comedian. . . . She is so fond of babies. She peeks into every pram we pass and would take every toddler she sees for a walk" (Schnabel 1961, 25).

In May 1940, when the Germans invaded Holland, their plans to eliminate all Jews were in the process of being finalized. On June 12, 1942, Anne celebrated her thirteenth birthday. Her parents gave her a red-and-white plaid diary, which became her most precious possession. Less than a month after her birthday, the family went into hiding to escape deportation to the East. They were soon joined by the Van Daam family and the dentist Dussel who shared Anne's room. For two years Anne's regular entries in her diary poignantly described the daily life of the eight occupants confined to the attic in which they hid. On Monday evening, November 8, 1943, she wrote in her diary: "I see the eight of us in the Annex as if we were a patch of blue sky surrounded by menacing black clouds. The perfectly round spot on which we're standing is still safe but the black clouds are moving in on us" (Frank 1967, 131).

In August 1944, the Green Police, the Dutch Gestapo, received a tip from an informer and raided the attic, surprising its occupants. In their haste to get ready, Anne dropped her diary. Fortunately for the world, Miep, their friend, who, along with others, had risked her life by smuggling food and other necessities into the attic, found the diary and eventually was able to return it to Otto Frank, the sole member of the families to survive.

On April 11, 1944, a few months before Anne and the other occupants were apprehended, she wrote, "If God lets me live. I shall not remain insignificant. I shall work for the world and mankind" (Friedlander 1999, 3). Her dearest wish—to be remembered after her death—came true. Her diary continues to be read by millions of people throughout the world.

Several accounts describe Anne's life after she was apprehended. Author Ernst Schnabel interviewed seventy-six people who had known her, among them Mrs. de Wieck. She told him how even in Auschwitz Anne retained her humanity: "She cried when we marched past the Hungarian children who had already been waiting half a day in the rain in front of the gas chambers, because it was not yet their turn. And Anne nudged me and said, 'Look, look at their eyes'" (Schnabel 1961, 136).

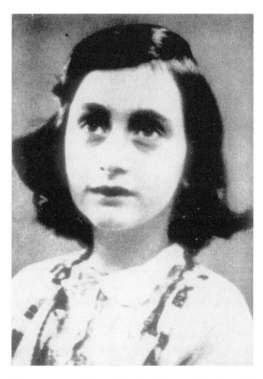

Photograph of Anne Frank taken on October 10, 1942. Yad Vashem Photo Archives, courtesy of USHMM Photo Archives.

In March 1945, at Bergen-Belsen concentration camp, just a few weeks before liberation on April 15, 1945, Anne, suffering from typhus, threw away her clothes because they were infested with lice and fleas and wrapped herself in a blanket. Anne's sister Margot, also ill with typhus, fell out of her bunk onto the stone floor and never got up again. Anne died a day later. (See Lindwer 1991, 74.)

LIFE IN GERMANY, THE FATHERLAND

Meanwhile, in Germany, the general population saw much of which to be proud. From early on, children were issued good-looking uniforms and required to meet regularly to march, sing, and camp out in the glorious German countryside. The clean, healthy children also engendered the admiration of many non-German visitors and correspondents.

Typical of many women's reaction to the changes in the Reich was Louise Solmitz, a conservative, who watched a procession of marching men in the streets of Hamburg: "20,000 brown shirts followed each other like waves in the sea, their faces shone with enthusiasm in the torch light. . . . they sang battle songs. . . . we were drunk with enthusiasm, blinded by the light of the torches. . . . and in front of us men, men, men . . . a torrent!" (Koonz 1987, 132).

There was a prevalent sense of optimism. Hitler had started to expand health, social security, and old-age benefits. His public works included the construction of a network of Autobahnen, the reclamation of swamps and wetlands, and reforestation—"all visible and inspiring signs of accomplishment and faith in the future" (Fest 1973, 434). To be sure, labor unions were banned. Instead there were so many pro-labor activities that few noticed or cared. Organizations provided vacation travel, sports festivals, art shows, dances, and training courses. Catchy slogans, such as *Kraft durch Freude* (Strength through joy) and *Schönheit der Arbeit* (Beauty of work), were given to the panels representing both labor and management (Fest 1973, 434).

In 1985 Dr. Theo Hupfauer, one of the early passionate party administrators who joined the central office of the Workers' Front, told Gitta Sereny when she was gathering information for her book on Albert Speer, "They [panels] actually succeeded in imbuing management and labor with the awareness of a common purpose . . . [yet] decisions were not freely negotiated but by politically supervised deliberations . . . we came to feel there was nothing we couldn't achieve" (quoted in Sereny 1995, 182).

Hupfauer explained further that, although salaries including management's were fixed, in his view offering ever more money with resulting spiraling price increases was less effective than being able to own a Volkswagen, enjoy cheap holidays, and obtain "above all cheap and good housing" (1995, 182).

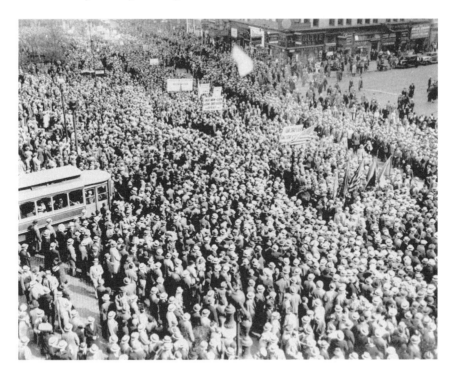

More than 100,000 demonstrators gather on May 10, 1933, in front of Madison Square Garden in New York City to take part in an anti-Nazi protest march through lower Manhattan. National Archives, courtesy of USHMM Photo Archives.

BOYCOTTING OF JEWISH BUSINESSES

Reports persisted in the foreign press that Hitler was clamping down on the Jews. A planned boycott of Jewish shops led to considerable protests abroad. On May 10, 1933, a mass rally was held in New York City's Madison Square Garden during which speakers threatened to counter-boycott all German-made goods. (Other mass protests were held at the Trocadero in Paris, on May 20, and at the Queen's Hall in London, on June 27.)

On April 1, the Nazis responded to the threat by enacting the planned boycott of all Jewish-owned businesses. The world witnessed the event, by means of photographs taken by foreign correspondents, in which armed storm troopers stood in front of Jewish businesses, some of them as simple as a corner grocery store. The armed storm troopers displayed posters stating: GERMANS! DEFEND YOURSELVES. DON'T BUY FROM JEWS (Gilbert 1987, 33)

One Jewish shop owner, Mrs. Arthur Seaman, recalled her anger when Nazi troopers stood in front of her home as well as her shop and prevented customers from entering. Later, gentile customers requested that Mr. Seaman make his deliveries at night, through the back door (Schulz 1981, 64). Amazingly, however, sales figures of Jewish-owned businesses did not show a decline (Shirer 1960, 422). The foreign press had a field day and the boycott, planned to last several days, was called off after twenty-four hours.

CIVIL SERVICE LAW: DISMISSAL OF ALL NON-ARYANS

A week later, on April 7, 1933, all non-Aryans—Jews—were to be dismissed from government service.

Defining the Jews

In order to define who exactly was a Jew, a new regulation was issued on April 11. Any person with either one Jewish parent or one grandparent associated with the Jewish community was considered a Jew. A *Mischling*, or part Jew, was a person with one or two Jewish grandparents who were not associated with the Jewish religious community. On the other hand, an Aryan was defined as a person with non-Jewish ancestors and was therefore of pure "Aryan" blood (Hilberg 1967, 46). These decrees, which were revised and refined as time went on, soon spelled the difference between life and death.

Dismissal from the Public Sector

Affected by the civil service laws were teachers, professors, judges, physicians, and personnel from the state-run radio, orchestra, and opera.

During that April, pianist Artur Schnabel, who had agreed to participate in a concert honoring the one-hundredth anniversary of the birth of Brahms, was told that plans had been changed and that he would have to renegotiate his contract. Schnabel understood the underlying significance of the change and made arrangements to leave Germany (Friedrich 1972, 384). The Communists were removed from civil service positions four days later.

These first laws—hundreds more were to come—started the process of isolating Jews and preventing them from earning a living. For a while the dismissed government employees tried to cope with the new realities.

Lorelei Lewis, who was born in Germany in 1897, immigrated with her husband and daughter to the United States in 1938. Her husband had worked as a dentist in an army hospital. After he was dismissed from this position, he maintained his private practice. At first, some of his gentile patients continued to come to his office; gradually they found other dentists. Others stopped honoring their financial obligations. One man, one of her husband's oldest patients, stopped paying, and when her husband ran into him on the street, he looked aside. "We had more such cases," she recalled (1980).

Some gentiles, however, were loathe to give up their trusted Jewish doctors. Nettie Allweiss, a Holocaust survivor, said her friend Dr. Krauss continued to see many of his patients including some members of the SA and SS. They simply took off their SA and SS uniforms and visited him under cover of darkness.

When Berthold Gaster's father, an obstetrician, was arrested, his women patients actually staged a protest in front of the jail. He was released, and the family left for America.

Dismissal from the Business Sector

Dismissal from service in the business sector was more complicated. Since there was no government office in charge of this process, each business had to make its own decisions about its Jews. In the beginning, Jews in the business community felt safe believing that, without outside pressure in the form of regulations, their employers would continue to value their contributions and keep them as a part of the workforce.

Eve Soumerai described her father's dismissal from his position as a managing director of a small comforter manufacturer:

He had been able to keep his job longer than most Jews in his position and this made him proud. When the original owner retired and his son, who joined the Nazi Party, took over, my father was given a "farewell" dinner and a long beautiful letter (from the original owner) about his service which he kept in his front pocket and would read to us on many occasions. He was cheered by the apparent decency of his former boss and for a while lured into wishful thinking that maybe "things" would turn around. (Soumerai 1980)

Because the Jews were officially discriminated against, the feeling caught on and unofficial discrimination began to emerge. Lorelei Lewis has described the behavior of her landlady who had recently purchased "her" apartment building from its Jewish owners who had been forced to sell:

At first, the new landlady was very nice. When my husband was in Dachau, she came up to see if we had enough food. But later when we were leaving, she wanted me to get out faster, even though the rent had already been paid. My leaving fit into their plans. I could see the change in attitude when there was something they wanted that they couldn't have in normal times . . . that really struck me as horrible at the time. (Lewis 1980)

BOOK BURNING

On May 10, 1933, while torchlight parades lit up the night sky and SS bands played patriotic songs, students accompanied by their professors followed the example of the SA instigator and tossed twenty thousand "un-German books" into bonfires in front of major universities throughout Germany. The occasions were festive and jubilant. German youths cheered and danced late into the night. Among the so-called un-German authors was Hugo Preuss, the principal drafter of Germany's blueprint for democratic government, the Weimar constitution; Albert Einstein, Sigmund Freud, and Lion Feuchtwanger; and American authors Jack London, Ernest Hemingway, Sinclair Lewis, and even Helen Keller. (Hitler did not appreciate Helen Keller's efforts to overcome deafness and blindness. He believed that handicapped people were imperfect, not of masterrace status, and therefore unworthy of life.)

Joseph Goebbels, the new propaganda minister in charge of German culture, addressed the students in front of Berlin University while they watched the burning books turn into ashes: "The soul of the German people can again express itself. These flames not only illuminate the final end of an old era; they also light up the new" (Shirer 1960, 241).

The book-burning ceremonies were widely reported in the foreign press, and people outside Germany expressed their outrage. American writers protested en masse in public rallies held in many American cities. A few days later, on May 17, Hitler once again mollified public opinion by delivering his famous Peace Speech before the Reichstag stating that "war was unlimited madness and that Germany was prepared to agree to any solemn pact of nonaggression" (Shirer 1960, 209). His apparent sincerity deeply moved the German people and also made a profound and favorable impression abroad. Hitler understood that it was necessary for

---

MARTIN HEIDEGGER (1889–1976)

Martin Heidegger was a widely known existentialist philosopher who once defined philosophy as the "search for the meaning of being." He, along with other luminaries took a public vow to support Hitler and the regime. The following words are from an address to German students:

> It is demanded of you that you become those who drive furthest and are most deeply pledged. Be hard and righteous in your demands. . . . May your loyalty and willingness to follow grow stronger every day . . . "Ideas" shall no longer govern your existence . . . The Fuehrer, and only he, is the current and future reality of Germany, and his word is your law . . . Heil Hitler.

Source: Martin Heidegger, "Aufruf an die Deutschen Studenten." Freiburg, Baden-Wurttemborg, Germany *Freiburger Studentenzeitung*, November 3, 1933.

people to hear these words so that they could happily continue to believe that everything would be all right.

MORE RESTRICTIVE MEASURES

On July 14, however, two ominous events took place: The National Socialist Party was declared the sole party in Germany, thus eliminating any political opposition to the Law for the Prevention of Hereditary and Defective Offspring, which was also proclaimed that day. It was said that Germany was in grave danger of *Volkstod* (death of the people), and harsh steps in the form of forced sterilization were required (Lifton *The Nazi Doctors*, 66). Later, a health tribunal was established to decide who would be sterilized. Teachers in schools for the deaf, for instance, were required to turn over to the Nazi authorities the names of their deaf pupils. Deaf and pregnant, Franciska Schwarz was forcibly locked inside a room with barred windows in the clinic of her town to undergo an abortion: "All night long I banged on the wall so that they would let me out. The nurse

A member of the *Shutzstaffel* (SS, security force) throws confiscated books onto the pyre during the public burning of so-called un-German books on the Opernplatz in Berlin on May 10, 1933. Courtesy of USHMM Photo Archives.

shoved me into a bed and gave me an injection. My baby is going to be on that tray. . . . The nurse handed me a notice when I left the hospital. 'You are to return to this hospital within ten weeks to be sterilized'" (Friedman 1990, 64, 73–74).

Under cover of World War II, Hitler planned to move from sterilization to extermination of those he considered unworthy of life. Dr. Karl Brandt, the physician in charge of the euthanasia project, admitted at his trial held at Nuremberg in 1946 that, in addition to the euthanasia, he had been involved in conducting inhumane medical research on inmates. He was sentenced to death and was hanged at Landsberg prison in 1948 (Lifton *The Nazi Doctors*).

EDUCATION IN THE THIRD REICH

Bernard Rust, a high official in the SA and a longtime friend of Adolf Hitler, was named Reich minister of science, education, and popular culture. Prior to his appointment, in 1933, the German public schools had been under the jurisdiction of the local authorities, but now all schools and universities were brought under the iron rule of the Reich Ministry of Education. Textbooks were hastily rewritten. The new rector of the University of Berlin, a storm trooper, instituted the core educational objective: twenty-five new courses in *Rassenkunde* (racial science), which specified in great detail the exact widths of Aryan skulls and noses as well as the prescribed pure Aryan eye color determined by "scientific" charts, to be taught by all educational institutions. The twin objectives were, after all, building the master race and their healthy bodies instead of filling young heads with the "ancient practice" of thinking (Shirer 1960, 248–50).

Education, starting with the very young, was revised for political purposes. The *Nazi Teachers' Gazette* (1933) published authorized versions of the tales of Sleeping Beauty and Snow White. Sleeping Beauty, Germany, was awakened by a kiss from the prince, Adolf Hitler (Raab 1961, 11).

The major goal of Nazi education was creating pride in being a member of the master race. *Rassenkunde* was taught from elementary school on. Students' skulls were measured according to prescribed charts, and their eye color was compared to Aryan eye-color charts. Students were taught that Jews were the ultimate inferior race. They were the typhus-spreading rats displayed in the movie *The Eternal Jew* (1940). They were the four-thousand-year-old enemy who spread their venom wherever they congregated. They, and the Communists, were responsible for Germany's defeat in World War I, the harsh Treaty of Versailles, and the economic disasters that followed.

In German history, students heard the story of Hitler's favorite mythological hero, Siegfried, who joyfully and fearlessly slayed the dragon (the enemy), fully aware that a flick of its massive tail might pulverize his bones and a drop of saliva might corrode his flesh. Courage and self-sacrifice unto death were Hitler's messages to 8 million young Germans.

In order to achieve these goals, an environment of total obedience was required. Every child said, "Heil Hitler," from 50 to 150 times a day: upon arrival at school, at the beginning of each class, and at departure from school. "Heil Hitler," became the greeting to the mailman, the policeman, and everybody else in uniform on the street, upon entering and leaving stores, and even greeting parents at home. Not saying the "Heils" was a punishable offense. In addition, hardly a week passed when, for one patriotic reason or another, flags and banners bearing the swastika were displayed from every window except those of Jews who were forbidden to participate (Stern 1982, 170–71).

Teachers were required to wear a swastika at all times and "command" their students to absorb Nazi ideology. Those who failed to conform to the beliefs of the Third Reich were dismissed or worse. Some tried, for a while at least, to remain fair to all the children in their charge. Eve remembers her third-grade teacher, Herr Weise:

During the summer of 1934, we heard that all Jewish children had to sit in the last row when school would start again in the fall. My mother rushed to speak to my teacher Herr Weise who assured her that as long as he remained a teacher, he would place children where he wished. At a time when all teachers had to wear the Nazi swastika, he wore such a tiny one that you could hardly see it. When I had to leave the school, he continued to keep in touch and assured me, "Storms pass, just look up into the sky, clouds move, don't they?" he said, always smiling. (Soumerai 1996)

Teachers were required to command instead of instruct. Discussion and thinking were avoided, because differing points of view would weaken resolve and discourage absolute obedience. Students were taught about the decadent Weimar Republic in particular and decadent democracy in general. Democracy was government by rich Jews. Democracy was government where people waste time, and democracy was weak and would perish. The fuehrer would lead the Germans to victory because race purity had made them strong. Nature was on the side of the aggressors and the victors—not the victims (Stern 1982, 176). A mathematics book posed the following problem: How many government loans to newly married couples could be granted for the money it cost the state to care for "the crippled, the criminal and the insane?" (Lifton *The Nazi Doctors*, 66).

Nazi ideology invaded poetry and literature. A book for students, entitled *Für Meinen Lebensweg* (For my life's journey), written by Dr. Walter Hawel and published by Justin Moser in Munich (no date), was widely distributed to youths of all ages. The book included poems written by the renowned German poet Johann Wolfgang von Goethe (1749–1832), prints of famous pastoral paintings of various German artists, and photographs of a loving Adolf Hitler wearing a civilian suit. In one photograph he is embracing a blond little girl; in another, he is smiling at an apron-clad mother while he gently touches the hand of the blond child in her arms. The caption reads, *Das Glüick der Mutter* (The happiness of the mother). On another page are the words intended to be spoken at the induction ceremony into the compulsory labor service: *"Was ich bin and was ich habe, dank ich dir mein Vaterland* (What I am and what I have I thank you my fatherland). One geography book includes a political cartoon with a "Jewish" octopus encompassing the globe of the world.

Julius Streicher, editor in chief of the anti-Semitic newspaper *Der Stürmer,* was so pleased that boys and girls were encouraged to read his paper every Monday by their teacher that he commissioned a book in 1937 entitled *The Jewish Question in the Classroom,* which was illustrated with repulsive anti-Semitic drawings made by children. This book was followed the next year by a best seller called *Poisonous Fungus* in which a young girl named Inge keeps an appointment with a Jewish doctor:

Anti-Semitic cartoon by Seppla (Josef Plank) circa 1938. An octopus with a Star of David over its head has its tentacles encompassing a globe. Library of Congress, courtesy of USHMM Photo Archives.

The door opens. Inge looks up. . . . Her eyes stare into the face of the Jewish doctor. And this face is the face of the devil. In the middle of this devil's face is a huge crooked nose. Behind the spectacles gleam two criminal eyes. Around the thick lips plays a grin, "Now I have you at last, you little German girl!" And then the Jew approaches her. His fat fingers snatch at her. . . . She smacks the fat face . . . breathlessly she escapes from the Jew house. (Rossel 1992, 114–16)

In most schools there was strict separation of the sexes. Educators were challenged to find ways to inspire Aryan pride in girls while reminding them that they were inferior to men in all activities except homemaking. The woman's body belonged to the *Volk*. It was their duty to bear blond, blue-eyed children for the fatherland (Koonz 1987, 201).

At age ten, after taking tests in athletics and Nazified history, a boy graduated into the *Jungvolk* (young folk). In order to become a member he had to take the following oath: "In the presence of this banner which represents our Fuehrer, I swear to devote all my energies and strengths to the savior of our country Adolf Hitler. I am ready and willing to give up my life to him, so help me God" (Shirer 1960, 253).

And youth did indeed thank their fuehrer. They believed and they listened. Albert Bastian, a member of the Hitler Youth, described the fuehrer's expectations: "The Fuehrer expects you boys to be quick as greyhounds, tough as leather, and hard as Krupp steel" (Steinhoff, Pechel, and Showalter 1994, 14). They adored him and were ready to die for him. Hitler had tapped into their overwhelming desire to belong. Whether rich or poor, from the countryside, the towns, or the cities, they were brought together as one all-encompassing community. They did not mind having their education interrupted so that they could spend six months tilling the land, living outdoors while they learned the value of manual labor. They developed faith in themselves, their country, and especially in the fuehrer for whom they were proud to die (Shirer 1960, 256).

They were also proud to make others die. Jan Karski, a courier for the Polish underground, described seeing two adolescent boys dressed in the crisp uniforms of the Hitler Youth in the Warsaw ghetto in 1942. They were there for "the hunt."

The boys stood in a deserted street, broad smiles on their faces, their blond hair glistening in the sunlight. One had drawn a pistol. His eyes canvassed the surrounding buildings. The other said something that made him laugh. Then the first boy raised his gun and fired. Jan heard the tinkling of broken glass and a moan of pain from an adjoining building. The boy who fired the shot let out a victorious whoop. His fellow "warrior" congratulated him. (Wood and Jankowski 1994, 123)

At the very end of the war, among the rubble of what had been Germany, it was the youths, some as young as twelve, who were enlisted to defend what was left of the fatherland.

One of the very last photographs of a bent, drug-addicted Hitler shows him shaking hands with members of the Youth Corps in Berlin shortly before his suicide. The faces of the young men show a sort of reverence in spite of the image of their fuehrer and the ruins all around them.

OTHERS CONSIDERED UNWORTHY OF LIFE

Besides Jews and the physically and mentally handicapped, others were considered unworthy of life: Gypsies, Freemasons, Jehovah's Witnesses, and homosexuals.

Gypsies

Gypsies, also called Rom, originally came from India. They were considered vagrants and vagabonds in the countries they wandered in, often in wagons, but usually they were not allowed to obtain land. They made their living as horse traders, tinkers, jewelry artisans, musicians, and fortune tellers. There were some 39,000 Gypsies in Germany and Austria who were not considered of "pure" blood. Eradication of the Gypsy family, considered a public nuisance, became another Nazi goal, and many of the women and their children were taken to extermination camps or became victims of medical experiments, while the men performed slave labor (Gutman 1990, 635–37). Dogs specially trained to attack people were used in Buchenwald, particularly against Gypsies who refused sterilization. After their hands were tied behind their backs, the dogs tore them to pieces (Yahil 1990, 536). The most accurate estimate of the number of Gypsies killed during the Holocaust is about half a million (Linenthal 1995, 38).

Jehovah's Witnesses

Jehovah's Witnesses, known in German as *Bibelforscher* (Bible students), were among the early victims of Nazism. In 1933 there were about 20,000 Jehovah's Witnesses in Germany. The first wave of arrests followed their refusal to say, "Heil Hitler," and, beginning in 1935, to serve in the army.

Elizabeth Kusserow, the youngest child of a Jehovah's Witness family, recalled her painful situation in school:

Every day the teacher reprimanded me for not saluting the flag. The big, black swastika on the red banner flew over the schoolhouse and hung on a pole in every classroom. My stomach churned as I tried to think of how I could avoid saluting it and saying "Heil Hitler." My parents had taught me to salute only Jehovah God. To salute a flag or a person was the same as worshiping idols. I wouldn't sing those horrible Nazi songs.

The teacher always watched me. "So, Elizabeth, you do not want to join in praise of our leader. Come to the front of the classroom." She turned to the others, "Children, Elizabeth thinks it is all right to insult our leader. Tell us why Elizabeth."

"Acts 4:12 of the New Testament says, 'There is no salvation in anything except Jesus Christ.'"

"Imagine, Elizabeth Kusserow believes in that ridiculous New Testament."

The children laughed. I couldn't understand why. All of them went to church. On the way home from school, they pushed me and threw my books to the ground. It got worse. (Friedman 1990, 52)

After the outbreak of war, many Jehovah's Witnesses were incarcerated in concentration camps because they refused to denounce their convictions, an act that would have spared them. The SS kept them apart from other prisoners lest they gain new converts to their faith (Gutman 1990, 742).

Freemasons

Right-wing organizations in Germany in the 1840s had linked Jews and Freemasons, a secret fraternal order, and accused them of secretly undermining Christian society in a sinister plot to control the world. This accusation lived on. In Nazi Germany an anti-Masonic museum was established, and members of the order were not permitted to join the Nazi Party. By September 1935, their property had been confiscated, and some were sent to concentration camps.

Homosexuals

In 1871, when the Prussian-dominated German empire was established, homosexuality was defined as an "unnatural form of licentiousness" that carried a prison term for persons caught in such an act. Under the Weimar Republic (1919–1933), the issue became a subject of free public discussion. After 1933, during the Nazi period, it was declared that homosexuality hindered the "preservation and continued existence of the *Volk*" and was incompatible with racial purity. "Protective custody" was the Nazi answer, and it included those acting on behalf of homosexuals as well as the "perpetrators." By 1935 chronic practitioners had been incarcerated in prison as well as in concentration camps. Hitler ignored his close associate Ernst Roehm's sexual preference until the Night of the Long Knives (Blood Purge) when Roehm and others were murdered for political reasons, rather than their homosexuality, which gave Hitler an excuse.

THE BLOOD PURGE (JUNE 30–JULY 1, 1934)

The SA Brownshirts continued to rule the streets and were quickly becoming an embarrassment to Hitler. One example occurred late in 1933 when American radio commentator H. V. Kaltenborn was in Germany assessing Chancellor Hitler and his movement. He was accompanied by his family, including his sixteen-year-old son, Rolf. The family, about to return to the States, was doing some last-minute shopping on the stylish Leipzigerstrasse in Berlin when a parade of Brownshirts turned into the street on the way to the Lehrte Bahnhof and the party rally at Nuremberg. The Kaltenborns did not wish to "Heil Hitler" the marching men and turned their backs pretending to look into a shop window, when a husky individual who identified himself as a party member whirled son Rolf around and slapped him sharply across the face for that lack of "courtesy." Because the Propaganda Ministry wanted to keep the incident quiet, they handed Kaltenborn a letter of apology just before the family left Berlin that night (Metcalf 1988, 157).

By June 1934, the army objected to the crude tactics of the 2.5 million Brownshirts under the command of Hitler's best and oldest friend, Colonel Ernst Roehm. Believing that he was expressing the fuehrer's wish, he asked to preside over a new People's Army consisting of his storm troopers and including the SS as well as the rest of the army. The officer corps could hardly imagine anything worse and appealed to the one remaining independent source of power—President Hindenburg—suggesting to him that the proud tradition of the army would be destroyed if the roughneck Roehm and his Brownshirts took charge. Some in the army even raised the possibility of restoring the monarchy and curbing the Nazi revolution after the aged President Hindenburg died. Hitler obviously had other plans.

At the beginning of June, Hitler made an attempt to talk sense to his friend Roehm, who had become a member of his cabinet, without reaching an agreement. A day or two after that conversation, Hitler asked the SA to go on leave during the month of July and not to wear the uniform or engage in parades or exercises. They agreed. Roehm and the SA leadership went on holiday at the resort town of Wiessee, near Munich, and invited Hitler to confer with them—to work things out. Hitler accepted and "worked things out" on his own terms.

Labeling the activities of the SA leadership as treason, Hitler and some carefully chosen accomplices sped out of Munich toward the hotel at Wiessee shortly after dawn on June 30, where Roehm and his friends were still fast asleep. They were awakened abruptly. Some were shot on the spot, but Roehm, Hitler's old comrade, was given special treatment: a dressing down by the fuehrer himself. He was then taken to the Stadelheim, Munich, prison cell where he had once served time for assisting Hitler in the aborted beer-hall putsch in 1923. There, as the promised special treatment, Hitler offered to leave a loaded pistol on the table of the cell so that Roehm could shoot himself instead of being shot. "If I am to be killed let Adolf do it himself," he is reported to have said, whereupon shortly thereafter, the deed was done "point blank" by some SA officers (Shirer 1960, 221).

In Berlin, meanwhile, Hermann Goering and Heinrich Himmler rounded up some 150 SA leaders and executed them on the spot. Given the unusual opportunity to get rid of opponents, Hitler's SS turned on countless civilians who "knew too much" or had opposed Hitler in the past and gunned them down in their homes, on the streets, or wherever they happened to be (Shirer 1960, 221–23).

Most of the killing was over by the next day. On Sunday afternoon, July 1, life was back to normal. Hitler returned to Berlin to host a tea party in the gardens of the Chancellery. On Monday, President Hindenburg thanked Hitler for his "determined action and gallant personal intervention which have nipped treason in the bud and rescued the German people from great danger" (1960, 224). Hitler, in turn, in his Reichstag address on July 13, stated that the army was "to remain the sole bearer of arms." He was proud to have gotten rid of the SA leadership that had dared to challenge that dictum (225).

HITLER BECOMES FUEHRER AND REICH CHANCELLOR

On August 2, 1934, at 9 A.M., President Hindenburg died. At noon, it was announced that, according to a law enacted by the cabinet the preceding day, the offices of chancellor and president had been combined and that Adolf Hitler had taken over as head of state and commander in chief of the armed forces. The title of president was abolished; henceforth, Hitler would be known as fuehrer and Reich chancellor. One of his first acts as commander in chief was to demand that all officers and men from the armed forces swear the following oath to him personally: "I swear by God this sacred oath, that I will render unconditional obedience to Adolf Hitler, the Fuehrer of the German Reich and people, Supreme Commander of the Armed Forces, and will be ready as a brave soldier to risk my life at any time for this oath" (Shirer 1960, 227).

Twelve years later, during the Nuremberg Trials, many officers tried to use this oath to defend themselves for the unspeakable crimes they committed following the orders of a supreme commander whose true nature they had seen for themselves during the butchery of June 30. However, it was determined at the trials that the defense of swearing the oath to the fuehrer was not valid because every individual was personally responsible for his own actions. Otherwise only Hitler could have been held responsible.

FINAL STEP IN THE ACQUISITION OF TOTAL POWER

The Enabling Act, which had been the legal basis for Hitler's dictatorship, permitted him to make laws that deviated from the constitution. But the act did specifically forbid tampering with the institution of the presidency, which Hitler had just eliminated. No one objected. On August 19, in a special plebiscite, the German people were asked to approve the usurpation of complete power by Hitler, and ninety-five percent of them voted approval of his total domination over every aspect of their lives; only 4.25 million people had the courage to vote against it.

SUMMARY OF FIRST YEAR'S ACHIEVEMENTS

When Hitler addressed the Reichstag on January 30, 1934, he could look back on a year of achievement without parallel in German history. He had legally replaced the Weimar Republic with his personal dictatorship, smashed the state governments, unified the entire Reich, and wiped out the labor unions. In foreign affairs he had taken Germany out of the League of Nations in Geneva and insisted that Germany be treated as an equal among the great powers, and he had given his well-received "peace" speech. Concerning the Jews, he had carefully and deliberately taken the initial steps on the road to their extinction. His grand plan was total dominion over Europe and eventually the world. He did not expect anything to stand in his way.

One incident is included here to symbolize foreign reaction to Hitler's achievements. The internationally famous German Jewish writer Lion Feuchtwanger, who had once dared to criticize Hitler's grammar and whose books were burned publicly in Germany, was living in exile. At

Adolf Hitler and Heinrich Himmler review SS troops during Reich Party Day ceremonies, September 1938, in Nuremberg. Estelle Bechoefer, courtesy of USHMM Photo Archives.

about the same time as the events described above, he was approached by a messenger from British Prime Minister Ramsay MacDonald with a suggestion that he prepare the screenplay for an anti-Nazi feature film. Feuchtwanger labored on the script and within two months had completed it. By then, however, His Majesty's government had decided on a policy of "accommodation" with Herr Hitler, which culminated five years later in "appeasement." Feuchtwanger converted his dramatic effort into a novel entitled *The Oppermans* (1934), which detailed the brutal and subtle pressures of the Nazi calamity during 1933. The book was widely read, and fifty years later, in 1983, it was made into a feature film by German director Eugen Monk to commemorate Hitler's ascension to power. This film was shown in the United States, Israel, the Soviet Union, and many other countries.

NAZI PROPAGANDA

Doctor Paul Joseph Goebbels, a short man with a crippled foot, became minister of propaganda and culture. As a youth, he had attended parochial schools and was the recipient of a scholarship from the Albert Magnus Society that enabled him to receive a Ph.D. from Heidelberg University in 1921 in philosophy, literature, and art. He went on to study Latin and Greek and fancied himself a writer. Among his plays was one called *The Wanderer* (about Jesus Christ), which, along with his other plays and novels, no one would publish or stage until he became nationally known as a Nazi leader. He was to emerge as Hitler's most loyal associate—unto death, which he and his family willingly underwent in the bunker, just before the end of the war. On April 8, 1926, he wrote in his diary: "Hitler phones. . . . At 2 o'clock we drive to the Bürgerbrau. Hitler is already there. My heart is beating so wildly. It is about to burst. I enter the hall roaring welcome . . . and then I speak for two and a half hours. . . . People roar and shout. At the end Hitler embraces me. I feel happy. . . . Hitler is always at my side" (Goebbels 1962, 233).

Goebbels believed that propaganda—lies and more lies—was necessary to achieve the goals set by the National Socialist revolution. He agreed with the fuehrer that the masses are stupid and will believe anything that is repeated in the simplest terms and appeals to the emotions.

In December 1930, before Hitler gained absolute power, he was very proud of being able to stop the showing of the American film version of Erich Maria Remarque's novel *All Quiet on the Western Front* (1930). The film and the book portrayed the blood, filth, and horror endured by young German soldiers during World War I. The novel had been a great success and had been read by hundreds of thousands of Germans.

Goebbels attacked the book and the film passionately as an invidious attack upon the honor of the German army. Both put in doubt the Nazi "stabbing in the back" version of the armistice. Books had not yet been publicly burned, but he was able to block the sales of the novel. The American film, however, gave Goebbels an opportunity to demonstrate his genius. He organized his henchmen to threaten those who wished to see the film and place stink bombs as well as mice under the seats of those who were trying to view the film inside the theater. Intervention by the police proved in vain. The fear and disgust of these activities, in addition to organized joint petitions of veterans' groups, were able to persuade the chief of the board of film reviewers to forbid any further showing of the film "because it would tend to endanger Germany's national prestige" (Eyck 1963, 295–96).

Goebbels, who knew the power of film, effectively used film to further his purposes. The propaganda film *The Eternal Jew* (1940) portrayed rats (Jews) scurrying from the sewers to spread infection among the population. Goebbels believed that people will believe anything they see and hear more than three times. He was in total control of the press, radio, and films.

Every morning newspaper editors and correspondents gathered at the propaganda ministry to be told what to print and how to write the news and headline it. So there would be no misunderstanding, printed guidelines were furnished. The Reich Press Law of October 1933 had made journalism a "public vocation" regulated by law, and it stipulated that all editors must be of German Aryan descent and not married to a Jew. When Goebbels once appealed to editors to make their papers less monotonous, one impulsive editor, Ehm Welke, took him seriously and complained about the red tape and the resulting dullness of the printed articles. This was not what Goebbels had in mind. He suspended Welke's paper, the weekly *Grüne Post*, for three months and had Welke deported to a concentration camp (Shirer 1960, 246).

Leni Riefenstahl, Hitler's favorite film director, was charged with instilling pride, and the notorious Jew-baiter Julius Streicher was responsible for enforcing hate and contempt for the Jews. His widely read tabloid *Der Stürmer* was, as already mentioned, dedicated to the damnation of the Jews as an evil force. Its banner headline read, *DIE JUDEN SIND UNSER UNGLÜCK* (The Jews are our misfortune), which became a well-worn phrase throughout the Nazi period (Gilbert 1987, 25). On May 1, 1934, a fourteen-page issue revived the medieval blood libel accusation against the Jews of using Christian blood in the baking of their Passover bread. One hundred thirty thousand copies were sold and displayed on public notice boards on the corners of public streets. Included in the text was the reproduction of an old engraving of four rabbis sucking the blood of a Christian child through straws. This issue also portrayed the Christian Holy Communion as yet another example of a Jew, in this case Jesus, drinking Christian blood in the Communion ceremony. Following protests from the Christian churches, Hitler ordered the issue banned, but copies were still widely available throughout the summer (1985, 43).

I remember seeing *Der Stürmer* display box at the end of our street. An ugly snake, meant to symbolize a Jew wrapped around a fair maiden. I heard somebody say *Jude Verecke* next to me and ran away as fast as I could and never looked at the box again. (Soumerai 1980)

Two weeks later, on September 4, William Shirer watched Hitler stride "like a conquering hero" down the center aisle of the rally terrain at Nuremberg, while an immense orchestra played the Egmont Overture and 30,000 hands were raised in the Nazi salute. Leni Riefenstahl, in charge of pride, immortalized these events on film. She called the resulting documentary *Triumph of the Will*, which is still considered by many to be the most effective propaganda film ever made. The opening shots of the film portray the fuehrer cruising in his small plane in and out of the clouds, almost touching the rooftops, spires, and clock towers of the medieval town of Nuremberg while the background martial music calls forth patriotism and pride. Like a god, Hitler descends from the plane to jubilant and ecstatic crowds lining the streets, swinging from trees, and hanging from windows. After cruising in an open limousine through the winding streets overflowing with cheering throngs, Hitler finally arrives at the rally to begin his oration—the centerpiece of the film—to an adoring crowd of thousands upon thousands who stand in neat columns, intent upon every one of his words, demonstrating their total devotion.

In her memoir, Leni Riefenstahl described the premiere of the film, on March 28, 1935, which was shown to a wide audience of party functionaries and diplomats:

We didn't even have time to screen it for the censors, a highly unusual situation, since no film could be shown in public until it was passed by the censorship board. . . . Hitler and all the guests of honor, including the diplomats, were already sitting in their boxes. No sooner had we sat down, the lights faded, an orchestra played a march, the curtains parted, the screen lit up . . . . Holding my eyes shut most of the time, I kept hearing more and more clapping. The end of the film was greeted . . . by endless applause. At that moment my strength ran out altogether. When Hitler thanked me and handed me a lilac bouquet I felt faint—and then lost consciousness.

After the war the German illustrated magazines with high circulations claimed that after the premiere Hitler wanted to present me with a diamond necklace and [claimed] that I gazed so deeply into his eyes and blacked out. (Riefenstahl 1992, 166)

Leni Riefenstahl went on to another triumph: the making of the film *Olympia*, which documented the Olympic Games held in Berlin in 1936, which gave the Nazis a golden opportunity to impress the world with their achievements. There they were, for the whole world to see: happy, healthy people united under their fuehrer, Adolf Hitler, competing with athletes from every corner of the globe.

During the Olympics, the signs "Jews Not Welcome" were temporarily removed from parks, hotels, and shops. Overt baiting and persecution were halted. Hitler's entrances and exits were carefully staged. Some controversy persisted especially in the United States. Did participation mean tacit approval of the Nazi regime? The argument that sports and politics should not mix won the day. In fact, so as not to offend their German hosts, two American Jewish sprinters were excluded from running even though they had qualified. President Franklin Roosevelt, who had remained silent throughout the Olympic debate, reassured his friend Rabbi Stephen Wise, president of the American Jewish Congress, that tourists returning from Berlin had told him that "the synagogues were crowded and apparently there is nothing very wrong" (Berenbaum 1993, 31).

Much to Hitler's displeasure, the African American sprinter Jesse Owens not only participated but set several world records and won four gold medals, an unprecedented feat. As a result, Jesse Owens, the tenth and last child of a dirt-poor Southern sharecropper, became the idol of millions worldwide. (His records stood until 1960.) There are some conflicting reports about whether Hitler snubbed him and the other black athletes or whether he merely was not present at their triumphs. There is no doubt, however, that the official Nazi newspaper *Der Angriff* called them "black auxiliaries" and that Martha Dodd, the daughter of the U.S. ambassador in Berlin, was told by an assistant of Foreign Minister Joachim von Ribbentrop that the United States had taken unfair advantage by letting "nonhumans like Owens and other Negro athletes" compete in the Olympic Games (Baker 1986, 100).

In July 1949, Leni Riefenstahl had to submit to a de-Nazification court. In her memoirs she wrote that she had to "defend herself alone without counsel all day. The decision was finally announced . . . it was unanimous" (350). The conclusion of the court was that she had had only "normal commercial intercourse" with party leaders. The making of *Olympia* was labeled an "international matter," and *Triumph of the Will* a "documentary." If it was used as an effective means of propaganda, the reasoning went, that was hardly Riefenstahl's fault. She further stated that "most of the notorious Jewish 'pogroms' had not yet taken place" and argued that she constantly maintained friendly relations with Jews. However, because of continuing French military government objections to the verdict, Riefenstahl was finally classified as a fellow traveler, in other words, a Nazi (Riefenstahl 1992, 354).

WORKS CITED

Baker, William J. *Jesse Owens.* New York: Free Press, 1986.

Benz, Wolfgang. *A Concise History of the third Reich.* Berkeley: University of California Press, 2006.

Berenbaum, Michael. *The World Must Know: The History of the Holocaust as Told in the United States Holocaust Memorial Museum.* Boston: Little, Brown, 1993.

Eyck, Erich. *A History of the Weimar Republic.* Cambridge, Mass.: Harvard University Press, 1963.

Fest, Joachim C. *Hitler.* New York: Harcourt, Brace Jovanovich, 1973.

Feuchtwanger, Lion. *The Oppermans.* New York: Viking, 1934.

Frank, Anne. *The Diary of a Young Girl.* New York: Doubleday, 1967.

Friedlander, Albert H. (ed.). "The Diary of a Young Girl." *Out of the Whirlwind: A Reader of Holocaust Literature.* New York: Union for Reform Judaism, 1999, 34.

Friedman, Ina R. *The Other Victims.* Boston: Houghton Mifflin, 1990.

Friedrich, Otto. *After the Deluge.* New York: Harper and Row, 1972.

Gilbert, Martin. *The Holocaust: A History of the Jews During the Second World War.* New York: Holt, Rinehart and Winston, 1987.

Goebbels, Joseph. *The Early Goebbels Diaries.* London: Weidenfeld and Nicholson, 1962.

Gutman, Israel, ed. *Encyclopedia of the Holocaust.* New York: Macmillan, 1990.

Hawel, Walter. *Für Meinen Lebensweg.* Munich: Justin Moser, undated. (Personal collection of Eve Soumerai.)

Hilberg, Raul. *The Destruction of European Jewry.* Chicago: Quadrangle Books, 1967.

Koonz, Claudia. *Mothers in the Fatherland.* New York: St. Martin's Press, 1987.

Lewis, Lorelei. Interview by Eve Soumerai, West Hartford, Connecticut, July 20, 1980.

Lifton, Robert Jay. "German Doctors and the Final Solution." *New York Times Magazine,* September 21, 1986.

———. *The Nazi Doctors: Medical Killing and the Psychology of Genocide.* New York: Basic Books, 1986.

Lindwer, Willy. *The Last Seven Months of Anne Frank.* New York: Pantheon Books, 1991.

Linenthal, Edward T. *Preserving Memory.* New York: Viking Penguin, 1995.

Metcalf, Philip. *1933.* New York: Harper and Row, 1988.

Raab, Earl. *The Anatomy of Nazism.* New York: Anti-Defamation League, 1961.

Riefenstahl, Leni. *A Memoir.* New York: St. Martin's Press, 1992.

Rossel, Seymour. *The Holocaust.* West Orange, N.J.: Behrman House, 1992.

Schnabel, Ernst. *The Footsteps of Anne Frank.* London: Pan Books, 1961.

Schulz, Carol. Jewish Accounts of the Holocaust Based on the Accounts of Survivors. Wesleyan University, unpublished thesis, 1981.

Sereny, Gitta. *Albert Speer: His Battle with Truth.* New York: Vintage Books, 1995.

Shirer, William L. *The Rise and Fall of the Third Reich.* New York: Simon and Schuster, 1960.

Soumerai, Eve. Interview by Carol Schulz, West Hartford, Connecticut, July 2, 1980.

———. Unpublished memoir, 1996.

Steinhoff, Johannes, Peter Pechel, and Dennis Showalter. *Voices from the Third Reich.* New York: DaCapo Press, 1994.

Stern, Margot. *Facing History and Ourselves.* Watertown, Mass.: International Educations, 1982.

Wood, E. Thomas, and Stanislaw M. Jankowski. *Karski.* New York: John Wiley, 1994.

Yahil, Leni. *The Holocaust: The Fate of European Jewry, 1932–1945.* New York: Oxford University Press, 1990.

4

THE CHANGING
LIVES OF JEWS

EFFECTS OF THE NUREMBERG LAWS

Overlooked by the world and most Germans in those glorious fun-filled summer days of 1936 were the ever-increasing humiliations suffered by Jews in the Third Reich. The Nuremberg Laws, prepared over many months by lawyers of the Ministry of Justice and enforced on September 15, 1935, deprived Jews of German citizenship, all its rights and privileges, and confined them to the status of subjects with no rights whatsoever. They were the recipients of ever-increasing laws and decrees, which invaded the most personal aspects of their lives, such as flying the German flag. In response, a patriotic Jewish veteran organization requested special permission to fly the flag in view of their status (Kahn 1981). Jews were also forbidden to employ maids younger than forty-five years of age. One explanation given was that they would therefore be less tempting to the male members of the household. Jews were forbidden to have sexual relations with non-Jews or to marry non-Jews. If they did, the non-Jewish partner would suffer ridicule and jail; their Jewish partners could receive the death penalty.

Eve Soumerai had two "Aryan" aunts. She remembers,

My mother's brother Adolf married Hete a month after the Nuremberg Laws were passed. My father's brother Karl had been married to Else for many years. Adolf and Hete escaped to Belgium, where they started a small stamp business and lived happily until a customer turned my uncle over to the Gestapo during the occupation. He was sent to Auschwitz. Hete waited two years after the war was over, in case her husband might return and look for her in Brussels. Else, on the other hand, once the Nuremberg Laws took effect, got a government sponsored divorce while her husband was incarcerated in a concentration camp. She stated that "she was ashamed to be married to a Jew." (Soumerai 1982)

Jews were excluded by law or terror from public and private employment, which meant many of them were unable to make a living. In small towns, Jewish families found it difficult to purchase the necessities of life—even milk for their babies. In addition, taunting signs could be found everywhere: JEWS NOT WELCOME, JEWS ENTER THIS TOWN AT THEIR OWN RISK. Some signs sprouted perverse humor: At a sharp bend of the road near Ludwigshafen, a sign read, DRIVE CAREFULLY! SHARP CURVE! JEWS 75 MILES AN HOUR! (Shirer 1960, 234). Each month the noose was tightening. Jews were forbidden to have pets or ride tram cars; they were forced to sit on special benches marked "For Jews" only and to wear the yellow star. Nobody was surprised anymore.

Hope had finally ebbed among most Jews in Germany. Some of the older ones tried valiantly to cling to shreds of hope such as memories of a happy past—good Germans they had known and who, in some cases, still did what they could to help their former friends and employees, at least, when no one was looking. Orthodox Jews had their own explanation; they

A German woman is forced to march through the streets of a town wearing a sign around her neck that reads, "I, [illegible word], have for years committed acts of racial defilement with the Jewish swine, Karl Strauss." YIVO Institute for Jewish Research, courtesy of USHMM Photo Archives.

believed they were being punished because of their acceptance of German values as opposed to traditional Jewish beliefs and the strict observance of ritual. Some of those fortunate enough to be able to emigrate had to make the heart-wrenching decision to leave their loved ones behind—not to mention home, hearth, and whatever possessions they might still own. Some others, as a way out, committed suicide. The synagogues overflowed. Jews were looking for solidarity and solace—a place to be together. Searching for answers became a preoccupation. Had Jews not celebrated Passover every year? Had Moses not led God's chosen people out of slavery in Egypt to the Promised Land? Almighty God had not forsaken his children then and surely he would not now. In order to live from day to day, people sold their belongings and pooled their resources.

I remember my mother weeping when she sold her precious crystal vase which had always sat in the middle of the dining room table and reflected the lights of the Sabbath candles into what seemed to be many twinkling diamonds. In the evening as usual the family got together, sat round the table without the vase and listened to Opa [grandfather] the optimist who had brought crusty pumpernickel bread and cheese supplied by Lieselotte, their former maid. My cousin Kurt, who was temporarily living with us in Berlin while waiting for his visa to go to Colombia in South America, wondered how to tell his mother in Dortmund that he was leaving the country. He was the only son. His father had died in the trenches during World War I. Kurt carried a letter in his wallet in which his father had written to his infant son "that he was proud to die for his country if need be." Tante Hans, Oma's [grandmother's] sister, who was also living with us, volunteered to tell Kurt's mother. Tante Hans was quite portly, but I would hear her run to the door when the postman deposited letters through the slot. She kept hoping for a letter from Australia from a niece she had raised who had promised to send her a visa from Australia. (Soumerai 1996)

In the early years of Hitler's consolidation of power, the mainstream of organizations representing the Jewish population looked for accommodation. After all, Jews were among the most law-abiding citizens. They had fought and died for their beloved Fatherland and had contributed greatly to its well-being. It seemed therefore inconceivable that what was clearly happening was more than a temporary aberration. Even after the Nuremberg Laws were passed, Jewish leaders still spoke of "creating a basis for a tolerable relationship between the German and the Jewish people" (Berenbaum 1993, 36). Life became ever more difficult, but everything at all possible was being done *far die kinder* (for the children). Jewish schools flourished. *Die Kinder* were taught Hebrew, English, French, Spanish, and rigorous academic subjects as well as vocational training in the various trades. Sports, too, were not neglected. No matter what, arrangements were made so that Jewish youths were able to meet regularly and engage in physical activities of all kinds. Some were fortunate and able to emigrate to Palestine in the program called Youth Aliyah.

Comments in the international press varied. Obviously the legislation, and the resulting treatment, of the Jews was unfair. But what could anyone do? Neither President Franklin Roosevelt nor the U.S. State Department made any public comment. To his credit Thomas Dodd, the father of Senator Christopher Dodd of Connecticut, the American ambassador to Germany, alerted Roosevelt that the new laws ensured complete subordination of the Jews. Dodd had hoped that the French, British, and American ambassadors would boycott the 1936 Nuremberg rally, but his proposal was rejected by the State Department. Dodd decided not to attend the Olympic Games, and he continued to send warnings to Washington, D.C., about the total separation of the Jews from the larger community.

DOROTHEA SCHLOESSER'S STORY

Born in 1921, half-Jewish Dorothea Schloesser survived the war as a singer.

My aversion to Hitler began with a remark made by the principal of my school. He said, "There are Jews and there are Christians, but worst of all are the half-breeds."

That really hit home! Usually I thought I stood above such insults, and more often than not I made fun of the Nazis. I didn't take them seriously. I considered them funny little brown delinquents, more comic than dangerous. And that was a mistake. . . . we failed to sense how dangerous the Nazis really were. But this time I was shocked . . . because they were obviously directed at me. I did get my *Abitur* (High School graduation certificate), but I cried a lot during that period. I used to look at myself in the mirror and think, "Are you really that horrible?" After a while I really almost believed myself to be inferior.

She was fortunate because many of the so-called half-breeds were sent to Auschwitz.

Source: Johannes Steinhoff, Peter Pechel, and Dennis Showalter. *Voices from the Third Reich* (New York: Da Capo Press, 1994), 45.

THE EVIAN CONFERENCE

By 1938 it was abundantly clear to the Jews in Germany, as well as in the annexed Austria, that war and worse was in store for them and that they must leave the two countries. Where they should go became the central question. In July mounting pressure in the United States coerced President Roosevelt to call for a conference at Evian, an idyllic spot by the Lake of Geneva in France. Representatives from thirty-two nations met to determine what they could do to help the persecuted Jews. Both German and Austrian Jews had obtained permission to send delegates to present a grand plan for systematic emigration (Dawidowicz 1975, 256). President Roosevelt, who had called for the conference, did not assert pressure on the international community to receive refugees beyond their already existing plans. He was well aware of the anti-immigrant sentiment in the United States. The Great Depression, he reasoned, deserved his complete attention because it affected almost one-third of the population of the United States. Hitler, accurately sensing the lack of willingness for serious intervention by the delegates, issued a statement expressing the hope that "the other world" would aid the "criminals." He would do his part and put the Jews on "luxury ships to wherever" (Berenbaum 1993, 49). To underline his point, Hitler ordered the synagogues of Munich, Nuremberg, and Dortmund destroyed shortly before the conference convened. He was right. There were very few offers of assistance. Holland and Denmark were willing to extend temporary asylum to a few refugees, and the Dominican Republic made a generous offer to receive 100,000 Jews, but very few were able to take advantage of the offer.

Hitler expressed great satisfaction that the countries represented seemed in no way anxious to take in any Jews. Hitler was now convinced that the rest of the world hated the Jews as much as he did.

KRISTALLNACHT: NIGHT OF THE BROKEN GLASS

At 3 A.M. on November 10, 1938, deliberate, organized terror was unleashed against Jews throughout the Reich, which now also included Austria. Jewish shops were trashed and looted, synagogues were set on fire, and thousands of Jews were arrested and sent to concentration camps. The official reason for what were called spontaneous demonstrations was the alleged German outrage resulting from the assassination of an official at the German embassy in Paris by a seventeen-year-old Polish Jewish refugee, named Hershel Grynszpan, who was seeking to avenge the persecution of his parents. The spontaneous demonstrations were, of course, planned well in advance.

Around midnight on *Kristallnacht,* Gestapo Chief Heinrich Muller sent a telegram to all police units informing them what was about to happen and asking them not to interfere. With methodical precision, the prepared Nazi storm troopers donned plain clothes and became members of the outraged civilian population. They fanned out to selected targets and, within forty-eight hours, had torched more than a thousand synagogues, destroyed hospitals and schools, and trashed businesses both large and small. So many thousands of Jews were rounded up and crowded into the concentration camps that immediate plans were drawn to expand the camps.

Eve remembers that night as though it were yesterday:

Mutti [Mother], Papi, Bibi my brother, and great-aunt were shaking, holding onto one another in the dark and looking out of the front window. There were sirens, screams and drumbeats all mixed up with shouts of "Death to the Jews." Flames were visible in the distance where our synagogue was. "Are they coming for us?"

my little brother kept asking. No one knew. The terror lasted throughout the night. In the morning, our neighbor downstairs, the laundry lady, came up and told us, obviously upset, that this madness would pass. *"Das ist nicht unser Deutschland"* [That's not our Germany], she said. She offered to do our laundry for no charge that week. A week later we heard that Papi's friend Herr Praeger was sent to Dachau. His wife received his ashes through the mail and was asked to pay for delivery. (Soumerai 1996)

The *Nationalist Socialist Courier,* a paper in Wurttemberg, deplored the reaction by Pastor Julius van Jan, who courageously denounced the pogrom from his pulpit:

Who would have believed the murder of one man in Paris could lead to so many murders here in Germany? . . . Passions run riot and the divine commandments are mocked. Places of worship, which some would regard as holy places, have been burnt without restraint and the stranger's possessions have been plundered and destroyed. Men who loyally served the German people have been thrown into concentration camps. (quoted in Thalman and Feinerman 1980, 73)

This sermon cost the pastor not only a term of imprisonment but internment in a concentration camp.

On November 12, Hermann Goering decided that "reparations" for the damage of 1 billion Reichsmark were to be imposed on the German Jews. They were also forced to clean up the rubble and instructed to hand over any insurance payments to which they might be entitled.

On November 23, all remaining Jewish businesses were closed, and a few days later, Jews were ordered to hand over their securities and jewelry.

Waves of suicides occurred. Lines in front of foreign embassies were long. People were desperate for any means to escape from hell.

THE VOYAGE OF THE *ST. LOUIS*

On May 13, 1939, 937 mostly Jewish passengers considered themselves most fortunate. They had booked passage on the luxury liner *St. Louis* destined for Cuba and freedom. They had been able to obtain American quota designations promising them eventual entry into the United States. In the interim, special permits had been issued to permit them temporary residence in Cuba while their American visas were being processed. A day before departure, however, the president of Cuba invalidated the landing permits, unknown to the passengers and Gustav Schröder, the captain of the German luxury liner, who was a decent individual who did everything in his power to make his passengers comfortable. He removed a picture of the fuehrer from the social hall of the boat and permitted religious services to take place, much to the consternation of some National

Socialist crew members. When the liner arrived and docked in Havana, the passengers gathered on the decks and joyfully greeted relatives below. Soon, however, they and the captain were advised that they would not be able to set foot on Cuban soil unless they came up with an unexpected million dollars, a sum impossible to raise in spite of furious negotiations between the Cuban government and members of the American Joint Distribution Committee in the United States.

In desperation, the passengers sent a telegram to President Roosevelt asking him personally for help. Captain Schröder also appealed to the U.S. government on behalf of his passengers. An editorial appearing in the *New York Times* expressed the sentiments shared by many: "We can only hope that some hearts will soften and some refuge will be found. The cruise of the *St. Louis* cries to high heaven of man's inhumanity to man" (cited in Berenbaum 1993, 58). All to no avail. The decision to bar the refugees from entering the United States reflected widespread feelings against immigrants, something that was difficult for the passengers to understand. Did they not have the necessary quota designations?

On the return journey to Europe, the passengers could clearly see the lights of Miami. They also noticed a U.S. Coast Guard ship patrolling the waters. The passengers at first erroneously believed it was there to assist them, but it instead was making sure none of them jumped overboard to freedom. Captain Schröder did what he could; he even devised a plan, if all else failed, to run the *St. Louis* close to the Sussex coast of England, set the ship on fire, and evacuate the passengers ashore. In the meantime, negotiators from the American Joint Distribution Committee had worked around the clock to make arrangements for the passengers to enter Belgium, Holland, France, and England—a miracle of sorts, given the tensions of the approaching war. Propaganda Minister Goebbels was upset. How could anyone accept Jews?

On Tuesday, June 13, 1939, the world learned that the "wandering refugees" would not be returning to Germany. In Berlin, Goebbels ordered that the British and French governments be heavily criticized in the German press for "selling out to the Jews" (Thomas and Witts 1974, 281).

Only the 288 passengers able to disembark in England survived the war; almost all the others ended up in Hitler's death camps after the Germans invaded their respective countries.

Captain Schröder, who had been so helpful, tried to make a living as a writer after the war. He used parts of his diary of the voyage in his writings. Some of the surviving passengers helped him by sending him food and clothing. They also spoke up on his behalf and helped to acquit him when he was put on trial under the de-Nazification process. In 1957, two years before his death, the West German government honored him for his important role in saving the passengers of the *St. Louis* on their ill-fated trip to Cuba (Berenbaum 1993, 58).

EXODUS TO SAFETY

The first Jews had reached German soil in Roman times. Jews had lived in Germany for more than a thousand years. There was a saying that Jews felt German first, German second, and German third, and then maybe Jewish. They resisted leaving their beloved country until it was too late for most of them. As more and more began to realize that their very existence was at stake, fewer and fewer opportunities became available—more and more doors to freedom closed. By the end of 1937, nearly 130,000, a quarter of the German Jews, had left; the rest were looking for havens—anywhere at all.

After *Kristallnacht*, during the first eight months of 1939, up until the outbreak of war in August, 78,000 Jews left Germany, the largest number in a single year since 1933. The number of emigrants from Austria totaled 55,000.

Between 1933 and 1943, the United States, the haven of choice, accepted 132,000 refugees from countries under Hitler's rule but left 400,000 immigration quota slots unfilled.

Kindertransport

Great Britain permitted the largest number of refugees to enter the country. The *Kindertransport* (children transport) program permitted 10,000 refugee children to go to England.

The World Movement for the Care of Children from Germany was the response of the British people to *Kristallnacht*. It was the umbrella organization for many groups, including the Jewish Refugees Committee, the Quakers, the churches, and countless individuals. What was missing was the necessary emergency legislation to give the operation legal status. A Quaker, Bertha Bracey, on behalf of the Quakers, accompanied Lord Samuel, the Liberal statesman, and persuaded Sir Samuel Hoare, then home secretary, to secure Parliament's urgent consent.

On November 21, 1938, only ten days after *Kristallnacht*, the House of Commons debated the refugee issue, and on the same day, the government announced its decision to permit "an unspecified number of children up to age seventeen from German-occupied lands to enter the United Kingdom as 'transmigrants.'" (*Kindertransport Souvenir Reunion Booklet* 1989, 3). A fifty-pound bond had to be posted for each child. On December 8, former Prime Minister Stanley Earl Baldwin issued a radio appeal: "'I ask you to come to the aid of victims not of any catastrophe in the natural world, nor of flood, nor of famine but of an explosion of man's inhumanity of man'" (*Kindertransport*, 3).

The English responded. Within a short time, more than 500,000 pounds had been contributed. Other gifts ranged from castles and farms to free shoes for all children (from the department store Marks and Spencer) to boxing gloves.

Another heroic individual responded. Thomas H. Wysmuller has this story to tell:

My grandaunt ("Tante Truus"), Mrs. Truus Wijsmuller, lived in Amsterdam, Holland, and was a member of the Committee for Jewish Affairs in that city during the 1930s. She worked day and night on behalf of Jewish children and negotiated with German authorities permitting literally thousands to escape via Holland to safety in England.

Tante Truus was extraordinarily persuasive. While visiting Westerbork, the Dutch transition camp to the death camps of Eastern Europe (where Anne Frank and her family also spent time) she came across fifty orphaned children ready to be shipped out. She immediately contacted the German authorities and insisted that these children were the illegitimate offsprings of Dutch girls and German soldiers—and should therefore be sent to Theresienstadt not Auschwitz—which they were. All of them returned after the war.

Even on the very last day of fighting on May 14, 1939, Tante Truus managed to save eighty children from the orphanage. All civilian traffic had been stopped but she found a bus ready to take the children to the port of Ijmuiden where ten minutes before the Dutch surrender, the last ship *Bodegraven* to leave the harbor took the eighty children aboard and thus to safety in England.

She wrote her story "No Time for Tears," which was her motto. The story has not been published in English. (Wysmuller 1998)

The news of the *Kindertransport* spread, and all parents tried to save their children. The committees in charge of rescuing the children tried to identify those in dire need, such as orphans, to give them priority. In some cases, German Quakers helped in the identifying process.

Eve was among those chosen.

My father was gone half the night to stand in line somewhere to make contact. Because he had already been rounded up by the Gestapo (and released because of the intervention of a well-known German lawyer who had been my father's World War I buddy) he had priority for at least one child. One day we heard from Reverend Josef Burton, the representative of the Quaker refugee committee in Ipswich, Suffolk, that Mr. and Mrs. George Rattenbury of nearby Foxhall were willing to be my temporary guardians, my new "uncle and auntie." There was muted jubilation because my ten-year-old brother was not able to make a connection. On June 30, I left Germany and my parents and brother forever. . . . It was a glorious summer day. Father, mother, and brother Bibi were jammed, along with hundreds of other parents and children, into a small room at a Berlin railway station. Everybody was in tears. It was supposed to be temporary—but in our hearts we feared that it might not be so. My mother's last words were, "Look at the stars and pray," and she kept repeating, say "thank you to 'uncle and auntie.'" My father hugged me one last time and said, "You have a beautiful smile, use it." And my little brother asked that I find him a home near me, and a pair of boxing gloves. My name was called over the loudspeaker, and I left them in that little crowded room. My new black patent leather shoes sounded like the beating of a hammer as I walked to the waiting train. (Soumerai 1996)

Kindertransport photograph of Eve Nussbaum
(Soumerai), 13 years old. Courtesy of Eve Nussbaum Soumerai.

Hanna, a high-priority orphan, was on one of the very first transports.
She was a German-born child of Polish parents. Hanna was twelve and
her sister thirteen when their parents were expelled in early November
1938 and taken away to the no-man's-land between the borders of Germany and Poland.

In the middle of the night, there were loud bangs on the door of our apartment. My mother started to sob, while my father opened the door. Two men in
uniform stood outside. *"Schnell machen* [hurry up], you have twenty minutes
to pack a suitcase each." While we watched in terror, my father tried to reason with them, saying he needed time to make arrangements for his children.
"Surely officer, you have children too," he pleaded. My sister and I were frozen in terror while our parents were led away. The apartment was sealed and
we were left sitting outside on the stoop alone. In the morning I tried to run
into the street. Someone pulled me away from the traffic and I can't remember
exactly how, but that evening my sister and I found ourselves in an orphanage.
(Hanna S. 1989)

The American Response

In the United States, early in 1939, Senator Robert Wagner of New York and Representative Edith N. Rogers of Massachusetts proposed the Child Refugee Bill that would have allowed 20,000 refugee children to enter the United States between 1939 and 1941. Support for this bill came from many quarters, including Eleanor Roosevelt, as well as from almost every religious denomination. The Quakers were again involved in working out transportation and distribution details. Within a day after announcing the plan, 4,000 families of all faiths had offered to take the children (Gutman 1990, 1262).

There were numerous opponents to the plan, including the Allied Patriotic Societies, the American Women Against Communism, the Veterans of Foreign Wars, and the Sons and Daughters of the American Revolution. The American Legion announced its support for Senator Robert R. Reynold's bill, which if passed, would have abolished immigration to the United States for the next ten years. One witness, representing an organization of widows of World War I veterans, declared at the hearing before the House Committee on Immigration: "I am the daughter of generations of patriots. . . . This nation will be helpless to guarantee to our children their rights under the Constitution if this country is to become the dumping ground for the persecuted minorities of Europe" (Gutman 1990, 1262).

President Roosevelt, reluctant to oppose an isolationist Congress, used his political capital to expand the Air Corps and construct naval bases; the bill died in committee.

Other Rescue Efforts

During the entire period from 1934 to 1945, only about 1,000 unaccompanied refugee children managed to reach the United States; 350 of them arrived after 1941 from France. Again, Quakers worked nonstop to overcome the numerous obstacles.

For a short time, the free port and cosmopolitan city of Shanghai, China, became a haven for refugees; it was the only place in the world refugees could enter without a visa. By the end of May 1939, 14,000 penniless refugees had arrived, usually on ships sailing from Italy. Funds were provided by Jewish relief organizations. But here, too, by the middle of August, restrictions were imposed by those in charge, and from then on only a very few managed to reach Shanghai. With Italy's entry into the war in 1940, passage to the Far East ceased altogether (Yahil 1990, 615–18).

Eve heard from her uncle Max, who was waiting in Genoa, Italy, to sail to Shanghai:

Soon after I arrived in Ipswich on the *Kindertransport,* I received a postcard from Onkel [Uncle] Max sent to me from Genoa, Italy, where he was waiting for his turn to go to Shanghai. The next time I heard from him was after the war was over. Instead of sanctuary in Shanghai, he ended up hiding in a cave. A family of peasants cared for him and a homeless cat kept him company. (Soumerai, 1996)

WORKS CITED

Berenbaum, Michael. *The World Must Know: The History of the Holocaust as Told in the United States Holocaust Memorial Museum.* Boston: Little, Brown, 1993.

Dawidowicz, Lucy S. *The War against the Jews: 1933–1945.* New York: Holt, Rinehart and Winston, 1975.

Gutman, Israel, ed. *Encyclopedia of the Holocaust.* New York: Macmillan, 1990.

Kahn, Lothar. Lecture at Teacher Seminar, West Hartford, Connecticut, 1981.

Kindertransport Souvenir Reunion Booklet. London, 1989.

S., Hanna. Interview by Eve Soumerai, London, June 1989.

Shirer, William L. *The Rise and Fall of the Third Reich.* New York: Simon and Schuster, 1960.

Soumerai, Eve. Interview by Carol Schulz, West Hartford, Connecticut, 1982.

———. Unpublished memoir, 1996.

Thalman, Rita, and Emanuel Feinerman. *Crystal Night.* New York: Holocaust Library, 1980.

Thomas, Gordon, and Max Morgan Witts. *Voyage of the Damned.* New York: Stein and Day, 1974.

Wysmuller, Thomas H. Interview by Eve Soumerai, Wethersfield, Connecticut, April 5, 1998.

Yahil, Leni. *The Holocaust: The Fate of European Jewry, 1932–1945.* New York: Oxford University Press, 1990.

5

PROLOGUE TO WORLD WAR II

HITLER VIOLATES THE LOCARNO TREATY

The Locarno Treaty, signed in 1925 by the Western powers and Germany, was intended to end war hatreds left over from the Treaty of Versailles and to ease Germany's economic situation resulting from World War I reparations. Germany agreed to submit any disputes to the League of Nations, which they joined in 1926, and promised to honor all territorial agreements, including noninterference in the demilitarization of the Rhineland.

A highly significant event occurred on March 7, 1936: Adolf Hitler decided to take the enormous risk of reoccupying the demilitarized zone of the Rhineland in direct violation of the Locarno Treaty, which, in contrast to the Treaty of Versailles, had been freely signed by all parties in preparing to admit Germany into the League of Nations. At 10 A.M., the German foreign minister called in the ambassadors of France, Britain, and Italy, told them what had happened, and handed them a formal note denouncing the Locarno Treaty, which Hitler had just broken, while proposing new plans for peace. "Hitler struck his adversary in the face," French ambassador Andre Francois-Poncet observed, "and as he did so declared: I bring you proposals for peace!" (quoted in Shirer 1960, 291). Historians believe that, had there been allied resistance to the takeover, the small German forces would certainly have been beaten. Hitler would have been embarrassed and lost the support of the army. Instead there was no resistance, and Hitler became bolder than ever (Kahn 1981).

On March 12, 1938, Hitler followed up by occupying Austria and incorporating it into the German Reich. He received a warm welcome from the population. It took only a year for Austrian Jews to be excluded from participation in Austrian life. The speed and efficiency with which the measures to accomplish these goals were executed served as models to be used later in other occupied countries.

In September 1938, Hitler bluffed the British and French leaders into the dismemberment of Czechoslovakia by insisting on pulling the Sudeten Germans (Sudetenland) back into greater Germany. Rather than go to war on behalf of Czechoslovakia, one of the most prosperous and democratic countries in Central Europe, British Prime Minister Neville Chamberlain went to Munich to appease Hitler and to agree to "peace in our time." Hitler promised once again that this would be his final territorial demand. Ivan A. Backer, formerly of Prague, Czechoslovakia, has this recollection:

My parents had shipped me off to stay with friends in the countryside. After the agreement with Chamberlain was signed, I returned to Prague. While there was a certain relief that the immediate crisis had passed, the air was thick with apprehension whether this agreement would stop Hitler or encourage him. The raging debate in the Jewish community was whether to get ready to leave or wait to stick it out. The uncertainty came to a crashing end on March 15, 1939, when German troops and armored vehicles came rolling into the city. It was a weekday morning and I was ready to go to school as usual when we heard the news that they were coming. By the time I was on my way to school, I saw German troops riding down the main street in our neighborhood on their motorcycles with seats attached to the side. It was cloudy and cold that day and the uniforms of the troops blended into the gray of the morning. I was overwhelmed by the numbing feeling that we were no longer free and the worst had come to be. (Backer 1997)

German troops poured into Czechoslovakia without resistance at 6 A.M. that day. That very evening Hitler was able to make a triumphant entry into the city and spend the night in the famous Hradshin Castle, the ancient seat of kings set high above the Moldau River. Shortly before leaving Berlin, he had proudly proclaimed to the German people, "Czechoslovakia has ceased to exist!" The country had fallen under full German "protection" (quoted in Shirer 1960, 291).

Only Joseph Stalin's opposition gave Hitler pause; therefore, on August 23, 1939, in a brilliant move, Hitler arranged for Joachim von Ribbentrop and Vyncheslav Molotov, the foreign ministers of Germany and the Soviet Union, to sign a nonaggression pact clearing the way for the dismemberment of Poland into Russian and German zones. Thus Hitler kept the Soviet Union out of his war, at least for the time being, until he was ready.

World War II began officially on September 1, 1939, when Hitler attacked Poland. The British, followed by the French, issued a last-minute ultimatum. Hitler's response was to leave Berlin. At precisely 9 P.M., a special train left to take him directly to the eastern front to assume his role as commander in chief. Part of his grand plan was to utilize the soon-to-be conquered Polish *Untermenschen* (subhumans) as slaves for the greater glory of the German Reich. Hitler's intentions and philosophy had been clearly spelled out a few days earlier, on August 23, 1939, when he addressed the commanding generals of the *Wehrmacht* at his Berchtesgaden retreat, the Berghof in Obersalzberg: "Our strength is our speed and our brutality. Ghenghis Khan drove many women and children to death, deliberately and joyously. . . . I will have any one shot who expresses even one word of criticism" (quoted in Czech 1990, 1).

Polish Jews, on the other hand, were a few steps below *Untermenschen*; they were considered vermin and, along with all other European Jews, were destined to be totally annihilated. Hitler was assisted in his attempt to achieve these goals by industrialists, trained engineers, chemists, railroad specialists, and physicians who were accumulating a lot of practical know-how in the operation of an efficient euthanasia program.

EUTHANASIA

In June 1939, three months before the outbreak of World War II, Hitler held secret meetings in his office to discuss implementation of what he called euthanasia. Among the psychiatrists, professors, and other experts who attended the meetings, only one, Gottfried Ewald, a professor of psychiatry at Goettingen University, tried to have the plan shelved.

First, handicapped children were considered *Lebens unwertes Leben* (life unworthy of life) and targeted for death. They were kept in specially designed institutions for several weeks to give the impression that they were being given some special form of therapy. The killing was generally accomplished via tablets of Luminal (a barbiturate) dissolved in tea. Pneumonia was listed as the cause of death. The criteria for the killing of children continually expanded to include not only various minor handicaps but also youths designated as juvenile delinquents and then expanded to include the killing of so-called impaired adults.

There was opposition from various clergy, both Catholic and Protestant, whose congregation raised their voices repeatedly. Dr. Hilfrich, bishop of Limburg an der Lahn near Hadamar, where one of the killing centers was located, wrote on August 13, 1941, to the minister of justice, "The local children now recognize the buses [transporting victims] with blacked-out windows . . . 'look there's the murderbox coming again'" (Yahil 1990, 309).

Perhaps the most famous sermon delivered in opposition was one given in early August 1941. Catholic Bishop Clemens Count von Galen, then Bishop of Münster, told the congregation:

"It is said of these patients: They are like an old machine which no longer runs, like an old horse which is hopelessly paralyzed, like a cow which no longer gives milk. . . . We are not talking here about a machine nor a horse, nor a cow. . . . No, we are talking . . . about our brothers and sisters . . . think of the horrible state we shall be in when we are weak and sick!" (Lifton *The Nazi Doctors,* 94)

Leaflets of the sermon were distributed throughout Germany and dropped among German troops by British Royal Fliers. It had great impact, and even those in charge of propaganda were unsure how to react to statements from such a popular figure (Lifton *The Nazi Doctors,* 94). No such leaflets were distributed on behalf of the Jews.

As a result of these protests, as well as appeals made by relatives of the victims, Hitler ordered the euthanasia operations discontinued. However, when the formal installations were closed down, the operations went underground. In a program of "wild euthanasia," (Yahil 1990, 310) the killing took place in special, locked-up institutions. Patients were put to death individually by injection, sleeping pills, or starvation; starvation was a particularly popular method in the case of mentally defective or physically disabled children. Again, concerned parents were informed that their child had been transferred to a special institution for treatment (Yahil 1990, 309).

Robert K. Wagemann, now living in New Jersey, was born in 1937 in Mannheim, Germany. Due to a difficult breech birth, he was born with a defective hip. When he was four years old, his mother was summoned to report to an annex of the university clinic on the outskirts of Heidelberg, run by Catholic nuns, so that he could be examined by a special team of doctors.

My mom was already suspicious and kept her ears and eyes open. They took off my clothes and put me into a gown. My mom waited in the hall. When the doctors left the examining room to go to lunch and passed her in the hall, she heard them say that after lunch they would give the boy an injection and put him to sleep. She waited until the doctors were gone, then ran into the room and asked one of the nuns for my clothes and, after an argument, was given them. Then she rushed me out of the hospital. At the exit she was stopped by another nun who also made objections. Mom threatened her and was able to leave with me in her arms. Mom and I went down to the banks of the Neckar river where the high grass was. There she put my clothes on and we were on our way. (Wagemann 1997)

Because the Wagemann family were Jehovah's Witnesses, they were doubly endangered. When Robert started to go to school and refused to salute the flag and say, "Heil Hitler," the family was visited by the Protestant priest in party uniform, an official, and a policeman. It was time to move, to leave, to go into temporary hiding. Robert explained that an additional reason for euthanasia was that it was a way for the state to cut costs. Money not spent on healing was better spent on furthering Nazi Party endeavors.

At the end of October, a circular was sent to relevant institutions, and the staff was ordered to fill out questionnaires on the condition of each patient within a month (Yahil 1990, 308). The renewed euthanasia operations were secret, and each participant took an oath of silence. Hitler had issued a rare

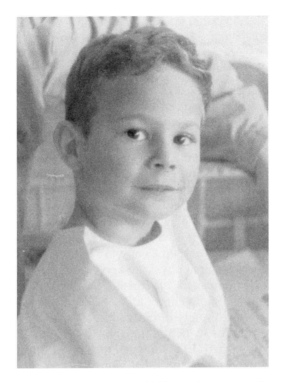

Robert K. Wagemann in 1941, age 4 years, nearly
a victim of the Nazi's euthanasia campaign.
Courtesy of Robert Wagemann.

written directive and predated it September 1, 1939, the day war broke
out. The name Adolf Hitler formed the only letterhead.[1] Hitler's signa-
ture was the equivalent of law and ensured that participating physicians
would be immune from legal consequences (Lifton *German Doctors,* 64).
The operations were to be carried out in steps:

1. The candidates were selected primarily from mental institutions.

2. From there, they were taken to transit centers.

3. From there, they were sent to special killing centers, equipped with carbon monoxide gas, to be gassed—about 20 at a time—in sealed rooms,
   and their bodies were burned in an attached crematorium but not before
   their gold teeth were removed and some of their brains were excised for
   "scientific research." These experiments were first conducted in January
   1940. (Yahil 1990, 308–9)

At first, Jewish mental patients were not included because they were
more "unworthy" than the afflicted German Aryans. Jews embodied not
only "dangerous genes" but also "racial poison." (Lipton *German Doctors,*
70) After a short time, those in charge changed their minds and included
Jewish patients.

Fred S. told about his father disappearing each Sunday morning apparently to visit [Fred's] mentally handicapped sister. The family had their visas for the United States. At the last moment the father felt he couldn't leave his handicapped daughter. The visas expired and the very next week, a package of ashes was delivered for which the father was asked to pay a considerable amount. Fred was able to leave at the last minute on the *Kindertransport* program to England; the rest of the family perished at Auschwitz. (Fred S. 1989)

The methodology of extermination in the death camps to come was in place—helped along by the medical expertise of German physicians who had one of the highest ratios of party membership of any profession: forty-five percent. They were present for the procedures used to determine the amount of corporal punishment a victim could absorb. They kept the extermination selections running smoothly, helped balance the costs and benefits of keeping prisoners alive, and contributed the necessary technical knowledge about the most efficient ways to burn the bodies (Gutman 1990, 1131). Hitler's personal physician and escort, Doctor Professor Karl Brandt, a gifted, distinguished surgeon and an authority on head and spinal injuries, became Hitler's choice to head the euthanasia program. He had at one time been strongly influenced by Albert Schweitzer and had hoped to join him in his work at Lambarene but, failing to be able to do this, joined the other hero in his life, Adolf Hitler (Lifton *The Nazi Doctors*, 114). Ironically, Brandt and other German physicians continued to administer the Oath of Hippocrates, the Greek physician and father of medicine (460–370 B.C.): "I will use treatment to help the sick according to my ability and judgment, but never with a view of injury and wrongdoing." These ancient words were simply recast into Nazi ideology, which no longer focused on the individual but rather on the *Volk,* the entire German nation, to prevent its *Volkstod* [death of the folk]—"doing this for the revitalization of our people" (Lipton *The Nazi Doctors,* 114).

NOTE

1. Robert Jay Lifton (1986) suggests that the reason for the predating was Hitler's belief that, during wartime, the German population would be more amenable to such a project. Why the private stationery? "He understood himself to be a prophet whose racial vision outdistanced ... the bureaucratic apparatus" (*German Doctors*, 63).

WORKS CITED

Backer, Ivan A. Interview by Eve Soumerai, Hartford, Connecticut, May 10, 1997.

Czech, Danuta. *Auschwitz Chronicle 1939–1945.* New York: Henry Holt, Owl Book, 1990.

Gutman, Israel, ed. *Encyclopedia of the Holocaust.* New York: Macmillan, 1990.

Kahn, Lothar. Lecture at Teacher Seminar, Madison, Connecticut, 1981.

Lifton, Robert Jay. "German Doctors and the Final Solution." *New York Times Magazine,* September 21, 1986 64–65, 70–75.

———. *The Nazi Doctors: Medical Killing and the Psychology of Genocide.* New York: Basic Books, 1986.

S., Fred. Interview by Eve Soumerai, London, at the *Kindertransport* Reunion, June 29, 1989.

Shirer, William L. *The Rise and Fall of the Third Reich.* New York: Simon and Schuster, 1960.

Wagemann, Robert K. Interview by Eve Soumerai, Fairfield, New Jersey, October 11, 1997.

Yahil, Leni. *The Holocaust: The Fate of European Jewry, 1932–1945.* New York: Oxford University Press, 1990.

6

WORLD WAR II BEGINS

LIFE AND DEATH IN EUROPE: THE *BLITZKRIEG*

On September 1, 1939, Germany invaded Poland. Less than two years later, on June 22, 1941, Hitler repudiated his pact with Joseph Stalin and sent troops into the Soviet portion of Poland and into Lithuania, Latvia, Estonia, Soviet White Russia, parts of the Ukraine, the Crimea, and Russia proper. As a result of the invasions of Poland and the eastern part of the Soviet Union, Germany gained control over some 5 million more Jews.

The Jews, along with the rest of the Polish people, suffered tremendous casualties during the early weeks of the invasion of Poland. City after city was destroyed.

Mark Sobotka and his fiancée, Bernice, were in their twenties when the Germans invaded their city of Lodz. Mark's father, who owned a small factory, considered his family lower middle class. There were six children in the family, and they were very religious but "not fanatics." Mark believed they were a "normal Polish family" who just wore different clothes, the traditional dress of the Hasidic Jews (Schulz 1981, 52).

Bernice's family, which was wealthier, was not as observant. She was one of eight children. Her father was a representative for a French company that sold silk. The family had several servants and was affluent enough to spend summers in the country. They had lived in Lodz for generations, spoke both Polish and Yiddish at home, and were fluent in German. Most of their neighbors were German. All of the children went to private schools, but Bernice's father could not afford to send them to college. It was almost impossible to get accepted into a Polish university, and going away to school was too expensive.

Both Mark and Bernice had experienced anti-Semitism throughout their childhoods, especially around Christmas and Easter: "Where my wife lived with her parents, I wouldn't even dare to go. I don't know how they managed to stay in that neighborhood. It was a strictly Polish neighborhood, and you were not safe there in the night" (M. Sobotka, 1980). "The most dangerous time was Christmas. You stayed in. You didn't look for trouble, and always somebody got beaten up" (B. Sobotka, 1980).

Although Mark and Bernice felt uncomfortable living in Poland, leaving the country was not a realistic option. It was difficult to get to Palestine (now Israel) or America. The bureaucracy was extensive, and the cost was very high. Also, without relatives living outside Poland, unless one could take a whole family including married children and their families, there was no compelling reason to say goodbye to the only people in the world one loved. Noted Bernice, "If you don't have anybody, anyplace in the world, what are you going to do? Where are you supposed to go? You don't run that quickly" (1980).

By the time the German army had advanced on their city, it was too late to escape. "I can remember the bombing of Lodz. We tried to run away to Warsaw, but the highway was bombed. So I went home," recalled Bernice (1980).

Many other Polish Jews, and non-Jews as well, tried to escape from the Germans. About 300,000 Jews fled to Soviet-occupied Poland. According to historian Lucy Dawidowicz, "Thousands upon thousands of Jews set out on foot, on carts, in wagons, seeking refuge" (1975, 536).

Chaim A. Kaplan, a schoolteacher in Warsaw at the time of the invasion, kept a diary of his life from 1939 to 1942. In his entry for September 4, 1939, just three days after the invasion began, he wrote, "Our world has turned into chaos. There is no mail; there is no train travel . . . there is no way to earn a living. All trade has stopped except for food stores and medical supply houses, which are being besieged by customers. . . . The Germans destroyed the Catholic church in Czestochowa, the most important Catholic shrine in Poland" (Kaplan 1973, 103).

On September 12, Kaplan described the destruction of the Polish capital, noting that the Polish government had fled the city: "Entire blocks have been turned into ashes and magnificent palaces into rubble" (1973, 105).

Incendiary bombs wreaked havoc in the city. Kaplan's diary noted: "No one knows where he is running . . . carrying babies and bundles, distracted and terrified . . . hundreds of families are left with nothing" (1973, 105). Five days later, he tells us, there is no more food: "Human beings spend all their energies and talents in pursuit of bread. Every day people are being dug out of the rubble and buried" (1973, 106).

Shmaryahu Elenberg, a survivor who had escaped from Lodz to Warsaw, later recalled "the horrifying scenes in the hospitals. They were crammed with the wounded, lying on the floors and in the corridors . . . physicians and nurses at their wits' end" (Elenberg 1973, 125).

Oddly enough, throughout this ordeal, German planes circled above taking pictures of the breadlines for their propaganda films. They wanted the world to see them as benevolent liberators, not as ruthless invaders.

In the small towns, the invasion of the Germans was just as shocking. "My father felt that it would be folly to try to outrun a modern, mechanized army and if death had to come, he wanted to be in his own home, not in somebody else's field or backyard," recalled Joseph Korzenik, who at the time of the invasion was only eleven (Korzenik 1980). Joseph lived in the Polish region of Bucovina, in a small Polish town of about 8,000 people, half of whom were Jewish. Although his town had electricity by 1939, most of the surrounding towns did not. Hot and cold running water was a luxury. Water was brought into the homes in buckets from a common well. Radios were at a premium, and possession of guns was against the law. In 1939 the horse was still the predominant means of transportation; only half a dozen townspeople owned cars or trucks.

Joseph's father was a butcher, and his mother helped in the operation of their store. The family was small, Joseph and his two sisters. Their ancestors had lived in Poland for a long time, though no one knew exactly how long. They did not live in a separate Jewish part of town, for Jews and Gentiles lived side by side. Joseph attended a regular public school in the morning and took Hebrew lessons in the evening. The family, who considered themselves Polish citizens, spoke and wrote in Polish at home.

Despite trying to assimilate, like Jews in the cities, rural Jews were subjected to anti-Semitic attacks.

For me it was difficult to strike up a true friendship with a Polish girl or boy. In school, boys always had to defend themselves. I remember that if I got caught on a street in which there were mostly non-Jewish boys, I was in constant fear that I would get beaten up. I was, on many occasions. But that was not just me. Most of the Jewish boys had to contend with this. We knew we lived in a hostile environment, but we learned to live with it, and we managed very well. (Korzenik 1980)

They managed very well, at least, until war broke out. Even then, Joseph's father did not want to run away. Joseph's older sister and her fiancé had succeeded in escaping to the east, but his father chose to remain in Poland.

People started to panic. . . . My father felt that, should we leave our home and get caught in the panicky evacuation, we would have nothing to come home to. He was equating the situation with his experiences during World War I when he was in the Austrian army. Whenever they invaded an area, the homes that were occupied were left alone. The homes that were empty, they would ransack and vandalize. (Korzenik 1980)

POLAND SURRENDERS

With the surrender of Warsaw on September 27, 1939, the occupation of western Poland was complete. It had taken the Germans less than one month to conquer Poland. The free city of Danzig (taken from Germany by the Treaty of Versailles following World War I) was annexed into the Greater Reich of Germany. This area was divided into two districts: Danzig–West Prussia and the Wartheland. The remainder of Poland was called the General Government of Poland and placed under German civil administration. Later, the western sector of German-held Russian territory was added to the General Government as well.

In the first few weeks of the German occupation, thousands of Jews and non-Jews were killed. At first casualties were the result of fighting. More than 60,000 Polish soldiers were killed, of whom about 6,000 were Jews. Many Jewish civilians were also singled out for special abuses. Jews formed a tenth of the Polish population but accounted for nearly a third of those killed during this time (Gilbert 1985, 32).

HITLER'S EARLY PLANS FOR THE JEWS

Even before Poland had been occupied, the Germans had formulated plans for the treatment of the Polish Jews. In a directive issued on September 21, 1939, by Reinhard Heydrich, head of the Reich Security Main Office (RSHA) and the Gestapo, and responsible to Heinrich Himmler (Reichsfahrer-SS and chief of German Police) for the execution of Hitler's "racial" program, these plans were set forth. The plans also included Gypsies and later non-Jewish Poles as well (Hilberg 1967, 137–13; Dawidowicz 1975, 154). The directive included four basic components.

1. First, the Jews were to be removed from the German Reich and the incorporated territories (except for Lodz) and concentrated in urban areas, mostly in the General Government.
2. Next, Jewish councils (*Judenräte*) were to be established that would be responsible for carrying out the orders of the *Einsatzgruppen* (mobile killing units) in each community.
3. Jews were then to be concentrated in ghettos.
4. Finally, "prompt Aryanization" (confiscation by the German government) of Jewish property, businesses, and labor was to be undertaken.

All this was to be accomplished by the *Einsatzgruppen*, under Heydrich's direction. As soon as Poland was occupied, this plan was put into operation. Frequently, events would happen simultaneously, as the German army, the *Einsatzgruppen*, or the Gestapo swept into each city, town, and village. (The *Einsatzgruppen* was a paramilitary police force that operated under the direction of Himmler. It was first used in the invasion of Austria to hunt down people suspected of opposing National Socialism.

Six *Einsatzgruppen* were attached to the army during the Polish campaign. Dawidowicz writes that "Their wholesale murder of Poles and their sadistic atrocities against Jews shocked some army generals" (1975, 152). Later, the *Einsatzgruppen* would be responsible for the "Final Solution to the Jewish Question" in the rest of Eastern Europe.)

HITLER ON THE "TRUTH"

On August 22, 1939, Adolf Hitler gathered his top military commanders, lectured them on his own greatness, and urged them to wage a "war without pity" against Poland. He claimed Poland planned to fight Germany and therefore must be liquidated. These were his words:

> I shall give a propagandist reason . . . never mind whether it is plausible or not. The victor will not be asked later whether he told the truth or not. In starting and waging war it is not right that matters, but victory. Close your hearts to pity! Act brutally!

Source: William L. Shirer, *The Rise and Fall of the Third Reich.* (New York: Simon and Schuster, 1960), 532.

IMPLEMENTING THE PLAN

Although Jews in prewar Poland lived in more than 16,000 localities, most of them (75%) could be found concentrated in the cities, where they made up a large portion of the population. This was true in the rest of Eastern Europe as well. In Kiecle, Poland, 24,000 Jews represented more than one-third of the population. One in four residents of Kovno, Lithuania (40,000), and Crakow, Poland (60,000), were Jews. In Minsk, in the Soviet Union, 80,000 Jews made up thirty percent of the people. In Radom, Poland, there were 30,000 Jews, also one-third of the population. Rounding them up and concentrating them into ghettos was not difficult. (The idea of the ghetto, referring to an enclosed section of a city reserved for Jews, dates back to the Middle Ages in Europe. The term itself comes from the Italian word for foundry, *gettare*, "to pour," because the first ghetto in the Jewish Quarter of Venice was near a foundry. By the start of World War II, though Jews frequently lived in Jewish neighborhoods, especially in the larger cities of Eastern Europe, they were no longer excluded from other parts of the city or confined to ghettos. All this changed as soon as the Nazis arrived.)

In Poland, ghettos were formed in the weeks following the start of the war, and, for the most part, the inhabitants remained there until the decision was made that the "Final Solution to the Jewish Question" was to take place in the extermination camps of Eastern Europe. In the areas of the Soviet Union that were occupied by Germany, the ghettos were formed after the first sweep of massacres following the June 22, 1941, Nazi invasion.

Given the fact that the Jewish people were already fairly well concentrated, the task of expelling them from their homes and forcing them into ghettos was fairly easy. But it was not peaceful. Expulsion from towns and villages was always accompanied by humiliation, terror, and death. Even in those areas in which Jews were allowed to remain, torture, shame, and death were daily occurrences.

What happened to Joseph Korzenik and his family in Bucovina provides a good example of the process of ghettoization. One week after the Germans invaded Poland, they occupied his town. He remembers that" the High Holidays were observed in hiding because the synagogues were destroyed. Torahs and prayer books were burned and worship forbidden." Joseph's uncle, who had lived for many years in Chicago, but had returned to Poland in 1939 to visit his children, "was shot in front of my eyes as he was coming to our home for the Sabbath meal" (Korzenik 1980).

Children, too, were the targets of Nazi brutality. Joseph also remembers seeing the Germans kill Jewish infants by tossing them into the air and shooting them. Although this was a common claim of anti-German propagandists during World War I, it actually did happen under the Nazi regime.

In the cities, similar events took place. In Lodz, Mark Sobotka was stopped in the street by a German SS officer and taken to a barbershop where he was forced to have his head shaved. Jewish law required men to wear their hair long. The incident shamed and embarrassed him so much that he left Lodz and went to Warsaw, where he attempted to escape to Russia. Unable to find a guide to help him reach Bialystok, he eventually returned to his family in Lodz.

Bernice also witnessed sadistic behavior: "They [the army] started catching Jewish girls and boys and men and women and forcing them to do filthy work. They caught my father once on the street, and made him pull a wagon like a horse" (B. Sobotka 1980).

This arbitrary terror continued during the first six months of the Nazi occupation. During this time, the Germans carried out a systematic plan designed to identify, isolate, and terrorize the Jewish community. To ensure that no Jew could escape identification, the Nazis required that all Jews over the age of ten wear the Star of David at all times. Failure to do so was punishable by death (Weiss 1977, 339). A twelve-year-old schoolmate of Joseph was shot to death because he forgot his star. (In the camps, other groups were singled out for "special treatment," including the Gypsies, who were also forced to wear an identifying badge.)

Jews were also restricted in their movement within the cities. In the General Government, they could not change residence without approval from the proper authorities, nor could they be out on the streets between 9 p.m. and 5 a.m. No Jewish children were allowed to attend school or to use public transportation (Weiss 1977, 346; Hilberg 1967, 145).

The Germans used additional tactics to isolate the Jews from the community and turn them into impoverished outcasts. As a result of the bombing, food was scarce. In the city of Warsaw, the Germans agreed upon the payment by the city government of 1 million zlotys to set up soup lines to feed the hungry. Although Jews were to be fed along with the rest of the population, the Germans arbitrarily ejected them from the lines, calling on Poles to do the same (Dawidowicz 1975, 269).

Bernice recalled how she and her sister were able to obtain food for their family:

I had a sister who was blond, and we worked together. We stayed in lines like the Poles and made believe we were German or Polish. We spoke German pretty well. My sister was blond with blue eyes; I was light-haired and my eyes are light. I would wear bright colors like blue and yellow to make them appear lighter. So I got away with it. I stayed in the lines, and when they came to pull out the Jews, they never pulled me out. I was lucky. (B. Sobotka 1980)

If one considers that the relations between Jews and gentiles in Eastern Europe during the years before the war had never been too friendly, it is easy to understand why the Germans believed, correctly, that they would be able to turn the non-Jewish population against their Jewish neighbors. One eyewitness wrote, "It was interesting to observe . . . how quickly the brotherhood born under the continuous danger of death disappeared and how quickly the difference between rich and poor, Christian and Jew, once again became apparent" (Dawidowicz 1975, 269).

Unfortunately, many Polish Jews were easily distinguishable from non-Jews by their appearance. Not only did they dress differently from their neighbors, but for many, their dark features or strange haircuts contrasted sharply with the blond, blue-eyed Poles. When this was not the case, especially with upper-middle-class Jews like Bernice who did not dress or wear their hair in traditional styles, gentile neighbors often pointed out the Jews to unsuspecting Germans.

When the Germans came, before we were shipped to the ghetto, we were still living among the Poles. The Germans really did not know who was a Jew except the Jews who wore Hasidic garb. But take a person like me. The Germans didn't know if I was Jewish or Polish or what. But the Poles told them which apartments belonged to Jews. They pointed them out. They worked hand in hand. They're the ones that told them, "That's a Jewish family, go ahead." So they helped the Germans. (B. Sobotka 1980)

THE "ARYANIZATION" OF JEWISH PROPERTY

In addition to making the Jews social outcasts and depriving them of food, the Nazis immediately began implementing their plan to "Aryanize" Jewish-owned businesses and industry, and to confiscate their private property. In large cities, such as Lodz and Warsaw, trucks were used to cart away Jewish possessions. In smaller towns, the Germans took Jewish hostages to guarantee that their orders would be obeyed, then demanded that the Jews turn over all their gold and other valuables. If the German orders were not obeyed, the hostages were executed. Even after the Jews complied with the orders, the hostages were rarely released.

By October 14, in Warsaw, the government had closed all the stores, but street vendors continued to sell food secretly purchased from store owners. Tens of thousands of people, with no other livelihood, took to selling everything from water, bread, potatoes, and chicken to rotten, spoiled, poisonous food. Despite the poor quality, prices were high. In addition, throughout the city, all electricity was shut off and newspapers and radio broadcasts were stopped. In his diary, Kaplan recorded that the city was plunged into "mental darkness" (Kaplan 1973, 110, 116).

During the third week in October, Kaplan recorded in his diary that the Nazis had decreed that trade among Jews in manufacturing clothing and leather goods was forbidden and that "violators will be severely punished, even by capital punishment" (120). The next day radios were confiscated. At this point Kaplan realized that, as awful as conditions were, events to follow would be far worse: "Blatant signs prove that some terrible catastrophe, unequaled in Jewish history, is in store for Polish Jewry" (121).

Two weeks earlier, the German government had begun expelling Jews from their apartment houses in Warsaw and the other larger cities of Poland. Orders had been given that the only property Jews were allowed to take with them were beds and photographs. People were not allowed "even a shoelace, or to put on an overcoat. . . . Within minutes, hundreds of families were left without a roof, without clothes, without food, without an apartment, without money" (108–9). As if this were not enough, while making their way to designated areas of the city, Jews were continually robbed at gunpoint by German soldiers (110).

After the Jews had been moved into the ghettos, the Germans confiscated their "abandoned" property as well. The final step in this process of impoverishing the Jews occurred in the ghetto itself. Jewish businesses were taken over by German authorities, thousands of Jewish firms were liquidated, and valuables were continuously hauled out of the ghetto districts by the German authorities (Dawidowicz 1975, 536).

Later, once the ghettos were liquidated and the Jews had been taken to concentration camps, German police and the local Polish population helped themselves to what little personal property was left. In the General Government, larger goods were confiscated by the governor, Hans Frank, but not before Himmler had removed machinery, taken over "choice real estate," and collected 11 million zloty in debts owed to the Jews by their Polish countrymen (Hilberg 1967, 157, 345).

FORCED LABOR OUTSIDE THE GHETTO

Despite having possessed what appears to have been large amounts of valuables, the Eastern European Jews were generally a rather poor group of people, particularly after anti-Jewish legislation passed in the prewar period had reduced their circumstances drastically. Their most valuable asset was their labor. By the 1930s, Jewry constituted a large portion of the middle class of Poland, and over seventy percent of the Jewish population were skilled laborers.

Two and one half million skilled Jewish workers did not go unnoticed by the German government. Just as the Germans benefited from the concentration of Jews living in cities, they benefited from this newly acquired source of highly skilled slave labor.

Soon after the city of Warsaw was taken, the general governor, Hans Frank, put up posters announcing that the Nazis had decided to train the Jews forcibly for a life of work. Jews were formed into forced labor troops and set to work wherever the Germans ordered. All males between the ages of fourteen and sixty were required to work. The Community Council of Warsaw was ordered to provide the necessary numbers of workers (Lenski 1959, 285).

The impressment of forced labor was conducted in several ways. During the initial phase, which occurred during the first few weeks of the German occupation, Jews were simply seized at random and put to work on emergency tasks. Later, this method of obtaining labor was replaced by a more orderly procedure in which Jews were organized into forced labor troops. Columns of laborers were put to work on special projects and then released, or not, depending on the whim of the authorities. Dawidowicz notes that "sometimes, they were released at the day's end and allowed to return home, but more likely, they were kept for a week or two, incommunicado, unable to inform their families of their whereabouts or even of their very existence" (1975, 271).

In Warsaw, Kaplan watched 150 men being pulled from a synagogue and herded into a truck. They were then taken to perform forced labor, cleaning toilets and scrubbing floors with no cleaning implements, merely their bare hands (Kaplan 1973, 112–14). Eventually, labor camps were established in which large-scale projects were undertaken. There were 125 Jewish labor camps in the General Government alone (Hilberg 1967, 165).

WOMEN AND WAR

Educator Frau Scholtze Klink, wife of an SS general, did some research for propaganda minister Josef Goebbels about "women and war." This is what Goebbels noted in his diary.

"On the problems of employing women. And there are all sorts. Who is to discipline the women? Female labor must become compulsory. Otherwise we shall never settle the issue. And camp life throws up so many problems for women. Frau Scholtze K. is quite despondent . . . And then, of course, there are the sexual aspects of separating millions of men and women. War means regression to a primitive state for human beings. We must seize victory as soon as possible, and then restore order and discipline" (Goebbels Diaries 1939–1944).

In 1943, Hitler ordered the importation of between 400,000 and 500,000 girls from conquered territories in the east to work as servants. But Hitler refused to conscript mothers.

Source: quoted in Claudia Koonz, *Mothers in the Fatherland.* (St. Martin's Press: New York 1987), 401.

FORCED LABOR

Joseph Korzenik participated in all of the labor situations described above:

In the beginning, each male Jew of twelve or over had to work for the Germans three days each week in order to qualify for food rations. Later, I worked for the German authorities almost all the time. The work varied from snow removal to road building, as well as removing the bodies of Jews killed in the Gestapo building area.

Eventually, I became a steady worker at the wood-processing factory near our town. At first, they used us for loading freight cars. This was a terrible experience, since the German in charge was a sadist and used to sic his German shepherd on us. The foreman used his whip to make us work faster. (Korzenik 1980)

After each day's work, the laborers were allowed to return home, but a few months later, Joseph and the other workers were forced to live in barracks within the factory limits. Joseph recalls that the "Living quarters were not heated; water was brought in barrels on horse-drawn wagons. Latrines were of a temporary, wooden type like an outdoor privy. We worked from sunrise until late at night" (Korzenik 1980).

Following the liquidation of his ghetto, in December 1942, Joseph was taken by truck to another labor camp in the mountains near the Czechoslovakian border. In April 1943, he was taken to a concentration camp outside an aircraft factory. Conditions were no better there than at the labor camps: "When we arrived, the inhabitants of this camp were just getting over a typhoid epidemic. Many died and the survivors looked more dead than alive" (Korzenik 1980).

Throughout this period, Joseph and his fellow workers experienced continual deprivation. They suffered from disease and hunger bordering on starvation. He explains that "we had no solid food, only grass soup twice a day. The only meat we found in this soup was worms." Exhaustion became normal too. "After working twelve hours a day in the factory, we were sent out to do field work around the factory." They also lived in constant fear, as they witnessed and heard about the murders of their fellow Jews. Joseph described one incident that took place before he left home:

One day, while I was working in the yard piling boards, a young Polish worker was bragging to me how he took part in a mass burial of about 900 Jewish people from a neighboring town. He made a special point of telling me how "some people were still alive when we covered them with dirt." I can still recall the fear within me, the sleepless nights and visions of mass executions. (Korzenik 1980)

Later, Joseph witnessed firsthand the killing of his fellow workers. One group of men was killed "for so-called sabotage." Another group was shot because someone escaped from a labor camp. "One night, during the night shift, we were coming back to the camp area for lunch. We saw many dead bodies lying in the road. We found out later that somebody had escaped."

These were not isolated cases.

There were many executions for no reason known to us. Gestapo from the nearby city would come into camp. Then we were lined up and one of them would count to ten as he walked by the ranks. Each tenth man would be pushed into a circle by men with machine guns. They would then be marched into the nearby woods where a pit had been dug. They were shot and dropped into the pit. Sometimes the pits were dug in the morning by the victims themselves though they were usually unaware of their intended use. (Korzenik 1980)

In an effort to bring order to their lives and stop the continual fear of being seized off the street or from their homes with no warning, the Jewish Council in Warsaw tried to organize a more orderly system. They offered to supply the Nazis with a specified number of workers if they were promised that the arbitrary roundups would stop. Eventually, the government agreed on 500 people per day, beginning on October 21, 1939. Each worker was to be paid four zloty per day from the Council treasury. (One zloty was worth about ten cents in today's dollars.) But it was not long before the arbitrary impressment of workers resumed.

WORKS CITED

Dawidowicz, Lucy S. *The War against the Jews: 1933–1945.* New York: Holt, Rinehart and Winston, 1975.

Elenberg, Shmaryahu, "Warsaw—Judenat: One view of Adam Czerniakow." *Hunter and Hunted: Human History of the Holocaust.* Edited by Gerd Korman. New York: Dell, 1973.

Gilbert, Martin. *The Holocaust: A History of the Jews During the Second World War.* New York: Holt, Rinehart and Winston, 1985.

Hilberg, Raul. *The Destruction of the European Jews.* Chicago: Quadrangle Books, 1967.

Kaplan, Chaim A. "The Beginnings: First Days of War." *Hunter and Hunted: Human History of the Holocaust.* Edited by Gerd Korman. New York: Dell, 1973.

Koonz, Koontz. *Mothers in the Fatherland.* New York: St. Martin's Press, 1987, 401.

Korzenik, Joseph. Interview by Carol Schulz, West Hartford, Connecticut, July 15, 1980.

Lenski, Mordecai. "Problems of Disease in the Warsaw Ghetto." *Yad Vashem Studies on the European Jewish Catastrophe and Resistance.* Edited by Shaul Esh. Jerusalem: Yad Vashem Martyrs' and Heroes' Remembrance Authority, 1959. Vol. 3, 283–93.

Schulz, Carol. *Jewish Accounts of the Holocaust Based on the Accounts of Survivors.* Middletown, CT: Wesleyan University, unpublished thesis, 1981.

Shirer, William L. *The Rise and Fall of the Third Reich.* New York: Simon and Schuster, 1960.

Sobotka, Bernice. Interview by Carol Schulz, West Hartford, Connecticut, October 18, 1980.

Sobotka, Mark. Interview by Carol Schulz, West Hartford, Connecticut, November 6, 1974, and August 8, 1980.

Weiss, Aharon. "Jewish Leadership in Occupied Poland." *Yad Vashem Studies on the European Jewish Catastrophe and Resistance.* Edited by Livia Rothkirchen. Jerusalem: Yad Vashem Martyrs' and Heroes' Remembrance Authority, 1977. Vol. 7, 335–65.

7

MOVING INTO
THE GHETTOS

By far the most productive form of forced labor, from the perspective of the Nazis, existed in the ghettos. Before explaining how this labor was extracted, it is necessary to describe the formation of the ghettos themselves.

Before the war began, the Germans had relocated nearly all the Jews in Germany, Austria, and Czechoslovakia to the urban areas of Poland. In October 1938, 15,000 Polish-born Jews, who had been living and working in Germany for from ten to thirty years, were forced to leave their homes, carrying only one suitcase, and told to report to the nearest train station. They were then taken to the Polish-German border and forced to enter Poland at gunpoint (Gilbert 1985, 26). (Living in France at the time was a young German Jew, Herschel Grynszpan, a member of one of the deported families. He was so shaken by the treatment of his family by the German government that he shot and killed a German diplomat in Paris. This action was used by the Nazis as an excuse for the terror of *Kristall-nacht* on the night of November 9, 1938.)

This expulsion occurred even though the Polish government had announced that anyone who had lived outside of the country for five years or more would no longer be considered citizens. Now these "stateless" Jews, along with others who had been expelled or had fled from Austria and the Sudetenland in 1938, and from Czechoslovakia in March 1939, were forced to live in Poland, where they were considered outlaws.

Most of the Czech Jews from Bohemia and Moravia were the descendants of families who had lived in the region since A.D. 970. Over the centuries, denied the right to own or work the land, or to enter the professions, they had excelled as craftsmen: shoemakers, tailors, hatters, furriers, goldsmiths, and, especially, musicians. They were even known to be excellent firemen. By the nineteenth century, Prague had become a center of Jewish learning and scholarship.

During the hundred years preceding the invasion of the Nazis, with religious freedom and the right to local self-government, they had built a vibrant culture. In 1939, after nearly a thousand years of increasing prosperity, they too were forced from their homes. Nineteen thousand of the 300,000 Czech Jews were able to escape from Europe and find sanctuary. The rest gained only temporary refuge, fleeing to an already-doomed Poland (Gilbert 1985, 24–28).

THE JEWISH COUNCILS

By September 1939, more than 3 million Jews lived in Poland. For over eight hundred years, Jews had made their homes in Poland. Although they lived mostly in cities, a significant number lived in small rural towns and villages, in communities as small as 8 and as large as 17,000. In order to ensure that all these people moved into the ghettos, and once there obeyed orders, the German government demanded that Jewish Councils (*Judenräte*) be established in each community throughout Poland—to supervise the carrying out of orders.

It was intended that these councils be composed of influential persons, rabbis and other community leaders, whom the people could be expected to follow. In some cases, recognizing the need for leadership, the Jewish communities formed their own councils, generally made up of leaders of local organizations. In other cases, the Germans appointed men to head the *Judenräte,* often from among those who had not previously been a part of the leadership or who were not even respected members of the community. (This was the case in Lodz where Mordecai Chaim Rumkowski was appointed head of the *Judenrat.* In *The War against the Jews* [1975], Lucy Dawidowicz notes that, though the story has not been substantiated, Rumkowski was chosen when the Nazis entered the offices of the *Kehilla,* the legally incorporated religious community, and asked who the "eldest" was, meaning the leader. Rumkowski, thinking they meant the "oldest," responded and became the appointed head of the *Judenrat* [305]. The same story was told by Mark and Bernice Sobotka [1980].)

Sometimes, when the Nazis threatened to shoot hostages unless a *Judenrat* was formed, Jews snatched people from the streets to form a council (Trunk 1972, 2). In some cases, the leaders of these communities fled, hoping to get help. In villages in eastern Poland, the occupying Soviets sometimes murdered the Jewish leaders before the Nazis arrived, and new people had to serve in the councils.

The first job given the Jewish Councils was to take a census of the Jews in their areas and then to supervise their evacuation from the countryside to the cities (Czerniakow 1979, 85). Joseph Korzenik recalls that there was a large influx of people to his town: "Little by little, they began [to encircle] the Jews, bringing them from the surrounding villages and herding them into the Jewish section of our town" (Korzenik 1980). Although the formation of the ghettos did not start for another six months in the larger cities, in the case described by Korzenik, it began immediately: "In the Jewish section, the Jews could be dealt with at will. Leaving the ghetto without a guard was punishable by death. Any Jew who did not have working papers on hand got the death penalty. There were only four to six Gestapo agents in our town, but they terrorized the entire vicinity" (Korzenik 1980).

Plans for the establishment of the first major ghetto, in Lodz, were devised in December 1939. The evacuations did not begin until February 1940, and the ghetto was not sealed off until May 1 of that year. Ghettos in other major cities were created as follows:

Warsaw (the largest ghetto)	October 1940
Krakow	March 1941
Lublin	April 1941
Radom	April 1941
Lvov	December 1941

By 1942, only a few ghettos were still to be established. In communities of less than 500, people were moved to the nearest city's concentration area (Hilberg 1967, 148).

THE HUNGRY CHILDREN

After each ghetto was finally closed, all types of problems arose. For instance, Jewish converts to Christianity were considered Jews by the Germans and renegades by the Jews, resulting in further torment. But saddest of all were the hungry children wearing loose clothing who tried to sneak out looking for food.

After the war, Eve Soumerai recalled:

While I was working as an interpreter/censor in Munich for the U.S. Third Army, I'll never forget a Nazi film I came across. Two of those children were caught and beaten with whips by the SS and a few hidden potatoes fell out, which increased the beatings.

Source: Eve Soumerai, *Unpublished diary,* 1945.

THE LODZ GHETTO

Mark Sobotka has described the process of ghettoization in Lodz. The Lodz ghetto, the second largest in Poland, existed for more than four years—the longest of any Nazi ghetto (Hilberg 1967, 149). Although the method of forcing people into the ghettos was not determined by an overall written plan, the pattern was basically the same in all cities (Trunk 1972, 543). In Lodz, the ghetto was created in the poorest section of the city. The district already contained 62,000 Jews, but 100,000 more were relocated there from other sections of the city, and the gentiles were moved out. The order was given on February 8, 1940, for the process to begin. People were purposely given little warning so they would be forced to leave most of their belongings behind (Hilberg 1967, 141).

They evacuated the Poles from the ghetto and near the ghetto because they didn't want the Poles to have any contact with the Jews. Jews were transferred from their homes to ghettos in blocks. Some were even brought from other cities. Everybody scrambled to get a room, bringing their goods in hand-drawn carts. (M. Sobotka 1980)

In all, 2 million Jews were concentrated into ghettos; at times, people were being moved at the rate of 10,000 per day (Hilberg 1967, 138).

When all the Jews had been moved into a ghetto, it was closed. "Warsaw and Lodz, with the largest Jewish populations, were the most tightly, almost hermetically, sealed ghettos" (Dawidowicz 1975, 276). The penalty for leaving the ghetto, or helping someone else escape, was death.

The Nazis even prohibited verbal communication with the world outside the ghetto. "They demolished all of the houses outside of the ghetto where the fence was, so nobody could be in contact with us" (M. Sobotka 1980). All printing presses and radios were confiscated, and possession of these things was punishable by death. According to Mark Sobotka, most of the time there was no communication with the outside world "whatsoever." Joseph Korzenik recalled the same: "For the most part, there was no contact with the outside world. No mail. There was nobody left to write to us anyway" (Korzenik 1980). (His parents and many others had been murdered.) Private telephones were also removed from Jewish homes, limiting their contact even with each other (Dawidowicz 1975, 279). In Lodz, one Zionist had a radio hidden in his office, which was discovered by Germans when the man was out. Upon hearing that he was wanted by the Nazis, he chose to commit suicide rather than be put to death (M. Sobotka 1980).

The Nazis used various types of police forces to enforce their directives. The fence surrounding the ghetto was guarded by the Order Police (Hilberg 1967, 150). "If you went too close to the fence, you just got shot. My grandfather got shot. He was too close to the fence and the guard just felt like shooting him. He killed my grandfather for just walking on the street near the fence" (B. Sobotka 1980). Movement within the walls of the ghetto was circumscribed as well. A curfew was established, prohibiting anyone from appearing in the streets from 7 P.M. to 7 A.M.

The purpose of the concentration and isolation of Jews was to cause as many as possible to die—of starvation, of disease, of suicide. The ghetto also served as a holding place or a "transition measure" until the Germans could decide what to do with its occupants. On April 5, 1941, the Cologne newspaper *Zeitung* said of the Lodz ghetto: "Although the ghetto of Lodz was intended as a mere trial, a mere prelude to the solution of the Jewish question, it has turned out to be the best and most perfect temporary solution of the Jewish problem." The same could be said for all of the other ghettos.

WORKS CITED

Czerniakow, Adam. *The Warsaw Diary of Adam Czerniakow: Prelude to Doom.* Edited by Raul Hilberg, Stanislaw Staron, and Josef Kermisz and translated by Stanislaw Staron. New York: Stein and Day, 1979.

Dawidowicz, Lucy S. *The War Against the Jews: 1933–1945.* New York: Holt, Rinehart and Winston, 1975.

Gilbert, Martin. *The Holocaust: A History of the Jews During the Second World War.* New York: Holt, Rinehart and Winston, 1985.

Hilberg, Raul. *The Destruction of the European Jews.* Chicago: Quadrangle Books, 1967.

Korzenik, Joseph. Interview by Carol Schulz, West Hartford, Connecticut, July 15, 1980.

Sobotka, Bernice. Interview by Carol Schulz, West Hartford, Connecticut, October 18, 1980.

Sobotka, Mark. Interview by Carol Schulz, West Hartford, Connecticut, November 6, 1974, and August 8, 1980.

Soumerai, Eve. *Unpublished diary,* 1945.

Trunk, Isaiah. *Judenrat: The Jewish Councils in Eastern Europe under Nazi Occupation.* New York: Macmillan, 1972.

8

LIFE IN THE GHETTOS
OF POLAND

As soon as the Jews of Poland were under the control of the occupying German government, their fate was almost entirely in the hands of the Nazis. In Poland, this meant concentration, isolation, and imprisonment in ghettos; starvation, slave labor, disease, torture, summary executions; and, for nearly twenty percent, death in the ghettos. Some Jews remained in the ghetto for more than 2.5 years.

Each of these ghettos functioned as a small city-state, with its own "government" (the Jewish Council, which was controlled, of course, by the German General Government), economy, and educational, medical, and cultural infrastructures. All were strictly supervised by the Jewish Council.

GHETTO GOVERNMENT

Within the ghetto, the Gestapo (state police) and the Kripo (criminal police) kept order. The Germans also created a Jewish police force that was required to enforce German orders. Some members of the Jewish police were known to have committed numerous acts of extortion, looting, and bullying, and they were often resisted by the general community (Ringleblum 1958, 155).

By September 1941, before evacuation to the camps, there were 144,000 people alive (out of an original 160,000) in the Lodz ghetto. With only 25,000 rooms available, an average of 5.8 people were crammed into each room. In Warsaw, with 445,000 people (out of an original 470,000) living in 1.3 square miles, 7.2 people lived in each room. Conditions in these cities were typical of those found in ghettos throughout Poland (Hilberg 1967, 152).

HUNGER STALKS THE GHETTO

The biggest problem for the inhabitants of the ghettos was hunger. It was necessary to have a ration card to obtain food. Denying ration cards to those who did not work was one means of enforcing compliance with Nazi demands; however, not everyone was *allowed* to work, and those who did not work were not given ration cards. Recalled Bernice Sobotka, "Naturally, children didn't work. Supposedly we were not to have children in the ghetto. We were not supposed to have old people either. So, these people did not get rations" (1980).

It became the job of the Jewish Councils to make sure that food was distributed throughout the ghetto to everyone, regardless of age or physical condition. In Lodz, food

was divided by the council. It was divided right. They knew the count [number of people] so they divided it right away so the kids and the older people would get it too. . . . Food came in train cars. You got so much a week and then you had to manage. If you ate it all in two days, you starved the rest of the week. That's why people were starving. Even if you knew how to manage it—each day a little bit—it was still a starvation diet. (B. Sobotka 1980)

By carefully curtailing food, medicine, and fuel, the German government was able to turn the ghettos into "death traps" (Hilberg 1967, 168).

Food, meant to suffice for a specified period, a week or a month, was shipped into the ghetto in bulk. There was no reason to provide enough food for the Jews, so even the small amount allotted to them was first looted by the Germans and sent to Germany. In addition, only the worst food was sent on to the Jews.

On October 25, 1940, in Lodz, local German officials met to discuss the problem of supplying food to the ghetto. The chairman of the group, Dr. Moser, stated that " 'the Jew community' was a necessary evil. The Jews, most of whom were living a useless life at the expense of the German people, had to be fed" (Hilberg 1967, 169). This meant that the quantity of food would be, at best, the equivalent of a "prison diet" (1967, 169). In reality, much less was delivered, and, as the supplies had to be divided among not only the workers who "counted" but those who could not work, rations were well below what was needed for survival.

The ration per person, in Lodz, for one month in 1941 was "less than one and one-half pounds of meat, one egg, 12 pounds of potatoes, and two ounces of cheese" (1967, 160–70). Even this meager diet was not free; it had to be purchased.

The amount of food one ate depended upon how much money one had to spend, not only for legal rations, but also for items available on the black market. The following are the prices per pound of staple foods in June 1941 (1967, 171):

Potatoes	3 zloty
Rye bread	8 zloty
Horse meat	9 zloty
Groats	11 zloty
Corn bread	13 zloty
Beans	14 zloty
Sugar	16 zloty
Lard	35 zloty

The daily wage in a workshop was from 20 to 35 zloty, so black-market food was not very affordable for workers, and nearly unavailable for non-workers (Dawidowicz 1975, 282).

NAZI RATIONING

In Warsaw, rations were allotted by the Germans by calorie count. German soldiers and other occupying forces were allowed 2,310 calories per day; other foreigners, 1,790; Poles, 934; and Jews, 183. These rations were paid for on a sliding scale: Jews were required to pay twice as much per calorie as Poles, twenty times as much as Germans (Gilbert 1985, 53). Before the ghetto was sealed, the Jews were able to supplement their diets and calorie counts by as much as 2,000 per day. At first, the problem was not the lack of calories, but the lack of protein and fat. Later, the calorie count also dropped, to about 800 (the ration plus food grown or smuggled in) per day (Lenski 1959, 292).

The diary of Stanislaw Rozycki, another resident of Warsaw, includes a monthly budget, from the fall of 1941. His family was considered "tolerably well situated" (Hilberg 1967, 173) compared to others.

Income

Father's salary	235 Zl.
Son's salary	120 Zl.
Public assistance	———
Side income	80 Zl.
	435 Zl.

Expenses

Rent	70 Zl.	Fees	11 Zl.
Bread	328 Zl.	Electricity, candles	28 Zl.
Potatoes	115 Zl.	Fuel	65 Zl.
Fats	56 Zl.	Drugs	45 Zl.
Allotments	80 Zl.	Soap	3 Zl.
			810 Zl.

This family balanced its budget this month by selling a clothes closet for 400 Zl. (Hilberg 1971, 39).

To supplement their diet, people planted gardens in tenement yards; political party organizations ran soup kitchens, as did the Jewish Councils; and begging and stealing were rampant (Dawidowicz 1975, 283–84; B. Sobotka 1980). Attempts to purchase food from non-Jews, if discovered, were severely punished. Poles caught selling food could be sentenced to months of hard labor, and Jews could be executed (Gilbert 1985, 55). But wholesale smuggling continued. Nazi soldiers could be bribed into allowing cartloads of food, even whole herds of oxen and cows, to be driven into the ghetto. People set up transfer points between two houses that straddled the wall separating the ghetto from the rest of the city, smuggling food between them. Each time the Germans changed the boundaries, the Jews found a new place to operate. Even death carts were used to bring food into the ghetto on their return trip from the cemeteries (Lenski 1959, 288).

The Jewish community as a whole tried to provide for those with no money. Before 1940, residents were able to form house committees whose job was to provide for those in greatest need. Soup kitchens, providing nutritious meals, were set up in each "house" or apartment building. Few people actually starved to death until the end of 1940. By that time even the committees had run out of money, and the cost of food was prohibitive. People then had to turn to community soup kitchens where food was much less nutritional, though cheap (Lenski 1959, 284).

Under such conditions, people who find ways to get a little more than their share live, and those who cannot die. Bernice was very lucky:

They needed office workers for bookkeeping. I was really pretty lucky. My grandfather was a councilman. He knew Rumkowski [the head of the Jewish Council], so I took advantage of this. This way, I could provide a little better for my family. Don't kid yourself, if you've got connections, it's like everywhere else. [Here not having connections actually meant starving to death.] At that time, you were desperate for help. So I had a little more than the majority. I would have a special ration once a month. You tried to survive any way you could. (B. Sobotka 1980)

S. Sheinkinder, a journalist living in the Warsaw ghetto, kept a journal of daily life from the first days of the invasion until his death, sometime between July 22 and September 21, 1942, when the Nazis rounded up and deported 300,000 Jews to the death camp at Treblinka. Writing of the scarcity of food, Sheinkinder lamented, "There is no sadder hour for me than when I finish my work and make my way home, where my hungry family is waiting for me. They have prepared no dinner for me. I did not leave them anything for lunch in the morning" (Sheinkinder 1963, 260).

Toward the end of the winter of 1942, the Gestapo office in Lodz sent a letter to the chief of the *Ghettoverwaltung* (ghetto administration), Biebow, suggesting that the Lodz ghetto was receiving too much food and that such food allocations could not be justified. Later, in a letter to *Oberburgermeister* Ventaki, Biebow pointed out that the food supply to the ghetto could no longer guarantee the continuation of production (Hilberg 1967, 173).

For months, the Jews had received no butter, margarine, or milk. In the soup kitchens, vegetables of B and C quality had been cooked in water with little oil, no meat, no fat, and no potato. The total expenditure for food had now (April 1943) dropped to 30 pfennige (12 cents) per person per day. No Jewish labor camp and no prison had hitherto managed with so little. In the words of the historian Raul Hilberg, "The ghetto starvation regime produced something more than the death of individuals; it spelled the doom of the community. . . . The death of an individual occurs every day. The death of a community is an event which happens much more rarely in history" (1967, 173).

MEDICAL CARE

Many physicians and other medical personnel lived in these ghettos. In Lodz, the second largest ghetto in Poland, in 1939, there lived 92 doctors, including specialists in gynecology, urology, surgery, otolaryngology, ophthalmology, internal medicine, dermatology, neurology, psychiatry, and venereology. There were three ambulances, free insulin, and free care for tuberculosis patients. Still, the mortality rate was high. In Warsaw, in March 1942, the death to birth ratio was 45:1 (Hilberg 1967, 173).

Medicine was nearly impossible to procure. When, in the winter of 1941–1942, sewer pipes froze, toilets became useless and excrement was dumped in the streets along with the garbage, causing widespread typhus epidemics, but "a single tube of antityphus medicine cost several thousand zloty" (Hilberg 1967, 172). By contrast, by May 1942, the price of a kilogram of bread was 15 zlotys, and an average wage was 22 zlotys per day (Dawidowicz 1975, 282).

Bernice's father was diabetic. For a time, her sister was able to smuggle insulin into the ghetto before it was sealed off completely, but it was not enough. Even before the doors were locked, their father died. Bernice acknowledged that "the hospitals tried their best, but they had nothing to work with" (B. Sobotka 1980).

Epidemics

Epidemics frequently began in synagogues, where thousands were forced to live in cramped quarters with grossly inadequate sanitary facilities. The councils organized disinfection brigades, steaming actions, and quarantine stations, but by the end of March 1942, people were collapsing at work and in the streets, dying at the rate of 5,000 per month. Beggars, desperate for food, snatched it from the hands of shoppers. Corpses were left lying on sidewalks, covered with newspapers, for cemetery carts to pick them up (Hilberg 1967, 172, 187–88).

The earliest epidemic, and the most common, was characterized by severe diarrhea and a fever, resulting in death. Its cause was never identified. An epidemic of abdominal typhus was caused by the destruction of the water-filtering station during the German bombing. This affected both Jews and non-Jews until the plant was fixed (Lenski 1959, 284).

A worse problem was the outbreak of exanthematic typhus, which spread unchecked from December 1939 until the end of 1940, and infected 1,727 (1959, 284). Until the ghettos were sealed, however, even these conditions were bearable, and few people died.

Once the ghettos were sealed, the uncontrollable spread of typhus became a major problem. Some estimate that there was a case of exanthematic typhus in every family in the Warsaw ghetto, affecting from one-quarter to one-third of the population. Most of these cases were not reported to the authorities, but were treated at home. The penalty for having a typhoid victim in one's family was severe. All residents of the house were isolated for two weeks, the house was locked and guarded by the police, and no one was allowed to bring in any food, thus condemning the rest of the family to starvation (although the mortality rate of the disease itself was only 15%). In addition, all the residents of the house, and of those in the two neighboring houses, were taken to the bath houses, where conditions were so inhumane that many healthy people became ill after the bath, and older, sicker people died (289).

By not reporting cases of typhus, this treatment could be averted. Despite the fact that doctors and nurses who treated patients risked deportation to the Auschwitz death camp, many participated in this form of passive resistance. The Nazis sent out mobile teams to make surprise visits to houses in an effort to catch lawbreakers (289).

Other diseases were prevalent as well. Tuberculosis left patients emaciated and feverish, with weak cardiac activity. Colitis, a painful inflammation of the large intestine, had a mortality rate of sixty percent. Its most probable cause was the filthiness of the carts used to transport foodstuffs. These carts were frequently used for carting dung as well as food (289).

Deaths from another "disease" occurred with increasing frequency: starvation. Before hunger kills there are other signs of malnutrition: weight loss (one woman, aged thirty, height four feet ten inches, weighed twenty-four kilograms, or about fifty pounds), low body temperature, cataracts in young people, low blood pressure, slow pulse, dysentery, anemia, fatigue, dizziness, nausea, and diarrhea (293). The lack of food affected the ability of the people to do physical labor and their ability to think clearly. Tempers flared, manners disappeared, and incidents of greed and dishonesty increased tremendously, particularly with regard to the theft and black marketing of food (Dawidowicz 1975, 289).

Thirty percent of all deaths in Lodz were caused by heart disease, the result of the tension and stress of ghetto life (1975, 289). The worst off were the very old and the very young who were least able to stave off hunger and disease. One other group, Jewish refugees from Germany and Western Europe forced to live in a hostile environment, away from home and family, housed in public buildings unsuited for such purposes, died in far greater numbers than the Poles. Their presence in the ghetto was greatly resented because it added to the overcrowding and lessened the food supply. Some even resorted to suicide (Trunk 1972, 369).

In addition to disease and starvation, there was one other cause of death: being shot for attempting to escape or merely for being in the wrong place at the wrong time. Below is an excerpt from a citation sent to an eighteen-year-old auxiliary policeman of the Protective Police department for acting "resolutely to frustrate the escape of five Jews from the ghetto" (Hilberg 1971, 42).

[The Jews] ducked out in a drainage canal which was strongly secured by barbed wire and, without the alertness and determination of the guard, would have disappeared in the dense terrain. The pursuit was extended over a distance of more than 1500 yards with the result that the 5 Jews were shot to death. Because of the vigilance, resolution, and good shooting of auxiliary policeman Schulz, the great danger of a spread of spotted fever and other epidemics to the German population was removed. (Hilberg 1971, 42)

RUNNING SHORT

Fuel, too, was in short supply. To obtain it, the council in Lodz dismantled stores, shops, and fences. One man was arrested for concealing the fact that he had an extra room in his apartment that he was dismantling and burning to keep warm. Children froze in the streets while the Nazis continued to confiscate clothing (Dawidowicz 1975, 281).

As noted, living quarters in the ghetto were extremely crowded. At times, the noise level was unbearable. "My ears are filled with the deafening clamor of crowded streets and cries of people dying on the sidewalks" (1975, 280), wrote one inhabitant. Plumbing, toilets, and sewage systems were used so much that they broke down. Disinfectants and soaps were practically nonexistent (Trunk 1972, 145). According to Mark Sobotka, "the only thing that relieved the congestion was death" (M. Sobotka 1980).

In a report filed by the Chief Field Headquarters in Warsaw District, signed by von Unruh, to the military commander in the General Government, dated May 20, 1941, conditions in the ghettos were described as follows:

The situation in the Jewish quarter is catastrophic. Dead bodies of those who collapsed from lack of strength are lying in the streets. Mortality, 80% from undernourishment, has tripled since February. The only thing alloted [sic] to the Jews is 1-1/2 pounds of bread a week. Potatoes for which the Jewish council has paid in advance of several million, have not been delivered. The large number of welfare agencies created by the Jewish council are in no position to arrest the frightful misery. The ghetto is growing into a social scandal, a breeder of illnesses and of the worst sub-humanity. The treatment of the Jews in labor camps where they are guarded solely by Poles, can only be described as bestial. (Hilberg 1971, 40)

A DESPERATE NEED FOR MONEY

Though money was needed to buy everything, from food to fuel to clothing, the Germans did not pay wages. Money was collected by the Jewish Councils from those who could afford to buy work exemptions; then it was redistributed as token wages to forced laborers, or used to pay for food rations for nonworkers (Dawidowicz 1975, 312).

Until the ghettos were sealed, one other source of funds existed, for those who were able to hold onto some of their property. Goods were taken to the Polish parts of the city and sold. The huge shortage of goods caused prices to increase daily. Artisans sold their products or bartered for food. People sold family heirlooms, such as silverware, furniture, jewelry, and household appliances. Those who had been evicted from their homes and forced into the ghettos without time even to dress properly, let alone to pack their possessions, and no way to transport property, did not have this option. What was left behind became the property of the Nazi occupiers (Lenski 1959, 283).

FORCED LABOR

Inside the Ghetto

On top of all these problems, the Germans added the hardship of forced labor. Of the more than 1 million Polish workers in war industries, over 300,000 were Jews. In Lodz, at the largest armaments manufacturer in Poland, between 50,000 and 80,000 Jews did ninety-five percent of the armaments work and sixty-six percent of the textile production (Dawidowicz 1975, 195–96; Hilberg 1971, 38).

According to Mark Sobotka, "There were thousands of workers producing shoes, ammunition, hats, clothing" (M. Sobotka 1980). To his list could be added uniforms, brushes, brooms, baskets, mattresses, containers, and toys. This work was tightly organized and run by a large ghetto bureaucracy (Hilberg 1967, 168).

None of these goods was used by ghetto workers. Bernice Sobotka worked for a "top-notch" clothing designer (B. Sobotka 1980). "Fancy" dresses, designed and manufactured by Jews, were worn by the Germans while inhabitants of the ghetto froze to death. In all, there were 117 factories, workshops, and warehouses in the Lodz ghetto (Dawidowicz 1975, 315).

In addition to this type of labor, the policy of providing specified numbers of workers "on demand" was continued by the councils even after the ghettos were created, presumably in order to lessen the threat of random roundups. Not surprisingly, the German authorities did not keep to their part of the agreement.

Jews lived in daily terror of being seized off the street and carted off. According to one German eyewitness, "Today in the *Gerneralgouvernment* [General Government], one can see Jewish troops, spades on shoulders, marching without any German escort through the countryside" (Hilberg 1967, 163). That he is ridiculing them is apparent, but also clear is the fear of disobeying Nazi orders and the uncertainty of the consequences.

Although not considered slaves, workers were paid erratically, if at all. When payment did come, it was inadequate. In some ghettos, the Jewish councils were reimbursed for the columns of workers they furnished. The councils, in turn, used the money to reimburse themselves for money spent on the poorest workers in the form of soup kitchens and community welfare. In other places, the councils were expected to pay workers out of their own funds, with no contribution from the German government at all. In cases like these, lists of workers were posted by the council, and wealthy Jews were allowed to buy their way out of working. This money was then used to pay the forced laborers (Hilberg 1971, 164).

Moving the Workers outside the Ghetto

This more or less haphazard supply of workers could be used only for emergency work and short-term construction projects. In addition to this system, small numbers of people were employed by army installations outside the ghetto (Hilberg 1967, 164).

Eventually, labor camps were established for more elaborate projects. It is interesting to note that none of these arrangements was caused by a shortage of workers. The disruption caused by the war itself created a large pool of unemployed, both Jewish and Polish. Historian Raul Hilberg notes that "to the Germans, the sight of thousands of Jews 'milling around' was a challenge that had to be met right away" (1967, 162).

These groups of forced laborers were put to work performing a number of enormous tasks. The first large-scale project, the creation of Reichsfahrer-SS and chief of the German Police Heinrich Himmler, employed several thousand Jews (though he originally envisioned using millions) to dig an antitank ditch between the Bug and the San rivers. Several major river-regulation and canalization projects were also implemented, along with land-restoration programs, road and railroad construction, and other outdoor projects (1967, 165). In addition to such large-scale projects, laborers were used in industrial enterprises, and some factories were even constructed in the concentration camps themselves (Lenski 1959, 286).

Conditions in these labor camps were deplorable. Dr. Mordecai Lenski, a resident of the Warsaw ghetto, recalls the descriptions of these camps from inmates who returned to Warsaw when they became ill and could no longer work. He wrote in his diary that "their words were those of despair, of people willing to work, but conditions were so difficult and the 'treatment' meted out to them so cruel, that they broke down, both physically and morally" (Lenski 1959, 286).

The laborers were forced to walk about six miles to their place of work, work for fourteen hours, and walk the six miles back to the camp. Their entire day's rations consisted of three hundred grams of bread, some jam, and a plateful of soup. In one camp, several workers came down with typhus. They were sent to the hospital, but the healthy persons, left behind, were shot to prevent the spread of the disease.

FEAR

The Jews in the ghettos were systematically deprived of food, clothing, fuel, medicine, sanitary facilities, living space, and sleep. They were forced to live in the bombed-out slums of Warsaw, Lodz, and other cities with no parks or even empty lots. In one ghetto there was only one tree (Dawidowicz 1975, 280). They also lived in constant fear of being deported and killed.

There were times when the Germans would surround the ghetto and pick up kids. They would go from house to house and from room to room and take away the kids. My younger brother, the one who survived, God knows how he survived, was all ready to be shipped out, but through connections I got him released at the last minute. Eventually he made his way to Italy and was rescued by Israelis, who took him to Palestine. (B. Sobotka 1980)

In Joseph Korzenik's small ghetto, the Germans decided to dispose of those for whom they had no use. Tailors, shoemakers, and members of the Jewish Council and the Jewish Police were saved. As for the rest: "The Gestapo and police went on a door to door search for Jews. All those found in hiding were shot on the spot" (Korzenik 1980). Out of a Jewish population of 4,000, a hundred families were spared. Joseph's family attempted to escape to a nearby village.

KEEPING A RECORD OF THE SUFFERING

The historian Emanuel Ringelblum and some fellow inmates recorded the suffering of the nearly half million Jews confined in the Warsaw ghetto and hid the resulting archives in milk cans, which they buried for posterity. These documents serve as a reminder to the world that Jews were not only victims, but a resilient people destined to once again live in peace.

[What their records reveal was that] [u]nfortunately the youth movements had been too disciplined. . . . for too long they had listened to adult leadership . . . They should have studied liberation movements in more detail. Throughout history . . . it was the young who led revolts, not those who had to worry about their family responsibilities.

Source: Samuel D. Kassow, *Who Will Write Our History?* (Bloomington: Indiana University Press, 2007), 371.

EFFECTS OF GHETTO LIFE

What were the effects of these inhumane conditions? The most obvious effect was, of course, a tremendous death rate. In the Lodz ghetto, 11,437 people died in the year 1941 (out of an original population, in 1938, of 225,000). By June 30, 1942, death had claimed 29,561 people. The most common causes of death were heart disease (28%), lung tuberculosis (22%), and starvation (19%) (Hilberg 1971, 41).

In Warsaw, out of a community of 470,000 people, 44,630 deaths occurred in 1941, and 37,462 during the first nine months of 1942, at the rate of 5,000 people each month. In all, between 500,000 and 600,000 Jews died in the ghettos and labor camps of Poland, or one-fifth of the Polish Jews (Hilberg 1967, 173–74).

In his diary, Isaiah Trunk reported:

You could see all day long. . . . There were those death wagons running back and forth constantly. When you walked down the street and you looked at people they were like skeletons. They were like dead people walking and they walked until they fell and they were dead. At times, we couldn't keep up with the burying of the dead. That's how it was. (Trunk 1972, 151)

WORKS CITED

Dawidowicz, Lucy S. *The War against the Jews: 1933–1945.* New York: Holt, Rinehart and Winston, 1975.

Gilbert, Martin. *The Holocaust: A History of the Jews During the Second World War.* New York: Holt, Rinehart and Winston, 1985.

Hilberg, Raul. *The Destruction of the European Jews.* Chicago: Quadrangle Books, 1967.

———. *Documents of Destruction: Germany and Jewry 1933–1945.* Chicago: Quadrangle Books, 1971.

Korzenik, Joseph. Interview by Carol Schulz, West Hartford, Connecticut, July 15, 1980.

Lenski, Mordecai. "Problems of Disease in the Warsaw Ghetto." *Yad Vashem Studies on the European Jewish Catastrophe and Resistance.* Edited by Shaul Esh. Jerusalem: Yad Vashem Martyrs' and Heroes' Remembrance Authority, 1959. Vol. 3, 283–93.

Ringleblum, Emmanual. *Notes from the Warsaw Ghetto: The Journal of Emmanuel Ringleblum.* Edited and translated by Jacob Sloan. New York: McGraw-Hill, 1958.

Sheinkinder, S. "The Diary of S. Sheinkinder." *Yad Vashem Studies on the European Jewish Catastrophe and Resistance.* Edited by Nathan Eck and Arieh Leon Kubovy. Jerusalem: Yad Vashem Martyrs' and Heroes' Remembrance Authority, 1963. Vol. 5, 255–69.

Sobotka, Bernice. Interview by Carol Schulz, West Hartford, Connecticut, October 18, 1980.

Sobotka, Mark. Interview by Carol Schulz, West Hartford, Connecticut, November 6, 1974, and August 8, 1980.

Trunk, Isaiah. *Judenrat: The Jewish Councils in Eastern Europe under Nazi Occupation.* New York: Macmillan, 1972.

9

COPING WITH LIFE IN A "CONCENTRATION" WORLD

An article written by Marc Dvorjetski (holocaust survivor and director of the Tel Aviv Institute for the Investigation of the Pathology of the Holocaust when his findings were published) on the adjustment of detainees to concentration camp and ghetto life describes how inhabitants attempted to cope in the concentration world in which they were imprisoned. He defines the concentration world as follows:

Life in ghettos, and in labour, concentration and extermination camps, life in the underground, life of those whose existence outside the ghetto boundaries depended on their forged "Aryan" papers, of those who hid with the peasants, and of those who lived in the constant expectation of imminent deportation . . . all forms of life-conditions during the Nazi reign of terror and mass-murder. (Dvorjetski 1963, 194)

The main purpose of forcing the Jews to live in such conditions was to cause them to die. *"Natural extermination* [italics added] of inmates by means of starvation, consuming their strength through forced labor under the indescribable conditions of the camps, illogical actions, and fatal illness" (1963, 195) was the goal. Jews were to be turned into "starving beasts," who would work until they dropped dead in return for a piece of bread. The Nazis used the term "productive extermination" to describe this process. Like the government in George Orwell's *1984*, to the Nazis "lawlessness was law," and appeals to justice, morality, or human compassion were "as futile as a voice in the wilderness" (195–96).

The chief means of coping with this existence, therefore, was to focus on the main objective: to stay alive. In order to do this, people followed certain rules of survival: being alert for unforeseen dangers, such as round-ups or new regulations that had to be obeyed; controlling one's nerves and emotions so that one could stay alert and avoid danger or fight against it; remaining calm in order to seize any opportunities to escape; tolerating all discomforts so as not to lose hope and give up; and forcing oneself to believe that life in the ghetto or camp was only temporary, that freedom would eventually come (196).

In the ghettos, in order to remain sane and hopeful, people forced themselves to create a normal life: to dress neatly and remain a human being, to attend theatrical performances in an effort to keep their spirits up, and to maintain the family structure whenever possible.

Fathers tried to find ways to save their families, obtaining permits to ensure temporary survival, arranging for food, fighting for space in a house or a place to hide in a bunker, an attic, or a cellar. Mothers continued to prepare what little food there was, waiting in long lines to collect food rations, searching for places to buy a few potatoes or a piece of horse meat. In addition, women were expected to keep their homes clean, even when it was one room shared by thirty others. When their husbands were taken, wives were forced to do the hard labor needed to retain their "work permit": digging holes, carting beams and bricks, or whatever was necessary (197).

Children continued to play, as children generally do, but the games reflected the life they were living. They would play "actions" (the term for mass roundups or executions), "blowing up bunkers," and "seizing the clothes of the dead" (198). Schools were also established to provide a place for the children to block out the ghetto world and for their elders to act out their hopes for the future. Most children understood that their parents could not save them, and they tried to find ways to provide for themselves. Some helped by smuggling food for their families or friends; others lied about their age and registered for work so that they could obtain "life-permits" (198).

According to the German authorities, old people were not supposed to live in the ghetto. Whenever they were discovered, they were taken out to be killed. In order to survive, they had to go into hiding. Knowing they were posing a threat to the rest of the community, they tried to make themselves as useful as possible, cooking, cleaning, or doing other unpaid work (199).

ATTEMPTS TO ESCAPE

Under conditions so horrible, one would think that people would try their best to escape, but escape was nearly impossible. The ghettos, particularly those in Lodz and Warsaw, were almost totally isolated from the outside world. Though a few people did escape, and some attempted to get help from the outside, most could not. Many of those who escaped were members of political parties who served as couriers bringing news, money, and moral support to fellow party members in other ghettos.

According to Mark Sobotka, Jews were supervised by other Jews, and thus few had any contact with outsiders, even with Germans, unless a person were caught on the street past curfew. In order to escape, one needed a safe place to go. The only people living outside the ghettos were non-Jews who were not likely to hide total strangers on the spur of the moment.

Mark recalled, "There was practically no way to escape. A few people got out through a connection in Warsaw, for which they paid a large sum of money. But these were isolated cases. On the whole, we had no means of escaping because we did not go on any work detail outside the city" (M. Sobotka 1980).

Inside the ghetto, movement was carefully monitored. The Lodz ghetto was split into two sections with a corridor in the middle for the street-car, which was used by the Poles living outside the ghetto. In order to go from one side of the street to the other, people had to walk on an elevated bridge. The gates to the bridge were guarded by the Gestapo. "At times, they would let you cross from one side to the other, but people tried to stay away from the gates because once in a while, if a Gestapo who stood at the gate didn't like your face, he would just shoot you" (M. Sobotka 1980). Both the gates and the streets were closely watched, prohibiting communication and travel to such a great extent that escape was hardly possible.

In the smaller ghettos, such as the one in Joseph Korzenik's town, escape was almost as difficult. Although Joseph and his family were able to escape death during the first house-to-house search, by hiding in a hay-loft for two days, others were not so lucky. "Across the street, a Jewish family was found and shot" (Korzenik 1980).

After almost three days without food, Joseph and his family were forced to leave the shelter of the loft. Joseph was able to protect his family for a while when he managed to obtain work papers, but eventually they had to flee again.

Although there were many in that village who knew my father well, there was nobody who would hide them. After walking aimlessly for a week they returned, broken in spirit and lacking in strength. The day after they returned, while I was at work, I saw a group of people being herded down the road. When I returned from work, I realized that those were my people. I never saw my father, my mother, or my second sister again. (Korzenik 1980)

Some people were able to escape to the forest and survive for a time, but this option was available to only a few.

MORALE AND RESISTANCE IN THE GHETTOS

It has been claimed that, as soon as the Germans took control of the Jewish populations of Europe, the Jews, for all intents and purposes, gave up. One reason given is that they hoped that, just like in previous times, the persecution would end and the Jewish community as a whole would survive. Others remind us that obtaining weapons was even more impossible than escaping.

In addition, the Nazis had executed their plans for the Jews in gradual steps (first identification, then impoverishment, then concentration, then starvation and disease) hiding their ultimate intentions. Once they were locked into the ghettos, the Jewish community was so weakened and demoralized by disease and starvation, random shootings and kidnappings, and torturous hard labor that rebellion was nearly unthinkable and escape practically impossible.

The Jews also knew that resistance on the part of one individual or group (e.g., a political party) would be met with large-scale reprisals against other members of the community. The choice between the slim possibility of freedom for some, with martyrdom for those left behind, seemed worse than the alternative: maintaining the status quo. Since it was not until the massive deportations began in 1942 that people even suspected that certain death awaited them, taking such a risk was considered foolish (Weiss 1977, 364; Dawidowicz 1975, 376).

Despite these dangers, the need to take up arms against the Nazis was often discussed by members of political organizations. In most cases, overt resistance was rejected by Jewish leaders at all levels, those on the Jewish Councils as well as those in political organizations, as being too risky to the community as a whole.

Staying Alive

All of these explanations for the failure of the Jews to resist have some validity, but they do not reveal what was really happening in the ghettos. Although armed uprisings were rare and mostly ineffectual, other forms of resistance were taking place in the ghetto.

Given the circumstances, and the German's stated intention of working them to death, just staying alive was a form of resistance. As early as December 10, 1939, one Nazi official stated: "The creation of the ghetto is, of course, only a transition measure. I shall determine at what time and with what means the ghetto—and thereby also the city of Lodz—will be cleansed of Jews. In the end, at any rate, we must burn out this bubonic plague" (Hilberg 1967, 149).

The inmates of the ghettos were continually exhorted by their leaders to "hold on and hold out" (Weiss 1977, 360). If it was the goal of the Nazis that Jews should die, they would defy their oppressors and survive. It was believed that "each Jewish survivor is a hero resisting the Nazis because he refuses to extinguish his precious life" (Dawidowicz 1975, 291). Suicide was discouraged and an astonishingly small number of people used it as a means of escape.

Strangely enough, there were very few suicides among religious Jews. There were suicides, but mostly among the assimilated Jews, because they couldn't take it. Their whole house of cards fell apart. They believed that the world was going to take some actions. They didn't have the strength to survive. Among the religious Jews, hardly a suicide occurred. (M. Sobotka 1974)

Whether more nonreligious Jews, most of whom had been uprooted from their homes and communities in Western and Central Europe, committed suicide because of their lack of faith in God, or because they were living in unfamiliar territory with few friends and family, is not really clear. According to at least one historian, however, there was a higher suicide rate among assimilated German and Czech Jews, and far fewer suicides overall than one might expect (Weiss 1977, 292).

There were also deliberate acts of sabotage. In Lodz, an underground movement continuously circulated the slogan "P. P.," symbolizing the Polish words for "work slowly." Fires were ignited in factories, and in other ghettos, similar acts of sabotage were perpetrated. Underground newspapers exhorted their readers to "work badly and slowly" (Dawidowicz 1975, 369).

Preserving Family and Cultural Life

Using their intelligence and ingenuity to outwit the Germans, the Jews were able to circumvent many of the restrictions and prohibitions meant to deprive them of their physical existence and their cultural heritage. They disobeyed decrees continually, by smuggling food and medicine into the ghetto, by publishing newspapers to keep people informed about dangers, by warning neighbors of forced-labor roundups, by refusing to report for deportation, by running underground schools, and by observing the traditions of their religion—all despite knowing the severe consequences they faced if caught.

Perhaps the most significant factor in their survival was their sense of family and communal solidarity. In each family, those who were able to work provided for the rest, often including aunts, uncles, grandparents, and cousins within the family circle. Even those with no family were rarely left to fend for themselves. Jewish organizations of all kinds flourished, providing social welfare, political leadership, cultural activities, and a strong sense of belonging, all to help build morale.

Close-up of two young girls in the Kovno ghetto in July 1943 wearing Stars of David that their uncle fashioned out of wood. Henia Wisgardisky Lewin, courtesy of USHMM Photo Archives.

The Jewish community fought death and despair in the same way Jews had always attempted to guarantee the survival of the community in extremity: by using their culture to transform their environment. When the Nazis prohibited education, Jewish schools went underground. Six months after the Germans invaded, 180 underground religious schools had been established in Warsaw. In other ghettos, thousands of children were taught their Jewish lessons in secret (Trunk 1972, 197).

Forty thousand children received their secular education in private homes and public kitchens in Warsaw. In some areas, the Germans did allow elementary schools at first, but these schools were soon closed. In Lodz, the *Judenrat* was responsible for the secular and religious education of the children. There were 10,000 students in fifty-five schools (1972, 197).

In spite of the continually worsening conditions, valiant teachers continued to teach children about a world few of them remembered. Teachers taught their children about apples and pears, in a place where there were none; about logic, even though nothing made sense; about happiness, where there was precious little.

A young unknown author at Theresienstadt (Terezin) wrote a poem entitled "Birdsong," bidding "us" to open up our hearts to the beauty of nature and of life itself:

He doesn't know the world at all
Who stays in his nest and doesn't go out.
He doesn't know what birds know best
Nor what I want to sing about,
That the world is full of loveliness.
When dewdrops sparkle in the grass
and earth's aflood with morning light,
a blackbird sings upon a bush
To greet the dawning after light.
Then I know how fine it is to live.
Hey, try to open up your heart
To beauty; go to the woods some day
And weave a wreath of memory there.
Then if the tears obscure your way
You'll know how wonderful it is
To be alive.

—(From *I Have Not Seen a Butterfly* n.d., 36)

Taking Part in Educational Activities

There were concerts, meetings, lecture series, courses in Yiddish language and literature, and theater performances. The inhabitants of the Warsaw ghetto held a "children's month" celebration in which hundreds of children took part and thousands of adults attended. The Zionist organizations were very active, trying to keep up peoples' spirits (Dawidowicz 1975, 341).

Warsaw, Lodz, Vilna, and Kovno even had orchestras. The orchestra in Lodz included twenty-five professional musicians and ten amateurs.

Many of the ghettos had libraries as well. Here again, in some areas, libraries were permitted: Lodz had one library with 7,500 books and 4,000 subscribers; and in some areas, they were not: Warsaw was forced to establish underground libraries, including a central library just for children (Meed 1974, 18).

The Jews of the ghettos also created their own literature. In Warsaw there existed a documentary center and intelligence service, code-named *Oneg Shabbat*. Headed by Dr. Emmanuel Ringleblum, the project encouraged people to submit to the center diaries, chronicles, photographs, essays, and even scientific research (such as a study done on the effects of hunger), depicting life under Nazi rule. Just before the final "liquidation" of the ghetto, these documents were hidden in large milk cans outside of the ghetto. They were dug up after the war and have become one of the primary sources of information about life in the ghettos.

Similar enterprises were undertaken in other ghettos. People wrote prayers, poetry, songs, even jokes. In this way, Jews not only vented their rage against Nazi oppression, fighting off despair through intellectual pursuits, but they also gained a small measure of immortality. Unable to tell the world of their sorrows while they were still alive, they could at least hope to be remembered after death.

Just before the uprising in the Warsaw ghetto, one man wrote in his diary: "I feel that continuing this diary to the very end of my physical and spiritual strength is a historical mission which must not be abandoned" (Kaplan 1973, 190).

Resisting Apathy

While searching for her family in postwar Europe, Eve Soumerai met Jakov, a survivor of the Warsaw ghetto and Treblinka concentration camp, who became her friend. He told her how he had resisted apathy, despair, and death:

> What did I eat? Don't ask.
> How did I survive?
> A miracle. I had a friend.
> You had to have a friend.
> I said *broches* (blessings).
> I shaved with a piece of broken
> glass and tried to keep clean.
> There was one tap of water
> for hundreds of us. A tiny trickle.
> But I am small. That helped.
> Less to survive. I sang about
> stars, shoes, a bit of bread. (Soumerai 1945)

Victor E. Frankl, psychiatrist and author of *Man's Search for Meaning* (1959), describes being driven "with the butts of rifles" through the icy winds to the work sites. To overcome the misery, he focused his mind on his wife's image: "I heard her answering me, saw her smile, her frank and encouraging look. Real or not, her look was then more luminous than the sun which was beginning to rise. . . . A thought transfixed me . . . that love is the ultimate and the highest goal to which man can aspire" (Frankl 1959, 58–59).

Frankl resisted the horrors by searching for personal meaning. He explored what happens to the human spirit when "there is nothing to lose except our so ridiculously naked lives?" (60). He found that survival is possible if one's life continues to have meaning through the exercising of a talent such as drawing, writing, or comforting others.

Frankl's talent was the art of observing and describing human behavior, which he had done in a precious manuscript that was taken away from him en route to Auschwitz. Yet despite suffering from typhus and high fever, he made himself remember bits and pieces of the script and note them down on scraps of paper, reassembling them, and adding to his original manuscript. After the war, the scraps formed the book *The Doctor and the Soul* (1965), a companion to his famous *Man's Search for Meaning* (1959), which sold more than a million copies.

Simple Acts of Defiance

A simple act of defiance gave fourteen-year-old, blonde and blue-eyed Auschwitz inmate Henry Klein a sense of self-worth. Because of his "Aryan" looks, he had been chosen to be an attendant to one of the commanding SS officers at Auschwitz. One of his duties was to wake "his" officer every morning with a strong cup of coffee and cream. Just before serving the coffee, he would gather all the spit he had available and add it to the cup. The officer was curious about all those bubbles floating on the cream. Henry was ready with a German rhyme he had composed for the daily ritual: "*Wenn die Sahne bricht, ein hfibsches Miidchen dich kiisst*" (If the cream "breaks," a pretty girl will kiss you). From then on, the "bubbles" pleased the officer and added to Henry's self-respect (Klein 1953).

There were many different responses to the question of resistance. Orthodox Jews, for instance, had their own beliefs and attitudes. They did not believe in physical force or individual acts of bravery. They believed in prayer, religious meditation, and devotion: "not by force but by the strength of the spirit" was their motto. They believed that Divine Providence was the only Judge, and that he decided between the forces of good and evil. It was therefore wrong, as well as useless, to resist physically.

According to an eyewitness account, Rabbi Isaak and his Hasidic disciples were discovered by Germans in an underground shelter in the Polish town of Dabrowa Tarnowska in June 1942. Because the men were dressed in their praying shawls, the Germans did not see the bottle of vodka one of them had hidden underneath his garment. The men were driven to the local Jewish cemetery. There, facing the murderers, they drank, held hands, and danced "le chaim" to life. The Germans were so enraged by the actions of the prisoners that they slit their bellies and trampled on them until their bowels came out (Gilbert 1985, 367).

It is clear that the Jews did not simply give up and give in to the outrageous demands made by the Nazis. They resisted by defying laws and regulations; by creating a rich, vibrant life of hope; and by refusing, whenever they could, to cooperate in bringing about their own demise. In doing so, they also preserved for posterity a record of their struggles.

WORKS CITED

Author Unknown. "Birdsong." *I Have Not Seen a Butterfly: Poems from Ter- ezine*. Prague: Jewish Museum, no date.

Dawidowicz, Lucy S. *The War Against the Jews: 1933–1945*. New York: Holt, Rinehart and Winston, 1975.

Dvorjetski, Mark. "Adjustment of Detainees to Camp and Ghetto Life: And Their Subsequent Readjustment to Normal Society." *Yad Vashem Studies on the European Jewish Catastrophe and Resistance*. Edited by Nathan Eck and Arieh Leon Kubovy. Jerusalem: Yad Vashem Martyrs' and Heroes' Remembrance Authority, 1963. Vol. 5, 193–220.

Frankl, Victor. *Man's Search for Meaning*. Boston: Beacon Press, 1959.

———. *The Doctor and the Soul: From Psychotherapy to Logotherapy*. New York: Alfred A. Knopf, 1965.

Gilbert, Martin. *The Holocaust: A History of the Jews During the Second World War*. New York: Holt, Rinehart and Winston, 1985.

Hilberg, Raul. *The Destruction of the European Jews*. Chicago: Quadrangle Books, 1967.

Kaplan, Chaim A. *Hunter and Hunted: Human History of the Holocaust*. Edited by Gerd Korman. New York: Dell, 1973.

Klein, Henry. Interview by Eve Soumerai, New York City, April 1953.

Korzenik, Joseph. Interview by Carol Schulz, West Hartford, Connecticut, July 15, 1980.

Meed, Vladka. "Jewish Partisans." *The Warsaw Ghetto Uprising*. New York: Congress for Jewish Culture, 1974.

Ringleblum, Emmanuel. "Cultural Activities in the Ghetto." *The Warsaw Ghetto Uprising*. New York: Congress for Jewish Culture, 1974.

Sobotka, Mark. Interview by Carol Schulz, West Hartford, Connecticut, November 6, 1974, and August 8, 1980.

Soumerai, Eve. Unpublished diary. Written in Munich, Germany, September, 1945.

Trunk, Isaiah. *Judenrat: The Jewish Councils in Eastern Europe under Nazi Occupation*. New York: Macmillan, 1972.

Weiss, Aharon. "Jewish Leadership in Occupied Poland." *Yad Vashem Studies on the European Jewish Catastrophe and Resistance*. Edited by Livia Rothkirchen. Jerusalem: Yad Vashem Martyrs' and Heroes' Remembrance Authority, 1977. Vol. 7, 335–65.

10

EINSATZGRUPPEN IN THE EAST

On June 22, 1941, the German *Wehrmacht* (army) broke its agreement with Joseph Stalin and invaded the Soviet Union. In doing so, the Germans added another 5 million Jews to their list of possible victims. Eventually, 2.5 million more Jews, living in the western parts of the country, came under Nazi rule. One and one-half million had escaped before the Germans arrived; the rest remained beyond their reach in the eastern part of the Soviet Union.

On the surface, the occupation of the Soviet Union and the subjugation of the Jews followed a pattern similar to that established in Poland: first, they were identified and terrorized; they were then stripped of their property; and, finally, they were concentrated within their cities, towns, and villages.

But sometime between the sealing of the Polish ghettos and the invasion of the Soviet Union, there was a major shift in German policy toward the Jews. In Poland, as we have seen, the Nazis expected that impoverishment, starvation, and disease would reduce the Jewish population significantly, while the government tried to decide what to do with those who survived. The Nazis even had a name for this starvation death: "clean violence" (Esh 1963, 138). Once the Germans moved to the Soviet side of Poland, the "final solution to the Jewish question" became something far more sinister than active neglect, however awful that had become.

Until then, terror as an accompaniment to the expulsion of Jews from their homes, and their concentration in ghettos, was more or less a random ingredient used to force the Jews to obey; but in the Soviet Union, from the very beginning, the aim of the Nazis was simply to kill them. In the spring of 1941, while making his plans to invade the Soviet Union, Adolf Hitler had decided that this invasion afforded a perfect opportunity to kill many Jews. "Small units of the SS [*Schutzstaffel*] and Police [were to] be dispatched to Soviet territory, where they were to move from town to town to kill all Jewish inhabitants on the spot" (Hilberg 1967, 177).

To accomplish this, along with the regular army, the Germans brought along four *Einsatzgruppen*, literally, "special action groups." These mobile killing units, referred to simply as *A, B, C,* and *D*, were each assigned a region in which to operate. With the exception of the killing centers themselves—which were yet to be invented—this Nazi innovation brought more terror and death to more people than any other method at any other time in history.

In fact, these plans were so horrifying, that a long list of euphemisms was created to mask their intentions: special treatment, special action, executive measures, cleansing, major cleaning action, work over in a security police manner, make free of Jews, resettlement, liquidation, finishing off, appropriate treatment, and the now infamous final solution to the Jewish question (Esh 1963).

To catch the Jews as quickly as possible, and prevent escape, the *Einsatzgruppen* were given the authority to operate anywhere the army was, even on the front lines. The army was instructed to supply them with living quarters, gasoline, food rations, and radio communication, but their "functional directives" (orders) came from the Reich Security Main Office (RSHA), headed by Reinhard Heydrich (Hilberg 1967, 187).

The men who served in these units were not drawn from a list of criminals, nor were they especially bloodthirsty soldiers, as one might expect. Most were ordinary citizens who had volunteered earlier for SS information or police work. They formed a highly cultured group of 3,000, with impressive academic credentials. There were teachers, artists, lawyers, physicians, dentists, journalists, even a clergyman and an opera singer. Most were in their thirties, and though a few members of the *Einsatzgruppen* asked to be relieved of their duties, and were transferred with no repercussions, most seemed content to carry out their orders. According to Michael Berenbaum, a noted Holocaust historian, they had "trained for murder, not for war," and they carried out their "housecleaning" duties with great efficiency (Hilberg 1967, 189).

STAGE ONE: THE MASSACRES OF THE FIRST SWEEP

In the first sweep, the *Einsatzgruppen* "moved with such speed behind the advancing army that several hundred thousand Jews [were] killed like sleeping flies" (Hilberg 1967, 192). *Einsatzgruppe A* reported killing 125,000 Jews on October 15, 1941. *Einsatzgruppe B* reported, on November 15, 1941, an "incomplete total" of 45,000. On November 3, *Einsatzgruppe C* reported shooting 75,000; and *Einsatzgruppe D* reported, on December 12, that they had killed 55,000 people (1967, 192).

Standardized Killing

The *Einsatzgruppen* were so effective because they simply overwhelmed their victims and shocked them into cooperating. At the same time, they adhered strictly to a carefully designed plan.

The soldiers first established a site just outside of town, usually one with an antitank ditch already dug. If there was no ready-made grave, the Germans had their victims dig one.

Next, all the males were told to report to a central location, the village square for example, and to bring with them all of their valuables: money, jewelry, religious or art objects, musical instruments, and family treasures, as if they were packing for a move. These goods were promptly confiscated for the coffers of the Third Reich. Next, the victims were loaded into trains, trucks, wagons, or some other form of transportation, or were marched to the waiting grave sites, and told to strip. In the winter they were allowed to keep their underwear on, in the summer they were not.

What happened next varied from place to place, depending upon the sensibilities of the murderers. Those who did not mind being close to their victims, lined them up along the edge of the ditch and shot each man separately, one bullet in the back of each head, as they had been trained to do. This was considered the most efficient means of execution, wasting the least amount of ammunition. Others preferred to kill at long range, using a machine gun to blanket the area.

Another method was also common. The Jews were told to climb into the ditch and to lie down, whereupon they were shot—already in their own graves. Layer upon layer of corpses, as many as five or six, were thus neatly buried.

In an effort to preserve the military character of these mass murders, outsiders and the curious were kept away. This was often difficult, and some people did witness and report these events, often members of the regular army. The soldiers were also told to administer no beatings along the way, giving the impression, almost until the end, that the Jews were merely being resettled—which was exactly what those remaining in the town were told. Once the men were gone, the peaceful cooperation of the next group of victims was more or less assured.

These actions were so horrific, and so extensive, that keeping them secret was impossible. Witnesses did exist, and did tell tales. The erroneous belief that the Jews went like sheep to the slaughter most likely arose in part because of the success of the *Einsatzgruppen*. Historian Oscar Handlin believes that the extent of the destruction was determined by the efficiency of the Germans, rather than the passivity of the Jews. Not only was the German bureaucracy extreme in its efficiency, it was also masterful in its ability to deceive. As noted above, at each step, the authorities offered a plausible explanation of the events that were happening and lied about the future. Given that there was very little one could do to stop these mobile killing units from carrying out their orders, the need to believe the lies was great (Handlin, n.d., 8).

In addition, Handlin believes that the behavior of the Jews was often misunderstood by witnesses. Most of the adult victims were not alone. Jewish children were not spared, but told to march right along with their parents. A Nazi eyewitness reported on the actions of one man: "The father was holding the hand of a boy about ten years old and was speaking to him softly; the boy was fighting his tears. The father pointed to the sky, stroked his head and seemed to explain something to him" (8).

The witness was baffled by this passivity, but it seems clear to Handlin that the father's goal was not to go down fighting, but to prepare his son for death and spare him from the extra suffering that would have been caused by fear and panic (8).

Despite this efficiency, whole towns and villages with Jewish populations still remained after the first sweep, and a second sweep was needed. Those who were missed the first time were herded into ghettos to await their death. In the fall of 1941, the *Einsatzgruppen* began again, this time in the Baltic. The terror spread to the south during the next year. Altogether, in the space of eighteen months, these mobile killing units succeeded in annihilating more than 1 million people (Berenbaum 1993, 95–98; Hilberg 1967, 192–95).

The Town of Belitzah

The story of Dr. Philip Lazowski provides a closer picture of the process followed by the *Einsatzgruppen*. At the time of the invasion, Philip was a young boy. On June 28, 1941, the Germans entered his home town of Belitzah, located on the Neiman River in Lithuania. The inhabitants of Belitzah found themselves caught between the armies of the Soviet Union and the armies of Germany. Philip's family hid in their basement, while above them, the Germans set fire to the village. The family was eventually discovered and forced out of their home so that it, too, could be burned. They spent the night in a field with hundreds of their neighbors (Lazowski 1975, 8).

As in Poland, the first response of many of the Jews was to flee from the invading German army. Estimates of the number of Russian Jews who succeeded in escaping to the interior of the Soviet Union vary tremendously, from a few thousand (Dawidowicz 1975, 541) to two-thirds of Russian Jewry or 2 million people (Sachar 1977, 443). Philip, his brother, and his father eventually escaped and became what were later to be called "forest Jews," but not before the arrival of the *Einsatzgruppe*.

The day after the invasion of Belitzah, *Einsatzgruppe A* arrived. According to Philip, "[T]hey randomly selected ten Jews, including our rabbi, and used them as horses to pull a wagon, whipping the men to make them go faster. Then, they cut the rabbi's beard in the middle, leaving two sides hanging. They made the rabbi wash some horses, then drink the water he used, forcing him to keep drinking, even as he vomited" (Lazowski 1975, 10).

Some of the men, including Philip's father, fled to the woods on the outskirts of the village. Philip made daily visits to his father, bringing him information about what was happening in the village.

Once I had to tell him that thirty men, some of the most intelligent and respected members of the community, were forced to work at hard labor. When they finished the job, the Germans made them dig a large hole. Then, the Germans killed the men, one by one . . . the hole they dug was their grave. (11)

The Germans killed most of the community leaders, then began killing the rest of the men in the town. Both his father and his grandfather remained in hiding. He recalls that "we lived in fear, and there is no way to adjust to living with fear, to accept death" (11).

The Massacre at Babi Yar

In September 1941, one of the most infamous events in history occurred just outside of the city of Kiev, the capital of the Ukraine, in the town of Babi Yar. On September 19, the German army captured Kiev and set up their headquarters. A week later the Soviet secret police blew up the occupied buildings. The 60,000 Jews of Kiev were blamed for the incident and an order was posted: "Kikes of the city of Kiev and vicinity! On Monday, September 29, you are to appear by 8:00 A.M. with your possessions, money, documents, valuables and warm clothing at Dorogozhitshaya Street, next to the Jewish cemetery. Failure to appear is punishable by death" (Berenbaum 1993, 100).

Both *Einsatzgruppe* C and the Ukraine auxiliary police were assigned to march the Jews to the suburb of Babi Yar where they were told to hand over their valuables and disrobe. Then, in small groups, they were led into a ravine and forced to lie down; finally, they were shot, each successive group falling on the previous one. In two days some 33,000 people had been murdered. A non-Jew, who witnessed the scene, later recalled:

This all happened very quickly. The corpses were literally in layers. A police marksman came along and shot each Jew in the neck with a submachine gun. . . . I saw these marksmen stand on layers of corpses and shoot one after the other. . . . I was so shocked by the terrible sight that I could not bear to look for long. . . . Masses kept on coming from the city to this place, which they apparently entered unsuspectingly, still under the impression that they were being resettled. (1993, 99)

One of the "marksmen" recalled the terror of the Jews when they reached the top of the ravine and saw the bodies below.

In the months that followed more were slaughtered at Babi Yar, including Gypsies and Soviet prisoners of war. Two years later, the Nazis decided to remove the evidence of what had transpired. Members of the same commando group that had killed the victims drafted concentration camp inmates to dig them up and burn the bodies. Bulldozers opened the mounds and machinery was used to crush the bones of the bodies. When they had completed their task, the concentration camp workers were killed. Unfortunately for the German government, 25 escaped and 15 survived the war and told what had happened (100–101).

"Jew Go Back to the Grave"

In her book *Hasidic Tales of the Holocaust* (1982), Yaffa Eliach tells a tale of a massacre that took place only days before the one at Babi Yar. By the first day of Rosh Hashana (the Jewish New Year), September 25, 1941, the Jews of Eisysky, a small town in Lithuania, had come to realize that they were doomed. Surrounded by Lithuanian guards, working for the Germans, 4,000 Jews and their rabbi, Shimon Rozowsky, dressed in his special Sabbath robes and yarmulke, were told to report to the horse market.

As they had done elsewhere, the authorities separated the men and women, and, in groups of 250, led the people to the Jewish cemetery where their open graves awaited them. The Jews were ordered to undress and line up at the edge of the ditches, and then they were shot in the back of the head.

Sixteen-year-old Zvi Michalowsky stood by his father, a teacher in the village, as they comforted each other and waited for death. But Zvi was also counting the intervals between each volley of shots, and just before he was fired upon he fell into the grave, feigning death. He felt the bodies piling up on top of him, the streams of blood surrounding him, and the trembling bodies below him.

He waited until the shooting had ended and proceeded to dig his way to the top of the grave. Naked, cold, frightened, and covered with blood, he headed for the houses of the Christians he had grown up with. At the first house, he knocked. The peasant who lived there came to the door and shined his lamp on Zvi.

"Jew, go back to the grave where you belong!" was Zvi's greeting, as the door was slammed in his face (Eliach 1982, 54). Next he tried the home of a widow he knew; but she chased him off with the same words, brandishing a burning stick after him as if he were the devil himself.

Soldiers with an unidentified unit execute a group of Soviet civilians kneeling by the side of a mass grave in Kraigonev, 1941. National Archives, courtesy of USHMM Photo Archives.

Zvi stopped abruptly, faced her, and shouted, "I am your Lord, Jesus Christ. I came down from the cross. Look at me—the blood, the pain, the suffering of the innocent. Let me in" (1982, 55). Awestruck, the widow believed him. For three days she cared for him and kept him hidden, in exchange for his promise to bless her and her children. Then, dressed in borrowed clothing, with a small supply of food, he left, swearing her to secrecy. He survived the war by living with other partisans in the forest.

More Killings

The killing units carried out similar operations all over the Soviet Union. In addition, non-German auxiliaries, particularly Lithuanians, Ukrainians, Latvians, and Poles, and more than 200,000 others helped them murder Jews. In the town of Pkyatin in the Ukraine, 1,600 Jews were shot in one day, mostly old men, women, and children, since the others had fled in an attempt to find help (Berenbaum 1993, 98). In Odessa, on October 23, 1941, 19,000 people were taken to a square, doused with gasoline, and set afire. Later the same day, 40,000 more Jews were taken to the village of Dalnik where some were shot and the rest were locked in a warehouse and burned (Berenbaum 1993, 102; Hilberg 1967, 201).

Close-up of a young mother with her two children, sitting among a large group of Jews from
Lubny in the Ukraine who have been assembled
for mass execution by the Nazis, October 16,
1941. Hessisches Hauptstaatsarchiv, courtesy of
USHMM Photo Archives.

In Iasi, Romania, 8,000 Jews were killed between June 22 and 30, 1941.
Then the Nazis created a "death train," loading 2,544 people onto a cattle
car bound for Calarasi, three hundred miles away. The train shuttled back
and forth from Iasi to Calarasi until everyone had died from hunger and
dehydration (Berenbaum 1993, 101).

With the aid of Romanian soldiers, *Einsatzgruppe D* managed to kill
tens of thousands in Bucovina and Bessarabia. Those who were not killed
immediately were taken on a death march to Transnistria, where 70,000
perished from famine, disease, or gunshot wounds in the space of three
years. By 1945, 350,000 Romanian Jews were dead, two-thirds of them
killed by fellow Romanian or Hungarian collaborators. For the 300,000
survivors, the Romanian general and dictator, Ion Antonescu, demanded
a ransom, but no one offered to pay it (1993, 102).

The Role of the Regular Army

Contrary to the belief that the regular German soldier was opposed to, or at the very least ignorant of, these killings, in some areas of occupied Russia, the German army was so eager to have the job of killing Jews completed quickly that they provided assistance. One memorandum from *Einsatzgruppe C* stated, "Armed forces surprisingly welcome hostility against Jews" (Hilberg 1967, 196).

Jews who were caught hiding in the forests were turned over to the killing units or were rounded up and placed in army-made concentration camps to await killing. In addition, the army made special requests that the *Einsatzgruppen* wipe out the Jews of a city. Army generals justified their actions by claiming that the Jews were a group of "diehard" Bolsheviks (1967, 201).

Non-German auxiliary police, especially in the Baltic and Ukrainian areas, helped, too. Local police were much better able to recognize and hunt out Jews in their own towns than were the Germans. In addition, local people were even willing to stage pogroms (organized attacks on Jews) at the instigation of the Germans, saving them some time and effort. Often, these pogroms were photographed so that the Germans could use them as evidence of the way in which the native populations treated their Jews (201–4).

Finally, as noted above, the Germans were adept at deceit, and even in the whirlwind action of the mobile killing units, they were able to create an appearance that all that was desired was the movement of the Jewish population to other areas of Europe. Simply doing nothing for a day or two allayed the fears of those who had fled the oncoming army. Since survival in the countryside and the forest was nearly impossible, and no one wanted to take in a Jewish refugee, returning home appeared to be the best option. Unfortunately, only death awaited them there (208).

STAGE TWO: FORCED INTO THE GHETTO

On November 10, 1941, the second stage of the invasion, expulsion from their villages and concentration in ghettos, began in Belitzah. Philip and his family were told to go to Lida, but his parents had heard that life was better in the city of Zetel, about twenty miles away. They went to Zetel, dragging a wagon loaded with their belongings and traveling at night so as not to be seen on the roads. When they arrived in Zetel, the Nazis put Philip's father to work in a flour mill (Lazowski 1975, 25).

Within a few weeks, the Germans began moving the Jews of Zetel into one section of the city, creating a ghetto, just as they had in Belitzah. As in Poland, the Nazis first took hostages and demanded that they be ransomed for gold and other valuables. Philip remembered seeing a soldier grab a woman, accuse her of not turning over all her gold, and then kill her (1975, 26).

Next, all the Jews were required to wear a yellow Star of David and were told to form a *Judenrat*. The Jews were then forced into the ghetto. On February 22, 1942, Philip's family of seven was put into a twelve-by-eight-foot room. The family was allowed little furniture, so they slept on the floor and "were constantly in one another's way" (26).

Once the Jews had been locked in the ghetto, the German authorities decided to eliminate those whose labor was not needed. On April 28, 1942, thousands of Jews were forced to gather in the marketplace. Philip recalls seeing Germans, Lithuanians, and Poles shooting people indiscriminately, in their efforts to round up all the Jews in the ghetto. He also saw one soldier bayonet a baby (33).

Once assembled, the Jews were told that some would be chosen to work in another city. This lie was frequently told to prevent panic and rebellion. In fact, the Jews were shot. People selected to stay in the ghetto and serve the Nazis were issued cards identifying them as workers.

Philip's family had dug a cave next to their house, and they remained in hiding during the roundup. Philip, who was sent to stand guard over the cave, was caught by the SS and taken to the marketplace. He was temporarily "adopted" by another family and thus saved from being shot (34).

The Second Sweep

A few months later, the *Einsatzgruppe* began the second sweep. In Zetel, the SS surrounded the ghetto shouting, "*Juden raus*" (Jews come out!) (36). Raiding parties were sent into the ghetto to collect the remaining Jews and bring them to a movie house. While the roundup was taking place, some Nazis searched abandoned homes for valuables. Then they opened the ghetto to the surrounding populace. Philip recalls that "villagers who had once been neighbors were looting our home, ripping it apart in the hope of finding hidden valuables, or taking doors and wood for their own places" (37).

Although most of his family managed to stay hidden for several days, they were eventually discovered and pulled from their cave. "The farmers went berserk. They began kicking grandpa, who fell to the ground almost immediately, weakened by the lack of food and five long days cramped in the underground shelter. . . . Then they turned on my mother, beating her to the ground" (37).

As soon as the family had been discovered, Philip's mother gave her older children instructions about what to do to save themselves. His brother escaped from Zetel but ended up in another ghetto in Dvoretz. Philip stayed with his mother, and they were taken to the movie house. His father had remained at the mill where he worked and thus managed to escape the roundup. He sent a gentile policeman, whom he had befriended, to rescue his family, but the man was unable to find them among the hundreds of people locked in the theater (39).

When the trucks with SS men arrived outside the theater, Philip tried to convince his mother to escape with him through the window. They had watched Jews being pushed into trucks and hauled away, and by this time they were quite certain that the Jews were going to be killed. Philip's mother had her youngest child with her, and she was afraid to jump out of the window for fear that he would be killed. She forced Philip to jump and escape without her (39).

Philip found his brother in the ghetto in Dvoretz. Several weeks later, their uncle, who had been hiding in the forest, learned that the boys were still alive. By joining a group of Jews returning after a day's work in the field, he snuck into the ghetto. He then smuggled the boys out, and they joined their father in the forest. The other members of Philip's family were all murdered (54).

Philip, his brother, and their father survived the war by remaining in hiding in the forests of White Russia. They were not alone. Although estimates of their numbers vary, thousands of Jews lived in the forests throughout the war. Three types of so-called forest Jews have been identified: individuals simply hiding from the Nazis; Jews who joined the Soviet partisan movement; and Jews living in special Jewish units (Dawidowicz 1975, 379).

In February 1942, the Germans began a campaign against these Jews. Within a few months, the *Einsatzgruppen* had hunted down most of them, leaving only a few thousand, Philip among them, to survive until the arrival of the Red Army (Hilberg 1967, 251).

"SUPERHUMANLY INHUMAN"

In a speech to the Einsatzgruppen, Heinrich Himmler, praised them for their bravery in taking part in the killing of Jews: "These are battles which future generations will not have to fight . . . against women, children, old people and other useless mouths. . . . We realize that what we are expecting from you is to be 'superhuman,' to be, in fact, superhumanly inhuman."

Those engaged in these wholesale murders believed that they were involved in something historic, grandiose, unique . . ."a great task that occurs once in two thousand years"

Source: Hannah Arendt, *Eichmann in Jerusalem: A Report on the Banality of Evil.* (New York: Viking, 1964), 105.

Rivka's Story

In 1961 in Jerusalem at the trial of Adolf Eichmann for crimes against humanity, Mrs. Rivka Yosselevseka recalled the harrowing events her family experienced at the hands of the *Einsatzgruppe.* Rivka, born in Zagrodski,

Russia, and married in 1934, had one child when the Germans invaded in August 1942. Just as elsewhere, the Jews of her town were first driven to the town square where they were forced to relinquish their valuables. Then, in smaller groups, they were taken by truck a few miles outside the village to ditches that had been dug earlier.

When Rivka arrived she saw naked people, lined up in front of the ditches, but she still hoped this would only be another form of torture. Then she realized that three or four rows of people had already been killed. Her daughter said to her, "Mother why did you make me wear the Shabbot [Sabbath] dress; we are being taken to be shot" (Hilberg 1971, 62). Some of the young people ran and were shot. "It was difficult to hold on to the children," she testified. "We took all children not ours, and we carried [them]—we were anxious to get it all over—the suffering of the children was difficult" (1971, 62).

Her father refused to take off his underclothes and was beaten, stripped, and shot. Then her mother was shot. Then her eighty-year-old grandmother, and her aunt, each holding two babies in their arms. Her younger sister and a friend went up to a German soldier and asked to be spared. He shot both girls.

Then her turn came. First her child was shot and then Rivka, but she was only wounded in the head. Not all of the others were dead either,

Naked Jewish women, some of whom are holding infants, wait in line before their execution by Ukranian auxiliary police in Mizocz, Ukraine, October 14, 1942. Main Commission for the Investigation of Nazi War Crimes, courtesy of USHMM Photo Archives.

especially some of the children, who were crying for their mothers and fathers. By the time Rivka struggled up from among the bodies, the Germans were gone. She found two other women, and they pulled out a third and some children. Some of the children who had escaped were recaptured and shot again.

Rivka recalled that she envied those who were dead. She had no one left and nowhere to go. She stayed at the site for three days, and then she was found by a farmer who took her in, fed her, and helped her join other survivors in the forest. There she remained until 1944, when she was rescued by the Soviets (61–66).

WORKS CITED

Berenbaum, Michael. *The World Must Know: The History of the Holocaust as Told in the United States Holocaust Memorial Museum.* Boston: Little, Brown, 1993.

Dawidowicz, Lucy S. *The War against the Jews: 1933–1945.* New York: Holt, Rinehart and Winston, 1975.

Eliach, Yaffa. *Hasidic Tales of the Holocaust.* New York: Oxford University Press, 1982.

Esh, Shaul. "Words and their Meaning: 25 Examples of Nazi-Idiom." *Yad Vashem Studies on the European Jewish Catastrophe and Resistance.* Edited by Nathan Eck and Arieh Leon Kubovy. Jerusalem: Yad Vashem Martyrs' and Heroes' Remembrance Authority, 1963.

Handlin, Oscar. *Jewish Resistance to the Nazis.* Florida: Documentary Photo Aids, no date.

Hilberg, Raul. *The Destruction of the European Jews.* Chicago: Quadrangle Books, 1967.

———. *Documents of Destruction: Germany and Jewry 1933–1945.* Chicago: Quadrangle Books, 1971.

Lazowski, Philip. *Faith and Destiny.* Hartford, Conn.: Fox Press, 1975.

Sachar, Howard Morley. *The Course of Modern Jewish History.* New York: Dell, 1977.

11

THE WANNSEE CONFERENCE: PLANNING THE "FINAL SOLUTION"

When Adolf Hitler came to power, few imagined that killing Jews was his first priority. Even today, no one is certain when Hitler decided that the "final solution to the Jewish question" was to take precedence over everything else, even winning the war. What eventually took place was a gradual tightening of the noose, until the fateful decision was made that the answer to the so-called Jewish question was to be total annihilation.

First, the Jews were forced out of Germany; then, after the war began, out of the entire Reich; and then they were crammed into ghettos in Eastern Europe. As the Nazi leaders of each region became more and more impatient to get rid of "their" Jews, they cut off the supply of food, clothing, fuel, medicine, sanitary facilities, space, and sleep, hoping the Jews would simply give up and die.

The Nazis next decided that all Soviet Jews, rather than be imprisoned like the Polish Jews and slowly killed through starvation and disease, would be gunned down and buried in ditches. Even after this had been accomplished, however, thousands of living Jews still remained in Europe.

THE DECISION IS MADE

On January 20, 1942, Reinhard Heydrich, head of the Reich Security Main Office (RSHA)—the same man who had so successfully directed the operations of the *Einsatzgruppen*—assembled the state secretaries of the most important ministries of the Third Reich to lay the groundwork for the systematic mass murder of the Jewish people. Thus we know that Hitler had, by this time, made his final decision regarding the fate of the Jews of Europe. This was to include not only the Jews who lived under Nazi control, but those the optimistic Nazi war machine expected to capture in Ireland and England as well.

Heydrich's invitation to the afternoon conference held in the scenic Berlin suburb of Wannsee contained a copy of a document signed by Hermann Goering, commander in chief of the air force, prime minister of Prussia, plenipotentiary for the four-year plan, and Hitler's number-two man, authorizing Heydrich to plan and coordinate the "Final Solution" throughout Europe. In order to implement any plan, Heydrich needed the cooperation of all of the men administering the regions now controlled by the Reich: the German leaders of the various occupied territories; the heads of the Justice Ministry and the Reich Chancellery; the state secretary of Goering's Four-Year-Plan Office; the head of the Gestapo; the head of the SS (*Schutzstaffel*) Race and Resettlement Main Office; the head of the SS and police in Poland; the commander of *Einsatzgruppe A* in the Baltic; the secretary of the Nazi Party Chancellery; and Adolf Eichmann, the so-called Jewish Expert, whose job at the meeting was to take the minutes. Eight of these fifteen participants held Ph.D. degrees (Arendt 1964, 83).

Prior to this time, Eichmann had specialized in forced immigration and expulsion of the Jews from Germany, and he had organized a network of officials in most of the occupied territories. On July 31, 1941, in anticipation of the role Eichmann would eventually play as director of the deportation of Jews to the death camps, he was summoned to a most important meeting with Heydrich.

Heydrich had received a letter from Reichsmarschall Goering, stating that "[t]*he Führer has ordered the physical extermination of the Jews* [author's italics]" (Arendt 1964, 83). He was also officially informed of the newest codeword, the most ominous in a long list of language rules (*Sprachregelung*): the Final Solution (1964, 83).

At his trial in 1961, Eichmann recalled his response to this extraordinary pronouncement: "I remember it even today. In the first moment, I was unable to grasp the significance of what he had said, because he was so careful in choosing his words, and then I understood, and didn't say anything, because there was nothing to say anymore" (83).

By the time of the Wannsee meeting, all of the participants had been informed of Hitler's decision. All were longtime Nazi Party members and trusted government officials. Everyone knew of the existence of the ghettos and of the activities of the mobile killing units taking place at that very moment. None were under any illusions about the nature of the task at hand.

Later, Eichmann was to testify that Heydrich had expected some "stumbling blocks and difficulties" (83) to be brought up at this meeting, but none were voiced. The representative from the General Government region of Poland, Undersecretary Josef Buhler, "welcome[d] the start of the final solution" (Hilberg 1971, 98) since, for him, transport posed no problem, but epidemics and the growing black market were endangering the health and disrupting the economic structure of his region (99). His superior, Hans Frank, had already announced to his leading officials that they "must destroy all the Jews. He [Buhler] had only one favor to ask: that the Jewish question in this territory be solved as rapidly as possible" (113).

When asked by the trial judge about the "spirit" of the conference, Eichmann would later recall that Heydrich had had a "relaxed attitude" (113). Buhler and Wilhelm Stuckart, Reich minister of the interior, had shown "extraordinary enthusiasm" (113) especially after the formal part of the meeting, when the participants chatted about such details as the best means of extermination, while being served their drinks and hors d'oeuvres during their "cozy little social gathering" (113).

This last part of the discussion was not explicitly recorded in the minutes. One of Eichmann's functions was to "translate" the language of the document according to the "language rules" (85) before completing the official minutes, which were carefully gone over by Heydrich before being submitted to Goering (113).

IRONING OUT THE DETAILS

Heydrich opened the formal meeting with reference to the progress of the "battle" being waged against their "opponents," (114) the Jews. He summed up for the participants the sequence of events that had occurred thus far: first, the Jews had been forced out of German life (e.g., from government, universities, the professions, and cultural life); then they had been pushed out of German living space (537,000 had emigrated to other countries within and beyond Europe's borders). He reminded them that the Reich Central Office for Jewish Emigration had been created to steer this flow of emigrants and to expedite their exit. But, he told them, "In place of emigration, the evacuation of the Jews has now emerged" (Gutman 1990, 1592).

In other words, escape from the Nazi regime would no longer be possible for the Jews. They were now to be involuntarily "evacuated to the east," the new euphemism for extermination. Then he continued:

Separated by sex, the Jews capable of work will be led into these areas in large labor columns to build roads, whereby a large part will doubtless fall away through *natural diminution* [author's italics]. The remnant that finally survives all this, because here it is undoubtedly a question of the part with the greatest resistance, will have to be treated accordingly, because this remnant, representing a natural selection, can be regarded as the germ cell of a new Jewish reconstruction if released. (1990, 1593)

His point was not missed: Not only were the Jews expected to die, by "natural diminution," but those "remnants" who failed to die would be killed, *every last one of them*. Evacuations were to be viewed "solely as temporary measures for 'practical experiences' were already being gathered that would be of great significance for the imminent Final Solution of the Jewish Question" (1592) (i.e., extermination methods were being tested). "The goal," he told them, was "to cleanse the German living space of Jews in a legal manner" (Hilberg 1971, 91).

Heydrich went on to discuss the steps that would be used to "treat accordingly" (Arendt 1964, 120) the Jews who survived the hard labor in store for them. First, Europe would be combed from west to east for Jews, though the Reich itself would come first as there was a shortage of apartments for the Germans. Then Jews would be brought, bit by bit, to specific ghettos identified as "transit ghettos," or to "transit camps," from where they would be transported farther east to the extermination camps.

WHO MUST DIE?

As soon as this had been explained, Heydrich raised the issue of which categories of Jews were to be taken where. It was expected that it might be difficult to cart off Jews living in the less anti-Semitic countries of Europe, and there was also the possibility that others might protest. Unfortunately, we now know, significant intervention in the destruction of the Jews of Europe did not happen. Nonetheless, some voices were raised in protest, especially those of church officials on behalf of baptized Jews (who were now, of course, Christians) or those living in mixed marriages with non-Jewish children. What to do in individual cases, in each country, had to be decided.

Going down the list of categories and countries, Heydrich conducted the discussion, asking for and giving suggestions. It was decided that old people (sixty-five and over), severely invalid Jewish war veterans, and decorated war veterans (Iron Cross First Class) would all be sent to the "old people's ghetto" at Theresienstadt. In this way, noted one conference participant, "Many intercessions will be eliminated in one blow" (Hilberg 1971, 95). Influential people also had their favorite Jews: valets, hairdressers, mistresses. It was believed that because these people were receiving special treatment, no one would complain (1971, 95).

The Foreign Office representative pointed out that the Nordic countries might cause a problem and recommended waiting awhile, especially since there was "an insignificant number of Jews" (95) living there anyway. The Romanian government, it was reported, had already appointed a "plenipotentiary for Jewish affairs" and were awaiting their orders. In France, Heydrich told them, the seizure of Jews should "in all probability proceed without major difficulty" (95). Regarding Italy, they were told, Police Chief Heinrich Himmler needed to be contacted.

The problem of what to do with *Mischlinge* of the first degree (half-Jews) and *Mischlinge* of the second degree (quarter-Jews) was never completely resolved. *Mischlinge* with no children, *Mischlinge* married to non-Jews, *Mischlinge* with non-Jewish children, *Mischlinge* too old to have children—all these posed special problems. Would Christian children with a Jewish mother cause trouble if she were carted off in the night? Would German (i.e., non-Jewish) spouses protest if their Jewish mates were arrested? How can the birth of more Jews be prevented if any Jews were allowed to live?

Some thought that "voluntary sterilization" (95) for *Misch linge* should be a prerequisite for staying out of the camps. It was decided that *Mischlinge* married to *Mischlinge* were Jews, and these would be evacuated along with all the rest. In addition, the group considered asking the legislature to dissolve all mixed marriages involving Jews, so that they could then be deported with no trouble, although this did not happen. Nor was there mass sterilization, although some people were sterilized, including non-Jews with congenital diseases or birth defects.

In the end, most of these problems were not solved; rather, it was determined that cases would be decided on the merits of the person: his or her looks (how Jewish a person looked was more important than any other consideration, even conversion to Christianity) and whether he or she behaved like a Jew, whatever that meant (96).

KILLING AND DISPOSING OF THE BODIES

Another issue that needed to be addressed was where and how to go about killing the people and disposing of all the bodies. This conversation was also not included in the official minutes, according to Eichmann, who admitted to listening very carefully while words like *liquidation* and *gassing* and *extermination* were being used. Although there had been little difficulty in conducting a campaign of mass shootings in the Soviet Union, this type of solution was not expected to work in Western or northern Europe for a number of reasons. One was that the actions of the *Einsatzgruppen* were being conducted in the middle of a war zone, which provided a certain amount of camouflage. There was much less chaos in the rest of Europe.

The participants at the conference also realized that the past record of anti-Semitism in Western and northern Europe was far less virulent than in Eastern Europe, which led them to believe that the type of brutality that took place at Babi Yar, for instance, would not be tolerated. Whatever was to be done had to be done in the east, and somehow the Jews would have to be taken there.

Transportation posed a few problems, but none that could not be solved. Coordination among the Ministry of Transportation, the army, and the Railroad Timetable Commission would enable things to move smoothly. Inside the Reich, regular passenger trains would be used until they reached the border, so as not to cause a panic. From then on, freight cars would be used because they provided the best means of surveillance.

As the shipping agent, Eichmann would have to pay attention to the capacity of the destination of each train, deciding whether the occupants would be sent first to a ghetto, a work camp, a transit camp, or a so-called direct operation (i.e., death camp). Cleaning the cattle cars would be a continual problem, one that they had already experienced in transporting people to the ghettos. In the winter, people froze to the benches, and they broke the windows in an effort to get at the ice since they were given no water.

Finally, the methods of killing and disposing of the bodies required improvement. Despite the fact that most members of the *Einsatzgruppen* continued to carry out their tasks willingly, the regular soldiers who had witnessed these atrocities were beginning to show signs of unrest. Some had even taken photographs or written letters home. Also, the local populations were getting upset, fearing that they might be next. Since the government preferred to keep the operations of the killing units secret, especially from the foreign press, a less visible, cleaner, and quicker means of delivering death was needed. Thus the idea of using gas chambers was born (Gutman 1990, 1592; Berenbaum 1993, 103–5).

WORKS CITED

Arendt, Hannah. *Eichmann in Jersusalem: A Report on the Banality of Evil.* New York: Viking, 1964.

Berenbaum, Michael. *The World Must Know: The History of the Holocaust as Told in the United States Holocaust Memorial Museum.* Boston: Little, Brown, 1993.

Gutman, Israel, ed. *Encyclopedia of the Holocaust.* New York: Macmillan, 1990.

Hilberg, Raul. *Documents of Destruction: Germany and Jewry 1933–1945.* Chicago: Quadrangle Books, 1971.

12

THE "FINAL SOLUTION": THE PLAN

The Jews of occupied Europe had struggled to stay alive, as individuals and as a people, for more than two horror-filled years before the fateful decision to annihilate them all was put into action. For the rest of the war, from 1942 until the defeat of Germany in May 1945, all through Europe, a state-sponsored policy of murder was carried out. In all, between 4 and 6 million Jews, and millions of other innocent victims, were slaughtered.

The "Final Solution" was unique to history. It was a deliberate, systematic, all-encompassing program of genocide, dictated wholly by state policy. The entire legal system participated, passing laws, decrees, and directives that condemned innocent people to death: Jews, Gypsies, Poles, Russians, Ukrainians, Czechs, Communists, and even Germans who were unlucky enough to have been born with physical or mental handicaps or congenital diseases.

All branches of the government that were needed to accomplish the task were enlisted. People at every level of German society and from every bureaucratic office participated. Churches and the Interior Ministry supplied birth records and prevented Jews from hiding their identities, even those who had been baptized. The newspapers and Post Office notified them of each new abuse: the loss of jobs, restrictions on whom they could marry or befriend, expulsions from their homes, and deportation to the ghettos and camps. The Finance Ministry confiscated all wealth and property and, ironically, used some of it to finance the Final Solution.

Private firms fired Jewish workers, company officers, and board members. The universities refused entrance to Jewish students, denied degrees to those already enrolled, and fired Jewish professors. Private industry bid on contracts to supply the gas for extermination and to build the ovens for cremation. One company supplied one camp with forty-six ovens capable of burning 500 corpses an hour. Pharmaceutical companies used camp inmates to test drugs without having to worry about negative side effects. Doctors performed experimental operations, many simply innovative methods of torture, with no legal repercussions. And the transportation bureau paid the railroad companies' bills for taking the Jews to their death.

Unlike instances of genocide in the past, the Final Solution was not incidental to some other national goal. The Jews did not stand in the way of national expansion, as settlers perceived the Native Americans, for example. Nor was there any way Jews could escape death by moving outside of Germany to some other European nation, or even by converting to Christianity as some had done during earlier times. Nor did the killing stop when Germany began to lose the war and needed the trains and labor to supply the troops.

PUTTING THE SYSTEM IN GEAR

The entire process of identifying and rounding up the victims and transporting them, by train, to the camps required careful planning and execution at all stages. Of all the operations conducted by the Third Reich aimed at the civilian population, this was the most costly and the most staggeringly complex. Millions of people had to be uprooted, transported, and delivered.

In charge of the operation was Bureau IV, Section B-4 of the Reich Security Main Office (RSHA), headed by Adolf Eichmann. An overview of the system shows its complexity.

First, the German Legal Department created legislation making the Jewish victims stateless, so that no country's government could effectively inquire into their fate after they had been taken away. This included not only German Jews but also the 5,200 foreign Jews living inside the Reich. The Germans soon discovered that foreign governments, who had relinquished their interest in the welfare of their own Jewish nationals living outside their country, were not too reluctant to turn over their native Jews living at home. This action made it possible for the Nazi government to confiscate property left behind, as well.

Second, the minister of finance and the Reichsbank prepared facilities to receive the huge supply of loot being confiscated from the victims, from gold fillings to typewriters to watches. These items were sorted out and then sent to the Prussian State Mint for distribution to the appropriate agencies or individuals.

Third, in addition, the minister of transport provided passenger cars and freight cars and saw to it that scheduled deportations did not conflict with regular train timetables.

Fourth, as soon as all these arrangements had been made, Eichmann, as overseer of the rounding-up process, notified each Jewish Council how many Jews had to report for deportation each day. This was determined by the capacity of both the trains and the camps to which they were headed. Transports were staggered, as there was a shortage of space in the trains and in the camps. The capacity of the gas chambers was also limited. The councils' job was to create the lists of names for deportation.

Fifth, as soon as their names appeared on the lists for deportation, the Jews were told to register with the authorities, and they were required to fill out pages and pages of questionnaires reporting on the extent and whereabouts of any property they still owned. This made it easier for the items to be confiscated. (Individual members of the SS were forbidden to help themselves to the loot because the Germans wanted to appear to be conducting their activities according to the law. Of course, the notion that the law itself was immoral, as were many of the laws of the Third Reich, did not seem to be a problem for the authorities.)

Finally, the Jews were assembled at a collection point and crammed into freight cars, as many as 100 or more per car. Those who tried to escape were hunted down, house by house, until they were found. Some were shot immediately; others were taken to the collection point and forced to board the train. When the victims arrived at their destinations, twenty-five percent were selected for hard labor, and the rest were immediately sent to the gas chambers. Frequently, as many as twenty-five percent of the passengers died before arriving at the camps from extreme heat, lack of water, or heart failure caused by stress and disease.

This gruesome process was conducted, step by step, first in Germany, and then, systematically, throughout occupied Europe and in countries that wished to remain in Germany's favor.

FINANCING THE MACHINERY OF DEATH AND DESTRUCTION

Who paid for the train tickets, the fuel to operate the trains, the gas used in the mobile vans and gas chambers, the machinery used to deliver the gas, the furnaces and the ovens, and the hundreds of offices of bureaucrats in charge of this production? Where did the money come from to pay for the salaries of all those involved in carrying out the Final Solution: the postal workers, the commanders and department heads, the clerical workers, the SS (*Schutzstaffel*) and police, the Gestapo, the conductors of the trains, the guards in the camps, the doctors who chose who lived and who died, and the operators of the gas chambers and the crematoria?

Much of the funding came from the victims themselves. As early as 1935, under the Nuremberg Laws, Jewish businesses and property were being *Aryanized*: turned into German property. Later, after the decision had been made to force the Jews to emigrate to the "east," special bank accounts—called Special Accounts "W"—were set up, into which Jews were forced to "donate" at least twenty-five percent of their liquid assets to pay for their transportation to the camps. This money also was used to pay for those too poor to contribute (Hilberg 1971, 113).

This procedure was spelled out in a memorandum sent to the Jewish Community Associates in Germany: "Subject: Evacuation IV Cash Levy 12/3/41" (1971, 113). Setting up these accounts in local banks was the responsibility of the Community Association and District Office, and a strict accounting of deposits and withdrawals was made (113).

The Jews were told that the money would be spent on equipping the transports with tools and food, although this was a complete fabrication as neither could be found in the train cars. As noted elsewhere, passenger trains were used to transport people within the Reich, so as not to alarm the Jews or cause any suspicions to arise among any non-Jews who might have been sympathetic. These trains, however, offered no amenities, and the cattle cars used, after the border was crossed, often did not even have a bucket for use as a toilet.

In addition to the twenty-five percent bank deposit, the Germans also confiscated pensions, both public and private. In a law enacted on June 29, 1941, it was decreed that as soon as a person had been evacuated and his property confiscated, the state did not need to "make pension payments to a third party for years and decades" (117) and that all money owed to Jews from private individuals and businesses went directly to the Reich. Here, too, the irony of the situation did not matter to anyone.

Finally, there were literally tons and tons of personal property that the Jews were forced to abandon when it was time for them to leave their homes. So many items were left behind that the government was unable to confiscate them immediately and worried about how to protect the loot. In a memorandum sent from the State Finance Office to the local Protective Police, "Financing the Solution of the Jewish Question," the police were advised to watch Jewish apartments "falling to the Reich" (117). They were cautioned to make certain to keep "unauthorized third persons" from "lay[ing] their hands on movable belongings" (117) before the government could collect them.

By 1943 most German Jews were dead. They had left behind personal property, apartments, Jewish communal property, blocked bank accounts, goods in customs houses, sequestered securities, business firms, real estate, credits, debts, pensions, insurance, and inheritances. The 11th Ordinance to the Reich Citizenship Law of November 25, 1941, paved the way for the mass looting of Jewish property by the German Reich. It stated that any Jew "who takes up his residence abroad could not be a Reich national, and that the property of such a Jew fell to the Reich" (Hilberg 1967, 301). Of course the fact that no one had voluntarily taken up residence abroad did not seem to matter.

Jews, forced to take up residence abroad in labor camps and death camps, were allowed to take with them a few pieces of personal property—clothing, photographs, and a small amount of money—in order to perpetuate the myth of resettlement in the east. However, once they arrived at the camps, all of their precious possessions, including the shirts on their backs and the shoes on their feet, were immediately, and brutally, appropriated.

WHO GOT WHAT: DIVIDING UP THE BOOTY

Theoretically, all property was to be used for the benefit of the German people, through direct use by government offices, or indirectly through sales and use of the money. Occasionally, goods or apartments were doled out to bombed-out Germans and civil servants, but much of the finer personal property went directly into the homes of Gestapo or SS members and their families. The Gestapo could "secure" property even before the Jews were deported and made use of such things as typewriters, adding machines, bicycles, cameras, film projectors, and binoculars (Hilberg 1967, 306).

The Finance Ministry got first choice of almost everything else: desks, bookcases, carpets, armchairs, pictures—even musical instruments and high-quality linens. Jewelry and stamp collections went to the Municipal Pawnshop of Berlin, and the money went to the government. Securities were sent to the Reich Treasury; phonographs and records went to the Propaganda Ministry. Sewing machines were sold to the administrators of the Lodz ghetto for the making of uniforms. Printing machinery went to the Reich Press Chamber. Even underwear was sold—to the Economy Group Retail Trade (1967, 305).

Deporting Jews was a very profitable business.

WORKS CITED

Hilberg, Raul. *The Destruction of the European Jews.* Chicago: Quadrangle Books, 1967.

———. *Documents of Destruction: Germany and Jewry 1933–1945.* Chicago: Quadrangle Books, 1971.

13

DEPORTATION AND THE BEHAVIOR OF JEWISH LEADERSHIP

The cold, efficient, businesslike approach to the Final Solution belies its reality. Each stage was accompanied by terror, violence, and unimaginable suffering. For the Jews, the first agonizing task in this process was to decide whether to obey the order to draw up a list of those who were to be deported in each transport. Would obeying orders make things easier or harder for the Jews? What were the consequences of compliance? Or refusal?

By agreeing to each set of demands, including reporting for deportation, some have accused the Jewish people of cooperating in their own destruction. Looking back, it is clear to us that supplying the lists of names, and later obeying orders to board the trains, certainly helped the Germans fulfill their mission. The question that needs be asked, however, is not whether the Jews cooperated in their own deaths but whether they understood what fate awaited them in the east.

Throughout the Holocaust, the phrase "going to the east," though understood by German officials to be a euphemism for killing, to the Jews and their neighbors meant simply relocating to Poland to perform more hard labor. To someone ignorant of the truth, each order leading to deportation was just one more in a series of painful, but not deadly, demands.

In general, what the Jews knew about the Final Solution depended on the location of their community; some knew more than others, although no one knew the full extent of the Holocaust until it was over. All Jews knew that throughout history their people had been persecuted, and, at times, even whole villages had been eradicated. They also knew that

European Jewry as a whole had survived by waiting patiently until each wave of anti-Semitism died down, and by finding ways to live with the fact that they were second-class citizens at best, with no influence over the behavior of their governments.

Before 1942 the Jews had never encountered a policy of total destruction and had no reason to believe that such was the policy now. They also had reasonable hopes that Adolf Hitler, unlike the Russian tsars or most other historical rulers, would soon be defeated. With that in mind, the effort of the Jewish Councils to avoid provoking large-scale retaliation by acceding to the Nazi demands was not cooperation, but an attempt to survive. Many might perish, but Jewry, as always, would survive.

WHO KNEW ABOUT THE CAMPS?

Unfortunately, as the war progressed, although many Jewish leaders were told about the death camps, they still obeyed orders to report for deportation. Why did this happen?

In his book *The Terrible Secret* (1980), Walter Laqueur argues that the facts about the Final Solution were known to the world at large, and even to the inhabitants of some of the ghettos themselves, as early as 1942. Witnesses to what was happening in the Soviet Union and in death camps like Chelmno, only forty miles from Lodz, had written to friends and family still locked in the ghettos. "Post offices in Poland continued to function, warnings continued to arrive from all over the country. . . . The existence of these letters shows that many Polish Jews did know at an early date about the Final Solution" (Laqueur 1980, 130).

Most people simply did not believe what they had read or heard. Some doubted the truth of the information they had received; others could not accept the fact that a similar fate awaited them. Throughout Europe, each Jewish community was convinced that, although the Germans had murdered some other group of Jews, in Poland, Greece, Russia, or Italy, their own community would be safe. "The information existed, but the psychological mechanism of suppression was also at work" (1980, 149). No one could believe that Hitler intended to kill all the Jews and that the Allies would not be able to stop him.

Thus, when forced to face the question of what actions were most likely to safeguard the lives of the greatest number of Jews, they were unable to make the correct decision. According to Laqueur, "In the case of East European Jewry the acceptance of reality might have induced more people to flee or to resist. Most would still have died, but less than actually perished" (1980, 155).

DECIDING WHAT TO DO

What happened in Lodz illustrates the dilemma faced by Jewish leaders throughout Europe as soon as the liquidation process began in earnest.

In June 1944, when the Germans announced the liquidation of the Lodz ghetto, the question of what to do arose. The Jews had been told by the Jewish Council that they were going to the camps where they would have a much better life. They had also been told that they were not going to be separated from their families. Although this was the line given to all the councils by the Germans, Mark Sobotka found it hard to believe. He and his friends decided to find out what they could.

People were sent out of the ghetto in cattle cars. Some of the cars came back and some people were given the job of cleaning them out. I had a friend who worked at the cars. Another of my friends was sent out in the car. We asked him to let us know what happened at the camps by putting a slip of paper under the window so it would be concealed. We marked the car so it could be identified when it returned. My friend wrote what happened. He said we are going to Auschwitz and families are being separated. (M. Sobotka 1980)

Mark and his friends went to the leaders of Lodz's Zionist organizations with their information, and again resistance was discussed. But, because the ghetto was so cut off from the rest of Poland, the residents had no weapons of any kind and were unable to get any support or guidance from anyone, anywhere. It was finally decided,

You cannot fight the German Empire with sticks. We could not, under any circumstances, obtain any weapons. And we did not have the slightest chance. At that time, there were still over 60,000 Jews in Lodz and we knew quite well that if we put up any resistance at all thousands and thousands of people would die. Sure they died later on anyway, but at that time, we didn't know that would happen. We just could not morally take the responsibility of jeopardizing those people. (M. Sobotka 1980)

Although Mark and the others firmly believed that fighting the Nazis would have been futile, they still felt guilty for not trying. Why? From our perspective, it is because the survivors later learned that almost everyone who had been deported was killed anyway, even though they "cooperated" peacefully. But Mark, and others like him, felt guilty *at the time* this was all happening. Did he know then what fate awaited them? The answer is yes and no. Many years later, Bernice Sobotka explained:

It was not that we didn't want to believe. It was that your brain—it was inconceivable. You can't believe that one human being can do this to another human being. It is beyond comprehension that people could be capable of such atrocities. So we actually did not believe it, no matter what we heard. (B. Sobotka 1980)

Not knowing for certain what their fate would be, most members of the Jewish Councils did what the council in Lodz did: they cooperated in the hopes that adhering to the demands of the Germans would lessen the violence and convince their captors that the Jews would cause no trouble.

Although the Jews assumed that whatever happened next would be worse than what they had already endured, they hoped that their good conduct would at least stave off death.

This policy caused much controversy, both then and now, about the nature of the Jewish Councils and the leadership they provided. As discussed earlier, the main job of the councils was to do their best to feed, clothe, house, and protect the Jewish community in a setting that made this task all but impossible. For example, when the Nazis demanded laborers, the councils found a way to lessen the terror of random kidnappings by providing a specified number of people. For a while, bargains such as these did provide some relief. Since the Germans had no intentions of making life easy for the Jews, however, none of these arrangements lasted for long. Regardless of how powerful the Jewish Councils may have appeared to the rest of the community—distributing jobs, food, medicine, living quarters, sanitation, schooling, police and fire protection, and more—in reality, they had no power at all. Everything they did was controlled by the German authorities.

Unfortunately, many ghetto inhabitants saw the councils as the source of their problems, especially when they were forced to give in to the Germans' demands. Some even accused members of the councils of collaborating with the Germans in an effort to save themselves. The opinion of historians regarding the role of the *Judenräte* is mixed (even contradictory), and as time goes by and as more information comes to light, it seems that most of the members of the councils have been judged wrongly.

Some historians, most notably Raul Hilberg, believe that much of the blame for carrying out the will of the Nazis lies with the Jews themselves. Had they not complied with orders—"to register their property, obtain identification papers, report at a designated place for labor or deportation, or shooting" (Hilberg 1967, 166)—the Final Solution could not have been pursued. These historians also believe that the Jewish Councils were responsible for the Jews' compliance. Others tell us that the Jews did not cooperate until it was obvious that disobedience would result in their instant death or, even worse, in the death of many others (Weiss 1977, 363).

JOINING THE COUNCIL

In most cases, the decision of whether to accept a position on the Jewish Council was cause for great soul-searching. Most leaders of the prewar Jewish community did not wish to serve as a tool of German oppression, but they were also reluctant to leave their communities defenseless. In some cases, when no one volunteered, councils were formed by lottery. In the end, those who joined the *Judenräte* did so with grave misgivings, and their fears were soon justified. In Lodz, for example, thirty leading members of the community formed a consultative council in October 1939. On

November 7, they were all arrested. Some were killed immediately; the rest were killed later, in the camps (Trunk 1972, 17, 327; Weiss 1977, 340).

On October 14, 1942, the entire *Judenrat* of Bereza Kartuska committed suicide rather than participate in a deportation. The others were deported anyway (Berenbaum 1993, 85).

On July 23, 1942, Adam Czerniakow, head of the Warsaw *Judenrat*, having refused to preside over the death of his fellow Jews, especially the children in Janusz Korzak's orphanage, committed suicide by swallowing a cyanide capsule (Hilberg 1967, 319). In his diary, Chaim Kaplan wrote,

He followed the Talmudic law: If someone comes to kill me, using might and power, and turns a deaf ear to all my pleas, he can do to me whatever his heart desires, since he has the power, and strength always prevails. But to give my consent, to sign my own death warrant—this no power on earth can force me to do, not even the brutal force of the foul-souled Nazi. (Kaplan 1973, 191)

Isaiah Trunk, in his book *Judenrat* (1972), wrote about the tenure of the members of the *Judenräte*. Most did not stay in office for long, especially those who refused to do what was demanded of them by the German authorities. Of 724 council members researched, only 6 percent served for three or more years, and 45 percent served no longer than one year. Only 11.9 percent of the 724 survived the Holocaust (Trunk 1972, 327).

In another study, historian Aharon Weiss evaluated the behavior of the *Judenräte* members in 146 communities. Of those serving in the first term of office (called by Weiss the first councils), 30.9 percent received a positive evaluation (assisted the community, refused to carry out financial directives, warned of approaching roundups), and 38.1 percent resigned because they were not willing to give in to Nazi policy, were removed from office by the Nazis, were killed for refusing to cooperate, or committed suicide. Of the remaining 31 percent, 4.3 percent served in some form of underground movement, 2.7 percent died soon after taking office, 0.7 percent were replaced by the Jews, 9 percent received a questionable evaluation, and 14.3 percent received a negative evaluation for having carried out German orders (Weiss 1977, 364).

Within a short time, most of the members of the first councils had been killed or removed from office. Research shows that the behavior of *Judenräte* members in the last councils was strikingly different from that of the first councils. Sixty percent of the members of the last councils in 101 communities earned a negative evaluation. Weiss concludes that those who resisted Nazi demands were "liquidated or removed" and replaced with those less concerned with the interests of the community. "During the stages of mass extermination and brutal terror, they carried out the Nazi orders" (1977, 364). Weiss believes that responsible Jewish leaders worked to protect the interests of the people, but those who had no previous leadership experience, and who had seen the horrifying consequences of refusing to cooperate with the Germans, gave in to their demands. They had no choice.

Finally, to the often-asked question, Why did the Jews appear to go to their deaths like sheep? the famous photograph "The Deportations," subtitled *"Mit Gewalt aus Bunkern hervorgeholttaken"* (Pulled from the bunkers by force), affords some answers. The photograph shows a group of mostly terrified women and children being rounded up for deportation. This particular group, having already suffered greatly in the walls of the ghetto, clings no doubt to a thin shred of hope that if they obey the soldiers—maybe, just maybe—they will be allowed to live. How could they have resisted? They possessed no weapons and were trying to protect their children. The guns were all on the other side. SS (*Schutzstaffel*) Major General Jurgen Stroop, who directed the destruction of the Warsaw ghetto from April 19 through May 16, 1943, was awarded the Iron Cross First Class for his role. The Stroop report, which included this photograph, contains his own proud description of the events, compiled for Heinrich Himmler, chief of the Gestapo, and for the fuehrer himself.

WORKS CITED

Berenbaum, Michael. *The World Must Know: The History of the Holocaust as Told in the United States Holocaust Memorial Museum.* Boston: Little, Brown, 1993.

Hilberg, Raul. *The Destruction of the European Jews.* Chicago: Quadrangle Books, 1967.

Kaplan, Chaim A. *Hunter and Hunted: Human History of the Holocaust.* Edited by Gerd Korman. New York: Dell Publishing, 1973.

Laqueur, Walter. *The Terrible Secret: Suppression of the Truth about Hitler's "Final Solution."* Boston: Little, Brown, 1980.

Sobotka, Bernice. Interview by Carol Schulz, West Hartford, Connecticut, October 18, 1980.

Sobotka, Mark. Interview by Carol Schulz, West Hartford, Connecticut, November 6, 1974, and August 8, 1980.

Trunk, Isaiah. *Judenrat: The Jewish Councils in Eastern Europe under Nazi Occupation.* New York: Macmillan, 1972.

Weiss, Aharon. "Jewish Leadership in Occupied Poland." *Yad Vashem Studies on the European Jewish Catastrophe and Resistance.* Edited by Livia Rothkirchen. Jerusalem: Yad Vashem Martyrs' and Heroes' Remembrance Authority, 1977. Vol. 7, 335–65.

14

THE ROUNDUPS

When the time came to report to the collection point to board the trains to the concentration camps, no one was foolish enough to *want* to go. As bad as conditions were in the ghetto, people were fairly certain that, at the very least, they would not be able to stay with their families after relocation. In many cases, family members were told to report on different dates for different trains. Many suspected far worse things to come.

In order to prevent panic and guarantee compliance, the Germans, as always, used lies, deceit, and threats. People were bribed with promises of food, and posters threatened dire consequences if the Jews did not obey were displayed. Some were told that they would find food on the train and to bring pots and pans. Others were instructed to bring twenty pounds of clothing, all their valuables, and money. The Germans even sent postcards from the camps, written by Jews on their way to the gas chambers, telling their loved ones that all was well (Hilberg 1967, 782, 194).

One notice, posted on the walls of the Warsaw ghetto (Hilberg 1971, 131–32), read,

Proclamation to the Inhabitants of the Jewish District

In accordance with official instructions of July 22, 1942 all persons not employed in institutions or enterprises will definitely be resettled.

Forcible removals are being continued uninterruptedly. I call once more on all members of the population subject to resettlement to report voluntarily at the railway siding, and will extend for three days, including August 2, 3, and 4, 1942, the distribution of 7 pounds of bread and 2 pounds of marmalade to every person who reports voluntarily. Families presenting themselves voluntarily will not be separated. Assembly point for volunteers: Dzika 3-Stawki 27

The Director of the Order Service Warsaw, August 1, 1942

In addition to these postings, notification was sent to each person; every decree came as a complete surprise so as to prevent attempts to escape. In her book *A Memoir: All but My Life* (1995), Gerda Weissman Klein noted that her family was told that, before they left to report to the station, they were to tag the keys to every lock in their house with the location of the locks they opened, and they were to leave them on a table in the front hall. The letter they received from the authorities read, "Violators of this order [will] be punished by death" (Klein 1995, 31).

When people refused to cooperate, buildings in designated blocks were surrounded, and the SS (*Schutzstaffel*) went from door to door hunting them down. Most of these roundups were conducted by the Jewish police, or Order Service, under the direction of the Germans, usually the SS and police. An anonymous letter of complaint to Adolf Hitler, from a German woman who had heard reports from a Polish policeman, describes a

A policeman stands guard as Jewish deportees, carrying a few personal belongings, march through Wuerzburg-am-Main, Germany, in 1942, before their transport east to the concentration camps. National Archives, courtesy of USHMM Photo Archives.

roundup: "During the dissolution of the ghettos children had been thrown on the floor and their heads trampled with boots. Many Jews whose bones had been broken by rifle butts were thrown into graves and covered with calcium flour. When the calcium began to boil in the blood, one could hear the crying of the wounded" (Hilberg 1967, 317).

In the Warsaw ghetto, the leader of the Order Service was a Christian who had converted from Judaism. He was highly successful in carrying out his charge. On July 22, 1942, when the liquidation began, 380,000 Jews were still alive in Warsaw. Seven weeks later, the number had dropped to 70,000. By December there were only 55,000. All had been deported to Treblinka. In his diary entry of July 27, 1942, Chaim Kaplan wrote that

people are being hunted down in the streets like animals in the forest . . . panic arises that is beyond imagination. Residents . . . hide in nooks and crannies in the cellars and attics . . . jumping over the roofs and fences at the risk of their lives . . . in the end the police take men, women and children. Their cries and wails tear the heart out.

   The old people . . . accept the judgment in silent submission and stand with their small parcels under their arms. But there is no limit to the sorrow and tears of the young women; sometimes one of them makes an attempt to slip out of the grasp of her captors and then a terrible battle begins. (Kaplan 1973, 192)

The sick are taken outside in their beds, babies in their cradles, old men and women half-naked and barefoot (1973, 202).

SPECIAL ACTIONS

Kaplan watched one woman try to fight back. "With wild hair and a torn blouse she rages with the last of her strength" (192). She was finally captured and carted away. "Before my eyes," he continued, "they capture an old woman who walks with a cane. A young mother of two little children from 19 Nowolipki Street was caught and sent off. The dear children are left orphans" (194). On one block, they captured 30 people in hiding and shot them on the spot (197).

ANOTHER EYEWITNESS FROM WARSAW

A resident of the Warsaw ghetto, Kalman Friedman, wrote about his neighbor, Mr. Nussbaum, who was paralyzed and unable to walk. He and his nephew lived upstairs from Friedman. Hearing loud noises upstairs, Friedman waited until things died down before going to investigate. "The bed had been moved from its place; all the household goods were spread on the floor and Nussbaum was lying under the bed—dead" (247). The SS had shot him and pushed him under the bed.

Friedman had looked for the nephew, Yezhy, but at first could not find him. Finally, Friedman was caught when his building had almost collapsed from exploding hand grenades. He was put into a building and guarded by "booted and armed wild beasts in the form of men" (247). Eventually, Yezhy appeared: "The child came closer, put his small head on me, snuggling up, and remained silent. I felt his quivering limbs, his burning cheeks, and I stroked his face that was wet with tears" (247). After twenty-four hours they were forced to walk to the train and loaded into freight cars, 100 to a car, to be taken to the camps.

Source: Chaim A. Kaplan, "Expulsion." Hunter and Hunted: Human History of the Holocaust. Edited by Gerd Korman. (New York: Dell, 1973).

"Special actions," as these were called, could occur as punishment for any number of offenses: for purchasing food and smuggling it into the ghetto, for failing to wear the yellow Jewish star, for possessing fake documents, for hiding outside the ghetto, for supposedly sleeping with a German soldier (after being raped by him), for being chronically ill, or for no reason at all (Arad 1976, 255).

These expulsions were so horrible that some residents of Warsaw looked forward to death. "One thorn," wrote Kaplan, "we shall not be privileged to witness the downfall of the Nazis" (Kaplan 1973, 190).

JANUSZ KORCZAK AND HIS ORPHANS

Orphans too were liquidated. In Warsaw, Dr. Henryk Goldszmit, famous throughout Poland as Janusz Korczak, writer of children's books and star of a popular children's radio program, ran a Jewish orphanage for over twenty-five years prior to the war. During the war, he continued his work, moving his orphanage into the ghetto and doing what he could to protect his children. Despite the attempted intercession of Adam Czerniakow, head of the Warsaw *Judenrat*, Korczak's orphans were denied an exemption from deportation.

On Wednesday, August 5, 1942, the SS surrounded the orphanage, blowing their harsh-sounding whistles and shrieking, "*Alle Juden raus*" (All Jews out). A few minutes later, they charged into the building. The children, who were eating breakfast, were given fifteen minutes to get ready. One hundred ninety-two children dutifully marched out of the building and lined up by fours, with Korczak and Stefa Wilczynska, his devoted assistant, at the head of the line, and their teachers, nurses, and caretakers with them.

Knowing that, regardless of their destination, the roundup and deportation that awaited the children would be a nightmare in itself, Stefa had

Group portrait taken on January 1, 1942, of children living in a ghetto orphanage in Kielce, Poland that was administered by the Judenrat. Rafal Imbro, courtesy of USHMM Photo Archives.

spent days preparing for the event. She packed their rucksacks with anything of practical use that would fit, and she dressed the children in their best clothes, as if they were going on an outing, trying to impart a festive atmosphere to the situation.

"Clutching flasks of water and their favorite books and toys" (Berenbaum 1993, 79) and carrying the green flag of the orphanage in front of them, the children marched to the assembly place. They were surrounded by whip-brandishing Nazis and Ukrainians.

One eyewitness, Jehoshua Perle, described the scene in his diary: "a miracle occurred, 200 children did not cry out, 200 pure souls, condemned to death, did not weep. Not one of them ran away. None tried to hide. Like stricken swallows they clung to their teacher and mentor, to their father and brother, Janusz Korczak, that he might protect and preserve them" (Perle, quoted in Perlis 1983, 96).

Another witness, Nahum Remba, Jewish secretary of the education department in the ghetto, also gave an account of that day.

No, I shall never forget this scene as long as I live. Indeed, this was no march to the carriages, but rather a mute protest organized against this murderous regime . . . it was a procession the like of which no human eye has ever witnessed. . . . They were going to their death with eyes full of contempt for the murderers. Seeing Korczak, the ghetto policemen jumped to attention and saluted him. The Germans asked: "Who is this man?" At this point I could no longer contain myself. With both hands I tried to hide the stream of tears running from my eyes. I sobbed and cried as I stood there, helplessly watching this cold blooded murder. (Remba, quoted in Perlis 1983, 97)

All the inhabitants of the orphanage were gassed at Treblinka.

SAVING A CHILD

Alexander Donat, a journalist, told about his efforts to save his son, Wlodek. First he wrote a letter to Polish friends, having it hand-delivered so that he would not be caught communicating with the outside world. He then alerted his friends that the letter would be coming, so they would not refuse it. He arranged a call to set up an appointment with a couple in the countryside willing to accept his son. He had saved the money to pay them by smuggling handmade kerchiefs out of the ghetto for sale. A Christian journalist friend agreed to take the child to the country, in two weeks.

> Two weeks: in which we tried to memorize our five-year-old son to the look and to the touch . . . while my son's mother taught him to disavow his connection with us. "Remember, you have never lived in the ghetto. You are not a Jew. You are a Polish Catholic" (1973, 236).

In one week, Donat's friend returned to take Wlodek; he had heard that a liquidation was to happen soon and wanted to save the child. He was right. Soon after he left, a new wave of roundups occurred (1973, 237).

Source: Alexander Donat, "Last Days," *Hunter and Hunted: Human History of the Holocaust.* Edited by Gerd Korman (New York: Dell), 1973.

LAST WORDS FROM WARSAW

On March 1, 1944, Dr. Emmanuel Ringleblum, leader of Warsaw's Oneg Shabbat (Joy of the Sabbath) project, wrote a letter to the Yiddish Scientific Institute and the Yiddish Pen Club, in the hopes of finding some Jews still alive and able to preserve the memory of those who had worked so hard to maintain Jewish life in the ghetto. He tells them that "To live with honor and die with honor!" was the watchword of the ghetto (Ringleblum 1958, 19).

He then described the fate of the artists, actors, writers, choir directors, scholars, musicians, composers, journalists, scientists, and children of the ghettos of Poland. He recalled Rosa Symchowitz, who worked extensively with homeless children and died of typhoid, and Menakhem Linder, a young economist, murdered by the Germans in 1942. He referred to the children as well: "Today there are no more Jewish children left in Poland. The Hitler criminals murdered ninety-nine percent of the children" (1958, 21).

Ringleblum told them that as soon as the Nazis had started to deport the Jews to the death camps, people knew there was no hope of survival in the ghetto. It was at that point that they began actively and overtly to resist.

In the forefront were our heroic youth of all groupings and the active corps of the working men. . . . The superb epic of the Jewish armed struggle in Poland began: the heroic defense of the Warsaw Ghetto, the magnificent struggle in Bialystok, the destruction of the annihilation centers in Treblinka and Sobibor, the battles in Tarnow, Bedsin, Czestochowa and other points. The Jews showed the world that they could fight with arms, that they knew how to die with honor in the struggle with the arch-enemy of the Jewish people and of all humanity. (22)

One week later, on March 7, 1944, the Gestapo discovered Ringleblum and his family in their underground shelter in the Aryan district of Warsaw. He, his wife, his son, and 35 others were tortured and shot (22).

TWO TEENAGERS PREPARE TO DIE

In late May 1943 when the buildings of the ghetto were about to be set on fire by the German military, two teenagers and two adults laid down on a blanket in the corner of an upstairs room. They held each other and shared a honey cake they had saved. They prayed and ended with: "May He Who Makes Peace Make Peace Upon Us." A few hours later their building was set on fire. I met one of the teenagers, Shlomo, in the Foerenwald Displaced Persons Camp. He had survived by hiding in the sewer. I have never forgotten this story.

Source: Eve Soumerai, *Unpublished Memoirs*, 1996.

BARGAINING FOR LIFE

Many people tried to survive by offering to set up factories and work for the Germans, as in Lodz. Tens of thousands produced goods for the German army. Apartment buildings were turned into factories and barracks for slave laborers. People were given certificates that said they held "worker status," which bought them some time, but eventually they too were taken. Actually, the certificates were meant to be used to classify people in categories for deportation and extermination. Those whose jobs were considered essential, such as armaments manufacturing, were spared for a longer time than other workers (Kaplan 1973, 197).

At times, disputes arose between the administrators of these factories, who wanted to save skilled artisans whom they were unable to replace, and the German authorities, who wanted them dead. One administrator, in a report sent home, wrote, "It is impossible to carry on work without Jews. . . . Every single artisan in this industry [leather making] is Jewish" (Arad 1976, 248). The authorities spared the workers and their families, temporarily, but insisted on liquidating all intellectuals and professionals.

One German official in Lithuania wrote to Berlin: "I have forbidden the wild executions of Jews in Liepaja because the manner in which they were carried out was not justifiable. . . . Of course the cleansing in the East of Jews is a necessary task; its solution, however, must be harmonized with the necessities of war production" (1976, 250). Berlin's reply: "Economic considerations should fundamentally remain unconsidered in the settlement of the problem" (1976, 250).

Private armaments firms, which wanted workers in steel and aircraft production, were also upset with the deportations. They even protested the deportation of the workers' families as this made the workers themselves too depressed to be productive (Hilberg 1971, 137). On August 5, 1942, when no one showed up to load six hundred cattle to be sent to the front, a memo was sent by the chief quartermaster to the Military Committee in the General Government: "The seizure of workers without full timely replacement harms the supply of the front and lengthens the time needed for loading the railroad cars—is therefore directed at the prosecution of the war. Help needed" (1971, 137). Apparently, no matter how necessary the Jews were for winning the war against the Allies, the war against the Jews took precedence.

Eventually one solution was devised to address the labor shortage and eliminate the Jews at the same time: factories, built and operated by private industrial firms, were established inside the concentration camps, where "free" labor was continually available. At a conference held on slave labor in September 1942, it was stated that the Jews would be used as a "living transport chain to the East" (Nuremberg Trial Brief 39). Notes on a September 1, 1942, meeting with Joseph Goebbels show that he favored extermination of the Jews through work. "Usable" Jews were to be separated from those considered worthless. One contingent of 45,000, for example, was expected to yield 10,000 to 15,000 usable laborers (39). A letter sent to Heinrich Himmler from the Reich Main Security office (RSHA) about the deportations in Galicia reported that "during this removal of the Jews into a certain quarter of the town several sluices were erected at which all the work-shy and asocial Jewish rabble were caught . . . *and treated in a special way* [author's italics]" (39).

A RANSOM NOTE

In May 1944, shortly after deportations began in Hungary, a strange message was delivered by Joel Brand, a Jewish emissary from Hungary, to the Allies stationed in Istanbul, Turkey. The message, which came from the Gestapo, proposed a deal. In exchange for ten thousand trucks, the German government would release the remaining 1 million Jews still in their control—100,000 Jews for every thousand trucks turned over to them. In the meantime, the Germans would continue the killings. They also promised to use the trucks only on the eastern front, most probably in Hungary.

The British government, the first to receive the message, sent word of it, along with their response, to the U.S. government. They called the request a "sheer case of blackmail or political warfare. Implied suggestion that we should accept responsibility for maintenance of additional million persons is equivalent to asking the Allies to suspend essential military operations . . . to give Germany 10,000 lorries [trucks] would bring important access of military strength to the enemy" (Hilberg 1971, 200–201).

In addition, the British were appalled that Hitler would get to choose who would be rescued (i.e., Jews) while the Allied governments would not be able to save their own prisoners of war. They did agree to accept some refugees, without payment of trucks, but only "Jews in position of extreme distress or danger" (1971, 201), and only if this would not affect the war effort. Of course, the Germans had already admitted that they would not only kill the Jews they were holding if the ransom were not paid, but that they were *at that very moment* killing Jews and would continue to do so until they received the trucks. Apparently neither the United States nor Great Britain thought this constituted enough "extreme distress or danger," and the deal did not take place (201).

THE SS VIEW OF THESE EVENTS

As the Jews became more and more aware of the viciousness of these roundups, they became even more frantic to escape. According to an SS report, they tried every means in order to dodge elimination. Not only did they try to flee, but they concealed themselves in every imaginable corner, in pipes, chimneys, even in sewers. They built barricades in passages of catacombs, in cellars enlarged to dugouts, in underground holes, in cunningly contrived hiding places in attics and sheds, within furniture. (Nuremberg Trial Brief 32)

The SS and the Gestapo responded with swift and immediate violence, "Howling raiders descended upon the ghettos with hatchets and bayonets" (32). For their work, they were given extra rations of brandy. A later report noted that the "mood and spirit of the men were extraordinarily good and praiseworthy from the first day to the last day" (32).

THE EFFECT OF THE EVENTS ON NON-JEWS

In his August 21, 1942, report on the mood of the population in Warsaw, Brigadier General Rossum, chief of field headquarters, wrote that the Jews were badly affected by their inability to get food, even on the black market. They were "no longer able to buy butter, fat, or meat" (Hilberg 1971, 132). Although no mention was made of the effect of the roundups, a statement about the reaction of the non-Jewish population to the liquidation of the ghetto was included: "The major part of the population is reacting to the resettlement of the Jews with a degree of satisfaction. Relatively few people are offended by it. To be sure, atrocity stories, in part exaggerated, are circulating about the manner of the resettlement" (132).

The memorandum ends there. It is difficult to imagine what part of these stories could possibly have been exaggerated, but it is not hard to understand why escape from the ghetto into the Christian side of Warsaw was nearly impossible.

WORKS CITED

Arad, Yitzhak. "The 'Final Solution' in Lithuania in the Light of German Documentation." *Yad Vashem Studies on the European Jewish Catastrophe and Resistance.* Edited by Livia Rothkirchen. Jerusalem: Yad Vashem Martyrs' and Heroes' Remembrance Authority, 1976. Vol. II, 234–72.

Berenbaum, Michael. *The World Must Know: The History of the Holocaust as Told in the United States Holocaust Memorial Museum.* Boston: Little, Brown, 1993.

Donat, Alexander. "Last Days." *Hunter and Hunted: Human History of the Holocaust.* Edited by Gerd Korman. New York: Dell, 1973.

Hilberg, Raul. *The Destruction of the European Jews.* Chicago: Quadrangle Books, 1967.

———. *Documents of Destruction: Germany and Jewry 1933–1945.* Chicago: Quadrangle Books, 1971.

Kaplan, Chaim A. "Expulsion." *Hunter and Hunted: Human History of the Holocaust.* Edited by Gerd Korman. New York: Dell, 1973.

Klein, Gerda Weissman. *A Memoir: All but My Life.* New York: Hill and Wang, 1995.

Nuremberg Trial Documents. Storrs: Thomas J. Dodd Research Center, University of Connecticut.

Perlis, Yitzhak. "Final Chapter: Korczak in the Warsaw Ghetto." Introduction to *Janusz Korczak: The Ghetto Years 1939–1942.* Israel: Ghetto Fighters' House, 1983.

Ringleblum, Emmanuel. *Notes from the Warsaw Ghetto: The Journal of Emmanuel Ringleblum.* Edited and translated by Jacob Sloan. New York: McGraw-Hill, 1958.

Soumerai, Eve. Unpublished Memoir, 1996.

15

DEPORTATIONS: COUNTRY BY COUNTRY

The Nazi roundups of Jews and other presumed undesirables occurred throughout occupied Europe, as well as in the Axis countries and others that wished to remain in Germany's good graces. The success rate of the deportations varied from country to country, depending largely upon how much control the Germans had over the home governments.

The history of the Jews in the region and the extent to which they had become part of the local community, as well as the behavior of the local non-Jews, also played a role in determining how the Jews were treated. In those countries completely dominated by the Nazis, almost all of the Jews were killed, if not during the roundups or on the journey to the east, then once they had arrived at the camps. In other countries, Jews were saved, either because their governments and their non-Jewish citizens refused to cooperate with the Nazis, or because they actively participated in rescue operations.

These resistance and rescue efforts are discussed in chapters 21 through 23. Here we offer a brief ov-erview of what happened in each of the countries of Europe when it came time to deport the Jews.

DEPORTATIONS FROM THE REICH

In October 1941 transports from the Reich began to arrive in the ghettos of Poland. Those people deported to Riga and Minsk were shot upon arrival. Others were sent to Theresienstadt or other concentration camps where they waited, in ignorance, to be sent to the killing centers.

DEPORTATIONS FROM EASTERN EUROPE

In Eastern Europe, special "advisors for Jewish affairs" were assigned to oversee the deportations. In a memorandum from Foreign Minister and head of the Division for Jewish Affairs Martin Luther, he noted that these assignments were to end "as soon as the Jewish problem in the country concerned can be regarded as solved in the German sense" (Nuremberg Trial Exhibit no. 1455, 128). (Luther was later sent to a concentration camp for writing a letter to Heinrich Himmler stating that Joachim von Ribbentrop, his superior, was insane.)

In discussing the issue of gaining cooperation from the governments of Eastern European countries, Luther had noted, "In general however it is apparent, that the States concerned are more egotistically interested in deporting their own Jewish elements than in any international solution" (Jackson Nuremberg Trial Brief 6). In other words, they were happy that someone else was taking away the Jews, and they did not really care what became of them.

Poland

In January 1942, deportations to Auschwitz began in Lodz. In September, the German authorities demanded that all children and old people be turned over to them. When the people refused to comply, the Nazis entered the ghetto and simply took them. Twenty thousand were deported to the death camp at Chelmno. After that the Germans stopped asking the councils to make up lists; they simply rounded up people. Many were simply killed on the spot (Gilbert 1985, 44).

Then the deportations stopped. Until May 1944, the entire ghetto of Lodz was turned into a huge slave-labor camp. Ninety percent of the inhabitants, including 5,000 Gypsies, now minus most of the young and the elderly, worked in the shops and factories of Lodz. On June 23, 1944, deportations resumed. Forty-six thousand of the remaining Jews had already perished; 145,000 more were killed in gas chambers or vans. In January 1945, the last 877 citizens of the Lodz ghetto were liberated (Berenbaum 1993, 269). (All statistics referring to the number of Jews who perished in each country or region of Europe are approximations. Although figures vary from source to source, individual estimates are fairly close. For each statistic listed, the source from which it came is cited.)

On March 27, 1944, in the ghetto of Kovno (which itself had been turned into a labor camp), an action was conducted against the children and the elderly. One thousand, mostly children, were taken by train to the death camps. On that same day, 200 children from Vilna were taken to be killed. The following day, 800 more were deported. One hundred thirty members of the Jewish police in the central camp in Kovno were arrested and told to hunt for the hiding places of other Jews, as well as to get information on the underground. The commander of the group, his 2 deputies, and 37 policemen refused to cooperate and were executed on the spot. Ninety others returned to the camp, and a new Order Service had to be created with members more directly controlled by the SS (*Schutzstaffel*) (1993, 270).

Six weeks later, the members of the Kovno *Judenrat* were arrested, tortured, and released. Then the entire ghetto was emptied. The inhabitants of Vilna suffered a similar fate. When liberation finally came, there were only between 150 and 200 people left in the ghetto out of the original 30,000. In the ghetto of Shavli, which had also become a labor camp, 7,000 Jews were taken to the death camps between July 10 and July 15, 1944. On July 27, when the Russians came to liberate them, there were no Jews left (270).

By January 1943, 70,000 people were still alive in the Warsaw ghetto. On April 23, Heinrich Himmler ordered the complete destruction of the ghetto. German soldiers managed to capture or kill 56,065; others were killed by means of blasting and fires set by the Germans. Twenty-four searching parties were sent to round up anyone still in hiding. In the end, SS Brigade Leader Stroop reported, "The Jewish Ghetto in Warsaw No Longer Exists" (Nuremberg Trial Brief 46). In all, approximately 3 million Polish Jews out of 3.3 million perished. (Exact figures are impossible to determine, but most counts are close to those reported here by Dawidowicz.)

Czechoslovakia

In Czechoslovakia, the list of Jews who were to be deported often included those who had died or escaped. In order to fill the quota, the police picked up people from the street or dragged them from their beds. The Slovak government did, however, manage to save thousands of baptized Jews (Nuremberg Trial Brief 44). Of the 253,000 Jews who lived in Czechoslovakia at the start of the war, approximately 25,000 remained alive at war's end (Dawidowicz 1975, 512).

Hungary

Jews in Hungary had such significant achievements that the period before World War I was known as the Golden Age of Hungarian Jewry. Large numbers of Jews had entered the professions; for example, 45.3 percent of all lawyers were Jewish, and 78.9 percent of the physicians. When Germany invaded, there were 740,000 Jews living in Hungary, 250,000 of whom lived in territory recently awarded Hungary by the German government. There were also 100,000 Christians considered "racial Jews" (*Historical Atlas of the Holocaust* 1996, 188).

Hungarian Jews remained safe until March 1944 when the Germans finally invaded Hungary. In May 1945 the deportations began. By mid-

July, 440,000 Jews had been shipped out, 400,000 of whom died at Auschwitz (Dawidowicz 1975, 513–17). Another 160,000 had died in ghettos.

The Balkans

Serbia

The largest number of Jews under German influence lived in the Balkans: 1.6 million. Both Serbia and Greece were ruled by the German military. In Serbia, all of the usual steps that preceded deportations (definition of Jews, removal from public office, registration of property, forced labor, rules against hiding Jews, and the order to wear the Jewish star) were accomplished in the space of one day.

In addition, any signs of rebellion on the part of the non-Jewish Serbs over the occupation by Germany were met with shootings of Jews and Gypsies. Eventually, what began as a small operation involving only a handful of people turned into killings by the army that strongly resembled the activities of the *Einsatzgruppen*. These activities were carried out with no opposition from the Yugoslavian government. Of course, the fact that the rebels were neither Jews nor Gypsies did not go unnoticed, but that was regarded as a bonus—a way of getting rid of the undesirables while retaliating for the killing of German soldiers (Hilberg 1967, 435–38).

Only men were killed by the German army, which did not believe in shooting women hostages. Eventually 15,000 Jewish women and their children had to be dealt with; by June 1942, they had all been gassed in mobile gas vans (1967, 442). By the end of the war all 20,000 Serbian Jews were dead.

Croatia

Croatia was created by Germany in March 1941. More than 30,000 Jews lived in Croatia, and by October 1941, most of them were serving as slave-laborers, were confined to concentration camps, or had been shot. In August 1942 approximately 9,000 Jews were deported to Auschwitz. During the next two years smaller groups were deported.

In all of prewar Yugoslavia there had been some 76,000 Jews. At the end of the war, approximately 16,000 remained.

Greece

The process of deporting the 55,000 Jews who lived in the German-controlled area of Greece was as easy and swift as it had been in Serbia, as soon as the Italian army, which had been providing protection, moved out. In just a few months, from March to May 1943, 45,000 Jews were deported from Salonika. In early 1944, Jews were rounded up from Athens and the rest of Greece. In all, 54,000 of the 70,000 Greek Jews were killed (Dawidowicz 1975, 530–31).

Bulgaria

Despite the fact that Bulgaria had become an ally of Germany in the middle of the war, it was not an anti-Semitic country. When anti-Jewish laws were passed, mainly to please the Germans, many protested, especially church leaders. When deportations did occur, they were of Macedonian and Thracian Jews living under Bulgarian control. The remainder of Bulgaria's Jews, some 50,000, were saved (1975, 527).

Romania

In 1939, 750,000 Jews lived in Romania, the third largest Jewish population in Europe. In June 1940, Russia acquired 300,000 of them, and Transylvania another 150,000, leaving 300,000. Most of the Jews in old Romania survived; those in Transylvania were deported with Hungary's Jews to Auschwitz. Those in the eastern provinces that had been ceded to Russia also suffered great losses. Many were killed by *Einsatzgruppe D*.

In Bessarabia, the Jews were driven out by the Romanian military and forced to cross a bridge into a German military area occupied by *Einsatzgruppe D*. The Germans attempted to push the Jews back across the bridge but were stopped by the Romanians, so they diverted the Jews to another bridge. This went on for some time, with Jews being sent back and forth between the two groups of soldiers, with thousands dying from exhaustion and bullet wounds.

While this was happening, the Romanian government ordered all Jews of military age to report for labor. Fearing that these Jews would eventually end up overwhelming the 600 men of *Einsatzgruppe D*, the Germans forbid the Romanian leadership from moving Jews beyond the Bug River and insisted they be placed in concentration camps. Thousands died from starvation or epidemics. In one camp of more than 50,000, nearly all were massacred by Romanian and Ukrainian troops. Eventually 350,000 Romanian Jews were killed (Hilberg 1967, 492).

By the end of the war, 750,000 Jews from the Balkan region had perished (Hilberg 1967, 767).

The Soviet Union and the Baltic States

Before the war started, about 2.8 million Jews lived in the Soviet Union (White Russia, the Ukraine, and Russia). In the Ukraine, although the Germans did not occupy all of the area, sixty percent of the Jews were killed, and in White Russia, sixty-six percent were killed (Dawidowicz 1975, 544).

In Galicia, "elimination" began in April 1942, and by June 27, 434,329 Jews had been evacuated. All but 21,156 died in the concentration camps (Hilberg 1971, 133). In the Baltic region (Latvia, Lithuania, and Estonia), home to 228,000 Jews, the Germans gave orders to puppet agencies to assist with the deportations. The SS brigade fuehrer reported to Himmler that nearly all Jews were "murdered in accordance with basic orders," about ninety percent (541). In Latvia, 30,025 of the 93,000 were deported to the camps; in Lithuania, over 80,000 of the 155,000 (Hilberg 1971, 134).

DEPORTATIONS FROM WESTERN AND NORTHERN EUROPE

Far fewer Jews lived in the north and the west than in the east, and the destruction process was therefore less extensive. In addition, as the Germans had predicted at the Wannsee Conference, there was far less cooperation on the part of native governments.

Norway

Norway's Jewish population was just 1,900 when the Germans invaded, but their presence caused the Germans a lot of consternation. Just as the Nazi government had successfully used propaganda to gain support from its own citizens, it also valued the good opinion of the rest of the world. Even before the war, the Germans wanted to look good to others and would make attempts to justify or cover up their actions.

When the neutral Swedish government expressed concern over the deportation of the Jews in neighboring Norway, the Germans were incensed, especially when they discovered that members of the Norwegian branch of the Nazi Party had passed on the information. In a memo to the High Command of the Armed Forces/Propaganda Division, from the Armed Forces Commander/Propaganda Group of Norway, the commander expressed his extreme dismay at the fact that the Norwegians displayed a "lack of understanding" (Hilberg 1971, 140) of the importance of deporting the Jews to Auschwitz. In a meeting of the party, Vidkun Quisling, the Norwegian leader who was collaborating with the Nazis, "addressed himself to the Jewish question once more, pointing out that *Jewry was the originator of this war* [italics added]" (1972, 142).

The commander also complained that the Swedes had turned the evacuation of the Jews into "an international sensation. The arrest and transport of the Jews was described [in the Swedish press] as a 'manhunt' which 'created dismay even in National Socialist circles'" (1971, 142). Of Norway's Jewish population, from 690 to 800 were taken to Auschwitz, between 900 and 1,100 were helped in their escape to neighboring Sweden by the

Norweigan resistance movement, and the fate of any remaining Jews is unknown (Dawidowicz 1975, 503).

Denmark

The Danish government refused to cooperate with Hitler's demands, in September 1943, to turn over their Jews. They did not provide lists, and German soldiers found it necessary to go from door to door hunting for Jews. Also, since the government was in sympathy with the Jews, the Germans had to avoid clashes with the Danish police. Only 477 people were shipped to Theresienstadt; 6,000 remained in hiding in Copenhagen. In October, the Germans expressed their fury with the Swedes for the bad publicity and their efforts to save the Jews, but the Swedes persisted and offered refuge to anyone who could be ferried across from Denmark. In the end, 5,919 Jews, 1,301 part-Jews, and 686 spouses of Jews were saved (Hilberg 1967, 358).

Finland

Although Himmler made a special visit to Finland's government to try to convince them to deport their 2,000 Jews, the Finnish foreign minister refused, and all were saved (Dawidowicz 1975, 505).

Sweden

Sweden was never invaded by Germany and remained neutral through-out the war. In addition to providing a refuge to Jews from neighboring Scandinavian countries, the Swedes even invited some Jews who had already been arrested in Norway to apply for Swedish nationality in order to protect them. When the Germans protested, a Swedish consular official revealed that he had been given an "official directive to extend to the 'poor Jews who, after all, are only human beings' his helping hand" (Hilberg 1967, 356).

The Netherlands

In February 1941, 1,000 Jews were arrested and sent to Buchenwald and Mauthausen. Their ashes were returned to Holland in return for 75 florins for each body. Of the 20,000 Jews who were married to Christians, 2,256 were not taken because they agreed to be sterilized. Deportations continued until September 1943. First, the full Jews were seized and taken to camps in Holland to await deportation; then those in mixed marriages and wives of munitions workers whose transport had been delayed were taken. Diamond cutters were sent to a special workshop in Bergen-Belsen.

Parents were told that their children were being sent to a "special children's camp," but actually they were sent to Sobibor and gassed upon arrival. Of the 140,000 Dutch Jews living in Holland at the start, 117,000 were deported, most to Auschwitz and Sobibor, and the remainder to Bergen-Belsen and Theresienstadt; only twenty-five percent of Holland's Jews survived (Dawidowicz 1975, 498).

Luxembourg

Luxembourg's prewar Jewish population was 3,000; an additional 1,500 had emigrated to France and Belgium before the Nazis arrived. Approximately 2,500 escaped to France or Portugal. Those still living in Luxembourg were sent to work in labor camps, or to transit camps, from which approximately 800 Jews were deported to Lodz or Chelmno (Dawidowicz 1975, 495).

Belgium

Belgium was controlled by the German military government. When the Germans invaded, 90,000 Jews were living in four major cities, including some 30,000 refugees from the Reich. A number had fled to France, and by December 1940, only 52,000 were left. Many of them hid with Belgian families or were provided with forged Belgian identification papers. When the Allies arrived in 1944, approximately 27,000 had survived (Dawidowicz 1975, 494).

France

France was the home of approximately 350,000 Jews, 200,000 of whom were nonnative refugees from Germany, Austria, Czechoslovakia, Luxembourg, Belgium, and Holland. This was the largest Jewish community in Western Europe. For a long time, the French governments in occupied and Vichy France tried to avoid deportations. Finally, they were forced to abandon foreign Jews, but they continued to protect French Jews. This strategy saved many. Some trains even had to be canceled for lack of passengers.

In Toulouse, the archbishop instructed the clergy to protest the deportations from their pulpits. In Lyon, priests were arrested for protesting and hiding Jewish children on church grounds. The German government asked the Vichy government to revoke the naturalizations of anyone who had become a French citizen after 1933, but they refused. Even so, thousands were deported, beginning in May 1941 (Dawidowicz 1975, 490).

The Jews in Italian-occupied France were also protected, at least until Germany assumed control. When the attempts to round them up intensified, many Jews tried to escape. Some went to Switzerland but were turned back: "We cannot turn our country into a sponge for Europe and take in for example 80 or 90 percent of the Jewish refugees" (Hilberg 1967, 410). Little Andorra did take in refugees, and it was reportedly "filled with Jewish refugees" (1967, 413).

By 1944 there were still approximately 250,000 Jews in France, about 100,000 of them were in Paris. On April 14, the Germans made an all-out effort to capture the remaining Jews. Their targets were children's homes, prisons, labor camps, residential neighborhoods, city blocks, and whole villages. They even paid rewards to Frenchmen who revealed hideouts or brought in victims. They eventually succeeded in deporting only twenty-five percent. In all, approximately 90,000 Jews were taken from France to die in the camps (413). Most of them were not native-born French citizens (491).

DEPORTATIONS FROM SOUTHERN EUROPE

Italy

Jews had lived in Italy since approximately the time of Jesus. By the twentieth century, Italian Jews were totally integrated into Italian society. When the Fascist government passed some anti-Jewish laws, the Italian Jews were shocked. But these laws were mild in comparison with those in other countries, and there were many exceptions for veterans, those in mixed marriages, and the elderly. In general, the Italian people and their government were not interested in solving the so-called Jewish question.

Deportations did not begin until after Italy had surrendered to the Allies and was invaded by Germany. By the spring of 1944, out of 57,000 Jews living in Italy in 1938 (including 10,000 refugees), 3,000 were now in labor camps, 7,496 had been sent to Auschwitz (where 6,886 were killed), 7,000 had emigrated, approximately 5,000 were in Italian labor camps, and the remainder were in hiding. Unfortunately, while all this was going on, the pope remained silent. Nevertheless, hundreds of individual priests, monks, and nuns did hide Jews in churches, and even in monasteries and convents. Eighty percent survived (Hilberg 1967, 424, 429, 430–31; Berenbaum 1993, 167–68).

WORKS CITED

Berenbaum, Michael. *The World Must Know: The History of the Holocaust as Told in the United States Holocaust Memorial Museum.* Boston: Little, Brown, 1993.

Dawidowicz, Lucy S. *The War against the Jews: 1933–1945.* New York: Holt, Rinehart and Winston, 1975.

Gilbert, Martin. *The Holocaust: A History of the Jews During the Second World War.* New York: Holt, Rinehart and Winston, 1985.

Hilberg, Raul. *The Destruction of the European Jews.* Chicago: Quadrangle Books, 1967.

———. *Documents of Destruction: Germany and Jewry 1933–1945.* Chicago: Quadrangle Books, 1971.

Historical Atlas of the Holocaust. United States Holocaust Memorial Museum. New York: Macmillan, 1996.

Jackson, Robert H., United States Chief of Counsel. *The International Military Tribunal Trial Brief: Persecution of the Jews,* Section 4. Storrs: Thomas J. Dodd Research Center, University of Connecticut, undated.

Nuremberg Trial Documents. Storrs: Thomas J. Dodd Research Center, University of Connecticut.

16

THE TERRIFYING JOURNEY TO THE EAST

That day the children were given no homework.
—Primo Levi, *Survival in Auschwitz*

Despite their efforts to hide or to escape from the powerful arm of the Third Reich, there came a day when the vast majority of Europe's Jews were forced to end their struggle to maintain a semblance of normality and report for evacuation to the concentration camps.

Among the prisoners crammed into freight cars for the journey "were mothers carrying newborn babies, frail old people on stretchers, seriously wounded people, small children" (Aroneanu 1996, 3). As many as 140 people were squeezed into one car, on trains carrying from 1,000 to 2,000 passengers. There were no amenities: no seats, no windows, no lights, no food or water, no sinks or toilets, not even any straw. In the middle of the car was a bucket for a toilet, and sometimes another filled with water. Getting to either bucket was nearly impossible. With no bathroom facilities and no privacy, people had to perform the most private actions in public, which caused great emotional suffering for many (Dvorjetski 1963, 200).

The weight of the train slowed it to barely thirty miles per hour, and the trip itself took from one day to as many as ten. In *Survival in Auschwitz*, Primo Levi described his experience in the freight car: "We suffered from thirst and cold, at every stop we clamored for water. . . . Two young mothers, nursing their children, groaned night and day, begging for water. The hours of darkness were nightmares without end" (Levi 1971, 11). Another

survivor recalled seeing friends so wracked with thirst that they resorted
to drinking their own urine or licking the sweat off fellow prisoners (Aroneanu 1996, 4).

Sometimes the victims were forced to travel naked, even in winter. At
other times people were told to bring their belongings, so they wore layers
of clothing, even in the summer, and carried their valuables into the cars
with them. World War I cars, built for forty men or eight horses, became
unbearably crowded and suffocatingly hot, and reeked from sweat, urine,
blood, and feces (1996, 4).

Many died of suffocation, thirst, or heart attacks before they even reached
the death camps. Others went mad, became violent, and attacked fellow
prisoners. In one "shipment," 64 deportees arrived dead, in another, 100;
in another boxcar, only 44 out of 126 were alive at journey's end. One train
from France lost 700 of the 1,200 deportees (Aroneanu 1996, 5; Dvorjetski
1963, 200).

At Auschwitz alone, there were forty-four parallel tracks with hundreds
of boxcars discharging their "freight" daily. Throughout Europe, 1.4 million railway workers and 0.5 million civil servants loaded and unloaded
their charges; there is no record that any railway worker ever resigned his
job or protested the nature of the work. Travel agents booked one-way
passages at four cents per kilometer, children at half fare, those under four
for free, with group rates for over 400 passengers at a time (Berenbaum
1993, 112).

ARRIVAL IN HELL

Boxcar doors were swung open, floodlights glared, guards bellowed,
gunshots reverberated, dogs howled, and babies shrieked—these sights
and sounds, and more, greeted the new arrivals to the camps. Outlandish
orders, shouted in strange languages, were accompanied by clubbings,
bullets, and dozens of questions—How old are you? Are you healthy or
ill? How many inmates in your car are dead or dying? Children were
snatched from loving arms, and husbands and wives and elderly parents
were hurled into lines (Dvorjetski 1963, 200).

Most survivors recall arriving in the dead of night. All remember feelings of total confusion and fear. Upon arrival, prisoners were immediately
separated into two lines: one line for work and the other line for death.
There were no pauses for goodbyes, no parting words of love or comfort,
just shouts and blows and bullets. Many women were so traumatized that
they stopped menstruating. Men too were shocked; some never recovered
their faculties. Other people, however, became even more determined to
survive (1963, 200).

In the midst of all this, the newest inmates got their introduction to what
lay ahead of them. The sign on the iron gate read *Arbeit Macht Frei* (Work
gives freedom), but the reality was otherwise. Levi recalls his first view

of the inmates of Buna, the labor camp section of Auschwitz, marching in columns past him:

with an odd, embarrassed step, head dangling in front, arms rigid. On their heads they wore comic berets and were all dressed in long striped overcoats, which even by night and from a distance looked filthy and in rags. They walked in a large circle around us, never drawing near, and in silence began to busy themselves with our luggage and to climb in and out of the empty wagons. (Levi 1971, 16)

INDUCTION INTO CAMP LIFE

Most likely to live were young, relatively healthy, men. The others, the "unusable," were taken to vans to be gassed, or, later in the war, to specially constructed gas chambers and then to the crematoria. By July 1944, "the ovens were working night and day" (Aroneanu 1996, 6). From Levi's transport of 500 (the other 500 had perished along the way), 96 men and 29 women were chosen to work. The remainder, including three-year-old Emilia, daughter of Aldo Levi of Milan, a "curious, ambitious, cheerful, intelligent child," were dead in two days (Levi 1971, 16). Most people who arrived were gassed and burned, and their clothes were packed and readied for shipment to Germany, on the first day (Hilberg 1967, 555).

Some people were forced to walk to the camps: a kilometer or two from a train station, or hundreds of miles from a ghetto to the camp. Regardless of how exhausted, hungry, injured, thirsty, or ill, all newly arrived inmates were treated with brutality.

Those chosen for life were given no time to mourn the loss of their loved ones nor to rejoice in their relatively good fortune. Despite the fact that they had received no food or water for days, they were first made to stand at attention and listen to a lecture on what was now to be expected of them: "You are not at home. . . . The only exit is by way of the chimney" (Hilberg 1971, 622; Levi 1971, 24). Recalled Levi, "We seem[ed] to be watching some mad play" (17).

More orders were given: to strip, to pile all clothing and shoes in special bundles that they were told would later be returned (a lie), and to stand naked (in summer or winter) until taken to be shaved and sheared. Next they were sent to the shower room, where they were made to stand in several inches of water while waiting for a shower. They were not allowed to sit down, though they had been standing for hours, and if they tried to talk to one another, they were reprimanded or beaten (Levi 1971, 20).

After a five-minute shower, they were out in the cold again, given their pajama-like uniforms, usually rags, and wooden-soled shoes but no socks. The wooden shoes prevented one from sneaking about without being heard. Their uniforms identified them to the guards. On the front were sown identifying triangles: green triangles were for ordinary criminals;

red indicated political prisoners; yellow and red triangles in the form of a star identified Jews; pink triangles were worn by homosexuals; and purple ones were worn by Jehovah's Witnesses. In addition, letters were stamped on the triangles to indicate the nationality of the prisoner (Aroneanu 1996, 26).

Since everything they were given was the property of the Reich, the inmates now had no belongings whatsoever: no shoes, no clothes, no photos, no letters, no handkerchiefs, no hair, no habits, no voices with which to protest or even to comfort one another ("There is no why here," Levi 1971, 25), no family, and no friends. Dehumanization was almost complete, but there was still one more step.

Each inmate was now tattooed on the left arm with a number that was to become the "name" to which he was to answer. If the prisoners failed to memorize their numbers, and did not respond immediately when called, they were punished. To get any food, they had to show their numbers.

The tattoos told their own stories: date of arrival, nationality, convoy. Numbers from 30,000 to 80,000 were among the first to be incarcerated; by 1944, only a few hundred of them were left. Those with high numbers were the so-called freshmen. People selected for death upon arrival were not given tattoos. There was no point (Levi 1971, 23).

When all the formalities were completed, the new residents of Auschwitz were marched to their barracks, accompanied by the sounds of German marching tunes being played by a Jewish band of inmates (1971, 25).

Once they were assigned a bunk it was important to find a way to make it livable. Sleeping in a narrow bed with a total stranger necessitated making some agreements: whose head went where, who slept on the outside, who could hang his shoes on the wall, and so on. There was a need to "nest," if one was not to give up in despair.

Nothing was easy: shoes hurt, buttons had to be found, and rules had to be learned. Most new arrivals were in shock, and some, even those chosen for the labor camp, did not survive even the first week.

WORKS CITED

Aroneanu, Eugene, comp. *Inside the Concentration Camps: Eyewitness Accounts of Life in Hitler's Death Camps.* Translated by Thomas Whissen. Westport, Conn.: Praeger, 1996.

Berenbaum, Michael. *The World Must Know: The History of the Holocaust as Told in the United States Holocaust Memorial Museum.* Boston: Little, Brown, 1993.

Dvorjetski, Mark. "Adjustment of Detainees to Camp and Ghetto Life: And Their Subsequent Readjustment to Normal Society." *Yad Vashem Studies on the European Jewish Catastrophe and Resistance.* Edited by Nathan Eck and Arieh Leon Kubovy. Jerusalem: Yad Vashem Martyrs' and Heroes' Remembrance Authority, 1963. Vol. 5, 193–220.

Hilberg, Raul. *The Destruction of the European Jews.* Chicago: Quadrangle Books, 1967.

———. *Documents of Destruction: Germany and Jewry 1933–1945.* Chicago: Quadrangle Books, 1971.

Levi, Primo. *Survival in Auschwitz: The Nazi Assault on Humanity.* Translated by Stuart Woolf. New York: Collier-Macmillan, 1971.

17

AUSCHWITZ

The Largest Death Center the World [Has] Ever Seen.
—Heinrich Himmler to Rudolf Hoess,
Auschwitz Commandant

Before describing daily life in the concentration camps, it is necessary to take
a broader look at the entire Nazi camp system. In all, there were more than
nine thousand concentration camps: transit camps, prisoner-of-war camps,
slave-labor camps, camps for "work-education," camps for political prisoners, camps for police detention, camps for children whose parents were
inmates of labor camps, camps for medical experimentation, and camps for
killing. Six of these camps were primarily killing centers: Chelmno, Sobibor, Belzec, Treblinka, Majdanek, and Auschwitz. Auschwitz was actually
three camps: Auschwitz I, for political prisoners, such as resistance fighters;
Buna, for slave laborers; and Birkenau, which housed the gas chambers,
crematoria, barracks for the waiting victims, and medical laboratories.

WHO WERE THE INMATES?

Jews were not the only victims who suffered in camps. In fact, most of the
inmates were not Jews, because Jews were usually sent to their death upon
arrival (approximately 3 million Jews were sent to the death camps) (Hilberg 1967, 555). Before the war there were three types of prisoners: political
prisoners, asocials (criminals and sex offenders), and Jews. As soon as the
war began, millions, in all sorts of categories, flooded the camps.

Inmates came from every country under the Nazi yoke: French resistance fighters, American prisoners of war (POWs), Polish slave laborers, Russian partisans, Italian Jews, and the Catholic priests who tried to save them. The number of prisoners in the political and labor camps grew from 21,400 in September 1939, to 160,000 in April 1943, to 524,286 by August 1, 1944 (1967, 556).

Gypsies were housed in Auschwitz (20,000), and thousands more were imprisoned in Bergen-Belsen, Buchenwald, Dachau, Mauthausen, and Ravensbruck. Five thousand were sent first to Lodz and then to Chelmno to be gassed with carbon monoxide in mobile vans. Birkenau contained a special Gypsy camp for families whose children were used for medical experiments by the infamous Dr. Joseph Mengele. On July 31, 1944, all of these children were killed (Berenbaum 1993, 123–30).

Ordinary Polish citizens were not held in much greater regard than the Gypsies and the Jews. Poles were also rounded up and sent to labor camps and concentration camps, where they were treated with brutality. In fact, proposals were made to limit marriages and births among the Polish people, and requests were made to eliminate Poles who were too ill to work.

Some were also assigned another category: ugly people. On November 16, 1944, after the transfer of asocials, a meeting was held by members of the German judiciary to discuss the "gallery of outwardly asocial prisoners," who "look like miscarriages of hell" (Hilberg 1967, 643). It was proposed

A group of Gypsy prisoners awaiting instructions from Nazi captors, sit in an open area near the fence in the Belzec concentration camp. Archives of Mechanical Documentation, courtesy of USHMM Photo Archive.

that they be photographed before being killed—as a picture was the only evidence needed to explain why they had been executed (1967, 643).

Soviet POWs made up another large proportion of the camp population. In all, 3.3 million Soviet soldiers died of starvation, exposure, brutality, or execution, most during their first year of imprisonment (Berenbaum 1993, 127).

Communists, unionists, Social Democrats—in short, active members of groups that were regarded by the Nazis as a threat—were also sent to concentration camps. Even Jehovah's Witnesses who refused to stop their proselytizing, or would not recognize Nazi authority, were rounded up and sent to the camps. Although they were not deliberately exterminated, one-third of these Jehovah's Witnesses died in the camps. In addition, German homosexuals, seen as a threat to the master race, were sent to the camps (1993, 130).

WHO WAS IN CHARGE?

The camps were run by a complex bureaucracy typical of German organization. Each camp had a commandant who was responsible for overall operations. Under him were a variety of administrators: first, the *Schutzhaftlagerfuhrer,* who was responsible for inmate control; next, the administration chief, who was in charge of financial matters; below him, an array of deputies, engineers, doctors, and others; and finally, several hundred guards. At Auschwitz the guards were German SS (*Schutzstaffel*) troopers not considered good enough soldiers to be assigned to the battlefield. At Treblinka, Belzec, and Sobibor, the guards were Ukrainians (Hilberg 1967, 576).

THE MOST NOTORIOUS CAMP

A look at Auschwitz, the largest, most complex, and most infamous of the concentration camps, will provide a fairly complete picture of what life was like for the inmates of all three of the main types of camps: concentration camps, labor camps, and death camps or killing centers. As noted, Auschwitz was really three camps, each of which housed different categories of prisoners and each of which subjected the inmates to different types of treatment.

The Commander

Rudolf Hoess, the commandant of Auschwitz, had been raised in a strict Catholic home. After he graduated from high school, at the age of fifteen, he volunteered to serve in World War I. Wounded three times, he also contracted malaria. He was decorated for his war activities. After the war, in 1921, Hoess was found guilty of murdering a French schoolteacher who had turned in a German comrade, during the period when France occupied the Ruhr. Hoess served five years in jail. In 1933 he joined the SS, and, prior to assuming command at Auschwitz, he worked in another concentration camp (Hilberg 1967, 576).

The Physical Plant

Built on approximately eighteen square miles of land that had been appropriated from Poland, the camp was "owned" by the Reich SS (Hilberg 1967, 565). In all, Auschwitz comprised three large camps and forty-five satellite camps in Upper Silesia and southwestern Poland. It was guarded by 6,000 men in twelve companies of SS Death's Head Units. Auschwitz I, a concentration camp for political prisoners and non-Jews, contained two- and three-story brick buildings, some of which were barracks and others of which housed laboratories for some of the medical experiments conducted under the supervision of Mengele (Berenbaum 1993, 130–35).

Buna: The Labor Camp

Auschwitz III, also known as Buna or Monowitz, was the labor camp. Here German companies, such as I. G. Farben, were able to solve the labor shortage created when Jews were expelled from their homes in the ghettos and were no longer available to work in factories. Well-known German companies, using monies from ordinary investments, simply relocated to Buna and other camps throughout the Reich and occupied territories. Decisions to run the factories right in the middle of the concentration camps were made by ordinary corporate executives eager to make a profit. These companies, some of which are familiar even today, included Daimler-Benz, Flick, Krupp, Messerschmitt, Siemens, Bayer, and BMW. Some 40,000 foreign workers, speaking nearly twenty different languages, were used as slaves for I. G. Farben at Auschwitz.

Each nationality had a different satellite camp: Ukrainian women, English POWs, French volunteers, and so on. These workers were intended to produce synthetic rubber for the war effort, but it took them four years just to build the plant, and ultimately, because of the poor treatment of the workers, and probably sabotage efforts as well, not a single pound of rubber was ever produced (Berenbaum 1993, 108; Levi 1971, 65).

The workers lived in one of sixty wooden barracks, called blocks. Each, originally built to house forty-eight horses, held from 250 to 800 people who slept on bunks, fitted "like cells of a beehive" (Levi 1971, 28). Each bunk held two men or women. With no pillows and only one blanket for two inmates, they slept on wooden planks, many layers high. In fact, they were so overloaded that they sometimes collapsed, crushing those below (1971, 28).

The bunks were divided by three corridors through which two people could barely pass. Only half the inmates could stand, while the others were forced to remain in bed, where even sitting up was impossible. Visiting someone else's section of the barrack, or another block, was out of the question, for there was no room. Some blocks had no lavatory or washbowl, only a bucket for washing and, at night, another for a latrine. Wooden latrines were shared by as many as eight blocks (Hilberg 1967, 581; Berenbaum 1993, 134).

At one end of Buna were eight blocks that served as an infirmary and clinic. One block was for German political prisoners and criminals; another was for the *Kapos* (the criminals who were put in charge of groups of workers). Another block served as the distribution center, and another was the quartermaster's office. Block 29 was a brothel that housed young Polish girls forced to serve as prostitutes for the SS (Levi 1971, 27).

Birkenau: The Death Camp

Auschwitz II, also called Birkenau, was the death camp or killing center, or the Charitable Foundation for Institutional Care (Arendt 1964, 109). The nine subunits that constituted Birkenau were surrounded by two barbed-wire fences, the inner one of which was electrified; chains of guard posts; and guard dogs two-thirds of the way out from the fences (Berenbaum 1993, 138).

There were four gas chambers at Birkenau, each capable of killing 6,000 people per day. These were built in special combination units, which contained an underground dressing room, the gas chamber itself, and a crematorium in which to dispose of the bodies—immediately and efficiently (1993, 138).

View of Auschwitz's double, electrified barbed-wire fence and barracks. Photograph taken immediately after the death camp was liberated in January 1945. Philip Vock, courtesy of USHMM Photo Archives.

The history of these buildings is worth noting because it reveals the cold, businesslike approach to the creation and the operation of the industry of murder. The earliest buildings were remolded peasants' houses, but as the Germans began to put into operation Hitler's Final Solution, more resources were devoted to the killing centers. Private companies supplied the doors, windows, gas, and ovens. Carbon monoxide, rejected as an inefficient means of killing, was replaced with hydrogen cyanide—the commercial name for which was Zyklon B. Firms specializing in large-scale fumigation of buildings, barracks, and ships, ridding them of rodents and insects, were the primary suppliers of Zyklon B (Hilberg 1967, 565).

Each one of Birkenau's gas chambers could hold 2,000 people at a time (1967, 566). Two of the combination units had elevators that were used to bring the corpses from the gas chamber to the ovens. Inside each crematorium were five furnaces, each capable of incinerating from forty-five to seventy-five bodies at once (Berenbaum 1993, 139).

A PROFIT-MAKING ENTERPRISE

Not only was supplying the raw materials for this death industry a profit-making enterprise, there were other ways to make money as well. Some earned contracts to receive goods, taken from the bodies of the dead, such as gold teeth or women's hair. Dried by the heat of the crematoria, hair was made into felt and then thread, and, eventually, socks for submarine crews, stockings for railroad workers, cords for ships, cloth, ropes, the ignition mechanisms of bombs, and stuffing for mattresses. One kilo of hair went for $1.09 (Berenbaum 1993, 149; Hilberg 1967, 609–10).

A PROFIT-MAKING ENTERPRISE

One ambitious university student wrote his dissertation on "The Possibilities of Recycling Gold from the Mouths of the Dead." His ideas were later implemented by the Reichsbank, which received most of this gold.

Source: Michael Berenbaum, *The World Must Know: The History of the Holocaust as Told in the United States Holocaust Memorial Museum.* (Boston: Little, Brown, 1993).

Among the designers and commanders of the six killing centers there was fierce competition as to who ran the most efficient operation. Rudolf Hoess even bragged about his important contribution: substituting Zyklon B for carbon monoxide (Hilberg 1967, 572).

THE KILLING PROCESS

The invention of killing centers, and of this machinery of death, marked a turning point in the history of man's inhumanity to man. Throughout

Bales of the hair of female prisoners found in the warehouses of Auschwitz during the liberation, January 1945. National Archives, courtesy of USHMM Photo Archives.

history, innocent people have been subjected to all manner of evil treatment, including genocide. During the Holocaust, those in the ghettos were starved to death or allowed to die of curable diseases, unnecessary exposure to the elements, or exhaustion. Others were subjected to random shootings, fatal beatings, and hanging. Outside the ghettos, the *Einsatzgruppen* were let loose upon unsuspecting victims, filling hastily dug mass graves with the populations of whole villages and towns.

Nevertheless, until the creation of the death camps, though thousands died, the methods used to kill them were generally haphazard, time consuming, and inefficient, using little or no advanced technology. The newly constructed killing centers were streamlined, high-tech operations capable of killing and disposing of thousands upon thousands of people in a day.

The procedure for carrying out this mission was very simple. First, upon arrival at the camp, those selected for death were told that they were going to the bath houses to be bathed and deloused. In an underground dressing room, approximately 107 feet by 25 feet by 9 feet, people were instructed to undress and leave their clothing neatly piled, and to remember where their clothes were placed so they could be retrieved after the showers.

Second, signs stating "To the baths and disinfecting rooms," "Cleanliness brings freedom!," and "One louse can kill you" were posted on the walls, contributing to the illusion that all was well. (These signs were also posted in labor camps.)

Third, the women and children, then the men, were ushered into the gas chambers that were disguised as showers. The SS guards remained in the chamber until the last minute to perpetuate the masquerade.

Fourth, as soon as the guards exited, the door was closed and screwed tightly shut, and the gas was discharged through ceiling vents. One-third of the people, those nearest the vents, died instantly. The rest screamed, staggered, and struggled for air. In twenty minutes all were dead.

Finally, the *Sonderkommando,* prisoners who were assigned to the task but who would soon be executed themselves, cleaned out the bodies, extracted any gold teeth (as much as 26.4 pounds per month), shaved off women's hair, and placed the corpses on elevators, ten to fifteen at a time, or carried them to the ovens, one floor up (Berenbaum 1993, 139, 149, 150).

The record for deaths per day probably belongs to Birkenau, which, toward the end of the war, was killing approximately 12,000 people a day.

MEDICAL EXPERIMENTS

Birkenau also housed the bulk of the so-called medical laboratories. Here the Nazis conducted thousands of experiments, mostly by people with little or no medical training, under the supervision of German doctors. Experiments were conducted for two different purposes. Some were more or less in the category of regular scientific experiments made to test a hypothesis, try a new serum, or solve a problem, particularly for the military.

For example, inmates were injected with diseases, such as tuberculosis, to test the effects of drug treatments. In other experiments, inmates were given typhus injections to preserve the bacteria for use in later experiments, since typhus cannot live in an artificial culture. In order to find ways to help soldiers, half frozen on the battlefield, prisoners were submerged in ice water for hours. To learn how to treat injured soldiers, perfectly healthy people were subjected to "experiments" in which surgery was performed on flesh, muscles, and bones. All types of substances (poisons, gasoline, air, petroleum, chemicals) were injected into healthy people just to see what effects they had (Aroneanu 1996, 85, 86, 88, 94).

What made these experiments especially horrifying was that no precautions were taken to protect the victim. No anesthetics or antiseptic techniques were used. All of these experiments were excruciatingly painful (1996, 91).

Some people were so hungry they volunteered for experiments in exchange for food, but the rest were forced to participate, and even if they survived the "treatment" they were gassed when the experiment ended.

The second purpose for experimenting on inmates was even more sinister, and its effects, had Germany won the war, could have been far more long range and destructive. The intention was no less than the complete subjugation of Europe.

These experiments involved the sterilization of both men and women deemed "unworthy" by the Nazi government. Groups targeted, in addition to Jewish people, were Poles, Gypsies, priests, and other so-called enemies. The plan was to sterilize people as quickly and as efficiently as possible, with the victim being unaware of what was happening. Some experiments focused on the introduction of a variety of chemicals into the bodies of unsuspecting women. The Bayer Company bought 150 Jewish women and forced them to participate in experiments with hormones. Men were exposed to high doses of X-rays while standing at a counter filling out forms. Eventually, these experiments proved to be impractical and much less reliable than surgery (Hilberg 1967, 604–6).

German universities took part in the experiments by collecting data, conducting autopsies, and making slides from amputated limbs and organs of healthy people who had been subjected to some type of experiment. Photographers took pictures of people in various stages of suffering, as well as of the dead, for record-keeping purposes. The Nazis, thinking they were doing a service to mankind, kept careful records of all these procedures. Doctors also worked on ways in which to increase the German population, including Mengele's work on twins. Mengele firmly believed that he would some day receive honors from the scientific community for his work (Berenbaum 1993, 134; Aroneanu 1996, 90).

WORKS CITED

Arendt, Hannah. *Eichmann in Jerusalem: A Report on the Banality of Evil.* New York: Viking, 1964.

Aroneanu, Eugene, comp. *Inside the Concentration Camps: Eyewitness Accounts of Life in Hitler's Death Camps.* Translated by Thomas Whissen. Westport, Conn.: Praeger, 1996.

Berenbaum, Michael. *The World Must Know: The History of the Holocaust as Told in the United States Holocaust Memorial Museum.* Boston: Little, Brown, 1993.

Hilberg, Raul. The *Destruction of the European Jews. Chicago:* Quadrangle Books, 1967.

Levi, Primo. *Survival in Auschwitz: The Nazi Assault on Humanity.* Translated by Stuart Woolf. New York: Collier-Macmillan, 1971.

18

LIFE IN THE LUNATIC WORLD OF THE CONCENTRATION CAMPS

Not all Nazi concentration camps were run the same way, and not all prisoners suffered the same treatment, but for all, daily life was a nightmare. In his memoir, Primo Levi described the camp's strange conditions.

Thousands of individuals, differing in age, condition, origin, language, culture and customs are enclosed within barbed wire: there they live a regular, controlled life which is identical for all and inadequate to all needs, and which is much more rigorous than any experimenter could have set up to establish what is essential and what adventitious to the conduct of the human animal in the struggle for life. (1971, 79).

This is how the young chemist described the "gigantic biological and social experiment" called Auschwitz. What was this experiment like?

THE DAILY SCHEDULE

Depending upon the time of year, inmates were awakened by a loud reveille any time from 3:30 A.M. to 8 A.M. Winter work hours were generally from 8 A.M. until noon and from 12:30 P.M. until 4 P.M. Summer hours were from 6:30 A.M. until 12 and from 1 P.M. until 6 P.M. Inmates worked only during daylight, not even in fog, so that if they broke the rules they could easily be detected. Every other Sunday, inmates worked on the upkeep of the camp, rather than at their assigned jobs. Rest days were rare. If they survived, people worked for years without a break.

As soon as reveille had been sounded the lights were turned on and frantic activity began. Prisoners had to make their beds, dress, rush outside to the latrines and washrooms, wash and go to the bathroom, all in five minutes. Some ran out of the barracks half dressed and others urinated on the way to the washroom to save time. If they were late, they did not get any breakfast (Levi 1971, 33).

Breakfast consisted of a gray slab of bread, made of flour and sawdust; it was "gigantic in your neighbor's hand, and in your own so small as to make you cry" (1971, 34). If one were served quickly enough there might be time to return to the latrine or the washroom.

Most mornings, before being ordered to work, the prisoners were forced to undergo one of the most dreaded procedures of camp life, the "roll call." Sometimes this took place after they were dressed; at other times, they stood naked. No matter how ill or tired they were, no matter how bad the weather was, they had to stand at attention, sometimes for hours. Inmates often had to prop others up so they would not fall and have to suffer beatings from the guards. Recalled one survivor: "At the first roll call a friend of mine was sick. Naively, I went up to our *Blockova* [block] and said: 'Excuse me for bothering you, but a friend of mine is very sick, can she be excused from roll call?' She answered: 'Here even the dying come to roll call'" (quoted in Aroneanu 1996, 41). Another recalled, "The Kapo [commander] of our unit killed a friend of mine because he was not standing up straight" (1996, 41). Roll calls were also held when inmates returned from work, and sometimes even in the middle of the night. Some roll calls could last an entire day.

Following morning roll call, the prisoners were marched to work, in *Kommandos* or work parties of from 15 to 150, headed by a *Kapo*, a criminal, or other German inmate. Their marching was accompanied by loud, incessant band music. Work could be close by or miles away. In winter, people worked for hours in the snow, with no boots, just their wooden shoes, which stuck to the snow and made walking awkward. Even when it was ten or twenty degrees below zero, the prisoners worked outside, sometimes with iron products that stuck to their hands. Fires were built for *Kapos* only. At the end of the day they were marched back to the barracks (49).

ALL TYPES OF WORK

The list of jobs filled by the camp inmates was as varied as that in the outside world. Contracts between the government and private German firms provided dozens of kinds of factory jobs. The workers did the labor and the companies paid their wages, about $1.50 a day, to the German authorities. In return for their work, the inmates earned only 10 cents worth of goods.

Jobs included finishing and assembling weapons, manufacturing aircraft and artillery, polishing lenses for military use, making steel nets for snaring submarines, doing masonry work, building railway tracks and unloading cargo, building underground factories for the construction of the V-1 rocket, making roads leading into the forest, carrying heavy stones (at times for no purpose at all), digging ditches, unloading boats and trucks, and building barracks and other buildings, including making doors and windows for the gas chambers (Aroneanu 1996, 49; Hilberg 1967, 590).

Inmates also served as electricians, smiths, brick layers, welders, mechanics, concrete layers, chemists, cooks, bakers, office workers, and prostitutes. Women were not spared hard labor; they worked as pipe layers, roofers, and wood choppers. They laid rails, built roads, pushed small trucks, unloaded sacks of concrete, felled trees, shoveled coal, drained swamps, wove cloth, sewed uniforms, and worked in offices (Aroneanu 1996, 57; Levi 1971, 92).

Sometimes the inmates were supervised by civilian foremen in factories that also employed people from the surrounding towns. Other jobs were supervised by the *Kapos* (Levi 1971, 31).

There was also lots of senseless work, undertaken solely to inflict suffering. *Kapos* and guards played games with peoples' lives. Some prisoners were forced to work in underground stone quarries for a year without seeing daylight. A group of Greek scholars, forced to lug heavy stones up a stairway of a hundred steps at top speed, were worked to death in

Buchenwald inmates standing during a roll call. Each wears a striped hat and uniform bearing colored, triangular badges and identification numbers. Robert A. Schmuhl, courtesy of USHMM Photo Archives.

five weeks. In fact, all work assignments had to be accomplished at high speed, and those who could not keep up died of exhaustion or were shot. Some became so desperate for rest that they committed suicide by provoking a guard to shoot them (Hilberg 1967, 595). The life expectancy of a Jewish inmate in Buna was three to four months; in the mines outside of Auschwitz, it was one month (1967, 596).

In addition to their daytime work, inmates were assigned regular camp duties such as taking food to the SS (*Schutzstaffel*), unloading food for the prisoners, cleaning and mending clothing, emptying night pails, and cleaning barracks. Despite the backbreaking work, no one was ever allowed to sit down or to rest (Aroneanu 1996, 53).

There was also one other set of tasks, which were performed by *Kommandos*—those related directly to the killing operations. The *Transportkommandos* cleaned up the freight cars after they were unloaded; the *Kommandos* sorted through the valuables taken from the victims; and the *Sonderkommandos* worked in the crematoria (Hilberg 1967, 588).

A TYPICAL DAY

The usual day consisted of approximately seventeen hours of work and from two to five hours of sleep. The remaining time was spent complying with arbitrary orders that subjected people to brutal punishments for doing nothing wrong. According to one survivor, a normal, healthy person might be able to last six months at most. "I saw how an American of Italian ancestry, called C. L., . . . was abused and killed. He had frostbitten feet and was forced to work . . . they bound his feet with paper and sent him back to work in the snow. He held out for 12 days before he died" (quoted in Aroneanu 1996, 54).

CLOTH AND CLOTHING

All the clothing that the inmates brought with them was confiscated, and anything valuable eventually made its way into the hands of an officer or his wife and children. Prisoners were issued thin, cotton, striped pajamas, and jackets in winter. Toward the end of the war, even these were scarce and people were given rags. They were not allowed even so much as a handkerchief, toilet paper, or a tissue. Even when they found something themselves, a sheaf of paper or an empty cement bag, if they were caught using it to bind their feet, or to place under their shirts to keep warm, they risked execution (Gelb 1997).

Needless to say, freezing to death was a strong possibility, and, in order to survive, people had to be creative and avoid getting caught. Cloth of any kind was a rare and valuable commodity. Even a small piece could have many uses as a patch, handkerchief, sanitary napkin, socks—or as a valuable item to trade for other necessary items. The only cloth available was on one's own back. Cutting even a small patch was dangerous and could be punished by severe beatings or death. Inmates had to find ways to ensure their "theft" would go undetected. One way was to cut a patch of shirttail or a piece of sleeve and hope that no one noticed. If this was done when needle and thread were available the damage could be hidden. One could also try to make a ragged shirt look like it was simply the victim of ordinary wear and tear, as long as it still had arm and head holes.

Another trick was to wait until "exchange" day, which happened infrequently and with little warning. On this day people were required to turn in their clothes to a tailor's workshop where they would be mended and disinfected, though not washed, and redistributed. This was a godsend because it meant one could cut a patch and quickly turn in the evidence and not even have to wear a shirt with a hole in it. Possession of more than one shirt was forbidden, but it could be very profitable (Levi 1971, 69).

FOOD RATIONS

It was never possible to survive on the amount of food that a prisoner was allotted. Breakfast amounted to a chunk of bread, made from flour and sawdust, and some hot, foul liquid that was called coffee. At midday there was a watery soup, made from turnips, potato peelings, nettles, cabbage, or pieces of wood. Even this food might be spoiled. For dinner, inmates were given another chunk of bread with margarine and "smelly" marmalade or putrid sausage. Generally one had to wait in line, sometimes for hours, to get one's food ration, which sometimes never came. Some days people received only one meal. Roll call was sometimes taken after food was distributed but before one was allowed to eat. Even children were expected to keep from eating the food already in their hands. It was not even possible to obtain a drink of water as none was served and the water used for washing was polluted (Hilberg 1967, 582; Aroneanu 1996, 14–17).

Any packages sent from home were confiscated upon arrival or stolen by the guards. *Kapos* also stole people's food rations. One survivor knew of an "18-year-old Kapo who killed more than 400 Jews for their food rations" (Aroneanu 1996, 38).

One result of the starvation rations was a strange process of trading of food among inmates throughout their meals. Those who were desperately hungry would eat the potato pieces in their soup bowls and trade the remainder of the soup for bread rations that others had saved from an earlier meal. They in turn would eat some of the bread and trade the rest for someone else's soup, until the food was gone or they got caught. Some were so hungry they were willing to exchange their only shirt for food, despite a potential beating if detected (Levi 1971, 71).

The effects of the lack of hygiene and nutrition, as in the ghetto, were much more than even the "living hunger" Levi refers to in his memoir.

Illness was rampant; the most common were dysentery, typhus, skin diseases, swollen bellies, and infected sores. People were emaciated, with yellow or gray skin. Feverish nightmares, often about food being taken from them, were ever present. Thousands died.

"THE MARKET" SYSTEM

In order to cheat death, inmates had to find more food. In addition, other items, essential to survival, somehow had to be procured. For example, having a spoon was required, but none were issued. "Polishing" one's shoes (with grease) was mandatory, but no polish was furnished (Levi 1971, 75).

Consequently, a system of bartering was created. Since all exchanges among prisoners, and between prisoners and civilians with whom they came in contact in the factories, were strictly forbidden, every transaction had to be completed in secret. In Auschwitz, trading took place in the corner of the camp farthest from the SS barracks, in the open during the summer, and in the washrooms in winter, usually right after everyone returned from work (1971, 71).

Their most desperate need was for food, and yet the only commodity most people possessed was the bread rations. As a result, bread became the medium of exchange. Not only could it be traded for other things, it could also be used as a form of credit card. One could "buy" something, such as a spoon, on the promise that when bread was handed out at breakfast it was turned over to the creditor. One could even buy more expensive items in return for several days' bread rations or sell high-priced items for the promise of bread in the future.

Some prisoners were luckier than others and had more to sell. According to Levi, the Greeks, the most cohesive group of inmates, were able to pool their resources and gain more goods. They frequently found means to obtain thicker soup and opportunities to steal from the kitchens. One could buy two pints of soup for one-half of a bread ration; more bread was needed if one wanted turnips, potatoes, or carrots (72).

Tobacco was another valuable item because it was often desired by civilians outside the camps who themselves had access to more food. A prisoner who worked in a factory employing outsiders could trade bread for tobacco within the camp and then exchange the tobacco for more bread when at work. He would then eat the surplus and start all over again, trading what he had left. A person with no outside contacts might even sell his shirt, to someone who worked outside, in exchange for food. The shirt could buy up to ten bread rations outside the camp. Sneaking out of camp wearing two shirts was very dangerous, however, and wearing no shirt at all earned one a beating (72).

People sold their own gold fillings or those from a new arrival desperate for food and not knowing the worth of the gold. A single filling could purchase from ten to twenty bread rations from a civilian, doled out at two per day (74).

The most bread one could get within the camp was four rations because credit could not extend beyond that and there was no safe place to store that much food. But the penalty for trading with civilians was always severe. It was acceptable to smuggle items into the camp, but since everything inside the camp was considered the property of the SS, taking anything out was a very serious offense. The inmate was usually hanged, often in public, as a warning to others. A lesser punishment was assignment to the coal mines, which eventually ended in death from exhaustion. Civilians caught trading with prisoners were also punished, though less severely. They were sent to camps, called the *Erziehunglager* (education camp), for up to eight months. Although the working conditions were the same for them as for the others, they were not tattooed, nor were their heads shaved; their possessions were saved for them until they were released, and there were no "selections" (74–75).

The list of articles stolen for use or for trading is astonishing. From their places of work both within and outside of the camp, inmates took light bulbs, brooms, paint, wire, grease for shoes, shaving soap, files, pliers, sacks, nails, petrol for lighters, methyl alcohol for drinking, pieces of tin for making spoons, sulpha drugs (from the infirmary), and even shoes and clothing from the dead (also in the infirmary) (77).

Spoons, manufactured within the camp, were another prized item. A regular spoon was worth one-half a bread ration, but a knife-spoon combination brought three-quarters of a ration. Persons released from the infirmary were not allowed to take their spoons with them and had to start all over again trying to find someone to make them a spoon. Dozens of spoons, abandoned in the infirmary by people who were supposedly cured or taken to the gas chamber, were thus ready for stealing. In fact, the infirmary was the source of many valuables: rubber tubing, colored pencils (for keeping the complicated records required by the Nazis), thermometers, glass instruments, and chemicals. Most of these items were initially stolen from Buna stores used only by civilians. Levi tells of Alberto, who signed out a large file from the tool store, exchanged it with a civilian for two small files, returned one to the tool store, and kept the other for further trading (133).

THE INFIRMARY

Even in a concentration camp, one would hope that treatment in the infirmary would be better than treatment elsewhere, but this was not the case. In fact, only when people reached a state of absolute desperation were they willing to go to the infirmary. At Auschwitz, *krankenbau*, or *Ka-Be*, as the infirmary was called, consisted of eight huts and two clinics, one for medical patients and one for surgical patients. It did not take long for prisoners to realize that few people emerged from the infirmary alive.

Primo Levi was one of the very few to emerge from the infirmary. He had sliced his foot on a large object. Since he had received no treatment, it had become swollen and bloody and he was no longer able to work. He went to *Ka-Be*. The procedures for admittance were torturous and time consuming, as long as ten hours just to get into the building. First, he had to remove his shoes and carry all his possessions with him: bowl, hat, gloves, and shoes. If these were removed too soon, one could freeze to death, but if one arrived at the entrance still in shoes it was necessary to go again to the end of the line.

Once inside there was another long line for the examination rooms. Waiting in this line could take as long as six hours. To enter these rooms one had to be completely naked, so people stripped along the way, trying to get the timing right. In the examination room, the patient's temperature was taken. Depending upon how sick a person was, he or she could be sent back to the barracks, to a *Ka-Be*, or to die.

Those who were admitted waited for up to six more hours for their examination, during which time they were still standing, and still naked. Eventually they were issued a gown and sandals and sent to Block 23, where they were asked all manner of questions, such as what their former job was, how many people were in their families, and what previous illnesses they had had (Levi 1971, 34–40).

Finally, they were assigned a bunk. Bunks were stacked in three levels of three rows, with two narrow corridors. In all, Levi counted 150 bunks, each two feet wide, holding 250 patients. Those on top were squashed against the ceiling; no one could sit up (1971, 40–47).

There were some benefits to life in the infirmary. It was not cold, there were few beatings, and the rules were less severe. Patients could eat in peace on their beds and go back to sleep after 4 A.M. reveille.

There were also daily selections, during which the SS came through the huts and decided who was fit to live and who would go to the gas chambers. Without saying anything, they simply placed an *x* by the patient's name. In his memoir. Primo Levi offers this ironic observation: "In this discreet and composed manner, without display or anger, massacre moves through the huts of Ka-Be every day, touching here and there" (47).

TREATMENT OF THE ILL

Those who remained in the infirmary were still not treated with kindness or care. Patients were frequently beaten and thrown out of bed. There were few medical supplies; the beds and blankets were filthy; and there were no disinfectants, bandages, towels, clean water, or adequate food supplies. Injured patients slept with those who had highly contagious diseases; diseased patients slept with the dead. Despite these conditions, the Nazis refused offers of help from the International Red Cross.

Source: Eugene Aroneanu, comp. *Inside the Concentration Camps: Eyewitness Accounts of Life in Hitler's Death Camps.* Translated by Thomas Whissen (Westport, CT: Praeger, 1996).

The death rate was about sixty percent per month. It would appear that this was deliberate. Inoculations were given to kill patients rather than cure them. Injecting phenol into the heart (an antiseptic that, when used in more than very tiny doses, causes burning) was the primary method of killing people before the gas chambers were built. One survivor recalled that "countless patients were brought to the infirmary where they were given an inoculation; the next day they would all be dead" (1996, 75).

Pregnant women were given abortions, no matter how close they were to giving birth. Even after the abortions, most were gassed, along with their children. Those allowed to live were sterilized, as were thousands of young men. None of these procedures were carried out with anesthesia (81).

Living in the infirmary had its psychological effects as well. With time to think about what had been done to them (memories of loved ones dying before their eyes while they were helpless to intervene, worries about what was happening to family members they had last seen alive, and thoughts of the pain and humiliation they had been subjected to), patients became homesick and depressed. Even those outside of the infirmary succumbed to despair when faced with the physical and emotional tortures they had undergone and the constant fear of the future (Dvorjetski 1963, 202).

They not only felt horrible, they understood how repulsive they looked to others—a calculated move on the part of the Germans to make them feel and appear less than human. They were either bald or had a "moldy" head and sickly yellow or gray skin. They had cuts and bruises from constant beatings, and sores and itching from insect bites, wooden shoes, and injuries at work. Their clothing was filthy, even when they tried to wash it, and they were covered with mud, grease, and blood. Diarrhea was a constant affliction, and everyone smelled awful (Levi 1971, 129).

While lying in *Ka-Be*, Levi realized that "our personality is fragile" (1971, 49). He and others had terrible nightmares. The most common was that they were out of the camp and back home, telling their story of life in the camp, but no one would listen. To Levi, this was even more frightening than his dreams of food that he was prevented from eating (54).

PUNISHMENTS

Added to all of this suffering were the continual punishments. Ironically, the German authorities did not approve of the arbitrary torture of prisoners by guards. Despite the surrealistic nature of camp life, the Nazi commanders were determined to run an operation that preserved the system they created. Therefore, orderly, systematic killing, by the book, was encouraged, but "excesses" on the part of individuals acting on their own, such as sexually abusing inmates, were not. This does not mean that such things did not often happen. Some sadistic behavior was tolerated— guards were expected to relieve boredom somehow—but they were not to get out of control. Corruption among administrators was actually considered a more serious threat to the orderly functioning of the camp (Hilberg 1967, 577).

When delivered as punishment for supposed "crimes," brutality was rewarded. Inmates were given orders they could not obey, such as to run to the washrooms when they did not know where they were located; or to carry bricks until they could no longer stand; or to get in and out of bed continually, all night long; or to stand for hours for roll call, naked and barefoot even in the snow. When these orders were not followed, beatings with clubs, wires, and rifle butts ensued. For meting out these punishments, guards were given brandy and extra food rations. Cigarettes were the reward for "legal" executions (1967, 577).

One guard was known for deliberately killing newly arrived Jewish men and young Jewish girls, whom he first raped. Pretty young girls were usually raped by the SS guards before being sent to the gas chamber. People were thrown into water (swimming pools, ice water tanks) and forced to remain there for hours, even until death (Aroneanu 1996, 30, 34).

Collective punishments, public executions or torture, were commonly used to frighten prisoners into obedience. Lashings with a cane or whip, two or three days of starvation, being locked in blacked-out barracks or in a dungeon where one could neither stand up nor lie down, hanging by one's wrists while they were tied behind the back; being stabbed with hot pins or handcuffed with pinchers on the cuffs—all these were considered legal punishments (1996, 42–45).

Inmates were often executed for ridiculous infractions of the rules. If one looked out the window, one could be killed; if one read a piece of newspaper that was meant to be used for toilet paper, one could be killed; if one stole bread or wire for shoelaces, one could be hanged, whipped to death, strangled, or drained of blood (42–45).

Levi reported witnessing seventy-three public hangings in one year— for theft, sabotage, escape attempts, and one for blowing up a crematorium at Birkenau (Levi 1971, 134).

One survivor, a priest, recalled that ministering to the inmates was also a capital crime. Religious items such as rosaries, holy pictures, and medallions were confiscated. Pages from breviaries, missals, and other holy books were used as toilet paper. The practice of any religion was punishable by death (1971, 31).

THE RETREAT AND THE SELECTION CAMP

In the March 17, 2008, edition of the *New Yorker*, Alec Wilkinson writes "Picturing Auschwitz," about a retreat held for German officers, including Rudolf Hoess and Dr. Josef Mengele, at the Auschwitz complex. In the accompanying photo, the participants in the retreat are smiling, listening to an accordion player. In the same article, is another photo of the "selection" camp at Auschwitz, used for the new arrivals (50).

In her memoir, Eve Soumerai tells the story of her friend Jakov who had been present during a selection at Auschwitz.

My friend Jakov told me a story he witnessed in front of him at selection time, [he watched] a father begging the officer-in-charge to let him and his son stay together, whereupon the officer raised his cane and shattered the glasses of the father. "Imagine," said Yakov, "remembering your father picking bits of glass out of his bleeding eyes, the very last time you saw him."

Source: Eve Soumerai, *Unpublished Memoir,* 1996.
Note: Photos of the retreat and selection camp appear on pp. 291 and 293.

THE "SELECTIONS"

Added to all of this were the so-called selections. Everyone was subjected to periodic selections, usually every two weeks. In the death camps that were not attached to labor camps, everyone was "selected" for death upon arrival, although sometimes people were forced to wait, even for days, locked in a barracks, until the gas vans or gas chambers were ready for them. At Auschwitz, where workers were needed, the first selection determined whether one went to Birkenau to die, or to Buna to work.

In order to prevent attempts at escape, the Germans tried to keep victims from learning the truth about what was to happen to them and their families, even as they were being led to the gas chambers. One survivor recalled watching a guard tell a mother who would not let go of her child to "Trust your children to us" (Aroneanu 1996, 124).

Selections usually took place during roll calls, though sometimes special selections were conducted right in the barracks. To be chosen for life an inmate had to demonstrate that he or she was fit for work. Often this meant being able to withstand hours of waiting in line while trying to look healthy. At other times, prisoners had to run as fast as they could, past the doctors, without looking weak or frightened. Even if these conditions were met, survival was not guaranteed. If there was a quota to be filled, people were sent to the gas chambers anyway (1996, 124).

Levi described a typical selection. As each man ran out one door and crossed toward another, handing a card with his number on it to the guard,

Polish children imprisoned in Auschwitz look out from behind the barbed-wire fence, July 1944. Main Commission for the Investigation of Nazi War Crimes, courtesy of USHMM Photo Archives.

The SS man, in the fraction of a second between two successive crossings, with a glance at one's back and front, judges everyone's fate, and in turn gives the card to the man on his right or his left, and this is the life or death of each of us. In three or four minutes a but of two hundred men is "done," as is the whole camp of twelve thousand men in the course of the afternoon. (Levi 1971, 116–17)

Even young children were subjected to selections, often done according to height: those shorter than 4 feet 3.18 inches were too little to live (Hilberg 1967, 626).

BEATING THE ODDS BY LEARNING THE RULES

Those who wished to remain alive in the world of the concentration camp had to learn quickly that obeying the official rules was dangerous. Like ghetto life, concentration life was intended to result in dehumanization, pain, and death, and the regulations of the camp were meant to achieve this.

Life in a concentration camp was far worse than anything the inmates had previously experienced, even those who had survived the ghettos of Poland. There was less food, less room, harder labor, hardly ever any friends or family to offer help or comfort, stricter rules about everything imaginable, and constant punishment. Inmates were told when to sit, to stand, to lie down, to speak, to walk, to eat, to wash, to go to the bathroom, to turn on the lights, and to turn off the lights. There were regulations that governed what inmates wore, how they were to take care of their clothing, what they were to sleep in, what they were to eat with, how they were to make their bunks, and on, and on, and on.

Yet obedience was even more dangerous than disobedience. The rules did not allow one to eat enough to prevent starvation; to wear enough clothing to keep from getting frostbitten, which led to gangrene and death; or to rest enough not to die from exhaustion or diseases for which one was not given medical care.

Only adherence to the unofficial rules made it possible to survive, and only those who learned them quickly had even the slightest chance. Those who failed to learn these lessons became the *mussulmans* (zombies) doomed to selection (Dvorjetski 1963, 207).

- Always pretend to understand orders, and always answer, "*Jawohl*" (yes).
- Never ask questions.
- Learn where to stand in the soup line so as to get the most nutrients (which had sunk to the bottom of the pot).
- Diligently scrape the bottom of the bowl.
- Hold the bread over your bowl to catch the crumbs.
- Waste nothing—wire ties serve as shoelaces, rags wrap the feet, waste paper pads a jacket.
- Avoid the infirmary at all costs: people go from there to the gas chambers.
- Sleep with your head on a bundle of all your possessions: your spoon, your bowl, your clothing, your shoes (everything can be stolen, as soon as you turn your head).
- Take care where you walk, and stay at least two yards from the barbed-wire fence.
- Keep your jacket buttoned if you pad it with paper; the punishment could be death.
- Do not lose a button or you will be punished; there must be five, tie them on with wire.
- Do not get caught sleeping in a jacket or pants or with a cap on your head. (Aroneanu 1996, 18; Levi 1971, 28–30)

Taking care of one's feet was another of the unwritten rules of great importance. "Death begins with the shoes," wrote Levi. The wooden shoes caused painful sores, which, once infected, would swell and worsen, causing unbearable pain and preventing one from working, or walking fast enough to obey the guards (Levi 1971, 29; Aroneanu 1996, 21).

THE OFFICIAL RULES

Obviously, one could not get caught disregarding the real rules when the punishment was death and obedience was not life threatening. There were many senseless rituals one had to go through that one could not afford to ignore. Inmates had to make their "beds" perfectly flat and smooth. Wooden shoes had to be smeared with grease; clothing was to be free of mud stains, an impossible demand in rainy weather. Lice removal and foot washing were demanded nightly, although blankets and barracks were themselves infested with lice, bedbugs, and fleas. People, constantly itching and scratching, developed pimples and painful skin rashes and diseases (Aroneanu 1996, 18; Levi 1971, 28–30).

Only certain latrines were to be used, and only at very short intervals during the day. Some camps had only buckets for latrines—12 buckets for every 700 people. Others had boards with holes in them, constructed above a ditch, or in fields out in the open (Aroneanu 1996, 18).

Cleanliness was both demanded and impossible. Showers and washrooms were to be used only when given permission. The water was filthy, as were the brick floors. Prisoners were expected to bring all their possessions with them to the washroom, including their bowls, and hold them between their knees while washing. Otherwise, they were stolen or simply taken away by the guards. In some camps there was only one spigot for 10,000 women, and washrooms built for 60 men were used by 1,400. Only dirty rags were available for feminine hygiene (1996, 18–19).

Even if one adapted to camp life quickly, no easy task, and learned to obey the unofficial rules and avoid the fatal official ones, death was still the most likely outcome. Most survivors were those who were somehow useful to the Reich: doctors, tailors, shoemakers, musicians, cooks, young attractive homosexuals, friends or countrymen of some camp authority, or "organizers" with superhuman energy. They were the ones who could manage to eat whatever they found no matter how inedible, to wash their clothing when this seemed impossible, to stay alert and avoid danger, to be incredibly self-disciplined and save rations for trading, to gain an extra minute's rest and not get caught—in short, to accomplish the impossible. Most survivors were non-Jews, even among those not initially selected for the gas chambers. They held the "good" jobs—cooks, nurses, *Kapos*, night guards—and were allowed extra privileges from the start.

WORKS CITED

Aroneanu, Eugene, comp. *Inside the Concentration Camps: Eyewitness Accounts of Life in Hitler's Death Camps.* Translated by Thomas Whissen. Westport, Conn.: Praeger, 1996.

Dvorjetski, Mark. "Adjustment of Detainees to Camp and Ghetto Life: And Their Subsequent Readjustment to Normal Society." *Yad Vashem Studies on the European Jewish Catastrophe and Resistance.* Edited by Nathan Eck and Arieh Leon Kubovy. Jerusalem: Yad Vashem Martyrs' and Heroes' Remembrance Authority, 1963. Vol. 5, 193–220.

Gelb, Ernest. Interview by Carol Schulz and Eve Soumerai, West Hartford, Connecticut, August 6, 1997.

Hilberg, Raul. *The Destruction of the European Jews.* Chicago: Quadrangle Books, 1967.

Levi, Primo. *Survival in Auschwitz: The Nazi Assault on Humanity.* Translated by Stuart Woolf. New York: Collier-Macmillan, 1971.

Soumerai, Eve. Unpublished memoir, 1996

Wilkinson, Alec. "Picturing Auschwitz," *New Yorker.* March 17, 2008.

19

THE COVER-UP

For a variety of reasons, the German authorities did their best to conceal what they were doing in the concentration camps, both from the victims themselves and from the outside world. They were intent on reaching their goal of making the world free of Jews and subjugating the rest of Europe to their will, without interference. Those who participated in the machinery of the Final Solution were sworn to secrecy, and even high-level officials were not privy to all the facts, especially information about the medical experiments and the gas chambers and crematoria (Hilberg 1967, 619).

The secrecy and deceit were carried out to great lengths, even to the extent of lying to a mother whose baby was about to be killed, or giving prisoners soap as they made their way to gas chambers labeled "Baths and Inhalation Institute" and outfitted with pipes and showerheads. Signs were posted at railroad stations saying "In transit to Bialystok," with a clock showing a departure time, when the true destination was Treblinka. Greek Jews who were sent to Auschwitz were first sold shops in the Ukraine; others were given letters of reference so that they could get jobs "in the East" similar to the ones they had held (Blumenthal 1957, 62).

THERESIENSTADT: THE MODEL CAMP

Consistent with the desire to camouflage their actions, the German government allowed foreigners to visit only one camp, Theresienstadt (Terezin). The carefully crafted propaganda surrounding Theresienstadt created the myth that the inmates, mostly the elderly and disabled, were

**VISITORS ATTEND THE OPENING
OF THE FIRST GAS CHAMBER**

Despite the efforts to deceive the public, the German authorities were not generally reluctant to hide their accomplishments. German visitors were allowed into the camps, although some were steered clear of certain areas. There is a record, however, of a group of sympathetic visitors attending the opening of the first crematory.

> On the "program" was the gassing and burning of 8,000 Jews from Krakow. The visitors—officers and civilians alike—were extremely satisfied with the results, and the window that had been specially installed in the door of the gas chamber was constantly in use. The visitors were full of praise for this latest novelty.

Source: Eugene Aroneanu, comp. *Inside the Concentration Camps: Eyewitness Accounts of Life in Hitler's Death Camps.* Translated by Thomas Whissen. (Westport, CT: Praeger, 1996).

treated with respect. This misapprehension was a deliberate fabrication on the part of the Germans in order to foster the belief that the other concentration camps were only labor camps. If the other camps were really death camps, they argued, who would care that the elderly and infirm could not work? This reasoning also explains why healthy, young women were sent to "work" at Auschwitz and not to Theresienstadt (Dawidowicz 1975, 184).

Theresienstadt was established in the spring of 1942 by Reinhard Heydrich, who designated it as the "old people's camp" (Hilberg 1967, 277). In addition to the broad deception explained above, Heydrich created the camp to avoid "interventions" (277) on behalf of people who had natural constituencies, groups who had an interest in the well-being of the inmates. Thus, the clientele was expanded to include Jewish war veterans who were severely disabled or had received the Iron Cross First Class or better and whose death would be noticed by veterans' organizations or the army. Also added to the list were prominent Jews whose disappearance might cause a stir in the outside world. People who were told that they would be sent to Theresienstadt considered it a "favored transport," and when interested parties were told of their destination they tended to stop their inquiries (Berenbaum 1993, 92).

In reality, Theresienstadt was not a "favored" place. Although it did house the elderly, they were not treated with kindness, and most died soon after arrival. The camp served as a way station on the trip to Auschwitz when the killing operation became overpopulated. Theresienstadt was also the favorite place to send orphans and other children whose parents had been sent to the killing centers: 15,000 children passed through the camp. The inmates set up schools for them and tried to make their lives more bearable. Only 200 survived (1993, 88).

Inmates, mostly Jews, came from Prague and the German Protectorate, from Austria, Holland, Denmark, Germany, and Slovakia. Since the prominent Jews comprised talented and highly educated people—scientists, jurists, diplomats, artists, writers, musicians, and professors—they created a rich cultural life for themselves while they remained. But few lived for long. Of the total population, estimated at from 139,642 to 144,000, more than 33,000 died at the camp—nearly 16,000 in 1942 alone. Between 86,000 and 88,000 were sent to the death camps, and only 19,000 survived the war. The death rate was so high that the authorities were forced to build a crematorium (Hilberg 1967, 278; Berenbaum 1993, 87).

A Visit from the Outside World

When 456 Danish Jews were transported to Theresienstadt, the Danes issued a protest and insisted on having the Red Cross visit the camp. The Germans responded by creating a fantasy atmosphere and perpetrating a hoax, not only on the Danes and the Red Cross, but on the whole world. First they deported many of the inmates, to make the camp more spacious. Then they forced the inmates to plant gardens, wash and paint buildings, and lay turf. Then they had them build a social center, a synagogue, a concert hall, and a monument to Jewish inmates who had died. When the Red Cross arrived, the visitors were greeted by a concert band of noted Jewish musicians. They were taken to a fictitious cafe filled with guests and then entertained at an inmate soccer game. Later they attended an opera performed by the children. They also visited the Danish inmates, housed in spacious quarters.

During this visit the Germans made a propaganda film that was used to further the myth of the model camp. After the Red Cross left the area, all the inmates who had taken part in the hoax were deported to Auschwitz (Berenbaum 1993, 88–89).

NAZI VOCABULARY

The Germans were also masters at using language to deceive. Since they felt the need to legitimize their behavior, this often led to bizarre legislation and legal jargon that sidestepped moral and ethical reality. The cruelest actions and crimes were justified by references to laws and statutes newly created or, better yet, taken from ancient traditions. For example, one whole category of words was used to describe methods for stealing Jewish property.

"Germanization" meant "to transfer" property into German hands.

"Verdeutschen" meant "to translate," as in translating Jewish property and land into German property, or Germanizing a group of people, such as Czechs, who were considered "worthy."

"Enjudung" meant "de-Judaization," or turning a Jewish business into a German one. *"Entjudungsprozeduren"* meant ousting Jews from economic life by taking their jobs or businesses. (Esh 1963, 138)

This theft was first accomplished through legislation, on February 6, 1939, and later by force. Property confiscated by the government was bought by non-Jews (1963, 138).

Other language hid more sinister behavior. The classification of people seems harmless until the purpose for these identifications is revealed. *Sterntrager* or "star-wearers," referred to *Mischlinge* (half- or quarter-Jews) who were to be *treated like full Jews;* in other words, deported to the death camps (119).

This Nazi perversion of the German language made for some ridiculous terminology. *Wiedereindeutshungwurdigkeit* (worthinessforre-Germanization) described former Germans, now living in Czechoslovakia or Poland, who did not need "special treatment" (i.e., killing) (140).

An entire branch of vocabulary was created to describe murder and the apparatus used to carry it out. *Vernichtungstelle* was an extermination station; *Vernichtungsanstatt,* an extermination institute; and *Vernichtungstellen,* an extermination center. Deportations to death camps were described as *Abwanderung,* or leaving a place or having been migrated, which was stamped on letters that could no longer be delivered. *Anwiserin* (usherettes) were the female *Kapos,* former criminals who guarded the concentration camp prisoners. *Hilfsmittel* was auxiliary equipment: gas vehicles used to kill people before the gas chambers were built (154–59).

In reports, letters, and memos sent from one Nazi official to another, carefully detailing mass shootings, forced evacuations, and the operation of the killing centers themselves, dozens of newly coined words were used to describe what was taking place. In one memo, an official wrote of "freeing" Lithuanian Jews. He calls the procedure an "organizational problem" that "necessitated thorough preparation" (Hilberg 1971, 56). The Jews had to be "collected, and a ditch had to be dug at the right site for the right number" (56). The marching distance from the collecting points to the ditch could average only three miles since opportunities for escape had to be minimized. The Jews were brought in groups of 500, separated by at least 1.2 miles to leave time for dispensing with the previous group. At the end of his report, the official remarked: "Escapes, which were attempted here and there, were frustrated solely by my men at the risk of their lives" (57). Of course, the Jews had no weapons.) During this so-called freeing of the Jews, 3 men shot 38 escapees. The official's conclusion: "Only careful planning enabled the

Commando to carry out up to five actions a week" (56). According to him, this was "nerve-scraping work" (Hilberg 1971, 56–57).

Once in a while a report would be blunt: "Kovno itself, where trained Lithuanian partisans are available in sufficient numbers [to help the Nazis], was comparatively speaking a shooting paradise" (1971, 57).

By far the most common use for euphemisms was in describing killings. The following is just a partial list: "very severe punishment," "brought to the pits," "threatened action," "liquidated," "destroyed," "systematic destruction" (as in the "destruction of Warsaw"), "has been rid of Jews," "radical measures are awaited," "unambiguous attitude toward Judaism," "bring a transport of Jews to their destination," and "removal" (e.g., "the steps planned for the removal of Jewry") (Blumenthal 1957, 50–61; Esh 1963, 159).

Perhaps most sinister of all is a letter to the commander of Security Police and Security Service, from the leader of *Einsatzgruppe 3*, SS-Colonel Jager, entitled "Recapitulation of Executions Carried Out in the Area of Strike Commando 3 Until December 1, 1941":

Today I can confirm that Strike Commando 3 has reached the goal of solving the Jewish problem in Lithuania. . . . I wanted to put the work Jews and their families *to rest* [italics added] but the Reich Commissar and the armed forces declared war on me and issued the prohibition: These Jews and their families must not be shot." (Hilberg 1971, 56)

(Evidently, their labor was still needed.) The author of the report suggests that, at the very least, the males be sterilized and the females be "liquidated" (56).

Language was also used to dehumanize the victims and make the business of killing more palatable. Jews were called *Scheisse* (excrement), "swine," "a stock of Jews," "a store of Jews," "Jewish material," "genuine Jew" (carved on a pocketknife made from human bone), "vermin," "lice," and the "Jewish infection" (Blumenthal 1957, 50–61).

Killing them was considered "political hygiene" (61). To rationalize the Nazi war against the Jews, the Jews had first to be turned into the enemy. Throughout the war, Nazi propaganda reiterated this theme. The Jews were enemy agents, spies, a security risk, inciters of revolts, organizers of the partisans, liaisons with the Red Army, saboteurs, and assassins, and all had criminal roots. Thus the Reich tried to justify their policy of making Europe *Judenrein*, or clean of Jews (Hilberg 1967, 656–57).

Slavs and Russians were portrayed in books as being devoid of physical feeling or intellect. Blacks were considered animals that could be trained but not taught. Gypsies fared only slightly better than the Jews (Blumenthal 1957, 55–56).

The tone used to describe the annihilation of others, even by high-ranking officers with impressive academic credentials, is not dry and official, but unnervingly enthusiastic: "I am very happy" [to dispatch a transport of Jews to their death]; "I am grateful" [for receipt of confiscated property from dead Jews] (1957, 54). This is a "labor of Love," Himmler wrote when reporting that 4,000 Jews were "laid to rest" on June 27, 1942, in the city of Slonim (Hilberg 1971, 58).

In a now infamous speech made by Heinrich Himmler, on October 4, 1943, to a unit of the *Einsatzgruppen,* we find the most remarkable example of this talent for self-deceit.

Most of you know what it means when 100 corpses lie there, or when 500 corpses lie there, or when 1000 corpses lie there. To have gone through this and, apart from exceptions caused by human weakness, to have remained decent, that is what has made us great. This is a page of glory in our history which has never been written and is never to be written. (Arendt 1964, 105)

Toward the end of the war, as the Russians were moving west and the British and Americans were marching east, the Nazi high command made one last effort to hide from the world what they had been about for five long years. They tried to destroy all evidence of the camps, the tortures, the deaths, the medical experiments, and the victims, those who had already been killed and those who were still barely alive.

WORKS CITED

Arendt, Hannah. *Eichmann in Jersusalem: A Report on the Banality of Evil.* New York: Viking, 1964.

Aroneanu, Eugene, comp. *Inside the Concentration Camps: Eyewitness Accounts of Life in Hitler's Death Camps.* Translated by Thomas Whissen. Westport, Conn.: Praeger, 1996.

Berenbaum, Michael. *The World Must Know: The History of the Holocaust as Told in the United States Holocaust Memorial Museum.* Boston: Little, Brown, 1993.

Blumenthal, Nachman. "On the Nazi Vocabulary." *Yad Vashem Studies on the European Jewish Catastrophe and Resistance.* Edited by Benzion Dinur and Shaul Esh. Jerusalem: Yad Vashem Martyrs' and Heroes' Remembrance Authority, 1957. Vol. 1, 49–66.

Dawidowicz, Lucy S. *The War Against the Jews: 1933–1945.* New York: Holt, Rinehart and Winston, 1975.

Esh, Shaul. "Words and their Meaning: 25 Examples of Nazi-Idiom." *Yad Vashem Studies on the European Jewish Catastrophe and Resistance.* Edited by Nathan Eck and Arieh Leon Kubovy. Jerusalem: Yad Vashem Martyrs' and Heroes' Remembrance Authority, 1963.

Hilberg, Raul. *The Destruction of the European Jews.* Chicago: Quadrangle Books, 1967.

———. *Documents of Destruction: Germany and Jewry 1933–1945.* Chicago: Quadrangle Books, 1971.

20

THE DEATH MARCHES

At 4:00 P.M., on January 19, 1945, approximately 66,000 inmates were marched out of Auschwitz (accounts vary from 58,000 to 66,000). Belzec, Treblinka, Sobibor, and Chelmno had all been destroyed, burned, and buried by the Germans. Lublin had been overrun by the Soviets. Auschwitz was the only killing center left. Between May and October 1944, 600,000 Jews had been sent to the camp, filling it to capacity. By January, only one-tenth remained (Hilberg 1967, 632–33; Berenbaum 1993, 181).

On November 25, Heinrich Himmler ordered the dismantling of the last killing institution, but it still held thousands of prisoners when U.S. States forces started dropping bombs on December 16. On January 16, the Soviets too began bombing. Three days later, the death march began.

Since fall, similar marches had been occurring, all over Europe, as the Germans tried to hang on to the prisoners they still needed to provide slave labor, while at the same time move their operations to Germany where they could conceal their activities. According to historian Michael Berenbaum, there were fifty-nine forced marches from concentration camps during that final winter. Some covered hundreds of miles. Prisoners were given little food or water and few breaks to rest or even go to the bathroom. Many died of exhaustion or were shot because they failed to keep up; others froze to death (Berenbaum 1993, 182). One way they found to rest was to speed up their marching in order to reach the front of the line, and then rest while waiting until the line was nearly past them before walking again.

THREE STORIES

A Young Girl Dies

In her memoir, Gerda Weissman Klein writes of the harrowing march she and her close friend Ilse experienced. At first, 3,000 girls, collected from other camps, arrived at Grunberg, the labor camp in which Klein was being held.

Although I had seen misery, I was utterly unprepared for the picture that the girls who had already been marching for a week presented. Covered with gray blankets, they reminded me of drawings of Death when, winged and garbed in loose sheets, he comes to collect the living. Some of them were barefoot, others wore wooden clogs. Many of them left a bloody trail in the fresh snow. (Klein 1995, 182)

Joined by another 1,000 from Grunberg, the girls were divided into two contingents. Klein was in the unlucky group: only 120 of 2,000 survived. After one morning's march from Grunberg, two girls could go no farther and refused to get up from the snow. As Gerda and her friend walked on, the two girls were shot (1995, 184).

After weeks and weeks of walking, with only an occasional drink of lukewarm liquid and some bread, both girls had severe diarrhea and were barely able to walk. For a while, between roll calls, Ilse rode in an open cart in the rain, but eventually she could not go any farther. While standing at yet another roll call, she collapsed. When Gerda begged a guard for some water for her friend, the guard merely kicked Ilse and swore at her. She lay, helpless, on the frozen ground.

It stopped raining. Before she fell asleep she licked the few drops of rain I had caught in my cupped hands. I dozed too.

After a while, she whispered, "Hold my hand."

I held her hand tightly, and we both fell asleep again. When I woke, it was getting light. Ilse's hand was cold. Her eyes were half-open. She no longer breathed. (205)

She was eighteen.

A Boy Survives

Like Gerda and Ilse, Ernest Gelb was a teenager when he was taken to the camps. He was born in Czechoslovakia, in a 150-year-old house that had been in his family since it was built. At one point his family had been fairly wealthy, but they had suffered a setback during the Depression. Still, he and his large family, which included three sisters, and several young aunts and uncles, were happy. Their dining table seated eighteen and was often full of family and guests, especially on the Sabbath, when his mother, after cooking all day, would ceremoniously collapse before dinner.

When the war began, Ernest's family was aware of what was happening in the rest of Europe. Although there was only one radio in the town, newspapers were available and everybody followed the progress of the war. In 1941 the Russians had allowed some Polish soldiers to stay in the town, and Ernest had heard them talk about what was happening to the Jews. The soldiers taunted the listeners, claiming that the same thing was going to happen to them.

In addition, foreign Jews living in Czechoslovakia had been deported to Poland, and some had escaped and made their way back home and told stories of what they had seen. Ernest's aunt had been arrested, and his mother had managed to rescue her by "paying bribes to anyone who asked" (Gelb 1997). She too came back with stories. Despite all of this information, no one was willing to believe how much danger they were in.

On Passover, in 1944, as he rode the train home from school, Ernest saw German soldiers at every stop. On April 21, a horse and wagon and two border police stopped at the Gelbs' house: "We had a half hour to pack. We were being taken 'for our own protection.' That we didn't want to be protected did not much matter (and why didn't the non-Jews have to be transported for safety?)" (Gelb 1997).

Ernest's family had known this was coming for several days, and Ernest had buried valuables in the yard with a note in a flask telling where everything was hidden. Nobody in the village thought to run—they had nowhere to run to—and no one asked to hide. Years later, he noted "I don't think anybody could possibly believe that anything really bad was going to happen" (Gelb 1997).

His mother had spent three days baking, while he delivered things that they had to leave behind to his relatives. His father had already been taken by the Hungarians to serve in a forced-labor battalion, and his mother was exhausted from trying to keep the family safe and fed.

They were taken to a ghetto about three miles from home where they stayed for about a week and then, "again for our protection," to a camp where some 50,000 Jews were being held prisoner. After three weeks, his mother was frantically worried about her children's future, and about her parents, whom she believed were in the camp, though she was not allowed to look for them. Ernest's uncle had been beaten by a guard and his shoulder was broken. (His injury healed just in time for him to be deported to Auschwitz.)

Finally, the time for deportation arrived. As always, the Nazis lied: "We were told we were going to the promised land, families would not be separated, nothing is going to happen to anybody, this place isn't so bad, the next won't be either" (Gelb 1997).

Ernest and his family, along with 95 others, their luggage, and their packages of food, were loaded into a cattle car.

There was one huge can in the center for going to the bathroom and another one for water. You sat down and spread your legs and the next person sat in the space. Once we were in there and the doors were locked there was instant panic, people with claustrophobia, and children, were frightened. There was one little window which was barred. . . . The train started moving. We didn't know where we were going. We realized there was a guard at the sides of each wagon. When there was too much noise there was hitting and yelling. At each station, the children were held up [to the window to identify where they were]. We went through Cracow and then we didn't think we were going in the right direction because Poland was not our favorite place. (Gelb 1997)

They were taken to Auschwitz, where Ernest, his older sister, and his uncle were selected for work. Happily, he and his uncle were assigned to the same barracks. He recalls that "We were greeted by a person with a name tag *schreiger* [boss]." They were given a "welcoming" lecture: " 'You are no longer people, you are prisoners. What you are wearing on your head is called a "mitzer" a cap. When I say "mitzer up" you obey.' As he was talking to us he pointed to the chimney. 'By the way, those are your relatives over there.' " Ernest was horrified. Looking back he describes this callous remark affected him. "And you know what, I don't know how a heart attack feels, but I had a rush of something and I knew that I believed him and I made up my mind that I did not want to be here. The next day they asked for volunteers to go somewhere, and I told my uncle I was going" (Gelb 1997).

He was taken to Buchenwald and from there to a series of labor camps. At Buchenwald he was assigned a number, 2562, and learned that during the previous winter 30,000 inmates had perished. This was the best of the camps to which he was taken. Explaining his situation, he later described going to work each day: "You went through the gates and walked ten minutes to work. The biggest factory I ever saw. Two huge tunnels that the trains went through, forty-six halls 200–300 feet long" (Gelb 1997).

Along with prisoners from France, Poland, and Russia, he was put to work building the scaffolding used to construct the walls of the camp. Although the food was good and the work was bearable, the seventeen-year-old boy still lived in constant fear.

At Auschwitz, when he was told to leave his clothes and shoes behind, he had managed to keep his shoes, his first pair of handmade shoes, a special present for his thirteenth birthday. It was the only piece of home he had. One day, during lunch, while doing his best to remain "invisible," he was accosted by a "seven-foot giant," a Gypsy *Kapo.*

Without even looking at me he says, "Take off your shoes." I think, should I give him my shoes? He's not even my Kapo. I had tried to keep my shoes dirty, covered them with dust. He was not yet forceful, so I asked my Kapo—"Do I have to give him my shoes? Who is he?" My Kapo just nodded. And that was the end of my shoes.

I want you to know, in the seventeen-year-old's mind in the concentration camp, I think I lamented the shoes as much as when I heard about my family. Seventeen is supposed to be quite aware, but this really punished me. The shoes were like a connection. There was still something. Now you're on your own. (Gelb 1997)

As winter approached, life became even more precarious. The ten-minute walk to the tunnel, in cotton pajamas, and the roll calls were increasingly harder to bear. Some prisoners used the inner shell of cement bags to line their pajamas, but even these had to be accounted for, and stealing them was very dangerous. Ernest recalled witnessing the punishments that made him stop stealing bags: "One day there was an inspection. On the way back, unfortunately, they started hanging people. For the next week or so, almost daily, there were two or three corpses. Right there when we got back there was a reception for us. So, I stopped [taking the bags]. I guess I wanted to live" (Gelb 1997).

In November, Ernest was shipped to a "bad camp." The grounds were muddy all the time and walking was very difficult. The work was hard, and they had to be up at 4:00 A.M., washed, dressed, and in line. Like other survivors, he vividly remembers the ritual morning roll calls: "The roll call was really punishment, almost a competition of endurance, whether the weather would outlast us or we would. Counting and looking and looking and counting. It was a game and there was no way out" (Gelb 1997).

The work was out-of-doors, building bridges, putting up telephone poles. The food was mostly water and a little piece of bread for supper. In February, some Russian prisoners of war (POWs) entered the camp:

They were fiercely independent and had a special spirit. One would go near the SS kitchen every day and bring a full set of potatoes and cook them and share them. Nobody asked where they came from. He was caught and killed—immediately sentenced and hung right in front of all of us. . . . You felt terrible, you felt bad, and then you went on immediately. We had to go back to work. You couldn't say because of this I can cop out. You couldn't. (Gelb 1997)

He tried hard to get a job in the kitchen. But, he recalled, "you had to pass a test peeling potatoes [quickly] with only a few eyes left." He flunked the test, but a friend who passed it brought him a carrot, a beet, and a couple of potatoes.

One day he felt so sick he had to do something to get some rest. He had a bad foot and was suffering from a gangrene-like vitamin deficiency.

I kept washing it, but it did no good. The cloth stuck to it, and it smelled terrible, and I decided I must take a vacation. So I lost my pants on purpose, in February. It was cold and I was standing outside with no pants. The guard says, "Where are your pants?" "I don't know, I lost them." "Twenty-five lashes." He started beating [me] and I passed out and the vacation started. (Gelb 1997)

Ernest was sent to the infirmary. A kind, French Jewish doctor helped him for a week, but he was in a tuberculosis ward and had to leave. The doctor put him in the typhoid ward—a huge barracks of naked men, allowed only blankets so they couldn't escape and infect others. "It was warm, corpses with eyes open in the beds. That's me and the whole bunch" (Gelb 1997).

He was given no treatment for his leg. Nonetheless, he survived for three weeks—just long enough to be ordered out. The inmates were being marched west. Unable to walk, even with help, Ernest was put in an open wagon. It was March and they were all freezing.

For nine days they traveled on bombed-out roads, in snow and rain. He was numb. There were continual requests for dead bodies to be thrown from the cart, but he kept some in order to stay warm. For five days there was food. For the next four there was none. There was constant shooting. When they arrived at their destination, another camp, of the 80 men in the wagon, only 9 were carried out. The rest were dead.

Ernest was still alive. He was served soup, "The best I ever ate in my life." It was April 1945. Finally the shooting had stopped. Ernest still rejoices at the outcome: "The Germans were out—the Russians were in" (Gelb 1997).

There was plenty of food. Everybody was running around with food, but Ernest remembered the lessons he had learned from the Talmud, and he proceeded to tell his friends a story:

Once, before the destruction of the Temple, one man, Reb Tzadek, fasted for forty years. He ate only at night, and only a small amount. His stomach was as thin as parchment. When the doctor went to feed him, he gave him only a little soup, a spoonful of flour. Slowly.
    If we eat now we will die. (Gelb 1997)

They boiled some potatoes and ate just a little. It was May 1, 1945. For Ernest, the war was over.

When he was feeling a little better, he made friends with a young Russian soldier. The soldier decided to celebrate the end of the war by killing a German. So they went to a nearby village and walked into a house. The Russian demanded rice, thinking the family would have none and he would then have an excuse to kill them. Astonishingly, he was given rice. The family cooked it, they chatted, had a little meal, and the Russian thanked them. Then the father asked them to sign a little book, to show to other soldiers so they would be safe. That the Russian would not do, but he did spare their lives.

Ernest spent the next two months in a Russian hospital, where he was operated on and recuperated from his wounds. Then he went home. His father, an old man at forty-four, and one sister, were alive and waiting for him. Ernest's sister, who was with their mother when she died, later told him of these last days:

In February 1945, after weeks of marching, my mother in the bitter winter weather became ill with typhus and severe frostbite. She did manage not to fall, because whosoever fell was summarily shot. They arrived at Proust near Gdansk, Poland, and found shelter in some barracks next to a makeshift air terminal. They considered themselves fortunate. There were about 1,000 women there—all waiting to die. There were no medications but a lot of kindness. Two days before my mother passed on, a friend from a previous labor camp was able to procure a bowl of hot oatmeal cereal with cinnamon which my sister fed her gently. A week later my mother died a peaceful death. The Russian liberators arrived three weeks later. By then, most of the women had died. (Gelb 1997)

Escape from a Concentration Camp

By the winter of 1944, Bernice Sobotka was living at Christianstadt, a labor camp in Germany. Being young, she had managed to stay healthy enough to survive the train trip to Auschwitz, and when the Germans began asking, "Who is a plumber? Who is a carpenter?" she realized that if she could do no useful work she would not be allowed to live. She pretended to be a carpenter, although, having grown up in a middle-class household in the city, she had never even held a hammer. Luckily she was put to work building houses, and she was able to watch others and follow their lead.

One night, several thousand prisoners arrived at Christianstadt. They had been marching for days, picking up more people at camps along the way; most likely Gerda Klein was among them. They described what they had undergone, and at that point, Bernice decided it was time to escape.

I felt I would take my chances. If I am to be dead, let me be dead right away. Let them shoot me dead. Why should I march and be hungry and thirsty and dirty and what not. So I take my chances. I broke into the tool shed and took out wire clippers. I knew when the light beams passed by. I watched when the guard was turning the beam the other way. So I cut the fence wire [unlike at death camps, fences at labor camps were generally not electrified], and I ran across the road into the woods. I took with me my girlfriend's younger sister. I couldn't leave her behind. (Sobotka 1980)

When he was about to be deported to Auschwitz, the father of Bernice's best friend had asked her to watch over his younger daughter, Lutka. Apparently, Bernice was the only one left that he could trust. Bernice had managed to protect the young girl, who was fourteen at the time, and they were still together.

We also stole some clothes from the warehouse. I had to take off the camp clothes, striped pajamas, and we stole some scarves to put on our heads because our heads were shaved and anybody would recognize us and would know just by that that we were from the concentration camp.

We got to the woods and it was December and the snow was neck high. I wouldn't dare go anyplace at night because I could end up back at the camp. So I said to Lutka, "Look, we have to stay overnight here and we'll see at daybreak where to go." We sat back to back to keep warm, and the amazing thing was that we didn't have a sniffle. We couldn't believe it. We thought we were going to get pneumonia. Nothing. We were just fine.

Daylight came. We started walking in the opposite direction from where the camp was. We got to a little town. The Germans were in [a] panic too. They had started evacuating toward Berlin because they knew that the Russians were coming. So nobody really paid that much attention to us.

But, would you like to know who [sic] I met in that little town? My German master, my foreman from the camp. They were liquidating the camp, and I come face to face with my German foreman. Would you believe it? (Sobotka 1980)

Fortunately for Bernice and Lutka, the German foreman was looking for a way to save himself, and he took the girls home, where he intended to claim that he had saved them. He fed them (they were very underweight), gave them German clothing, and kept them hidden in the cellar when anyone came to the house. After a few weeks, Bernice was anxious to get out of his house and convinced him to let them go. He took them to an abandoned *Luftwaffe* (air force) cabin in the woods and brought them food and water and told them to stay there until the Russians came and it was safe to leave.

After two weeks, Lutka was becoming more and more frightened ("getting a little mental" [Sobotka 1980]) and insisted upon returning to the village. For a time, they were forced to work for the German army, although they were free to live where they wished. Most of the village had been evacuated.

For the next month, the girls made their way toward Lodz, sometimes on foot, sometimes by horse and buggy, and once they tried hopping a coal train, but were thrown off. Twice they were arrested by the Russians as spies and spent several days in jail before they were able to convince their captors to let them go.

Lutka got sicker and sicker as they went on, and Bernice was forced to leave her in a hospital. Eventually, Bernice arrived in Lodz. In the months after the war, she worked for an agency in Lodz that assisted returning Jewish refugees in their search for missing loved ones. She herself had just about given up hope of ever finding anyone in her family still alive.

One day at work, she happened to look up at the window where newcomers came to report their return and make inquiries. There was her fiancé, Mark. Later, she learned, almost by accident, that her younger brother had been rescued in Italy and taken to Palestine.

"WE WERE SAVED."

Celina and Genia, survivors of the camps, remember:

"It was the last days of January 1945. We were on the march, exhausted. We'd stop thinking . . . We were covered with a white layer of ice . . . We couldn't go further . . . Shooting all around. We came to a small village . . . Germans lived in every house."

They, Polish Jewesses, decided to knock at a door, hoping against hope they wouldn't be betrayed.

"A woman stood in the doorway . . . frightened to death . . . A man appeared:
    'What d'you want?'
    'Hide us please, . . . Don't send us away, please.'
    'I'll get shot . . . '
    'Please give us something to eat.'
    'Come on, then.' He glanced quickly in all directions . . .
    They were led to the attic.
    There was a pile of straw in one corner . . . We threw ourselves down . . . We were saved."

Source: Azriel Eisenberg, *Witness to the Holocaust.* (New York: Pilgrim Press, 1981), 490–91.

THE RED ARMY ARRIVES

When the Soviets arrived at Auschwitz, about 6,000 inmates, too sick and weak to march, were still in the camp. The Red Army found twenty-nine of the thirty-five storerooms burned to the ground. In the six that remained were 368,820 men's suits, 836,255 women's coats and dresses, 5,525 pairs of women's shoes, children's clothes, toothbrushes, false teeth, pots and pans, and seven tons of hair (Hilberg 1967, 633).

The starving inmates had been left on their own. The patients in the infirmary were dying of typhus, severe diarrhea, and starvation. Corpses were rotting where they lay, and rats ruled the barracks. Although Himmler had earlier ordered that evacuations be stopped and the camps be turned over to the Allies, Hitler had overruled him (1967, 633).

It was not until the Russians arrived that any help was given to the inmates.

WORKS CITED

Berenbaum, Michael. The World Must Know: The History of the Holocaust as Told in the United States Holocaust Memorial Museum. Boston: Little, Brown, 1993.

Eisenberg, Azriel. *Witness to the Holocaust.* New York: Pilgrim Press, 1981.

Gelb, Ernest. Interview by Carol Schulz and Eve Soumerai, West Hartford, Connecticut, August 7, 1997.

Hilberg, Raul. *The Destruction of the European Jews.* Chicago: Quadrangle Books, 1967.

Klein, Gerda Weissman. *A Memoir: All but My Life.* New York: Hill and Wang, 1995.

Sobotka, Bernice. Interview by Carol Schulz, West Hartford, Connecticut, October 18, 1980.

21

RESISTANCE

Resistance to the Nazis took many forms. Often overlooked was defiance—simply not to die as ordered. Among the many acts of defiance in the concentration camps described in previous chapters were singing "Ani Mamin" (I know that my Redeemer liveth) on the way to the gas chamber, keeping oneself clean with drops of water, teaching children about goodness where there was none, and sharing morsels of bread. These acts attested to the strength of the human spirit and enabled some to continue living—one hour at a time.

In addition, planned and organized resistance occurred in every occupied country—in its ghettos, camps, and forests. Even in Germany itself there was resistance, although it was ineffective and limited. Horrific forms of retaliation were inevitably the German response.

GERMAN RESISTANCE

The best-known act of resistance was Count von Stauffenberg's unsuccesful attempt on Adolf Hitler's life on July 20, 1944, late in the war. Stauffenberg and his fellow conspirators, who would pay the ultimate penalty for their treachery, being hanged like cattle on meat hooks, a film of which Hitler enjoyed viewing most evenings, believed that Germany's unconditional surrender was inevitable and that it was their responsibility to free Germany from Hitler's tyranny (Shirer 1960, 1048).

The White Rose

Less well known is the story of a group of young people—university students—who felt compelled to make a difference. Deeply religious, Sophie Scholl, her brother Hans, and other students at the university in Munich founded a nonviolent resistance group: the White Rose. They had heard of the mass deportations and shootings in the occupied areas from a young Munich architect, Manfred Eickemeyer, who traveled regularly to Poland and the Soviet Union on business. Hans Scholl, a medical student and soldier in the German army, had worked in army hospitals in conquered France and seen firsthand the suffering the Nazis imposed on people. These young people knew the difference between right and wrong and took the passage from the Epistle of St. James to heart: "Be ye doers of the word, and not hearers only" became their call for action.

Hans, along with other idealistic students, decided to act: to print and distribute leaflets. Fellow student Alexander Schmorell had the biggest allowance, which he used to pay for a typewriter, a mimeograph machine, stencils, and paper. Manfred Eickemeyer offered his studio located in a rear building in the Leopoldstrasse in Munich.

During May, June, and July 1942, a few hundred copies of the first four leaflets were run off anonymously. The opening sentence read: "Nothing is so unworthy of a civilized nation than to be governed by an irresponsible clique given to sinister instincts" (Scholl 1983, 73–74). At the bottom of the leaflet was the message: "Offer passive resistance wherever you may be . . . before the last cities, like Cologne, have been reduced to rubble, and the nation's last young man has given his blood on some battlefield for the hubris of a subhuman" (73–74).

When the leaflets appeared in Munich and its suburbs, they created a sensation. Nobody dared to say such things in public. Some who found a leaflet in their mailbox took it to the police at once; others disposed of it quickly hoping no one would notice. Others, however, took the suggestions seriously and passed the leaflets on. One of them said later, "Today no one will believe how happy we were to do something against the regime at last" (Vinke 1980, 113–16).

The next three leaflets were more specific: " '300,000 Jews have been bestially murdered in Poland.' The entire aristocratic youth of Poland has been annihilated" (1980, 117). And again, accompanying these words was the message: "No one who goes on watching these crimes without doing something can acquit himself of guilt. . . . The White Rose will not leave you in peace!" (117).

At the end of July, Hans and some of his friends were ordered to leave for the Russian front, but before they left, they met once more in the studio to discuss ways in which to resist after their return.

A few very difficult months followed for Hans' sister Sophie. Her father, convicted of malicious slander of the fuehrer, was in prison; her mother had a heart condition; and both her brothers were on active duty in Russia. She was assigned to a two-month armament job, which she described to a friend as "mindless and lifeless labor . . . with its horrifying purpose" (124–25).

Early in October 1942, Hans Scholl and his friends returned to Munich. They had witnessed more horror and were ready again to do their utmost to carry on their form of resistance. Sophie became a very active member in the group. She, her brother, and Christoph Probst, another idealistic student, helped raise funds and shuttled between Munich and other cities to spread the leaflets and organize White Rose groups in other universities. Wherever they traveled, their backpacks were tightly packed with leaflets. Had their bags ever been checked, they would have been arrested on the spot. To prevent that possibility, they left their packs in one compartment on the train during the trip and collected them at the very last minute, just before they got to their destination.

When, on February 3, 1943, the radio newscast reported that the battle of Stalingrad was over, members of the White Rose believed that time was on their side. Little did they realize that they were about to compose their very last leaflet:

> Fellow Fighters in the Resistance!
> Shaken and broken our people,
> behold the loss of the men at Stalingrad.
> 330,000 German men have been senselessly
> and irresponsibly driven to death and
> destruction by the inspired strategy of our
> World War I Private First Class Fuehrer.
> We thank You! . . . The day of reckoning has
> come—the reckoning of German youth
> with the most abominable tyrant our people
> have ever been forced to endure. (Scholl 1983, 93)

February 18, 1943, was a mild day. Sophie and Hans were on their way to the university carrying a suitcase. Classes were conducted in the lecture halls; the stairways were empty. It seemed safe to scatter most of the leaflets. They decided to toss a few through the window into the courtyard below.

They were stopped unexpectedly by Jakob Schmid, the janitor, yelling, "You are under arrest." The president of the university, SS-Oberführer Professor Walter Wüst, called the Gestapo who immediately interrogated them. Composed and resigned, Hans and Sophie stuck to their story that they happened to be passing by and had nothing to do with the distribution of the leaflets. The Gestapo, however, found telling evidence in their rooms: several hundred new postage stamps (Vinke 1980, 161).

In the end, Sophie and Hans took full responsibility, hoping that they could save their friends from the fate awaiting them: death by guillotine. Their surviving sister, Inge Scholl, described their last moments:

Hans asked his parents to remember him to his friends. As he mentioned one last name, a tear ran down his face and he bent down over the bar to hide it. . . . Then Sophie was brought in by a woman warden. She wore her own clothes and walked slowly and easily and very upright. . . . She kept smiling as if she were looking into the sun. Gladly and cheerfully she accepted the candy Hans had refused. "Oh yes, of course. Why, I haven't had any lunch yet," she said. (Vinke 1980, 186)

Their parents were allowed to visit them one last time. Their mother spoke, " 'Remember Sophie: Jesus . . .' Sophie replied, 'Yes—but you must remember too.' Then she too left—free, fearless, serene" (187).

While many other members of the White Rose group were subsequently arrested and executed, the only other one to die with Sophie and Hans was Christoph Probst. The prison wardens decided that they would permit the three of them to be together for a few moments before the executions.

They were so incredibly brave. The entire prison was impressed. That is why we took the risk. . . . We wanted them to smoke one last cigarette together. "I didn't know dying could be so easy," said Christoph Probst. "In a few minutes we meet again in eternity." Then they were led away, first the girl. She went without batting an eyelash. None of us could understand how such a thing was possible. . . . And Hans before he put his head on the block, cried in a loud voice—you could hear it reverberate throughout the large prison—"Long live freedom!" (188)

Inge Scholl ends her book with the following words: "It was an instance in which six students took it upon themselves to act while the dictatorship was totally in control . . . It is rare that a man is prepared to pay with his life for such a minimal achievement as causing cracks in the edifice of the existing order" (1983, 110).

DEATH OF HEYDRICH AND REPRISAL: LIDICE

Reinhard Heydrich, head of the SS (*Schutzstaffel*) Intelligence Service, deputy chief of the Gestapo, designer of the Final Solution, and acting protector of Bohemia and Moravia, was driving his open Mercedes sports car to Hradschin Castle in Prague during the morning of May 29, 1942, when, suddenly, two Czechs, Jan Kubis and Josef Gabeik of the free Czechoslovakian army in England, who had earlier parachuted from a Royal Air Force (RAF) plane, tossed a bomb into the Mercedes that blew the car to pieces and inflicted fatal injuries on Heydrich. The two Czechs were given temporary refuge by the priests of the Karl Borromaeus Church in Prague.

Savage reprisals followed: 1,331 Czechs including 201 women were immediately executed. The two assassins, along with 120 members of the resistance hiding in the Karl Borromaeus Church, were found and killed. Jews were also targeted for reprisal: 3,000 Jews were shipped to extermination camps from Theresienstadt. In far away Berlin, in another immediate reaction to the assassination, Joseph Goebbels rounded up 500 of the few remaining Jews in the city and executed 152 of them on the spot (Shirer 1960, 991).

That was not all. To educate the world that such acts of sabotage would never be repeated or forgotten, the village of Lidice, located ten miles outside of Prague, was chosen to demonstrate once and for all the price exacted for such a deed.

At dawn on June 9, 1942, ten truckloads of German Security Police arrived and surrounded the village. The entire male population was locked up in the barns, stables, and cellar of the mayor. The next morning, in batches of ten, they were taken in back of the barns and shot. Most of the women were transported to the Ravensbrück concentration camp in Germany. Four of them, about to give birth, were first taken to the maternity hospital in Prague where their newly born infants were murdered. The village children were sent to a camp at Gneisenau, Germany. A few of them, after suitable examination by "racial experts," were sent to Germany, to be brought up as Germans.

The village of Lidice was wiped off the face of the earth, burned down and dynamited. There were other "Lidices"—in Poland, Russia, Greece, Norway, and France. Stunned by Nazi brutality, the Czechs looked askance at overt resistance. So unpopular was the Heydrich assassination that the Czech government-in-exile denied all responsibility, even after the war was over (Shirer 1960, 1991–93).

As a tribute to Heydrich, the SS command gave the code name Operation Reinhard (Heydrich's first name) to the Final Solutions carried out in the death camps of Belzec, Sobibor, and Treblinka (Berenbaum, 1993, 171).

GHETTOS AND DEATH CAMPS

Warsaw Ghetto Uprising

Despite the odds, armed uprisings did occur. They were carefully planned over long periods of time—mostly by young people. They required contacts on the Aryan side for arms and supplies. The Warsaw ghetto uprising was one of the most successful attempts. Prior to the uprising, between October 1940 and September 1942, almost 400,000 Warsaw ghetto Jews had died of hunger, epidemics such as typhus, superhuman slave labor, and mass executions. Some 50,000 remained—waiting their turn to be deported to the death camp.

A few days after the "Deportation" photograph was taken (Monday, April 19, 1943, in honor of Hitler's birthday on April 20), armed German, Latvian, and Ukrainian patrols began to encircle the Warsaw ghetto. Their plan called for the total liquidation of the ghetto in three days. After the firing began, the Germans believed, the Jews would go willingly. To accomplish this task, the Germans had assembled what resembled a military operation: more than 2,000 soldiers and officers of the Waffen SS, three *Wehrmacht* divisions including artillery, two German police battalions totaling 234 officers and enlisted men, 367 Polish police called *Granatowa*, enlisted men and officers, 35 security policemen, and hundreds of Ukrainian and Latvian Fascists selected from SS auxiliary troop detachments (Mark 1976, 13).

While the Germans and other participants met to plan the details of the attack, ghetto fighters, under the leadership of Mordekhai Anieleicz, also held strategy meetings in their staff bunker. Weapons, including grenades, ammunition, and bottles of incendiary fluid, as well as food and cyanide pellets, were distributed. Anieleicz and other leaders believed that face-to-face confrontation would end in disaster and opted instead to attack the enemy from behind windows, in buildings located at crossroads, while specially prepared underground bunkers were used to store the ammunition and food.

The next morning, at precisely 6:00 A.M., 2,000 SS troops entered the ghetto with tanks, rapid-fire guns, and three trailers of ammunition ready to oust the remaining Jews. But, to their surprise, they found themselves in the line of fire. By mid-afternoon, the German attackers withdrew having

A young boy stands with his hands raised among a group of Jews discovered in underground bunkers in the Warsaw ghetto. They are being led away for deportation by the SS. Main Commission for the Investigation of Nazi War Crimes, courtesy of USHMM Photo Archives.

suffered many dead and wounded. Later in the afternoon, the Germans vented their anger by going through the wards of the ghetto hospital shooting and killing the sick without mercy (1976, 26).

This savagery was taking place during Passover, which celebrates the miraculous delivery of the Jews from slavery, an event not lost on the ghetto fighters. Ghetto fighter Simkha Korngold described the event taking place in the midst of battle: "Five men stand watch outside with weapons in hand. My father sits in the bunker conducting the Seder. Two candles illuminate the cups of wine. To us, it appears the cups are filled with blood. All of us who sit here are the sacrifice. When 'pour out your wrath' is recited we all shudder. We've awaited a miracle but none appears" (29).

SS General Jurgen Stroop, who took charge of the operation after the first disastrous day, wrote daily reports of the battles: "After a few days it was already clear that the Jews would under no circumstances consider voluntary resettlement [deportations] but were determined to fight back by every means" (quoted in Yahil 1990, 482).

The determined ghetto fighters were prepared to die. They knew their chances were nil, but there was the forlorn hope that help would come from non-Jews in Warsaw. After all, they reasoned, Warsaw was also under German occupation. But this help never materialized.

For several days, battles raged between the well-armed German forces and a handful of fighters who decided to open fire first from one roof, then another. Their losses were minimal, and the Germans were unable to stop the barrage.

After a week, the Germans regrouped and decided on a new tactic. They began to burn down the buildings from which the shots were fired. This destruction blocked the secret passages leading from the bunkers to the attic. Nevertheless, the resisters did not surrender. They created new passages. Finally, the Germans turned to informers and promised them life as a reward for revealing the locations of the bunkers. This stage, accompanied by armed clashes, lasted for weeks. "We were happy and laughing," said one Jewish fighter. "When we threw our grenades and saw German blood on the streets of Warsaw previously flooded with so much Jewish blood and tears, a great joy possessed us" (Altschuler 1978, 166).

Gradually, however, the Jews ran out of ammunition, even though, for a while, they were able to confiscate weapons from dead German soldiers in the midst of battle while being bombarded by flame throwers, artillery, and even aircraft dropping bombs. Building after building was reduced to rubble. On May 16, after four weeks of continued fighting, there still was no formal capitulation. Nevertheless, German commander Stroop sent an official report to his superiors claiming that the ghetto no longer existed and celebrated this "great historic victory" (Suhl 1967, 75) by blowing the magnificent Great Tlomackie Synagogue to pieces. The explosion reverberated throughout Warsaw. On that very day, however, new Jewish fighting groups reassembled. They were young and tall, wore German uniforms, and were armed with pistols and hand grenades. At night they ambushed German patrols. Clashes between Jews and Germans continued into July. Some of the resisters continued to hide in the underground ruins. Very few used the cyanide pellets given to them in case they wished to end their lives (75).

Partisans in the Forest

Ghetto archivist Emmanuel Ringelblum described the uprising as "a struggle between a fly and an elephant" (quoted in Suhl 1967, 15); the end result was a foregone conclusion. But what has been handed down to us are examples of incredible courage and determination by the resistance fighters who held out and continued their struggle in the forests. These were the first civilians in all of occupied Europe to carry out a major revolt against the German military machine—a revolt that lasted longer than the entire 1939 Polish campaign, or, for that matter, the 1940 French campaign.

News of the Warsaw uprising spread and inspired Jewish fighters everywhere and filled them with pride. Hirsch Glick, in the Vilna ghetto, composed what has become the hymn of the Jewish resistance fighters: "Oh, never say you have reached the very end." It also gave encouragement to the Jewish partisans in the surrounding forests.

At one point, a young woman from Warsaw, Vladka Meed, left the ghetto to meet with a small group of partisans in nearby Wyszkow Forest where they were living in the crudest of circumstances. She was guided by a gentile peasant woman who served as the liaison between those on the outside and those inside the ghetto, delivering food, clothing, letters, and sometimes even money to those in the forest. The Jewish soldiers came at night to her house on the edge of the woods to collect their supplies and news of life in the ghetto. She also warned them whenever she learned of any impending German raids.

Meed notes that it was very easy to get lost in the woods, but that the partisans had lived there long enough to find their way, even in the dark. "The swamps are our allies," they told her (Meed 1974, 25). "Almost all of them were sunburned and disheveled. Some wore jackets without shirts, others shirts without jackets; not a man was fully dressed. Most wore leather belts, some were armed with revolvers, others with carbines. The three women in the group differed little in appearance or armament from the men" (1974, 25).

The group included Gabriel Frishdorf, who had once rescued 3 captured resistance fighters from German headquarters in Warsaw; 2 doctors; a fugitive who had escaped from Treblinka's death camp; several fugitives from small Polish towns; and several other fugitives from Warsaw. They lived in a shanty in the trees and stored food in a dugout kitchen with a hole for a chimney and another hole for water. They slept on the ground with no coverings. In response to Meed's query about their diet, one young man replied: "Most of the time we thrive on a varied diet; one day we eat; the next day we do without" (27). In the winter, they could not wash or change their clothes because everything froze, and lice plagued them constantly.

Always guarded by sentries, they tried to maintain a liaison with the Polish underground in an effort to remain safe from the Germans. The local peasants feared them, however, because earlier a wild group of Polish-Ukrainian partisans had plundered their homes and raped the women. So, the Jewish partisans, who in the minds of the peasants were associated with the Polish-Ukrainians, lived in danger of being turned over to the Nazis. The previous winter, the Germans had attacked and killed 12, but the rest had escaped.

Between raids, the partisans carried out acts of sabotage: They set fire to German estates, cut phone lines, raided outposts, and generally harassed the enemy.

A few days after Meed's visit, Gabriel Frishdorf was killed in a German raid. Ironically, many of his group were later killed by the Polish-Ukrainian partisans (29).

On April 19, 1985, an official ceremony marking the forty-second anniversary of the Warsaw ghetto uprising took place in the square of the Heroes of the Ghetto Monument:

On the benches sat mothers and their small children in the sun while old men read newspapers. Off to one side, a small group of mostly young people hold children by the hand. The men have yarmulkas on their heads. They formed a column and moved towards the monument, carrying a large beautiful wreath. The inscription on the ribbon, in Hebrew and Polish read, "We are Your Children." (Niezabitowska 1985, 107)

Rescue from the Lvov Ghetto

Today Lvov is called Lviv and is part of the Ukraine. In 1941, however, it was part of the eastern section of Poland under Russian control, as agreed upon in the Ribbentrop-Molotov agreement. Then, on June 21, 1941, the Germans invaded the Soviet Union, and the Russian soldiers retreated to the east to defend their country.

In August the family of Dr. Leon Chameides, along with the rest of the Jewish population, were forced into the newly created ghetto. "Survival became more and more questionable," (Chameides 1997) said Leon, and for that reason, Leon's father, Rabbi Chameides, accompanied by his friend Rabbi Kahana, arranged a meeting with an acquaintance, Metropolitan (Archbishop) Andrew Sheptytsky, the head of the Eastern Right Catholic Church in Western Ukraine, to ask him to hide their holy Torahs.

The Metropolitan told them that he would try, but that they would have to be brought to him. This turned out to be hopeless, since carrying Torahs through the streets up the hill to the church residence would be impossible in occupied Poland.

The two rabbis then asked whether the Metropolitan would help save their children. They all knew such a deed might result in death. The Metropolitan thought he might be able to hide girls; however, the boys, Leon and his brother, were circumcised, which was an immediate giveaway. He felt he needed to consult with his brother, also a priest. After due reflection, he agreed to take seven-year-old Leon and find a place for his nine-year-old brother. The entire family of Rabbi Kahana was also given shelter with yet another group of priests.

Leon, now a "war orphan" called "Levko" and torn from his family, remembered Father Marco, in charge of prayers, patiently teaching him day after day the customs, rites, language, and prayers of the Church—and constantly reminding him not to bathe or go to the toilet in public. While the ghetto was being liquidated and Leon's parents sent east to their deaths, Levko helped tend the pigs, cows, and sheep at the church's farm. The fathers were constantly on the alert, and Leon had to hide in the loft when the Germans "visited." One day, the Germans confiscated the animals and the bells of the church, and the residents had to learn to survive on berries and the plants of the fields. They were helped by their neighbors as well. "The nice thing I remember were the peasants who came on Sundays and brought us eggs and cheese" (Chameides 1997).

The church became a hospital, and Leon washed bandages from those who had no further need of them. After battles between Germans and Russians, Leon remembered searching for dead German soldiers in the woods because they always had good bandages in their packs.

When the Russians drove the Germans out of Poland, Leon remembered the morning when his life took another significant turn. Brother Josef was celebrating Mass, and there, without any warning, his brother had walked into the church. "I recognized him immediately. And unbeknownst to me, he had been in touch with the Kahana family. We had breakfast. And I remember leaving with him to join the Kahanas. In our case, the Ukrainian Church not only saved our lives but returned us to our Jewish roots," he concluded (Chameides 1997).

FATHER PASSELECQ

Père (Father) Georges Passelecq was a Belgian priest who knew misfortune and imprisonment for nearly four years until his liberation from Dachau by the U.S. Army on 29 April 1945. He was active in the resistance saving many Jewish children. At the first organizational meeting of the resistance movement after Germany had invaded Belgium, he had a great surprise: his brother and sister were also present.

In Dachau, where there was a compound for about 1,000 priests and nuns, he would say Mass even though it was punishable by death. His assignment was making brooms for the German army. He made sure the bristles would fall out after one or two uses.

His brother and sister both died. "You never get over the pain, the loss, the injustice," he told me. Yet the experience made his faith stronger. How? By reaching out to all others, in any way possible, to be a peacemaker, not a judge. "

Source: Eve Soumerai. Unpublished interview of Père Georges Passelecq, 1971.

Sobibor Death Camp

By the end of the summer of 1943, most of the ghettos in the cities and towns had been liquidated, and their Jews had been sent to different death camps including perhaps the least known of all of them, Sobibor, located in eastern Poland. Sobibor became the scene of one of the most dramatic revolts to occur. The camp, completed on May 8, 1942, lay close to several forests. It was surrounded by four layers of barbed wire over ten feet high, a ravine filled with water, and a minefield. Several dozen SS men and hundreds of armed Ukrainian guards presided over thousands of Jews who arrived daily from all over Europe. Escape seemed virtually impossible.

On February 12, 1943, Heinrich Himmler, accompanied by a group of high officers, inspected Sobibor, its defenses and operations. To welcome the important visitors, the commandant and other high officials polished their uniforms and boots, and ordered the selection of 200 attractive, young Jewish women. They were forced to undress and march to the gas chambers—to demonstrate the Final Solution in process. Then a great banquet was given in honor of the visitors.

One young inmate, Eda Lichtman, recalled being asked to decorate the tables with flowers. She noted that Himmler seemed overjoyed with the visit and the next day, she noted, "our" executioners wore new decorations. Production of the number of bodies burned went up to 15,000 a day (Suhl 1967, 7; Novitch 1980, 59).

There had been previous attempts to revolt. In one, a Jewish sea captain from Holland led a group of inmates. They planned to set the camp on fire and escape in the general confusion. Somehow the Germans found out about the plan, and the captain was immediately tortured in public. Still he refused to give the names of the others involved. In response, the Germans marched every man out of his block and beheaded each in turn in front of the sea captain, whose turn was last. The Germans increased their roll calls to three times daily and placed more mines around the camp.

In September 1943, a transport of Russian prisoners of war arrived from Minsk, the first from the Soviet Union. Among the prisoners was a thirty-four-year-old Jewish Red Army officer, named Alexander (Sasha) Pechersky, from Rostov-on-Dov, who had studied and composed music in his native Russia. His arrival made a great impression on the prisoners. Although they all knew that there was a war going on, they had never met Russian prisoners, men who were actually fighting the Germans and knew how to handle arms. They were looked up to with curiosity and hope. Perhaps they could help some to escape from the hell called Sobibor. Sasha decided to do just that and started to keep a diary describing the events of each day (quoted in Suhl 1967, 12).

September 24

We arrived in camp yesterday and today we were roused at five in the morning. Each of us received a cup of hot liquid but no bread. At half past six we were counted . . . and lined up three in a row. The Russian Jews who had arrived yesterday were placed in front of the column. Oberscharfuehrer Franz ordered the Russian Jews to sing Russian songs. "We don't know which songs we're allowed to sing," I said. "Sing what you know," Franz replied.

(We sang) If war comes tomorrow
Tomorrow we march
If the evil forces strike . . .
United as one
All the Soviet people
For their free and native land will arise

In this camp of death and despair, the song rang out like a clap of spring thunder (1967, 13–14).

Within three weeks, Sasha, aided by Polish-Jewish inmate Leon Feldhendler, had planned the revolt. Sasha provided the energy; Leon and others provided the knowledge of the daily rituals and procedures. They set to work. Sasha drew a map of the camp. He and the other Russians had been assigned barracks in Sector I. Within that same area were also the shops of the tailors, shoemakers, cabinetmakers, the smithy, and the kitchen. These artisans worked for, and at the discretion of, the German and Ukrainian guards. Farther north was Sector II where inmates sorted out the belongings of the victims. Still farther was Sector III and the gas chambers.

Sasha explored various options with the artisans in his block and with others on the work detail. They decided that one of the blacksmiths would make hatchets. Others would collect knives. There was much debate and many presented their ideas of what to do. On October 12, Sasha described one of the many planning meetings in his diary:

"So comrades," I said . . . , "first we must do away with the officer group . . . one by one without a sound. The task of killing will be assigned to our Soviet prisoners. . . . Behind the officers' house the wire fence must be hacked through. Those assigned to the front lines will hurl stones as they advance. Where the stones fall, the mines will explode . . . clearing the mine fields." (Suhl 1967, 31–32)

On October 14, the day of the revolt, much happened as planned. Relying on the proverbial German punctuality, the tailors, shoemakers, and storekeepers had arranged appointments with individual commanders at fifteen-minute intervals. It happened to be the time for the Germans to order new uniforms and boots for the winter season, and they were asked to come to be measured. Each turned up at the exact time and was greeted with an ax blow on the head. Within thirty minutes, the leaders of the revolt were armed with revolvers taken from the SS officers. Next, after whispering the agreed-upon password, "Hurrah," Sasha gave the order to advance and seize the armory. The prisoners started to pour out from all sides of the camp. They were subjected to heavy fire from the Ukrainian guards and the two SS officers who had not had measurement appointments.

Sasha described the scene in his diary:

At that moment the column from Sector II was advancing toward us. Several women began to scream. One prisoner was on the verge of fainting. Another began to run blindly, without any direction. . . . "Comrades forward!" I called out loud. "Forward," someone on my right picked up the slogan. . . . The slogans reverberated like thunder in the death camp and united Jews from Russia, Poland, Holland, France, Czechoslovakia and Germany, six hundred pain-racked, tormented people surged forward with a wild "hurrah" to life and freedom. . . . And there we were on the other side of the fence and minefield. And running faster, faster through the barren strip of land. . . . Faster, faster into the woods, among the trees. (Suhl 1967, 39–40)

About 300 prisoners succeeded in escaping, and about 100 of them survived. Many joined the partisans and continued to fight for freedom.

The next day, October 15, the following report was issued by the Security Police in the Lublin district:

On October 14, 1943, at about 5 P.M. there was a revolt of the Jews in SS-camp Sobibor, 25 miles north of Chelm. They overpowered the guards, seized the armory, and after a firefight with camp garrison, fled in unknown directions. Nine SS men murdered, 1 SS man missing, 2 foreign guards shot to death. Approximately 300 Jews escaped; the remainder were shot to death or are now in camp. Military police and armed forces were notified immediately and took over security of the camp at about 1:00 A.M. (quoted in Novitch 1980, 168)

Two days after the revolt, Himmler ordered Sobibor liquidated. The Nazis could not continue the work of death on a spot where life had suddenly flared up.

CONTINUING THE FIGHT FROM THE FORESTS

About 15 Sobibor survivors joined a large Jewish partisan unit in the Parczew Forest and joined the activities of the group who were in touch

with the Russian army and, in the latter part of 1943, were informed that
they would be the recipients of a parachute drop of weapons. They were
to drive their wagons into the woods and wait in a previously designated
clearing until dark and then light bundles of wood to signal their location.
They kept scanning the sky for hours, while one of them, a "clown," kept
them amused with jokes and imitations to keep up their spirits. Finally,
after hours of waiting, they saw a parachute descend and a man land
who cut himself lose keeping everybody at bay with his revolver until
they exchanged their prearranged passwords. The group received much
bounty: bags containing fifteen brand-new submachine guns and ammunition. One of the bags was filled with German ammunition, which was
badly needed for the rifles and pistols acquired during ambushes. Another
bag contained various mines and explosives for blowing up bridges and
trains. Harold Werner described the feelings of the group: "Receipt of this
airdrop was a tremendous lift to our morale. for the first time we felt there
was a friendly hand to encourage us to go on fighting. It made us feel
we were an important part of the Allied armed struggle" (Werner 1992,
198–99).

WORKS CITED

Altschuler, David. *Hitler's War against the Jews.* New York: Behrmann
House, 1978.

Berenbaum, Michael, ed. *I Never Saw Another Butterfly.* New York: Schocken
Books, 1993.

Chameides, Leon. Interview by Eve Soumerai, Hartford, Connecticut,
July 15, 1997.

Mark, Ber. *Uprising in the Warsaw Ghetto.* New York: Schocken Books,
1976.

Meed, Vladka. "Jewish Partisans." *The Warsaw Ghetto Uprising.* New York:
Congress for Jewish Culture, 1974.

Niezabitowska, Malgorzata. *Remnants: The Last Jews of Poland.* New York:
Friendly Press, 1985.

Novitch, Miriam. *Sobibor.* New York: Holocaust Library, 1980.

Scholl, Inge. *The White Rose.* Middletown, Conn.: Wesleyan University
Press, 1983.

Shirer, William L. *The Rise and Fall of the Third Reich.* New York: Simon and
Schuster, 1960.

Suhl, Yuri. *They Fought Back.* New York: Schocken Books, 1967.

Vinke, Hermann. *The Short Life of Sophie.* New York: Harper and Row,
1980.

Werner, Harold. *Fighting Back.* New York: Columbia University Press,
1992.

Yahil, Leni. *The Holocaust: The Fate of European Jewry, 1932–1945.* New York:
Oxford University Press, 1990.

22

THE LIVES OF THE RESCUERS AND THE RESCUED

Judaic teaching declares, "Whosoever saves a single life, it is as though he saved an entire world." Six million "worlds" perished in the Holocaust. Yet some—a few—were saved by Gentiles who throughout occupied Europe risked their lives and those of their families to save their Jewish fellow human beings.

The rescuers included Catholics and Protestants. They lived in cities, small towns, and villages. They were men and women from all walks of life, from the highly educated to the working poor and illiterate. They included priests and unbelievers.

The most common question asked of them after the war was why they risked their lives. Their responses varied: It was the right thing to do; what would you expect me to do?; I'd do it again; it was the human thing to do. Some did not know why. Père Georges Passeleqc, a Belgian Benedictine priest interned at Dachau for aiding Jews, told high school students at Conard High School, in West Hartford, Connecticut, "Something in me told me to, I just had to—that's all" Then he added with a smile, "Besides, I didn't think I would get caught. I thought I was too smart" (Soumerai Unpublished interview of Georges Passelecq 1973).

On a hillside in the western part of Jerusalem is a memorial to the martyrs and heroes of the Holocaust. It is called Yad Vashem, Hebrew for "place or monument" and "name." The words come from a verse in Isaiah 56:5 in which God promises that even childless Jews shall not be forgotten by future generations. In God's "place" and in God's walls, "I will give them an everlasting name that shall not be effaced."

In order not to "efface" the events of the Holocaust and the names of their victims, the main museum at Yad Vashem houses the largest collection of archival materials of the Holocaust, and the nearby Hall of Names holds the names and biographical information of millions of victims. Across the courtyard from the main museum is the Hall of Remembrance, a heavy, brooding building in which the names of the death camps are inscribed on grey slabs of stone. It is here that the perpetual flame disperses its light. Next to the flame is a vessel containing ashes of the martyrs.

To always remember the rescuers, tree-lined paths, named Avenues of the Righteous, wind their way to the museum complex and beyond. Bathed in Jerusalem's golden light, these evergreen carob trees bear witness to the individuals who risked their lives to rescue Jews. The individuals are called the "Righteous of the Nations of the World." Psalm 1:3 is the source for the expression "Righteous One" who is "like a tree planted by streams of water that yields, its fruit in its season, and its leaf does not wither."

The carob tree was chosen because of its toughness. Its shiny and leathery leaves do not wilt in the dry, hot winds of summer or wither in the damp, cold winds of winter. At the base of each planted tree is a small plaque with the name and nationality of the honored Christian. Among the many trees are those for Raoul Wallenberg of Sweden, Jan Karski of Poland, and Oscar Schindler of Austria.

HUNGARY

Holocaust historian Raul Hilberg described the Hungarian pro-German government as a reluctant collaborator who used anti-Semitic rhetoric to extract material benefits from their German ally while, at the same time, trying to protect their own Jews from deportation. In 1941 between 15,000 and 20,000 non-Hungarian Jews (many of them Polish Jews who had resided in Germany and Austria) were driven across the border into Poland. Reports of their massacre filtered back to the Reich. The 650,000 Hungarian Jews remained relatively free until the German forces invaded on March 19, 1944, to prevent Hungary's defection to the Allies. Adolf Hitler then expected the full cooperation of the Hungarian Fascist forces in rounding up all of Hungary's Jews (Fein 1979, 107).

Raoul Wallenberg: The Life of One Protector

On January 22, 1944, President Franklin Roosevelt, acting under considerable pressure, issued Executive Order 9417, which established the War Refugee Board. Its mission was "to take all measures within its power to rescue the victims of enemy oppression who are in immediate danger of death." The Jewish community of Hungary, once the third largest in Europe, was about to become "in immediate danger of death" as a result

Hungarian Jews selected for death in Auschwitz-Birkenau's gas chamber wait in a nearby wooded area, May 1944. Yad Vashem Photo Archives, courtesy of USHMM Photo Archives.

of the appointment of a pro-German cabinet and SS *Schutzstaffel* Lieutenant Colonel Adolf Eichmann as the Jewish Affairs specialist. Eichmann was proud that between May 15 and July 9, 1994, 147 sealed cattle trains had already carried over 400,000 Jewish men, women, and children from the Hungarian provinces to their death, and he planned to showcase his ability by deporting the remaining 200,000 Jews still in Budapest to Auschwitz in one stunning twenty-four-hour blitz.

President Roosevelt pleaded with the neutrals to open their gates. "It would be a major tragedy," he said, "if these innocent people . . . should perish on the very eve of triumph over the barbarians" (Feingold 1970, 252). His newly created War Refugee Board would supply the necessary funds primarily from Jewish organizations.

The Swedes responded that they were willing to enlarge their diplomatic mission in Hungary for that purpose. They found a perfect candidate for the task: Raoul Wallenberg, a thirty-two-year-old, wealthy member of an aristocratic Swedish family who was willing to assume the responsibility. He had studied architecture and had traveled widely, including a stint at the Holland Bank in Haifa, then Palestine, where he had met Jewish refugees fleeing from persecution. He had been shocked by their stories, and the shock spilled over into passionate concern.

On July 8, 1944, on the eve of Wallenberg's departure for Budapest, some of his best friends joined him in a farewell dinner. They knew him as intensely patriotic and proud of the name Wallenberg. They also remembered that, as a young boy, he so despised hunting and killing that he had broken into the kennels of a neighboring estate to release the hunting dogs the night before the hunt was to take place. They also recalled how he had run outside his house in the middle of a severe thunderstorm to "see God's fireworks" while his friends cowered under the bed (Werbell and Clarke 1982, 25).

The day after his farewell dinner, Wallenberg found himself on a southbound passenger train to Budapest filled with returning German troops. From the opposite direction, a northbound freight train passed filled to capacity with thousands of Jews from the Budapest suburbs on their way to Auschwitz. Wallenberg had neglected to book a seat and therefore spent the entire journey sitting and dozing on his knapsack in the corridor of the train. As well as the knapsack, he carried a sleeping bag, a windbreaker, and a small revolver to give himself courage. He later confided all this to

Passport photo of Swedish diplomat Raoul Wallenberg issued in Stockholm on June 30, 1944. Courtesy of USHMM Photo Archives.

Per Anger, his friend and fellow Swede at the legation, who thought these belongings a rather odd assortment for a diplomat.

In the meantime, the Hungarian regent, Admiral Miklos Horthy, had decided to exercise some independence, particularly since conditions in Europe were changing rapidly. The Red Army was advancing, and the deportations were in full view of the world press. Perhaps Horthy thought he could put a stop to, or at least slow down, the deportations, much to the annoyance of Eichmann.

Unfortunately, from Eichmann's point of view, Auschwitz was unable to handle the thousands of Jews arriving daily from Hungary and the rest of Europe, despite the extra gas chambers and ovens that had recently been added. Auschwitz commandant Rudolf Hoess had personally rushed to Budapest to tell Eichmann to slow down. In addition, the German army demanded the use of the deportation trains to move soldiers.

Eichmann cried foul and appealed to Hitler's general headquarters. The immediate response was that the army could claim priority only if soldiers were advancing. Since they were retreating, Eichmann was able to procure some of the trains but not nearly enough to carry out his plans.

The just-arrived Wallenberg sized up the situation. He had $100,000 at his disposal with which to start rescue operations, and he realized that, despite the delays and difficulties facing Eichmann, each of the 200,000 targeted Jews was in great danger. He wasted no time and immediately established his Section C at the Swedish embassy—a space set aside for the sole purpose of rescuing Jews. Next, he used his architectural skills to design an impressive looking Swedish passport in yellow and blue that prominently displayed the triple crown of the Royal Swedish government. He made sure there was a designated space for the "Swedish" holder's photograph, as well as other pertinent passport information. Understanding the bureaucratic mind-set, he marked the passport with generous amounts of seals, stamps, signatures, and countersignatures. Although these passports had no validity, they engendered respect, unlike those issued by Swiss and Vatican authorities. Wallenberg mass-produced the passports—many more than originally planned. A staff of first 250 then 400 Jews worked in shifts around the clock to prepare and distribute the protective documents.

Problems abounded. So many Jews fled for safety to the Swedish embassy—700 crowded into Section C alone—that it became necessary for Wallenberg to rent thirty-one safe houses. He declared them to be inviolable Swedish property and therefore protected by international law.

He began to surface everywhere and soon became a living legend. Sleeping fewer than four hours each night, he managed to supervise his staff, roam the streets dispensing passports, procure food and medicine for specially set-up clinics and soup kitchens, and arrange meetings with the active Swiss consul, Charles Lutz, and the Swedish Red Cross representative. Though he was overworked, he still found time for individuals in need.

Letter of protection (*Schutzpass*), issued by the Swedish legation in Budapest on August 25, 1944 to the Hungarian Jew Lili Katz. The document bears the initial "W" for "Wallenberg" in the bottom left corner. Lena Kurtz Deutsch, courtesy of USHMM Photo Archives.

All hospitals were barred to Jews and conditions in the houses were atrociously overcrowded and insanitary. Wallenberg heard that the wife of a young Jew, Tibor Vandor, who was working [with him] was about to have a baby. He swiftly rounded up a doctor taking him and the young couple to his flat. . . . There he turned over his own bed to Agnes, the young mother-to-be, and went out into the corridor to sleep. In the small hours of the morning he was awakened by the doctor, and told that Agnes had given birth to a healthy baby girl. Wallenberg went in to inspect the new arrival and the Vandors begged him to be the godfather. He consented happily and the child was named Yvonne Maria Eva. (Bierman 1981, 97)

After three months, Wallenberg thought that conditions had much improved and that the "passports" had done their job. There was a deceptive lull. Eichmann was temporarily out of the country. Wallenberg thought that he might return to Sweden in advance of the Russians about to enter Hungary. But, on October 12, 1944, everything changed. Admiral Horthy, who had been attempting to negotiate a separate peace with the Allies, infuriated the Germans. They immediately sent SS troops back into Hungary and forced Horthy to leave Budapest for Berlin where he became a virtual prisoner.

Horthy's replacement was Ferenc Szalasi, the leader of the vicious Hungarian Nazi Party called the Arrow Cross. Eichmann returned in triumph, and from the very first night, terror resumed. Jews were arrested and disappeared. The Arrow Cross gangs invaded their homes, including the safe houses, and brutalized—often killing—the inhabitants. Wallenberg immediately organized groups of strong, young Hungarian Jews who tried to protect the blockaded Jews and bring them food and medicine.

Meanwhile, a busy Eichmann decided not to fight the German army for every locomotive and cattle car, but to take more creative measures: working or walking the victims to death en route to Germany and away from the advancing Russians.

Men between sixteen and sixty were driven to the outskirts of Budapest to dig trenches and erect earthen walls to stop the advancing Russians. Many died of exhaustion and ill treatment. The old, sick, handicapped, women, and children were rounded up and forced to make the death march. They were whipped along the 120-mile route from Budapest to the Austrian border town of Hegyeshalom by Hungarian gendarmes. It was bitterly cold, and when some fell or lay down on the road, they froze to the icy ground. Others, not able to keep up, were beaten to death.

When those who survived the march reached the border town, Eichmann and members of the SS were waiting for them. They counted the prisoners one by one, like cattle, and gave the Hungarian officer in charge of the march a receipt with the numbers. Wallenberg and his friend Per Anger traveled back and forth along the route, bringing van-loads of food, medicine, and clothing. Wallenberg also carried lists of the names of Jews who had received passports, as well as blank ones, which he issued on the spot.

Zwi Eres, one of the "death marchers" remembered the event:

At the end of the march we saw two men by the side of the road. One of them, wearing a long leather coat and a fur hat, told us he was from the Swedish legation and asked if we had Swedish passports. If we hadn't perhaps they had been taken away from us or torn up by the Arrow Cross men. We were on our last legs but alert enough to take the hint, and we said, yes. . . . A group of Hungarian officers and Germans in SS uniforms were there, too. Wallenberg was brandishing his list. There was a tremendous amount of arguing going on. . . . In the end, to our amazement, Wallenberg won his point and between 280 and 300 of us were allowed to go back to Budapest. (Bierman 1981, 84)

At the beginning of December 1944, Wallenberg reported to Stockholm that, during the death marches, "it was possible to rescue some 2,000 persons from deportation," (86) and he added that the Swedish mission had also secured the return of fifteen labor service men holding Swedish and other protective passes.

Shortly before the Russians liberated Budapest, 5,000 Swedish-protected Jews were marched out of their safe houses into the walled-in ghetto in order to be executed. In a last-minute joint operation between the German army and Arrow Cross, the decision had been made to massacre every last Jew by blowing up the ghetto.

Wallenberg immediately intervened. He sent a messenger to SS General August Schmidthuber, the officer in charge, to tell him that if he did not stop this outrage, he, Wallenberg the Swede, would personally make sure that Schmidthuber would be charged with murder and genocide by the War Crimes Tribunal to come. With 500 SS men and 22 Arrow Cross members on alert to kill, time was of the essence.

The SS general, concerned about his own future, picked up his telephone and ordered the German commander and the Arrow Cross chief to appear in his office immediately. He told the disappointed men that there would be no massacre and, just to make sure, he placed the military commander under arrest, saving the lives of thousands of Jews.

Wallenberg had, once again, displayed an uncanny ability to come up with the right solution at a moment's notice. Even though Wallenberg considered his survival thus far miraculous, he was for the very first time concerned about his own safety. He had made powerful enemies. But, for the time being, he busied himself compiling the necessary paperwork for the restoration of property for "his" Jews. He was also envisioning a Wallenberg Institute for Rescue and Reconstruction in the postwar era.

On the morning of January 13, 1945, the Russians arrived. Wallenberg introduced himself and, in the elementary Russian he had been practicing, asked to make contact with military headquarters. His intent was to negotiate proper care for the liberated Jews. Little did he realize that the Russians might be highly suspicious of the Swedish mission and that the large number of Swedish documents in circulation would add to their doubts.

They agreed to take him to their headquarters in Debrecen. His friend and chauffeur, Vilmos Langfelder, accompanied him in their Studebaker. Wallenberg returned the next day, escorted by two Soviet soldiers, and was overheard to say that he did not know whether he was a guest of the Soviets or their prisoner. Wallenberg stopped at the office and asked one of his assistants, George Wilhelm, to return several thousand dollars in Hungarian currency that he had given him for safekeeping. He said that he had secured Soviet permission to make the trip to Marshal Rodion Malinovsky's headquarters. Still under escort, he stopped off at the offices of the Swedish legation where he dispensed funds to his Hungarian assistants and told them that he expected to return in about a week, after having established contact with the Russian military and the new Hungarian government. He insisted that the operation be kept going.

He then stopped at the Swedish hospital he had helped establish. In front of the door, he slipped on the ice. Paul Nevi, the hospital manager, helped him up just as two elderly men, with yellow stars still stitched to their coats, went by. Wallenberg told him that he was glad that his mission had not been in vain. Those were some of the last words he spoke in what might be called relative freedom. He did not realize that, although the Germans had been defeated, the Grand Alliance between the Americans, the British, and the Russians had begun to crack and the cold war was in the making.

In the eyes of the Soviets, Wallenberg's protective passports, some of which had ended up in German hands, were highly suspicious. He was also responsible for Swedish flags flying from thirty-two buildings, purchased with funding he had obtained from the War Refugee Board in the United States—another suspicious activity, given that the Russians expected to see their flags flying above the houses of Budapest.

Wallenberg's obvious courage, convictions, and, above all, initiatives were not qualities appreciated by a totalitarian, bureaucratic state built on Communist Party ideology. It is assumed that for these reasons (although the truth has never been known) Raoul Wallenberg and his driver disappeared into Russian protective custody from which they never emerged.

The Swedish government was more worried about Mother Russia and the danger she posed to neutral Sweden than about Raoul Wallenberg who, they had been assured by the Soviet ambassador in Stockholm, was safe under Russian protection.

January 16, 1945, the Soviet deputy foreign minister dispatched an official note to the Swedish envoy in Moscow that said, "First Secretary Raoul Wallenberg of the Swedish delegation in Budapest has gone over to the Russian side." Signals were decidedly mixed regarding his whereabouts because, in the spring, Radio Kossuth, the voice of Russian-liberated Budapest, announced that Raoul Wallenberg was "most probably assassinated by agents from the Gestapo" (Marton 1982, 219)

Enquiries continued from throughout Europe and Israel. From America, Secretary of the Treasury Henry J. Morgenthau, Jr. (son of former Ambassador Henry J. Morgenthau, who had objected to the Armenian genocide), added his voice to others trying to discover Wallenberg's whereabouts; the Russian authorities continued to stonewall. Some believed that Wallenberg had broken too many rules and had stepped on too many toes and that it was therefore conceivable that he did not want to come home.

In the summer of 1946, a new Swedish, Social Democratic government was elected. The new foreign minister, Osten Unden, a Marxist, believed that the Soviets were misunderstood by the rest of the world. He arranged to see Joseph Stalin personally in regard to Wallenberg. Stalin assured him that he would look into the matter and find out whether Wallenberg was still in the Soviet Union. The foreign minister, who suggested that Wallenberg might have been the victim of robbers or have had an accident in Budapest, provided Stalin with a handy excuse. Three months later, the Soviet foreign minister declared they would no longer accept enquiries about Wallenberg. This directive came straight from the desk of Stalin. There was no higher appeal.

However, reports continued to surface. Returning German, Austrian, and Italian prisoners of war claimed they had met Wallenberg. Finally, in April 1956, Swedish Prime Minister Tage Erlander, armed with this "evidence," faced Communist Party Chairman Nikita Khrushchev and said, "Raoul Wallenberg is casting a giant shadow over Swedish-Soviet relations" (224).

Ten months later, Foreign Minister Andrei Gromyko responded in a memo explaining that, after an exhaustive inquiry, a document had been located from the health services of Lubyanka prison. The handwritten document was signed by Smoltsov, Chief of Prison Sanitary Ward, on July 17, 1947: "I report that the prisoner Wallenberg . . . died suddenly in his cell this night, probably as the result of a heart attack" (226). An additional notation declared "that the body was cremated without an autopsy" (226).

Unfortunately, Smoltsov had died on May 7, 1953, and could therefore not furnish any more information. The memo did confirm, however, that Wallenberg had been arrested by Soviet troops and that incorrect information by certain leaders of the security organs had been transmitted over the years, as a result of someone named Abakumov, who had inflicted upon the Soviet Union all kinds of damage and was executed after receiving a guilty verdict from the Supreme Court in the Soviet Union. The last paragraph expressed Gromyko's sincere regrets and profound sympathy (223–31).

Although biographies and films detailing the events of Wallenberg's life have been written, statues have been erected, and trees have been planted, Wallenberg's biggest memorial resides in the hearts of the thousands of individuals he saved. Two of them, Annette Lantos and her husband Congressman Tom Lantos of California, both children in Budapest during the war, were saved by Wallenberg's protective passports. Annette Lantos organized a committee, including her husband Tom, Senator Daniel Patrick Moynihan of New York and Senator Claiborne Pell of Rhode Island, to sponsor the necessary legislation to award Raoul Wallenberg honorary United States citizenship. On October 5, 1981, President Ronald Reagan signed the resolution, and Raoul Wallenberg joined Winston Churchill, the only other recipient so honored.

In 1981 Per Anger published *With Raoul Wallenberg in Budapest,* a memoir of their collaboration in the rescue operations. He mentioned how difficult it was for all of them at the legation to have thousands of Jews jam the streets outside the courtyard of the legation, considering that the legation had numerous other assignments, and how difficult it had been to set priorities.

How many passports would be safe to issue? How far did we dare to bend the bow when we had no support from home? . . . all of us were aware, that in the worst event, it could end up costing us all our lives. Good triumphed, however, and the work was enabled right up to the end with utterly heroic contributions, especially by Wallenberg. (Anger 1981, 164, 165)

During the six short months he spent in Budapest, Wallenberg was able to save between 50,000 and 100,000 lives. He could have stayed in secure, neutral Sweden where he could have led a comfortable life; instead, he chose to travel to Budapest during the very last months of the war on a seemingly impossible mission: to save Jews.

He is remembered not only by those he saved, but also by those he inspired. One of them is Imre Varga, an internationally known sculptor—a former officer of the Hungarian Aircorps—who, through several visits made to Auschwitz in 1978 and 1979, has become what he calls "physically" involved with the Holocaust. Varga has created several commemorative sculptures, the most famous of which shows Raoul Wallenberg standing between the sections of a huge, split, pink granite rock (imported for this purpose from his birthplace in Sweden). The monument was erected on the Buda side of the city in 1987.

Eve Soumerai visited the monument and the sculptor in November 1997. Varga spoke of an artist's obligation to do what he believes. "It's

Raoul Wallenberg Memorial in Budapest. Courtesy of Eve Nussbaum Soumerai.

necessary to work on your dreams," he said. Many people aided Varga's efforts, including the American ambassador to Hungary, Nick M. Salgo, the well-known philanthropist Edgar Bronfman, and the actor Tony Curtis, whose parents came from Hungary.

Jewish Artifacts in Budapest

During her visit to the Jewish Museum in Budapest, Eve was told that the Judaic cups, Torah crowns, and other artifacts were saved by curators of the National Museum who packed the Jewish objects into boxes and labeled them "Religious Objects of the Roman Catholic Church" and stored them in the basement of the museum. Some of the Torah scrolls were saved by Franciscan monks.

FRANCE

The French Revolution of 1789 promised Liberty, Equality, and Fraternity to its people, including the Jews who lived in France, who went on to contribute to, and to prosper in, French society. Between the two world wars, France experienced a large influx of foreign Jews from Russia, Poland, Greece, and Turkey, and, during the Nazi period, Jewish refugees added to the numbers of foreign Jews. At the beginning of World War II, there were an estimated 350,000 resident Jews (1% of the entire population) in the country, about 165,000 of them who were foreign born.

At 6:30 P.M. on June 22, 1940, the French capitulated to the Germans, and France was divided into two zones: The Germans occupied the north; and Vichy, the "free" unoccupied zone in the south, was headed by the eighty-four-year-old Marshal Philippe Pétain, a World War I hero, who had accepted the terms of surrender on behalf of France. (After the end of World War II, Pétain was condemned to death, a sentence later commuted to life imprisonment.)

Although the Germans in the zone of occupation started the process of identifying Jews almost immediately, it took them almost two years, until May 29, 1942, until Jews over the age of six were ordered to wear the yellow star. Some objected. The BBC in London reported that French university students wore badges inscribed with JUIF (Jew), signifying Jeunesse Universitaire Intellectuelle Française (French intellectual university youth). Others chose to become informants. Anonymous poison-pen letters were sent to the authorities: "I have the honor to draw your attention, for whatever useful purpose it may serve, to the fact than an apartment at 57 Boulevard Rochechouart, belonging to Jew Gresalmer, contains very fine furniture" (Joseph 1989, 75).

On Thursday, July 16, 1942, La Grande Rafle (a roundup) of 12,884 Jews—men, women, and children—took place in Paris. By the end of that year, more than 42,000 had been deported to Auschwitz; about a third of them were from Vichy. The Pétain government had cooperated fully with the Germans and had instituted its own version of anti-Jewish laws. With one stroke of Marshal Pétain's pen, Jews had become an ethnic minority stripped of rights.

Serge Klarsfeld, head of the Association of French Jewish deportees, claimed that of the 76,000 Jews, including 10,000 children, who were sent to the camps, only 2,500 returned. Those who were saved managed to hide and escape, often illegally, to safe havens in Switzerland, Spain, and Portugal. What made deporting Jews from France difficult was that they were dispersed all over the country, unlike the Jews of Eastern Europe who were congregated in ghettos; roundups were much more difficult and time consuming.

Rescue operations also played a significant role. It is interesting to note that, in the Italian occupied zone of France, the Italian Fascist troops provided sanctuary for Jews and did not comply with German demands for deportation or with Vichy's anti-Semitic legislation.

Madame Marie-Rose Gineste

Madame Marie-Rose Gineste was born in a village near the small town of Montauban in what had become the occupied zone of France. Her house was only fifty meters from Gestapo headquarters, and she could hear the commotion of cars leaving and returning. She knew when they were rounding up Jews.

In August 1942, when the persecution of Jews intensified and the French Catholic Church debated whether to protest officially, Marie-Rose, though fearful for her own life, volunteered, at the urging of Monsignor Théas, head of the diocese, to ride her bicycle to hand deliver a letter of protest to every priest in a one-hundred-kilometer area. The letter stated that actions against the Jews were abhorrent and asked that the priests share these thoughts with their parishioners during services the next Sunday. All but one of the priests complied.

Monsignor Théas then asked Marie-Rose to find hiding places for every Jew in Montauban. Marie-Rose, who had become a member of the Resistance, put all of her energy into the search for shelters. She visited the convents in the area.

They wanted to take only children, but I convinced them to hide families. The Resistance stole food from farms and brought it to me in suitcases and I took it to the convents that were hiding Jews. A Jewish man named Levi came to me to ask if I could find friends . . . who could give money. I was able to find some money at the university to send to them. I acquired false documents from a comrade in the Resistance in Toulouse. . . . After October 1943, I had to begin to make the documents myself. . . . There was a vicar at the cathedral who gave me real baptism certificates. And on two occasions I even brought plastic explosives on my bicycle to Monsieur Ginesty, a painter in Moissac, who made them into bombs to blow up railroads and trains . . . . People still ask me why I helped. I guess it was a question of temperament . . . . The hardest thing for me was that I was putting my mother in danger . . . . Before the war I wasn't so patriotic, but during and after the war I was. I always said that if anything happens to me, put a tricolor flag in my coffin. (Block and Drucker 1992, 128–31)

Le Chambon-Sur Lignon: Pastor André Trocme, His Wife Magda, and Their Friends and Relatives

In 1976 the late Wesleyan University professor, Philip Hallie, was weary. As a teacher of ethics, after studying cruelty and patterns of persecution for so many years that he was beginning to feel damned himself, he came across a short article about a little village in southern France where, in his words, "goodness happened." As he read the article, he was surprised to find himself weeping. Thirty years after the liberation of France, he decided he had to visit the village "to seek good and not evil" (Hallie unpublished lecture, 1976). The result was his book *Lest Innocent Blood Be Shed* (1979) about a small Huguenot village that found the courage to save hundreds of Jews.

Le Chambon, in the "free" zone of France, a village of 3,000 inhabitants, was a Protestant enclave in a country of Roman Catholics. Less than one percent of the French population, they were descendants of the Huguenots who had come in the 1500s to practice their particular form of Christianity. Their ancestors, too, had suffered persecution; some had been hanged, others burned. For these reasons, and because they had lived their lives as pacifists, opposed to war, the villagers in Le Chambon wanted to help others escape persecution.

Why then, wondered Hallie, was the adjacent Protestant village of Le Mazet "dead" as far as aiding Jewish refugees was concerned? Hallie discovered that it was the leadership of Pastor André Trocme, who chose to resist evil actively that had attracted committed followers, *les responsables*, and succeeded in saving some 5,000 refugees, 2,000 more than the entire population of Le Chambon. About 3,500 of the refugees were Jewish, many of them children.

When the family of Pastor André Trocme and his wife Magda arrived in Le Chambon in 1934, the village seemed to be moving toward "death, death, death," noted Trocme in his notes. The villagers considered their lives to be *"neuf mois d'hiver, trois mois de misères"* (nine months of [bitterly cold] winter and three months of misery). The three months of "misery" meant they had to procure all the funds necessary to survive all year during the three short summer months when the tourists visited the area (Hallie 1979, 78).

Trocme decided to bring life to the village during the long winter as well as during the short summer months: With the help of his close friend Edouard Theis, he started the Cevenol School. Their goals were to prepare teenagers for higher learning while providing an infusion of moral concepts, including the practice of nonviolence.

Soon Jewish children from Central and Eastern Europe flocked to the school, where they too were taught how to be creative in resisting *le mal* (the evil) exemplified by Adolf Hitler and Germany. Classrooms were scattered throughout the village and beyond. Every small place was utilized. Magda Trocme, for instance, taught Italian, her mother tongue, in a large bathroom in the boardinghouse of *la famille Marion.*

In the winter of 1940, when the effects of Pétain's anti-Jewish decrees were being felt, the first Jewish refugee arrived at the door of Le Chambon's presbytery. It was a snowy, bitterly cold night when Magda Trocme heard the knock and opened the door. Outside stood a shivering woman covered in snow. She was visibly frightened and explained that she was a German Jew and in great danger. Magda, in spite of being aware that Pétain had ordered the surrender of foreign refugees and that the village might become a target for destruction, did not entertain a moment's doubt about what to do. She invited the woman to come in and eat and sit by the fire, while she searched for a home. The news spread and men, women, and children continued to arrive. Soon every home in the village harbored one or more of the refugees (obituary of Magda Trocme, *New York Times,* October 19, 1996).

At the same time, more and more Fascist decrees were issued by the Vichy government. Symbols of the French Revolution were to be taken off school walls and replaced by the portrait of *le chef de l'État Français le Marechal* Pétain, to whom allegiance was to be sworn daily. The flag of France was to be raised each morning, and students as well as teachers were obliged to stand at attention and to give the Fascist salute.

None of these decrees were ever obeyed in Le Chambon. The villagers were inspired by these acts of courage, and for a while the authorities at Vichy seemed unaware of their disobedience. Then, in the summer of 1942, Pétain insisted that youths spend eight months in training camps similar to the ones set up in Germany. Le Chambon's students ignored the request. When Vichy's minister of youth, Georges Lamirand, personally visited the village to find out why there was no compliance, a dozen students—some of whom would later become theologians—handed Lamirand a formal protest against the recent deportations of Jews:

Mr. Minister

We have learned of the frightening scenes which took place in Paris three weeks ago. We are afraid that the measures of deportation of the Jews will soon be applied in the Southern Zone. . . . We feel obliged to tell you that there are among us a certain number of Jews. But we make no distinction between Jews and non-Jews. It is contrary to the Gospel teaching. If our comrades, whose only fault is to be born in another religion, received the order to let themselves be deported, they would disobey the orders received and we would try to hide them as best we could. (Hallie 1979, 102)

Two weeks later, on a Saturday night, some khaki-colored buses, flanked by police motorcyclists, entered the village square. The chief of police of the department of Haute Loire confronted Trocme and told him that he must supply lists of names of the hidden Jews. They had twenty-four hours to supply the lists. Trocme refused, even though the police chief threatened him with deportation. Trocme was prepared for this sort of emergency. He had met with his Boy Scouts and Bible class leaders and had sent them out to warn the refugees and tell them to hide in the woods. The police searched every house without success. The buses left empty.

But the police continued to pay frequent visits to Le Chambon and to search the houses in the village, where they were received with food on the table and accompanying discussion on the merits of each human being. Only once were the police able to capture a person, who happened to be half Jewish, and was therefore released. There are many who remember, with much amusement, the khaki-colored buses returning with their catch—one lone passenger.

In 1943 Vichy's orders grew increasingly severe and almost put a stop to the activities at Le Chambon. One evening, Pastor Trocme had returned home from his pastoral duties when he found the chief of the gendarmes waiting for him with a "gloomy face and unpleasant news." He had come to arrest the pastor and his friend Edouard Theis. Madame Trocme remembered:

The police told me to take my time and collect everything he'd need, but they wouldn't allow me to inform any of the villagers. . . . Everyone found out what was going on that evening. And while we were sharing our dinner with the gendarmes . . . a procession of people came to the house with gifts; candles, tins of fish and meat all those things people put aside. . . . The most valuable gift to my husband turned out to be a roll of toilet paper into which had been put verses of the Bible—someone had taken the time to unroll the paper and conceal the pages. The presents made a small mountain on the table. Though there were candles, there were no matches: "Here," the chief of police said and lit the candles. When they left [with her husband and Theis] the whole group followed them down the little road singing the Lutheran hymn: "A Mighty Fortress is our God." (quoted in Latour 1981, 144–45).

Despite these arrests, the villagers were more dedicated than ever to the task of sheltering the Jews. Although Pastor Trocme and Edouard Theis were soon released, they were quite aware of the great danger they were facing and decided to hide in the mountains, where they kept themselves busy by smuggling refugees into Switzerland.

Daniel Trocme, a cousin of the pastor, was not so fortunate. He was in his mid-twenties and had a heart condition when he came to Le Chambon to help the cause. He had been put in charge of children whose parents had been deported, and he worked "like a madman" on their behalf, spending many evenings resoling their shoes using old automobile tires, and preparing vast amounts of soup for "his" children.

In the summer of 1943, the Gestapo arrived. By then, the Germans were in charge of the entire country. They arrested Daniel and his students. After the war, one of the former students returned to Le Chambon and told the Trocmes what had happened. Daniel had been questioned incessantly about his attitude and feelings toward Jews. Time and again he had affirmed his compassion and love for them. Soon, they were all sent to the death camp of Maidanek in Poland where, on April 4, 1944, at two o'clock in the morning, Daniel was killed. Even after his death, the Gestapo continued their investigation of Daniel Trocme. In May 1944, they sent an inquiry to the city hall where he was born to verify whether he had not in fact been born a Jew (Hallie 1979, 216).

Pastor Trocme was dedicated to absolute honesty. He refused to baptize Jews simply to escape anti-Semitic laws. He would convert people only as a result of religious conviction. There were other ways to escape anti-Semitic laws, he claimed. As for the children in his care, "During the Occupation, not one Jewish child received improper Christian upbringing. To not respect the consciences of children who had been entrusted us by parents who had disappeared, would have been abuse. What would give us such a right?" (quoted in Latour 1981, 141).

Au Revoir Les Enfants: Père Jacques of Le Petit Collège

Louis Malle's film *Au Revoir Les Enfants* (1987), considered by some to be his masterpiece, is an autobiographical account of a traumatic incident that occurred during World War II, during his youth in occupied France. The incident occurred when young Louis Malle was a student at the Petit Collège d'Avon, a Carmelite boarding school, fifty miles south of Paris, where he had been sent by his parents to escape the bombing raids made on the French capital. Three Jewish boys had been sent there in order to escape Nazi persecution. One of them, Hans Helmut Michel, known as Jean Bonnet in the film, had been born in Frankfurt, Germany. He and Louis enjoyed a growing friendship that was "all-to-brief, awkward, often silent" and ceased one bright day in January. Malle explained that the local chief of the Gestapo, acting on a tip, barged into their classroom to remove Michel and the other two boys. They also "collected" Père Jacques, the school's headmaster and took them all away.

This was the day young Louis Malle discovered "evil" and said farewell to his childhood. "The event burned" in his memory all of his life. It took him forty years to transform the experience into the film. On February 7, 1988, prior to the opening of the film, Malle was interviewed by Richard Bernstein of the *New York Times:*

"I was a very good student but he [Michel] was always a little in front of me. We were both very shy, and he stayed away from having any sort of deep relationship because he didn't want to give away who he was, but I know that I felt he was going to become my best friend."

Mr. Malle remembers what happened in every detail. At the school, a stairway led from the courtyard up to a platform, and eventually out of the school, and it was from that dramatic elevated point that Père Jacques, accompanied by Bonnet, the two other boys, and his Nazi guards turned toward the school and bid the children: "Au revoir et à bientôt—Goodbye and see you soon."

"He gave us a great smile," said Mr. Malle, "and then something took place which was very bizarre. Somebody started to applaud and then everybody was applauding, despite the shouts of the Gestapo to keep quiet."

Only in 1945, when the war ended and the three Jewish boys did not come back—the priests, Mr. Malle remembers, led the students in prayers for them.

Years later, people at the school found out what had happened. The group was sent to Drancy, the French transition camp, and two weeks later, on February 3, 1944, the three boys were put on convoy 67, consisting of 1,214 people, destined for Auschwitz. When the Russians liberated Auschwitz in January 1945, only 26 of the people on that convoy were still alive. The three boys from Le Petit Collège had been sent to the gas chambers upon arrival.

Père Jacques, born Lucien Bunel in 1900 and ordained a priest in the Carmelite order in 1925, who had also been arrested that day, was not singled out for extermination. He was sent instead to the Mauthausen camp in Austria where he became well known as a result of his tireless efforts to help and console other inmates. When the camp was liberated by American troops, an exhausted Père Jacques was sent to recuperate in a hospital in the city of Linz. He died there on June 2, 1945, one week after being freed from captivity.

The Carmelite order in Paris published a brief biography about his life that contains some of his quotes including, "We are Carmelites only for this: to love, to love of course, but to do so giving proof of our love" (Bernstein 1988).

POLAND

One of the reasons Germany chose Poland as the site of the death camps was, with 3.5 million Jews (out of a population of 33 million), it had the largest, most vital Jewish community in all of Europe. The Germans reasoned that the concentration of the large numbers of Jews would save on transportation costs. In addition, Poland's long tradition of anti-Semitism would most likely ensure that few objections to the mass murders would be raised. A telling example of this anti-Semitism can be found in the memoir of Alexander Donat in which he describes the reaction of ordinary Poles— bystanders—to the burning of the Warsaw ghetto on Easter Sunday: "Mass over, the holiday crowds poured into the sun-drenched streets . . . . Bemused the crowd stared at the hanging curtains of flame . . . and whispered to one another. 'But the Jews—they are being roasted alive.' Pain-crazed figures leaped from balconies and windows to smash on the streets below . . . and the crowds cheered" (Donat 1965, 153).

Nevertheless, more than 2,000 Polish rescuers have been honored at Yad Vashem, and there were doubtless many more. They were peasants, intellectuals, housekeepers, and sometimes strangers who happened to be in the right place when they were needed.

Stefan Raczynski

Stefan Raczynski belonged to a farming family of devout Catholics living near Vilna. He remembered seeing the Nazis shoot the Jews from a nearby town and how they fell into the ditches "like matches" (quoted in Block and Drucker 1992, 199). Some of the people who managed to escape knew that the Raczynski family were good people and would shelter them. In spite of being afraid that they would be found out, the family took in forty people at various times. For the very religious Jews the family provided special plates of dairy food. One of them prayed so loud "you could hear him two kilometers away" (200). Stefan said. The neighbors knew and there were constant searches, which meant the Jews in hiding had to run regularly to the forest and disappear into holes dug for this purpose in the earth. The holes were hidden by trees and leaves so no one would notice.

Stefan remembered happy occasions, such as his mother's preparing a Hanukkah ceremonial dinner and everybody sitting together enjoying the food and singing songs in Polish, Yiddish, and Hebrew, while Stefan volunteered to stand guard outside. He said, "It was like gambling . . . we only lived until tomorrow" (199–200).

Irene Gut Opdyke

Irene Gut Opdyke, a Polish Catholic, liked helping people. Her mother had never turned away anyone in need. During the German occupation, Irene risked her life hiding 12 Jews. She met them while doing laundry for the Gestapo at Ternapol, where she was a housekeeper for a German major. In the half-hour film *The Courage to Care* (1986), a United Way production for the United States Holocaust Memorial, she tells her story:

At that time I was serving breakfasts and luncheons to the German officers and their secretaries. . . . Behind that hotel there was a ghetto and for the first time I realized what was happening to the Jewish people. . . . They pushed them like cattle through the middle of town. I did see old men that looked to me like rabbis with the white beards and white hair and most of all the children all sizes, all ages . . . crying, "Mama, mama." And I remember their eyes searching and asking, "What did I do?" And then I prayed and promised I would help. . . . And then I met twelve Jewish people and we became good friends. But when the time came for the total liquidation of the ghetto, they had no place to go. And you know the next day in the morning the major called me to his office [and said] "I would like you to be my housekeeper." . . . When I did see the villa, I made a decision . . . to put those twelve in the cellar. In September I was in town and all of a sudden the Gestapo was pushing the people to the marketplace [to] witness a Polish family hung together with a Jewish family. And we did have to stay to watch, to be a warning, what happened when you befriended a Jew. When I came home I locked the door. But usually I leave the key in the lock because when the major came home unexpectedly, he couldn't unlock the door. I was so shook up. I came to the kitchen and there were Ida, Franka, Clara, Miriam. The women came out because that's what they usually did, to help me. I was white as snow. They asked me what happened. I said, "Nothing." I could not tell them. We were talking and the major stood in front. I can still see his chin shaking and his eyes with unbelief. We were all frozen like statues. . . . I have to go and face him. There was no other way. He yelled, "Irene how could you do it? I trusted you, gave you protection." "I know only one thing, they are my friends . . . I do not have a home. I do not have a family. Forgive me but I would do it again. Nobody has a right to kill or murder because of race or religion." "You know what will happen to you?" "I know I just witnessed." I was crying. I could hardly talk. [He said] "I cannot do this to you. I just cannot let you die. . . . " When he said that, believe me, I knelt down and kissed his hand. Not for me but for these people. They were alive and they had hope. (*The Courage to Care* 1985)

Instead of being killed, as the 12 hidden people had feared, they were able to stay on, but for a price Irene was willing to pay; she became the major's mistress. Irene never told her friends. Life went on. The major became accustomed to the "guests" and started to enjoy their cooking and baking. He called them by their first names. They in turn called him "Grandpa." They stayed together until February 1944, when the Russians marched into Poland and the villa had to be evacuated. They escaped into the forest where they stayed until the Russians arrived and freed them (Fogelman 1994, 168).

Jan Karski

Jan Karski, an intellectual and an academic, was born in 1914 in Lodz, Poland. He had lost his father while he was a child, but at the age of twelve he acquired a mentor—a Jesuit priest—who taught him the importance of individual choice and responsibility to society and the Lord.

While a student at the gymnasium (high school), he established close friendships with Jewish students. He studied law and political science at Lvov University, and after graduating with high honors, he accepted an important position in the Polish Foreign Office, which in 1942 led to his involvement with the Polish underground and the Polish government in exile in London.

One day he was visited by two Jewish leaders who asked him to take word about the systematic killing of the Jewish population to the Allied leaders. They suggested that he visit the Warsaw ghetto to see for himself. He reported that "the streets were packed with humanity and its remnants . . . The cries of the mad and hungry echoed through the streets, mingled with the voices of residents offering to barter scraps of clothing for morsels of food. . . . Strewn in the gutters were the bodies of the old and the young, all as naked in death as they had been in birth" (Wood and Jankowski 1994, 122).

That night, sickened by what he had seen, he vomited blood and decided he had to do whatever he could to help. He would inform the leaders that if they waited to do something until the war was over, it would be too late for millions of Jews. Money, too, was essential for rescue efforts. Furthermore, he suggested that millions of leaflets be dropped all over Germany to inform the population that if these killings did not stop, their cities would be bombed.

In London, he was able to meet with Foreign Minister Anthony Eden who told him that Great Britain had already done all it could by accepting 100,000 Jews. In Washington, D.C., Supreme Court Justice Felix Frankfurter arranged a meeting between Karski and President Franklin Roosevelt. Karski was most impressed by the president even though he offered no specifics about what he might do. Roosevelt did ask Karski to tell the Jews that they had a friend in the White House and to reassure them that the war would be won and the perpetrators punished (Block and Drucker 1992, 172–73).

Karski often wondered whether his mission had accomplished anything, but, thirty-five years later, he happened to read the comments of John Pehle, a key player in the creation of the War Refugee Board. Apparently, four months after Karski's visit, the president had given the go-ahead for the War Refugee Board. Although there were many reasons for this development, Karski's words, according to Pehle, had shaken the president and had had a significant impact. It was this board that had made possible Raoul Wallenberg's heroic efforts on behalf of the Hungarian Jews.

Karski spent his life teaching. He became a professor of Eastern European political studies at Georgetown University, in Washington, D.C. He also spent much of his time encouraging Jewish children to believe in humanity, in the many individuals—priests, nuns, peasants, and intellectuals—who had actively helped the Jewish people. He also reminded non-Jews that everyone is vulnerable, including Catholics. The pride and joy of his life was the medal and the tree he planted at Yad Vashem, honoring him as a righteous gentile.

In October 1981 an International Liberators' Conference, sponsored by the United States Holocaust Memorial Council, brought together former Allied soldiers who had taken part in the liberation of the Nazi camps.

The "star" was Jan Karski who spoke publicly about his Jewish mission for the first time:

The Lord assigned me a role to speak and write during the war, when—as it seemed to me—it might help. It did not. Furthermore, when the war came to an end, I learned that the governments, the leaders, the scholars, the writers did not know what had been happening to the Jews. . . . Then I became a Jew. Like the family of my wife—all of them perished in the ghettos, in the concentration camps, in the gas chambers—so all murdered Jews became my family. But I am a practicing Christian Jew. I am a practicing Catholic . . . my faith tells me the second original sin has been committed by humanity; through commission, or omission, or self-imposed ignorance, or insensitivity. . . . This sin will haunt humanity to the end of time. (Wood and Jankowski, 1994)

Emanuel Tanay

Most of the individuals whose stories are told here have been honored at Yad Vashem, but there are also many who helped save Jews but remain unrecognized. The following story is about such an individual.

Emanuel Tanay, a Polish-born Jew, told the story of how he was saved, in the film *Courage to Care* (1985). A teenager, he had been hidden in a monastery outside of Cracow. After a year and a half, someone denounced him and he had to run for his life. On his way through a village not far from the monastery, he tried to contact some friends by telephone. The public telephone in the village was located at the house of the village elder, a total stranger. Suddenly, the police arrived and, because of partisan activity in the neighborhood, asked Emanuel to raise his hands while they searched his pockets. Then one of the men said, "This kid looks like a Jew" and asked him for the documents that everybody had to carry. Emanuel said he had left them at home. The village elder volunteered the information that the boy was the son of so-and-so in the village and that he personally knew him well. There was a fine for such forgetfulness, which the village elder paid for Emanuel, without hesitation. "Another close call," said Emanuel. "Without people who helped it would have been impossible to survive." (*The Courage to Care* 1985)

Oscar Schindler

Oscar Schindler, who is the subject of the film *Schindler's List* (1993), directed by Steven Spielberg and set in Cracow where these events took place, was born in 1908 in the small industrial town of Zwittau, then part of the Austro-Hungarian empire. Ten years later, in post-World War I Europe, it became part of a new nation, Czechoslovakia, and Schindler became a German Czech—a Sudeten German.

Tall and handsome, Oscar loved women, wine, gambling, and making lots of money. When Hitler invaded Poland on September 1, 1939, Schindler attached his swastika pin to the lapel of his silk suit and followed the fuehrer to Cracow, the beautiful medieval city in southern Poland that was home to 60,000 Jews, twenty-six percent of the city's population.

Within a few weeks, the Jews had lost the right to attend school, keep bank accounts, or own businesses, transforming Poland into a land of economic opportunity for German entrepreneurs such as Schindler, who took charge of an idled enamelware plant, the Rekord factory, and renamed it the Deutsche Email Fabrik (DEF) (German Enamel Factory). Bribes in the form of lavish gifts—cognac, jewelry, expensive clothing, and sumptuous dinner parties—brought him many contacts as well as contracts, especially from the German army. Because his aim was to make a lot of money, Schindler asked for and received the necessary permission to expand "his" plant. Soon, with the help of the plant's original accountant, Itzhak Stern, a Jew, the number of employees swelled to 250 including many Jews and their families, who were looking for safe havens.

In March 1941, Jews from the city and countryside were forced from their homes into the Cracow ghetto, which was sealed off from the rest of the city by a wall topped with a barbed-wire fence. The ghetto was extremely crowded, but bearable. Occupants were given special permits to work outside the ghetto, sometimes scrubbing latrines in the German barracks, sometimes working in German-run plants such as Schindler's. Soon the sick, the old, and the young began to disappear and, by October 1942, the number of deaths had increased. Thousands had been sent to the Belzec death camp; many had died of malnutrition and other diseases; still others had been killed outright. Well aware of the ever-increasing horror engulfing the Jews, Schindler added several hundred more Jews to his company (named Emalia by its workers) and also added a new line of products, the manufacture of antitank shells, to his ever-expanding operations. No one would ever have the slightest doubt about his plant's usefulness to the German war machine.

Two events had led Schindler away from his focus on personal gain and toward helping Jews. One event occurred during a glorious June morning when Schindler and his mistress were riding horses in the hills above the ghetto and stopped to witness an "action" happening below them. A crowd of human beings was being driven into the streets and separated into columns. In one column, women and many children were being led away by a guard who walked in front while another brought up the rear. Suddenly Schindler noticed a toddler in a red coat, all by herself, dawdling behind.

Adding to the confusion were SS teams and their dogs sniffing out those trying to hide and shooting them on the spot. While one woman was being shot, a crying boy slid down a wall, apparently trying to reach her. An SS officer jammed his boot down on the boy's head, as if to hold it in place, and put the barrel of his gun against the back of his neck—and fired. Schindler looked again at the little girl in red who had stopped to see the boot descend on the boy's neck. And in one of those moments of total comprehension, Schindler realized that the little girl in red was permitted to see this sickening spectacle because the Germans' grand plan included the killing of every single Jew, including the toddler in the red coat (Keneally 1993, 129).

The other pivotal event was the return from the Belzec death camp of a young pharmacist named Bachner. He told Schindler what he had witnessed: naked victims being driven to their deaths down a barbed-wire passage to bunkers labeled "Baths and Inhalation Rooms" while SS men reassured them that by inhaling deeply they would be disinfected. Somehow Bachner had been able to save his own skin by hiding for three days, inside a latrine, up to his neck in human waste. His face, he said, had been a hive of flies (1993, 136).

March 23, 1943, was the set date for the liquidation of the Cracow ghetto. During January and February, Jews had been forced to work on the construction of Plaszow, a new slave labor camp located two or three kilometers from the ghetto (Weitz 1993, 30). The entire operation was under the command of the newly arrived SS Untersturmfuehrer Amon Goeth.

Murray Pantirer, one of Schindler's workers, remembered Goeth's first day on the job: Goeth came on a Friday morning and the first thing he did was to take everybody on the Appellplatz and [there] shoot Katz the OD [Ordnungsdienst or Jewish policeman] and Goldberg [another OD]. He took a hatful of [their] blood and put it over one of our friend's head that he should be the successor. (Brecher 1994, 185)

(Amon Goeth was captured by the American forces in February 1945. At the time, he was a patient in an SS sanitarium at Bad Tolz. He was imprisoned at Dachau and, at the end of the war, he was handed over to the new Polish government and tried before their supreme court on a charge of committing mass murder. He was sentenced to death and hanged in Crakow in 1946. He was thirty-six years old.)

Although the Plaszow camp was not far away from the factory, Schindler's workers were now forced to live behind barbed wire and were unable to arrive for work on time, which provided Schindler with an excuse for proposing that a subcamp be built in the backyard of his factory. He argued that this would be more advantageous to the war effort because his workers would be closer to their work. Even though he had begun to abhor Goeth, Schindler was able to hide his feelings, drink with him, throw parties for him, and shower him with lavish gifts—all designed to get Goeth's support. During one of their meetings, Schindler witnessed teams of women hauling limestone. Those who stumbled or were too slow were trampled upon, a sight that filled Schindler with a nausea similar to what he had experienced while watching the toddler in the red coat (Keneally 1993, 171).

Unlike the major extermination camps like Belzec and Auschwitz, Plaszow did not have gas chambers or crematoria, but mass killings occurred there nonetheless. People were shot on a hill called Hojowa Gorka, and their bodies were dumped in a nearby ravine.

In August 1944, the breakup of the camp was underway and Schindler was ordered to reduce his workforce by 700 people. Prisoners were being transferred to other camps and extermination centers, including Auschwitz, the largest one, which was located thirty-seven miles west of Cracow (Weitz 1993, 37).

In September 1944, Schindler was told that the Emalia subcamp must be closed and the remaining 300 workers sent to Plaszow for "relocation." There was very little time to save anybody, yet Schindler managed to devise a way. First, he drew up a list of the 300 workers still reporting to him and then added 700 additional names, replacements for those shipped out in August. In all, he came up with the names of 800 men and 300 women. He met with Goeth to ask for permission to relocate his skilled workers to a site in Brinnlitz, a village in Moravia near the town of his birth. He was willing to accept responsibility for all costs. Goeth had no objections as long as Schindler obtained the necessary permission from SS headquarters in Berlin. Again substantial bribes helped put this plan into operation.

By mid-October, the men and women on Schindler's list were able to board freight trains destined for Brinnlitz, with intermediary stops in Auschwitz for the women, and camp Groess-Rosen—originally built for criminals and political prisoners—for the men. Schindler was aware of the stops, but he did not expect them to be as lengthy as they turned out to be. Again he needed to come up with substantial bribes to free "his skilled workers."

Chaskel Schlesinger recalled his experiences at Groess-Rosen. He particularly remembered the showers: the barrels with detergent and the few drops of water that made "your whole body red."

We stood outside naked. The bosses were German criminals from jail. They gave you a nightgown, a pair of striped pants, a jacket and a pair of shoes. . . . One of the soles was open. [We] went from freezing outdoors to sweltering inside an over-crowded barrack. . . . They had fifty bowls for the whole group. You had to stand in line, come and get it and pass it to the next one and if you didn't do it fast enough, they knocked the bowl from your hands. The beating was all day long. Finally they took us to the train and gave us soup. It was grass and water not cooked. (Brecher 1994, 134–35)

The women were forced to stay for three weeks at Auschwitz and worried about whether they would ever be able to leave. In one of the most dramatic scenes from Spielberg's film, based on Thomas Keneally's thoroughly researched account also called *Schindler's List,* the women are stripped, shaved, and locked into a windowless room. Above them are shower heads. Somebody pulls a switch; the lights go out. The women scream. Water blasts from the jets. There is sudden relief and joy. Women later interviewed confirmed that this event actually happened (Brecher 1994, xxxi).

Rena Ferber Finder, one of "Schindler's women," recalled these events:

We could actually sit on the train. I remember cradling the head of a young sick girl on my lap. Someone caught snowflakes which I put on her parched lips. The men had already arrived and there waiting for us was Oscar Schindler wearing a Tyrolean hat in honor of his native mountains. As usual he was smiling. He was so dashing. He reminded me of Clark Gable. Many of the girls had a crush on him. You could tell he liked us—that's why he did the most unpopular thing—saving us. He also liked gambling, winning. The Auschwitz commandant let us go because [Schindler] dispatched a young beautiful secretary with diamonds to bribe him. (Finder 1997)

In spite of the camp, the barbed wire, and the presence of the SS, Schindler's workers felt safe under the direction of their Herr Direktor. "We were hungry but not starving. We were cold but not freezing and he was always there," (Finder 1997) explained Rena.

Sometimes Schindler did extraordinary things. Cantor Mosche Taube, one of the workers, recalled how somehow he was able to secure a single *tefillin* (a black leather case with straps within which is a prayer written on parchment) for the extremely religious Mr. Jereth, who was then able to organize daily prayer sessions. Many of the workers waited patiently for their turn and passed the *tefillin* from one to the other while reciting the customary benedictions and blessings (Brecher 1994, 212).

Oscar Schindler's wife, Emilie, became a welcome presence to the worker-prisoners at Brinnlitz. She helped comfort and nurse the sick and the anxious. According to Canadian journalist Herbert Steinhouse, who interviewed Schindler extensively, Oscar and Emilie never spent a single night in their comfortable villa at Brinnlitz. They preferred to sleep instead in a small room in the factory because Oscar understood how deeply the Jews feared late-night visits by the SS (1994, xxxiv).

On January 29, 1945, Schindler was told about a locked goods wagon marked "property of the SS" at the station near his factory at Brinnlitz. The wagon had been traveling for days and was covered with thick ice. Inside were more than 100 Jewish men and women from Birkenau in a frozen state resembling corpses. Schindler had no authority to claim the wagon, but again he demonstrated his skill and daring. He approached the railway official in charge for the bill of lading, and, while the man was checking to see whether this was proper, Schindler quickly scribbled "Final destination Brinnlitz" on the bill and declared that the wagon was

Group portrait of female office workers employed by Oscar Schindler at his Emalia enamelware factory in Cracow, Poland. Prof. Leopold Pfefferberg-Page, courtesy of USHMM Photo Archives.

intended for his factory. He then ordered the railway authorities to transfer the wagon to his factory siding. When he and some helpers pried the doors open, they found 16 of the occupants had frozen to death and none weighed more than thirty-five kilos (less than sixty pounds) (Gilbert 1985, 777). Emilie arranged for beds, nursed them, and fed them teaspoons of farina until they were able to digest more (Finder 1997).

The guns ceased firing and the bombs stopped dropping at midnight on May 9, 1945. The Third Reich, responsible for the slaughter of millions upon millions of human beings, had simply ceased to exist. Herr Direktor Schindler, now considered an enemy wartime profiteer, was ready to leave the camp at Brinnlitz to avoid being captured by the Russians who were about to arrive. He set up radio loudspeakers and called the workers together to listen to Winston Churchill's dramatic announcement declaring an end to hostilities. Schindler said farewell: "The unconditional surrender of Germany has just been announced. After six years of the cruel murder of human beings, victims are being mourned. I would like to turn to all of you who together with me have worried through many hard years" (Keneally 1993, 385). His workers had a surprise for their Herr Direktor: a gold ring made out of Mr. Jereth's gold tooth and bridgework. Inside the ring, one of the workers had carefully engraved the Hebrew words of the Talmudic verse: "Whosoever saves a single soul, it is as if he had saved the whole world." Touched by the gift, Oscar Schindler asked for a translation of the verse and wanted to know where the gold had come from. Jereth opened his mouth wide and showed the empty spaces that had housed the gold.

Armed with a letter attesting to his good deeds and signed by "his" workers, Oscar, his wife Emilie, and eight "worker-volunteers" to protect them left Brinnlitz. A few days later they ran into a group of American infantry men, including several Jewish soldiers and a field rabbi, who were deeply touched by the story they were told. The regimental commander and the rabbi hosted the Schindler party for two days at the Austrian border. They enjoyed quite a feast—and were safe.

There was one more surprise. Schindler had made arrangements to give out three yards of cloth and a bottle of vodka to his "children." Rena Finder called it "our dowry." With these items she managed to bridge the gap between nothing and a new life.

The *Schindlerjuden* (Schindler Jews) became Oscar's family. When, after the war, Schindler's various attempts to start new businesses failed and he became penniless, the "family" took over. He made many trips to Israel. On July 18, 1967, Yad Vashem, a Holocaust memorial museum and center for study in Jerusalem, decided to recognize Oskar Schindler as Righteous Among the Nations.

In October 1974, Schindler collapsed and died in his small apartment in Frankfurt, Germany. He had asked to be buried in Jerusalem, and, within two weeks of his death, his leaden casket was flown to Jerusalem. It was carried by some of his "workers" through the crammed streets of the Old City to the Catholic cemetery that overlooks the Valley of Hinnom, called Gehenna in the New Testament. Among those who paid their last respects were many *Schindlerjuden*, including his accountant Itzhak Stern. Schindler was mourned on every continent. He saved more than 1,100 lives. If one adds their descendants, the number becomes 6,000 (Keneally 1993, 397). It is worth noting that, in the whole of Poland, once the country of 3,250,000 Jews, there now live approximately 4,000.

RIGHTEOUS MUSLIMS

Robert Satloff, the executive director of the Washington Institute of Near East Policy, wrote a book entitled *Among the Righteous* targeting audiences in the Arab world: "not the jihadists but the vast middle who are either ignorant or disinterested. They are the people on the front lines." The reaction from them has been overwhelmingly positive. One of the most poignant responses from an Arab was, "Thank you for telling the stories of heroes, but thank you also for telling the stories of villains. It is important for the world to know that we Arabs are not cardboard cutouts."

On 9/11, the puff of smoke emerging from the north tower reminded him of the chimneys of Auschwitz. His book tells stories of Arabs whose unusual kindness for Jews involved taking them into their homes, nursing Jewish babies, saving Jewish lives. He hopes his book will kindle curiosity about the persecution of Jews in North Africa during World War II as well as about Righteous Muslims.

Source: U.S. News and World Report, December 11, 2006, 28.

DENMARK

Denmark was the one occupied country in Europe that went all out, from king to commoner, to save her Jewish population.

Before dawn on April 9, 1940, Germany invaded Denmark. Foreign Minister Joachim von Ribbentrop, in an outrageous pronouncement, declared that the Reich had come to the aid of Denmark in order to protect it against Anglo-French occupation and then asked "would they accept on the instant and without resistance, the 'Protection of the Reich'?" (Shirer 1960, 697). Pleasant little country, incapable of defending itself against the German military might, had little choice. Because the Danes were considered Aryans by the Germans, their country would become the model protectorate. The king, the courts, parliament, and the press were, at least in the beginning, allowed a great deal of freedom. So were Denmark's 7,000 Jews (697–700).

Nevertheless, the Germans were busy ferreting out names of Jews. They searched through birth registers, telephone books, and other directories to compile their lists. This was a difficult task because Danes were not listed by their religious affiliation, and it was not always possible to tell by names alone who was a Jew.

By the fall of 1943, the possibility existed that Germany might lose the war. Danish resistance increased, and German activities took an ominous turn. On September 17, the Gestapo confiscated a list of names from Jewish community records, signaling that trouble was brewing. On September 28, Hans Hedtoft, a leader of the Danish Social Democratic Party, was alerted by a German naval attaché, Georg Ferdinand Duckwitz, that an "action" was about to take place. The German plan was to ship all the Danish Jews to the Theresienstadt concentration camp. Immediately, members of the growing resistance movement went to work. The chief rabbi, Marcus Melchior, of the Copenhagen synagogue, who was preparing the Rosh Hashanah (Jewish New Year) service, was alerted. The very next day, on September 29, the rabbi told the startled congregation during services to leave Copenhagen at once and go into hiding (Werstein 1967, 68–69). Within two days, rescue operations went into full swing with the full cooperation of the entire population:

The Gestapo could not make a move without being reported. Children playing in the street spied on the Germans. Policemen, postmen, street sweepers, housewives, shopkeepers, bankers, bakers, students, doctors, the old, the young, the healthy, the sick—an entire population—closed ranks to foil the Germans and to save the Jews. (Werstein 1967, 70)

A good example of the sort of ingenuity and dedication exercised was a plan conceived by Dr. K. H. Koster, a junior surgeon on the staff of the 1,200-bed Bispebjerg Hospital just outside of Copenhagen. He and his colleagues contacted every general practitioner in Copenhagen to ask them to advise their Jewish patients to come to the hospital. From there, arrangements were made to transport them to Sweden. Since the Germans used their own medical facilities, hospitals were a safe gathering point. Every detail was planned carefully, such as warning taxi fleet owners not to dispatch pro-German drivers to transport Jews to the hospital. As a result, not a single Jew was captured en route. Hospitals throughout the area joined the effort. Ambulances transported the men, women, and children to the coast.

Students closed down Copenhagen University and secondary schools to search for and alert Jews who might be hiding in the countryside. Danish ministers broadcast appeals to their parishioners not to cooperate with the Germans (Fein 1979, 148–49).

Swedish and Finnish vessels, operating between Copenhagen and Swedish ports, stood by, ready to receive and shuttle their human cargo to safety.

Jewish refugees being ferried out of Denmark aboard a Danish fishing boat bound for Sweden in October 1943. Frihedsmuseet, courtesy of USHMM Photo Archives.

Every type of vehicle, from farm carts to Red Cross ambulances, was employed to bring the refugees from hospital hideouts to the seacoast where they were picked up by trawlers, fishing boats and a motley flotilla of seaborne conveyances. A Copenhagen man who fled to Sweden . . . recalled years later . . . that he would not have been surprised to see "Noah's Arc crossing the Sound, there were so many strange-looking craft on the water." (Werstein 1967, 7273)

On Friday night, October 1, 1943, the German action began. The results were disappointing from their point of view. Their records show that a mere 284 (out of 7,000) Jews were seized that day, which included 30 from an old-age home next door to the synagogue. The Danish writer Erling Foss wrote:

The old-age home next to the synagogue in Krystalgade was surrounded by 150 men and all the inmates aged from sixty to ninety, were taken away. . . . They burst into the room of an old lady who had been bedridden for eleven years and since she could not get up, they bound her with leather straps and dragged her to the synagogue where all the old people were assembled. (quoted in Meltzer 1988, 93–94)

Immediately after the action, on October 2, Bishop Fuglsang-Damgaard of Copenhagen declared that Jews and Christians were people related by sacred history:

Wherever persecutions are undertaken for racial or religious reasons against the Jew, it is the duty of the Christian Church to raise a protest against it for the following reasons: Because we shall never be able to forget that the Lord of the Church, Jesus Christ, was born in Bethlehem, of the Virgin Mary into Israel, the people of his possession . . . the Old Testament is part of our Bible. (cited in Fein 1979, 114)

It was not the first time the bishop had spoken up. After *Kristallnacht* in 1938, he publicly denounced the persecution, which he described as the "poisonous pestilence of anti-Semitism," and he added these words, "Those who love Him cannot hate His people" (quoted in Fein 1979, 115).

Because of the Danes' determination and support of their Jewish population, some Germans, beginning with G. F. Duckworth, actually followed their example. One commander grounded the German Coast Guard vessels patrolling the ports so that apprehension of "illegal" fishing vessels was delegated to the Danes (1979, 50).

Some Danish collaborators and informers threatened death to anyone caught in the rescue operations; they were told that "first informers would be sent a funeral wreath; if this did not help, they were sent a card on which was drawn a cross of the type engraved on tombstones; then they were sent a tiny model of a coffin" (quoted in Fein 1979, 151).

Less than two percent of the Jews were caught in flight. Some who participated in the rescue efforts were rewarded in ways they could not have

Group portrait of Danish-Jewish children living in a Swedish children's home after their escape from Denmark (1943–1944). Frihedsmuseet, courtesy of USHMM Photo Archives.

foreseen. Aage Bertelson, leader of a resistance group, recalled his and his wife's reactions:

I remember particularly one night late in October. We were walking along the beach after having sent the last boat off to the ship. . . . For fourteen days in succession we had shared the same experience, but nevertheless the finished embarkation filled our souls each time with this peculiar intense feeling of happiness. . . . My wife participated only once in an embarkation, bound as she was night and day by the hard toil at "the office" [resistance]. We agreed no matter what happens to us, we could not have done without that period. "No, because it's like this," said [wife] Gerda very quietly, "It's as if we never realized before what it means to live." (quoted in Fein 1979, 151)

Approximately 400 Jews were sent to Theresienstadt from Denmark. The Danish government kept track of them. They lodged complaints with the German authorities, sent them packages, and asked repeatedly for permission to allow members of the Danish Red Cross to inspect the camp. This was finally granted in June 1944. Because of the persistent interest shown, not one of the interned Danish Jews was sent to Auschwitz. At the end of the war, 51 had died of natural causes; the others were able to return and resume their normal lives. Rabbi Melchior remembered the day he returned to Denmark: "When we returned, our fellow Danes did say 'welcome back' . . . with open arms and hearts. Our homes, our businesses, our property and money had been taken care of and returned to us. In most cases we found our homes newly painted, and there were flowers on the table" (Melchior 1963, 254).

There is a Talmudic saying that it takes 36 righteous individuals to save the world. In every occupied country, including Germany, there were many more than 36. It is also true that they were vastly outnumbered by the many who seemed to enjoy torturing and murdering the many millions of men, women, and little children. And the murderers were again outnumbered by those who watched, who knew and did nothing. They argued that it was not their problem. It was a Jewish problem. Still others—anonymous individuals—gave water to a nursing mother begging for water, gave a home to an outcast family, gave reassuring words to a frightened child, and gave a warm coat to a prisoner in Auschwitz.

The Bible tells us that God created man in His image and gave him free will—the ultimate gift.

WORKS CITED

Anger, Per. *With Raoul Wallenberg in Budapest.* New York: Holocaust Library, 1981.

Bernstein, Richard. "Malle Confronts Haunting Memory." *The Arts. The New York Times*, February 7, 1988.

Bierman, John. *Righteous Gentile.* New York: Viking Press, 1981.

Block, Gay, and Malka Drucker. *Rescuers.* New York: Holmes and Meier, 1992.

Brecher, Elinor J. *Schindler's Legacy.* New York: Penguin, 1994.

The Courage to Care. PBS Video, 1985.

Donat, Alexander. *Holocaust Kingdom: A Memoir.* New York: Holt Rinehart, 1965.

Fein, Helen. *Accounting for Genocide.* New York: Free Press, 1979.

Feingold, Henry. *Politics of Rescue.* New Brunswick, N.J.: Rutgers University Press, 1970.

Finder, Rena Ferber. Interview by Eve Soumerai, Framingham, Massachusetts, August 8, 1997.

Fogelman, Eva. *Conscience and Courage.* New York: Anchor Books, 1994.

Gilbert, Martin. *The Holocaust: A History of the Jews During the Second World War.* New York: Holt, Rinehart and Winston, 1985.

Hallie, Philip. *Lest Innocent Blood Be Shed.* New York: Harper Colophon Books, 1979.

Joseph, Jeremy. *Swastika over Paris.* New York: Arcade, 1989.

Keneally, Thomas. *Schindler's List.* New York: Simon and Schuster, 1993.

Latour, Annie. *French Jewish Resistance in France 1940–1944.* New York: Holocaust Library, 1981.

Marton, Kati. *Wallenberg: Missing Hero.* New York: Ballantine, 1982.

Melchior, Marcus. *Rescue in Denmark.* New York: Holocaust Library, 1963.

Meltzer, Milton. *Rescue.* New York: Harper Trophy, 1988.

"Obituary of Magda Trocme." *The New York Times,* October 19, 1996.

Shirer, William L. *The Rise and Fall of the Third Reich.* New York: Simon and Schuster, 1960.

Soumerai, Eve. Unpublished interview of Georges Passelecq. Brussels, Belgium, August, 1997.

U.S. News and World Report. December 11, 2006, 28.

Weitz, Sonia. *I Promised I Would Tell.* Brookline, Mass.: Facing History and Ourselves, 1993.

Werbell, Frederick, and Thurston Clarke. *Lost Hero: The Myth of Raoul Wallenberg.* New York: McGraw-Hill, 1982.

Werstein, Irving. *That Denmark Might Live.* Philadelphia: Macrae Smith, 1967.

Wood, Thomas E., and Stanislaw M. Jankowski. *Karski.* New York: John Wiley, 1994.

23

LIBERATION

APPROACHING DEFEAT

By the winter of 1944, it had become clear to Germany that the war was lost. The Soviets were advancing from the east, while the British and Americans were advancing from the west. Even in defeat, the Nazis were determined to carry out their mission of death. They forced the prisoners in various stages of starvation to march west through freezing mud, ice, and snow. Some had wooden shoes, others only rags covering their feet. If they fell or slipped, they were shot dead on the spot. In their hurry to move and cover their tracks, the SS (*Schutzstaffel*) tried to shoot everyone too sick to move—a task too vast to accomplish.

MAJDANEK: THE FIRST CAMP TO BE LIBERATED

On July 23, 1944, Majdanek in Poland was liberated by the Soviets. What they found there was a gigantic murder plant where the gas chambers were so tightly packed that people remained standing after they had been gassed, and individuals, too sick to move, had been tossed into the ovens along side of the corpses. Photographs taken by the Soviets, too horrible to view, were carefully censored by the Western press. Adolf Hitler, still in power at that time, along with some of the Allies, dismissed these early reports and accused the Soviets of fostering Communist propaganda (Berenbaum 1993, 183).

SOVIETS LIBERATE AUSCHWITZ AND OTHER CAMPS

In the afternoon of January 27, 1945, soldiers of the Red Army entered the vicinity of Auschwitz's main camp. They met resistance from retreating German units, which resulted in many Russian casualties, including two soldiers who were shot in front of the *Arbeit Macht Frei* sign on the main entrance. A Russian military physician organized assistance for the victims left to die, and the soldiers distributed their own bread (Czech 1990, 804). Still, many inmates died just before, during, or after the liberation of the camps. Eve Soumerai's brother and mother were among the victims.

In the confusion of those days some of the prisoners tried to escape. One of them was my seventeen-year-old brother Norbert, who had worked in the coal mines of one of the subcamps. He and a friend had made their way into Germany. They were apprehended and shot by German soldiers on May 18—ten days after the war had ended.

My mother died at Stutthof on January 5. Stutthof had once been a labor camp, but had become a death camp. I will never know whether she died in the camp or on one of those death marches. I do know she had just had her forty-fourth birthday. [Information about these events came in the form of a letter from the Service Internationale de Recherches, Comite Internationale de la Croix Rouge, on February 9, 1956.] I searched for years for news of my father. He simply disappeared. (Soumerai, 1980)

Full press coverage on the death camps and labor camps did not appear until May 1945. By that time, Russian troops had liberated Sachsenhausen, Ravensbrück, Stutthof, and Theresienstadt (Berenbaum 1993, 183–84).

GERDA WEISSMAN KLEIN DESCRIBES LIBERATION DAY

"Within an hour Red Cross trucks arrived and soldiers of the Fifth U.S. Infantry Division arrived. Their uniforms, their language, their kindness and concern made it true: we were finally free. Some soldiers carried girls in their arms like babies, speaking to them soothingly in words they did not understand."

Gerda was given a bath in a round wooden tub something that had not happened for years. She was able to save her most precious belonging: "a dirty shapeless package" containing the photos of her family before her clothes were burned. A nurse gave her a drink of milk.

Milk! She had not had for years. As she drank it, something happened. Her body shook convulsively. She wanted to stop it but could not. Then she heard a doctor say "let her cry it out."

> There was a sudden commotion. Nurses hurried in and cried, "Germany has capitulated. The war in Europe is over!"
>
> *Source:* Gerda Weissmann Klein. *All but My Life.* (New York: The Noonday Press 1957), 216–17.

THE BRITISH LIBERATE BERGEN-BELSEN

The British liberated Bergen-Belsen on April 15, 1945. Typhus, which killed Margot and Anne Frank, had ravaged the camp. Thousands of bodies lay rotting in the sun. Tank commander Robert Daniell and his crew had smashed through the gates of the camp on April 12, three days earlier. He had been given two hours to check out the camp, which was located a few miles north of Hanover. While walking around with a revolver in his hand, he shot the lock off one building, which turned out to be the hospital. What he saw affected him for the rest of his life.

"It was crammed with tiers of bunks on which lay starving sick and helpless people. Those in the bottom tiers had drowned in urine and excrement coming down from those on the top. . . . Five little children sat on the bare bloated corpse of a woman, playing. . . . I noticed an extremely well dressed woman, with an Alsation on a lead, behind me. She was Irma Grese, the guard who got her dog to tear little children to pieces." (She was later sentenced to death by a British military court.)

He then heard shots . . . there were Hitler Youth shooting prisoners so they would die in agony, the men in the groin and the women up the backside. . . . "I was so disgusted I shot them with the last four rounds I had. There was a huge trench with probably 3,000 corpses in it. Putrefying bodies give off gases which make the bodies move and the pile was heaving as if the dead were alive." (*Hartford Courant,* January 5, 1997)

The British took films of everything they saw during liberation. These films, shown throughout the world, brought the full extent of the events to the attention of the world community.

AMERICANS LIBERATE DACHAU AND OTHER CAMPS

The American forces liberated the camps of Dachau, Buchenwald, Nordhausen, Ohrdruf, Landsberg, and others in April and May 1945. Wherever they went, these men who were trained for combat tried to heal the victims, to give them a chance to live. In spite of these efforts, many died during and after liberation. Most of the inmates were infected with typhus and other diseases, and their bodies were too weak to process the sudden intake of food.

American soldiers of the U.S. 7th Army force German boys—believed to be Hitler Youth—to examine boxcars containing bodies of prisoners starved to death by the SS in Dachau, April 30, 1944. National Archives, courtesy of USHMM Photo Archives.

As they entered each camp, the Americans and other liberators began to understand "what they were fighting for," a phrase often heard and repeated. How could this have happened? Why was this allowed to happen? These questions were asked by both victims and liberators. To educate German and Polish civilians, the liberators ordered thousands to visit the camps and see the horror up close: the bald, emaciated, foul-smelling, living and dead corpses strewn everywhere. "We didn't know," was a common response, even though many lived within sight of the camps and would have seen the prisoners at work. Many of the visitors fainted. Even seasoned journalists were deeply affected by what they saw.

GENERAL DWIGHT DAVID EISENHOWER AT OHRDRUF

On April 12, 1945, General Dwight David Eisenhower, accompanied by General Omar Bradley and General George Patton, visited the slave-labor camp at Ohrdruf, not considered one of the worst. Bradley was overwhelmed, and George Patton refused to enter a room where piles of

General Dwight D. Eisenhower, accompanied by a group of U.S. Army officers, including General Omar Bradley and Lt. General George Patton, examines the corpses of prisoners executed by the SS prior to the evacuation of Ohrdruf, a sub-camp of Buchenwald, April 12, 1945. National Archives, courtesy of USHMM Photo Archives.

rotting bodies were stacked. It was the supreme commander of the Allied forces, Dwight David Eisenhower, who insisted on seeing "every nook and cranny" of this hell on earth. He recorded what he saw. It was important, he said, to testify to the world that these examples of Nazi brutality did indeed take place, in case anyone then, or in the future, ever doubted their occurrence or term them mere propaganda stories (Berenbaum 1993, 8, 9).

MAUTHAUSEN ON LIBERATION DAY: ONE VICTIM'S VIEW

Sonia Schreiber Weitz, a survivor of Mauthausen concentration camp, was liberated on May 5, 1945. She described the event in the following poem, entitled "Liberation Day" (later called "My Black Messiah"):

> A black G.I. stood by the door
> (I never saw a black before)
> He'll set me free before I die,

I thought he must be the Messiah.
A black Messiah came for me . . .
He stared with eyes that didn't see,
He never heard a single word
Which hung absurd upon my tongue.
And then he simply froze in place
The shock, the horror in his face,
He didn't weep, he didn't cry
But deep within his gentle eyes
A flood of devastating pain,
his innocence forever slain.
For me, with yet another dawn
I found my black Messiah gone
and on we went our separate ways
For forty years without a trace.
But there's a special bond we share
Which has grown strong because we dare
To live, to hope to smile . . . and yet
We vow NOT EVER TO FORGET. (Weitz last unnumbered page)

WORKS CITED

Berenbaum, Michael. *The World Must Know: The History of the Holocaust as Told in the United States Holocaust Memorial Museum.* Boston: Little, Brown, 1993.

Czech, Danuta. *Auschwitz Chronicle, 1939–1945.* New York: Henry Holt, 1990.

Hartford Courant, January 5, 1997, obituary of Robert Daniell who died on December 11, 1996, in Bury St. Edmunds in England, at the age of ninety-five

Klein, Gerda Weissmann. *All but My Life.* New York: The Noonday Press, 1957.

Soumerai, Eve. Interview by Carol Schulz, West Hartford, Connecticut, July 2, 1980.

Weitz, Sonia Schreiber. *The Poetry of Sonia Schreiber Weitz.* Brookline, Mass.: Facing History and Ourselves, 1983.

24

THE NUREMBERG TRIALS

PREPARATION FOR THE INTERNATIONAL
MILITARY TRIBUNAL

On August 8, 1945, the Allies met in London to prepare for an International Military Tribunal and to develop a charter to establish the procedures for the trial of those responsible for the atrocities committed during the Nazi regime. The tribunal would consist of four judges and four teams of attorneys, representing France, Britain, the Soviet Union, and the United States. For the first time in history, the victors decided to prosecute their defeated enemies for alleged violations of criminal law. Secretary of War Henry L. Stimson, a friend and advisor to Supreme Court Justice Robert Jackson, was chosen to lead the American prosecution. On September 15, 1944, he announced that the objective of the trials was continued peace, not whether the United States should be soft or tough on the German people (Smith 1963, 12).

A Fair Trial

Not everyone was in favor of the painstaking trial. There were those among the Allies, especially among the British and the Soviets, who recommended summary executions without trials—the evidence was overwhelming. Robert Jackson strongly dissented. He spelled out the American view, upholding each man's right to a fair trial. What he meant by a fair trial he had previously addressed in a speech delivered to members of the

American Society of International Law on April 13, 1945: "The ultimate principle is that you must put no man on trial under the form of judicial proceedings if you are not willing to see him freed if not proved guilty" (Conot 1983, 14).

One of the most important and most controversial issues raised was the question of the criminal responsibility of the individual under international law. Does, in fact, international law apply to individuals as well as states? If so, for what acts may an individual be held criminally responsible? The International Military Tribunal's response was spelled out thus: "Crimes against international law are committed by men, not by abstract entities, and only by punishing individuals who commit such crimes, can the provisions of international law be enforced" (Woetzel 1960, 96).

The Setting

The site chosen for the trial was Nuremberg, then in total ruins, but formerly the showplace for Nazi Party pageants demonstrating might, unity, and splendor. Rebecca West, who attended the Nuremberg Trials as a correspondent, described the scene as "a trench of nothingness" with bits of paper pinned on the ruins written by families begging for news (Neave 1978, Foreword).

The defendants were to await trial in a specially prepared wing of the prison at the Palace of Justice, located close to the courthouse where the tribunal would take place. The defendants were lodged individually in small cells, isolated from each other and prevented from conversing with one another or their guards. They were given a varied diet of from 1,500 to 1,800 calories daily.

DEFINITION OF THE CRIMES

Three kinds of crimes were specified in the indictments of the charter: (1) Crimes Against Peace, which focused on Germany's conspiracy to unleash total, aggressive war against its neighbors; (2) War Crimes, which targeted violations of accepted international laws and customs of war (according to Article 46 of the Geneva Convention), including murder, ill treatment, and deportation of populations in the conquered territories, the killing of hostages and prisoners of war, the seizing of private property, and the wanton destruction of villages, towns, and cities; and (3) Crimes Against Humanity, which included murder, extermination, enslavement, deportations, and other inhumane acts committed against any civilian population before or during the war. All three counts of the indictments were interrelated by what is sometimes called the fourth indictment: the conspiracy—the carefully planned execution of all of these acts.

Every count in the indictments was backed up by the words, photographs, and films the Germans had meticulously put together with evident pride. While witnesses might have had their own agendas as well as faulty memories and be therefore subject to dispute, the German documents not only presented the strongest possible irrefutable evidence but also supported the witnesses called to testify. These documents would also ensure a fair trial for the defendants.

Preparations

The tribunal was scheduled to begin on November 20, 1945, after only eight months of preparation, arguably short for such a major trial and therefore a bone of some contention among some. There were 403 court sessions for which lawyers had gathered and studied more than a 100,000 captured German documents. Piles of these documents were waiting to be filed in floor-to-ceiling racks. Help was desperately needed to stack and sort them. For this purpose, members of the Waffen SS (*Schutzstaffel*) were recruited from a nearby prisoner-of-war camp. They also built shelves, cleared away the rubble, and repaired the roof of the Palace of Justice.

Since there was only one guard for every fifty prisoners, they could easily have escaped, but none did. The American officer supervising them boasted that they were his troops now. If he told them to go out there and fight, they would, without asking who or where (Conot 1983, 37).

THE DEFENDANTS: A SAMPLING

Hermann Goering

In all, twenty-two major, high-ranking Nazi leaders were indicted and placed on trial. Among them was Hermann Goering, Adolf Hitler's deputy, who, upon surrendering to the commander of the U.S. Thirty-sixth Infantry Division on May 7, 1945, insisted that he speak to no one but General Dwight Eisenhower; however, he then agreed to talk to General Carl Spaatz, commander of the American Strategic Bombing Force, who threw a party for him. At that occasion, Goering presented a photograph of himself to another American general with the inscription: "War is like a football game, whoever loses gives his opponent his hand, and everything is forgotten," which may suggest Goering's concept of justice (1983, 37).

When Goering, next to Hitler in importance, surrendered, he was so large that it took two men to lift him out of his car. He was accompanied by four aides, his personal nurse, two chauffeurs, a five-member kitchen crew (headed by a chef), his wife, his wife's maid, his young daughter, and his daughter's nurse. He had left behind in Berchtesgaden an entire train loaded with art objects "collected" from all over Europe, along with enough champagne, caviar, and pâté de foie gras to last a lifetime (31). His luggage contained his medals, 81,000 marks in cash, and enough jewelry to open a small shop. One of his suitcases was filled with 20,000 paracodeine pills, which he consumed at the rate of 40 a day. His fingernails and toenails were lacquered bright red. He also carried with him two glass vials of cyanide. He was upset that he—a man of his stature and importance—was assigned a three-room working-quarter apartment, which, unbeknownst to him, he would soon have to vacate to move to still smaller quarters—a cell in Nuremberg. In spite of these developments, Goering never lost his appetite; he would use his bread to soak up every little drop of gravy from the mess kit (33–36).

Hans Frank

Hans Frank, a lawyer by profession, had joined the Nazi Party in 1927 and two years later became the party's principal lawyer. In 1933 Hitler named him Reich commissioner for justice. On October 26, 1939, Hitler appointed him governor-general of the remnant of prewar Poland not annexed to Germany or occupied by Russia, a position he held until the end of the war. Frank was intelligent, a patron of the arts, and a skilled pianist. He preferred to make his headquarters in beautiful, slightly damaged Cracow, rather than in war-torn Warsaw. He was also a writer, and he willingly submitted forty-three volumes of his diary to the American soldiers who had arrested him because he thought he had the responsibility to reveal to the world what had transpired during his tenure in Poland.

Albert Speer

Albert Speer, the architect, considered himself Hitler's closest friend. He explained, "Here was hope. Here were now ideals, a new understanding, new tasks" (Speer 1970, 45). He impressed his friend with the design of the "cathedral of light," which consisted of hundreds of searchlights pointing upward into the night sky accentuating the splendor of the Nuremberg rallies (Sereny 1995, 131). Hitler in turn chose Speer as the architect to take charge of totally redesigning Berlin into what would be called Germania, the future capital of the world. The central dome of the new Reichstag building alone would be sixteen times the size of St. Peter's in Rome. Speer created a model in Hitler's chancellery in which the Fuehrer, often accompanied by his architect, would stroll, relax, and dream.

When Speer became armament minister, he demanded and presided over millions of forced laborers in factories all over Europe, including Auschwitz.

Julius Streicher

Julius Streicher did not hold an important governmental position or issue any orders. His contribution was as editor in chief of the hate-filled paper *Der Stürmer*, displayed on most street corners, bus stops, and public parks. His "crime against inhumanity" was incitement, not direct action, such as the statement he made on December 25, 1941: "If one really wants

Nazi defendants before the International Military Tribunal at the Nuremberg Trials (October 18, 1945 to October 1, 1946) are seated in the prisoners' dock. Front row from left to right: Hermann Goering, Rudolf Hoess, Joachim von Ribbentrop, Wilhelm Keitel, Ernst Kaltenbrunner, Alfred Rosenberg, Hans Frank, Wilhelm Frick, Julius Streicher, Walther Funk, and Hjalmar Schacht. Second row from left to right: Karl Doenitz, Erich Raeder, Baldur von Schirach, Fritz Sauckel, Alfred Jodl, Franz von Papen, Arthur Seyss-Inquart, Albert Speer, Konstantin von Neurath, and Hans Fritsche. John W. Mosenthal, courtesy of USHMM Photo Archives.

to put an end to the continued prospering of this curse from heaven that is the Jewish blood, there is only one way to do it, to eradicate this people, this Satan's son, root and branch" (Gutman 1990, 1415). He was loyal to Hitler who claimed that *Der Stürmer* was the only paper he ever read from cover to cover.

Wilhelm Keitel

Field Marshal Wilhelm Keitel was the chief of the High Command of the armed forces. Although he was not highly regarded in terms of personal stature, he participated in the detailed preparations of every Nazi attack and invasion and signed nearly every order that led to military war crimes and crimes against humanity. He considered himself Hitler's "shield-bearer." This would cost him his life.

THEY THOUGHT THEY HAD DONE NOTHING WRONG

In *The Rise and Fall of the Third Reich,* William L. Shirer describes some of the defendants at the end of their lost war:

Heinrich Himmler, the former SS chief, who had held the power of life and death over countless millions, tried his very best to escape from death. He had shaved off his Hitler mustache, donned a black patch over his left eye and wore a private's uniform. When he was stopped and after intensive questioning, he confessed his identity to a British Army captain. After being stripped of his clothes to search for a hidden vial of poison, he was asked to open his mouth, that's when he managed to bite into a vial of potassium cyanide hidden behind his teeth and was dead within twelve minutes in spite of frantic efforts to keep him alive.

Julius Streicher, "the Jew-baiter of Nuremberg . . . a sadist and a pornographer, who had often [been] seen brandishing his whip, while walking along a street, seemed to have wilted. A bald, decrepit old man, he sat perspiring profusely, glaring at the judges and telling his guard, that they were all Jews."

Source: William L. Shirer. *The Rise and the Fall of the Third Reich* (New York: Simon and Schuster, 1960), 1141–43.

THE TRIAL BEGINS: PRELIMINARIES

On November 20, 1945, the trial began. The defendants sat side by side in the dock—a group of weary, ordinary-looking men who a few months previously had wielded extraordinary power over millions of people. One was missing: SS General Ernst Kaltenbrunner, Reinhard Heydrich's "bloody" successor in charge of the Final Solution. He had suffered a minor cerebral hemorrhage and did not appear in the dock until December 10.

The first day was taken up by a full reading of the indictments. The day before, all the defense counsels had jointly issued a petition that challenged the legal foundations of the trial. They claimed that neither the Kellogg-Briand Pact (also known as the International Treaty for the Renunciation of War as an Instrument of National Policy, signed by fifteen nations in 1928 in Paris), nor any other international body, had ever established the criminality of "starting an unjust war." Nor was it fair, the defense attorneys stated, that all the judges were drawn exclusively from the victorious powers. In response, the court agreed that, even though Article 3 of the charter stated that neither the tribunal nor its membership could be challenged by the defense or the prosecution, they would give consideration to these issues at a later time (Taylor 1992, 166).

The defendants were called upon to plead guilty or not guilty. One after the other pleaded not guilty. Goering was not allowed to read a statement he had prepared, but he was permitted to give it to the press. In it he acknowledged "political responsibility" for his acts, denied they were criminal, and challenged the jurisdiction of the tribunal. He also rejected responsibility for "acts of other persons which were not known to me" and of which he did not approve, but claimed he could not have prevented (1992, 167).

JACKSON'S OPENING ADDRESS

As the chief prosecutor for the United States, Robert Jackson considered his address, which lasted more than a day, the most important task of his life. It won wide acclaim and is frequently quoted. Some of the following excerpts will give the reader a taste of the thinking and feeling of this truly great American:

The privilege of opening the first trial in history for crimes against the peace of the world imposes a grave responsibility. The wrongs which we seek to condemn and punish have been so calculated, so malignant, and so devastating, that civilization cannot tolerate their being ignored, because it cannot survive their being repeated. . . . Unfortunately the nature of these crimes is such that both prosecution and judgment must be by victor nations over vanquished foes. The world wide scope of these aggressions carried out by these men has left but few real neutrals. . . . If these men are the first war leaders of a defeated nation to be prosecuted in the name of the law, they are also the first to be given a chance to plead for their lives in the name of the law. Realistically the Charter of this Tribunal, which gives them a hearing, is also the source of their only hope. (*International Military Tribunal Film,* taken by the U.S. Army Signal Corps) (Taylor 1992, 167–68)

Among the 100,000 meticulously kept official German records, Jackson found evidence to support all the charges leveled against the defendants: Goering's active participation in the consolidation of absolute power by the regime; his exploitation of the Reichstag fire, which put an end to the democratic principles of the Weimar Constitution; the wholesale arrests of those who opposed these methods; the creation of Dachau; and the deliberate, ever-increasing series of laws and events that stripped the Jews of all the freedoms that they had enjoyed under the Weimar Republic.

Jackson believed that the charge of launching an aggressive war was at the core of the entire case. He read from the records of the military attack against Poland that began World War II. In May 1939, Hitler had told his military leaders: "It is a question of expanding our living space in the East and securing our food supplies . . . and we are left with the decision: To attack Poland at the first suitable opportunity" (Taylor 1992, 170).

Jackson also read from the records of the SS *Einsatzgruppen;* he cited SS General Jurgen Stroop's report on the destruction of the Warsaw ghetto, the incredible account, beautifully bound in leather, of the resistance put up by the "Jews and bandits"; and he showed the photographs of people jumping from the flaming windows and being shot on the spot. He read, from carefully kept records, of the freezing and starving to death of millions of Soviet prisoners (Persico 1994, 137).

The description of the medical experiments carried out by the SS physicians startled the tribunal. A Czech doctor and inmate of Dachau, Franz Blaha, testified for the prosecution. He was in charge of autopsies to "flay skin off bodies" that were chemically treated and placed in the sun to dry to be made into saddles, riding breeches, house slippers, and ladies' handbags. Tattooed skin was especially valued. If on any given day there was a shortage of good "young" skin, fresh bodies were promised and delivered the next day after they had been "leather inspected" by Dr. Sigmund Rasher, the doctor in charge, who would grab a man by the buttocks or thighs and pronounce the word "good"—his death sentence (Conot 1983, 288).

Jackson's final words were about Civilization writ large:

The real complaining party at your bar is Civilization. In all our countries it is still a struggling and imperfect thing. It does not plead that the United States or any other country has been blameless. . . . But it points to the dreadful sequence of aggressions and crimes I have recited . . . and the destruction of everything that was beautiful and useful in this world. . . . Civilization asks whether law is so laggard as to be utterly helpless to deal with crime of this magnitude. . . . It does not expect that you [the tribunal] can make war impossible. It does expect that your juridical action will put the forms of international law, its precepts, its prohibitions and, most of all its sanctions on the side of peace so that men and women of good will, in all countries may have "leave to live by no man's leave, underneath the law." (Taylor 1992, 171–72)

Jackson was aware of the many difficulties surrounding the trial. He stated, "Never before in legal history has an effort been made to bring within the scope of a single litigation, the developments of a decade covering a whole continent, a score of nations, countless individuals and innumerable events. Despite the magnitude of the task, the world has demanded immediate action" (Taylor 1992, 172).

THE DEFENSE

Because the charter did not permit the defendants to plead "higher orders" or "You did it, too" as their defense, the defendants tried hard to refute the evidence. They pleaded ignorance. If that seemed impossible, they tried to shift the blame. A case in point came when Goering admitted establishing the first concentration camps, which, he claimed, had been for "sequestering rather than punishing political enemies" (Conot 1983, 334). But he said, after Himmler took over in 1934, he stopped having anything to do with the camps and had little knowledge of what was going on in them.

It was difficult for them to plead ignorance; not only were the incriminating documents written and signed by the defendants, they were also corroborated by high officials in the Nazi hierarchy who testified as witnesses both for the defense and the prosecution.

Hermann Goering

Hermann Goering took twelve days to present his case. He stated that he had done everything within his personal power to strengthen the National Socialist movement as the one and only authority. He admitted that he had set up concentration camps in which opponents of the Reich were incarcerated and that he had been responsible for the huge financial burden imposed on the Jews as the result of *Kristallnacht*. He argued that it was justifiable for Germany to rearm and to seize the territories lost under the Treaty of Versailles and other lands because they were essential for the growth and greatness of the Reich, and that, in his opinion, The Hague and the Geneva Convention rules limiting the rights of an occupying power to seize properties and displace workers were not justified because of "the technical expansion of modern war" (Taylor 1992, 333–34).

He voluntarily furnished more than enough evidence for convictions under counts one and two. When asked for his input by counsels on behalf of the other defendants, he was condescending: The General Staff was timid and Ribbentrop definitely had no influence. In reply to the question of whether there was any conspiracy among the Nazi leaders, Goering said that no one but he could even approach working closely with the fuehrer. It was he who was familiar with Hitler's thoughts and therefore able to exercise the greatest influence (Taylor 1992, 334).

Hans Frank

Hans Frank claimed that he had had no knowledge of the atrocities that he heard about during the trial, even though Cracow, where he had spent five years, was only thirty miles from Auschwitz. The many passages in his diary that revealed his participation in atrocities were, he thought, taken out of context (Taylor 1992, 369). He was quite passionate, and he swore to God that he was a believing Christian and that he neither directly nor indirectly had ever had anything to do with the extermination of the Jews (Conot 1983, 80–81).

Albert Speer

Albert Speer also claimed that he was unaware of the Final Solution, which he called a well-kept secret. Unlike the other defendants, he admitted his responsibility and did not try to justify or deny his involvement. His intelligent, well-articulated statements culminated into a form of collective penitence—much to the annoyance of the others in the dock. In a letter to his wife, written in June 1946, he wrote, "What matters most to me is that I tell the truth" (Speer 1970, 650). In his final speech, he repeated a frequent theme: the role of modern technology and how the radio and public address system made it possible to address millions and have them obey. He spoke of the inhumanity of the weapons used by both the aggressors and the victors.

Julius Streicher

Julius Streicher remembered hearing "inner voices," which told him what to do, and seeing a halo on Hitler's head the first time he heard Hitler speak. He denied that his actions had incited violence and led to the mass killings of Jews, something that he had only heard about when taken prisoner in 1945. He acknowledged ordering the destruction of the main Nuremberg synagogue in 1938, but he insisted that the purpose was architectural not anti-Semitic. He also admitted that he had visited the Dachau concentration camp four times, but only to select noncriminal inmates for an annual trip to the Hotel Deutscher Hof in Nuremberg for Christmas dinner (Taylor 1992, 378–79).

Wilhelm Keitel

In his testimony and cross-examination, Keitel admitted his weakness: his inability to object to orders. He thereby admitted his guilt, which, in the view of many, produced one of the most honest and touching defense presentations. In his final plea, he said he wanted to die like a brave man (Smith 1963, 186). He wrote his memoirs from his cell during the six weeks prior to his hanging at Nuremberg. His description of the strain of his last months gives insight into the daily life of the prisoners as well as into Keitel's attitudes and personality:

I know nothing at all of what has become of my country or my family, and indeed what is to become of myself. For the last two months we have been permitted to write letters and postcards, but we have received no replies. . . . Since May [1945] I have lost two stone [about 28 pounds] in weight. . . . I can well understand that we soldiers are to be called to account . . . and that we have to be kept apart. . . . I mention only a few of the deprivations. From 5:30 P.M., or when it grows dark— one must sit and brood in darkness, because they have taken away my glasses and it is impossible to read even by the glimmer of light coming in from the corridor outside. Secondly, one has only a bunk and a small table, with no desk or shelf and even the wooden chair is taken out. Thirdly there is nothing to hang or lay ones clothes on . . . so it is impossible to keep one's clothes clean. Fourthly, the window which ventilates the cell and regulates the temperature cannot be operated from inside. Fifthly one is restricted to ten minutes exercise in the open air each day. . . . I must stress that by drawing up a list of reasons for my unchecked physical and mental decline I am not raising any complaints because I have no doubt as to the basically good intentions of my immediate custodians [the Americans] and because I have benefited personally from the manifold help of the American military surgeons, I must make my gratitude to them quite plain. But my permanent back pains are physical torture to a man of sixty who is not even permitted a chair with a back to it. (Keitel 1966, 30–31)

THE VERDICTS

Hermann Goering

Goering, the only one permitted to take twelve days of court time to deny knowledge of events he ought to have known about, was found guilty on all counts and condemned to death by hanging. Major Airey Neave, a member of the British War Crimes Executive Team, had been chosen to act as legal advisor to the defendants and was therefore in a position to visit with them on many occasions. He was also responsible for amassing evidence on the treatment of slave laborers by the Krupp Works. On one of his visits to Goering in his cell, Neave described seeing the photographs of Goering's wife and small daughter, Edda, on the table: "The photograph of Goering's daughter so like her father touched me. Then I felt suddenly angry. It was impossible to forget the Krupp guards who caught a prisoner trying to keep a snapshot of his parents. They seized it, tore it up and beat him till he bled" (Neave 1978, 68).

Hans Frank

Hans Frank was also condemned to death by hanging. His own diary, he admitted, bore witness against him. He referred to the tribunal judges and prosecuting attorneys as "such noble figures" sitting across from where *he* sat among such "repulsive characters as Streicher, Goering and Ribbentrop." He embraced his Roman Catholic religion and noted in his diary, "Religion is such a comfort now. I look forward to Christmas like a little child" (Neave 1978, 114).

Albert Speer

Albert Speer, who had admitted that the ties between himself as armament minister and those in charge of slave labor were very strong, was given twenty years because of his apparent repentant attitude and his strenuous efforts to prevent Hitler's "scorched earth" policy, designed to annihilate what was left of Germany, from taking effect. On March 19, 1945, Speer had handed to Hitler the last of the memoranda he had written explaining that the war was lost and that what was important was to preserve Germany's infrastructure for the sake of the people. Hitler had responded that it was best to destroy even these things, that "the garbage left over will only be the inferiors because the good ones will be dead" (Speer 1970, 83).

Julius Streicher

Julius Streicher, whose newspaper *Der Stürmer* was judged to incite murder, was sentenced to death by hanging. Streicher, upon hearing the verdict, was furious, and he stomped his feet all the way to the elevator.

Wilhelm Keitel

For Wilhelm Keitel, the deliberations were the shortest of all the defendants. All the judges agreed that he was guilty on all four counts and sentenced him to death. During most of the trial, he was viewed as a pathetic instrument of crime. In the words of Francis Biddle, an American member of the tribunal, he was the "prototype of the criminally pliant general" (Smith 1963, 186).

OTHERS ARE SENTENCED

Eight other defendants were sentenced to death by hanging: Joachim von Ribbentropp, foreign minister; Ernst Kaltenbrunner, secret police chief; Wilhelm Frick, Minister of the Interior; Alfred Rosenberg, commissioner of the Occupied East-European Region; Fritz Sauckel, in charge of foreign workers from the occupied territories; Alfred Jodl, Keitel's immediate deputy; Dr. Arthur Seyss-Inquart, who was instrumental in policies governing areas of occupation; and Martin Bormann, private secretary to the fuehrer, sentenced in absentia because he had not been captured.

Rudolf Hoess, deputy for party affairs and Hitler's confidant; Walter Funk, minister of economic affairs; and Admiral Erich Raeder, commander of the German navy, were sentenced to life imprisonment. Albert Speer; Constantin von Neurath, the first foreign minister and voice of "moderation"; Admiral Karl Doenitz, commander in chief of the navy; and Baldur von Schirach, leader of Hitler Youth, were given sentences ranging from ten to twenty years. Franz von Papen, former ambassador to Austria; Hjalmar Schacht, financial advisor; and Hans Fritsche, a high official in the Propaganda Ministry, were acquitted.

PUNISHMENT

The executions were scheduled to begin early in the morning of October 16, 1946, in the prison gymnasium. Goering escaped the gallows by swallowing a cyanide capsule during the night. The chaplains visited the condemned prior to the executions. They went to their deaths with relative calm, except for Streicher who spat at Master Sergeant Woods, the executioner, and told him that the Bolsheviks would hang him one day, followed by the words "Heil Hitler." All of the corpses were photographed and then carried in trucks to a crematory in or near Munich. Some believe the destination was Dachau. It is believed that the ashes were emptied into the river Isar (Taylor 1992, 610–11).

More trials took place at the conclusion of the military tribunals. Physicians were tried for their involvement in the selections, murders, and medical experiments; judges were tried for transforming German law into a new set of laws permitting mass murder; top executives of I. G. Farben were tried for manufacturing Zyklon B and constructing factories at Auschwitz; Alfred Krupp and other executives were tried for their use of slave labor.

The unfolding of the cold war between the United States and the Soviet Union shifted attention away from the trials and resulted in the sentences being reduced and pardons being granted. Germany became central to American economic and political interests.

The chief perpetrators—Hitler, Joseph Goebbels, and Heinrich Himmler—all committed suicide and escaped the trials. Many others took on new identities and escaped to South America or the Middle East; in addition, thousands entered the United States claiming to be anti-Communists fleeing from Soviet persecution. Hundreds of scientists, including war criminals, were brought to the United States to work for the military and the National Aeronautics and Space Administration—just as Jewish refugees such as Alfred Einstein had done prior to the war. Thousands of others who participated in the "crimes against humanity" were never tried.

WHAT WAS ACCOMPLISHED BY THE TRIALS?

For the very first time in history, individuals were held responsible for their particular crimes against humanity. Swearing allegiance, taking an oath, or taking orders were no longer acceptable reasons for their defense. Also, the masses of German recorded evidence presented at the tribunal will make it almost impossible for present and future revisionist historians to claim that these crimes did not occur or were exaggerated—*almost impossible,* because there are always those who try to distort or deny the evidence. In the continuing struggle for freedom from persecution and unbridled hate, the Nuremberg Trials played a significant role and as such must be remembered.

POSTSCRIPT

Adolf Hitler, the chief defendant, was absent. On the night of April 28, 1945, he had married his faithful mistress Eva Braun. Shortly before 4:00 A.M., on April 29, he called in his secretary and dictated the final sentence of his political testament: "Above all I obligate the leaders of the nation and their following to a strict observance of the racial laws, and to a merciless resistance to the poisoners of all peoples, international Jewry." Eliminating Jewry was his passion (Trevor-Roper 1947,

179); dominating all of Europe, his goal. Had they obeyed his decree, what would have happened to morality?

The next day, April 30, 1945, between 2:00 and 3:00 P.M., Hitler put his Walther pistol against his right temple, bit into a cyanide capsule, and pulled the trigger.

WORKS CITED

Conot, Robert E. *Justice at Nuremberg*. New York: Harper and Row, 1983.

Gutman, Israel, ed. *Encyclopedia of the Holocaust*. New York: Macmillan, 1990.

Keitel, Wilhelm. *Memoirs of Field-Marshal Keitel*. New York: Stein and Day, 1966.

Neave, Airey. *On Trial at Nuremberg*. Boston: Little, Brown, 1978.

Persico, Joseph E. *Nuremberg: Infamy on Trial*. New York: Penguin, 1994.

Sereny, Gita. *Speer: His Battle with Truth*. New York: Alfred A. Knopf, 1995.

Shirer, William L. *The Rise and the Fall of the Third Reich*. New York: Simon and Schuster, 1960.

Smith, Bradley F. *Reaching Judgment at Nuremberg*. New York: Basic Books, 1963.

Speer, Albert. *Inside the Third Reich*. New York: Avon, 1970.

Taylor, Telford. *The Anatomy of the Nuremberg Trials*. Boston: Little, Brown, 1992.

Trevor-Roper, H. R. *The Last Days of Hitler*. New York: Macmillan, 1947.

Woetzel, Robert K. *The Nuremberg Trials in International Law*. New York: Frederick A. Praeger, 1960.

25

AFTERMATH

World War II was over: The concentration camps had been liberated, the Nazi war machine had been disassembled, and the soldiers had been sent home. The world beyond the camps was beginning to learn about what many had known for some time—the Jewish world of schools, libraries, universities, hospitals, synagogues, concert halls, museums, trade unions, industries, business and professional firms, butcher shops, bakeries, tailors, shoemakers, political organizations, theatres, clubs, neighborhoods, friends, and, most of all, families had all but disappeared.

The remnants, those who had survived the camps or had spent the years in hiding, should have been rejoicing. Perhaps, had this been today there might have been hundreds of medical personnel there to provide aid, to help them heal, both physically and emotionally, if not spiritually. And perhaps then they might have been able to feel joy. But this was the aftermath of World War II, and everyone, even Americans safe at home, believed their own wounds needed tending.

The world that had found no room for the Jews while they were being hunted by Nazis seemed to have even less sympathy now that they were in competition for precious resources.

READJUSTING TO LIFE AFTER THE CAMPS

It is nearly impossible to imagine the condition the survivors found themselves in after the war ended. To begin with, the physical condition of most of them was so bad that many continued to die despite medical care. They suffered from tuberculosis, typhoid, infections, extreme malnutrition (some adults weighed as little as 60 pounds), crippling injuries caused by accidents and overwork, and the effects of ghastly medical experiments. Some had been castrated, others simply rendered sterile (Dvorjetski 1963, 211).

In the months following liberation, other illnesses developed as a result of the severe strain on their bodies and their minds: cardiovascular and pulmonary diseases, endocrinological and metabolic illnesses, surgical problems, and, of course, neuropsychic illnesses (1963, 217). People were dirty, demoralized, depressed, haunted by nightmares, fearful of authorities—even the Americans—argumentative, lonely, and sick (Berenbaum 1993, 205).

Emotionally traumatized, they not only missed their loved ones, and wondered whether anyone was still alive, but developed guilt complexes over the loss of their families. Parents who had hidden children with non-Jews or had thrown them over the walls of the ghetto frantically tried to find them. Children who did not know their own names, or who their parents were, published advertisements with their pictures, trying to find answers.

Crate full of gold wedding rings confiscated from prisoners in Buchenwald and found by American troops in May 1945 in a cave adjoining the camp. National Archives, courtesy of USHMM Photo Archives.

With no clothing, no money, no possessions, no family, no home, and no country, most Jews felt truly abandoned. The overwhelming response to a poll taken of Jews in the Displaced Persons Camps showed that if they were barred from entering Palestine, they preferred the gas chamber to going home. They no longer had faith in anyone's humanity.

Those who did try to return to their cities and villages found they were not wanted. In August 1945, anti-Jewish riots occurred first in Cracow and began to spread to the rest of Poland. In the first seven months after the war, 350 Jews were killed in Poland by their Polish compatriots. In one instance, a Jewish hospital for orphans was attacked. In some towns, anyone who even looked Jewish was attacked (Rossel 1992, 161).

Of the 24,000 Jews who had lived in the city of Kielce in Poland, only 150 returned. Fears that the Jews would try to reclaim their homes precipitated a renewal of the ancient scourge of anti-Semitism. Rumors spread throughout the city that the Jews had kidnapped a Christian child. As a result, on July 4, 1946, Jews were dragged from their homes, shot, stoned to death, murdered with axes, and beaten with blunt instruments. In all, 42 were killed, and 50 more were wounded. Another 100,000 Jews fled to neighboring Hungary and Czechoslovakia. Despite appeals, the Church was silent (Berenbaum 1993, 208; Rossel 1992, 161).

Afraid of similar pogroms, Jews began to flee to occupied Germany. Knowing what awaited them, few wanted to go home. Despite the illegality of such action, 100,000 poured into the American Zone. Walking, hitch-hiking on trucks, hopping trains, some even traveled the 700 miles from Cracow and Silesia.

Others were able to gain entrance to France, England, Canada, Latin America, Australia, and the United States, but even these countries did not open their doors very wide. Survivors made everyone feel bad. They were too quiet, they looked awful, they were visibly fearful, and their presence made others feel guilty. The governments of most countries treated the defeated Germans better than they did Germany's victims (Rossel 1992, 163).

THE DISPLACED PERSONS CAMPS

Most survivors were forced to stay where they had been found when the war ended, in the same concentration camps in which they had been imprisoned by the Third Reich, only now they were called Displaced Persons (DP) Camps and were under the jurisdiction of the Allied Occupation Forces and operated by the representatives of the United Nations Relief and Rehabilitation Administration (UNRRA). Aside from the absence of deliberate torture, conditions in these camps were hardly better than they had been during the war. Although no one went without food, the camps lacked sufficient medicines and medical personnel, housing, clothing, and sanitation. In the beginning, there was no one to help people look for their families or to find the means to leave the camps and restart their lives. In addition, many of the non-Jewish DPs were openly hostile to the Jews, frightening them even more.

Hundreds of thousands were living in deplorable conditions. In October 1945, at the age of nineteen, Eve Soumerai joined the U.S. Third Army as an Allied civilian employee, working as an interpreter and censor.

Soon after my arrival in Munich, I started to search for my parents and my brother. Accompanied by a U.S. Army captain and a Jeepful of food and medicine, I traveled to Förenwald DP Camp located not far from Munich.

What I saw is forever etched in my memory. What seemed like hordes of young-old-looking skeletons approached the Jeep and matter-of-factly began to help themselves. A harried UNRRA official rushed over and tried to restore order. I apologized to the captain—I didn't know what else to do—these were my people.

The official invited us for lunch in the barrack's dining hall, where I sat next to a ravaged individual who kept describing gas chambers and crematoria while he slurped watery spaghetti. I was speechless. I could not identify the loving family I had left at a Berlin train station six years earlier with the skeletons I saw. The pain was overwhelming—a mixture of the horrific reality I saw in front of me with the feelings of overpowering guilt. Maybe I should never have left. Why had I survived? My father, my mother, and my brother were better than I. What made me special?

Slowly . . . gradually. I began my search for answers, and never stopped. (Soumerai 1945)

In April 1945 when General Eisenhower visited the DP camps, he demanded that immediate improvements be made. General George Patton had been in charge of this work but was opposed to doing anything to alleviate the sufferings of the Jews. Eisenhower quickly relieved Patton of his command.

In a report sent to President Harry Truman, Earl Harrison, dean of the University of Pennsylvania Law School, stated, "We [the United States] appear to be treating the Jews as the Nazis treated them, except that we do not exterminate them" (Berenbaum 1993, 206). He recommended that Jews be evacuated from Germany immediately and that the United States admit 100,000 Polish Jews. Truman endorsed the report, chastized the army, put pressure on England to take in more refugees, and opened the United States to more immigrants—but not a lot more. Americans did not want refugees competing for jobs with returning soldiers.

In the fall of 1945, Jewish relief organizations were finally allowed into the camps. They set up schools and occupational and agricultural training programs and taught Hebrew—all in preparation for the establishment of a Jewish state in Palestine. Things started to pick up in the camps. Survivors married and started families. More than seventy newspapers were published, and youth groups were formed. One hundred schools, housing 12,000 students, were established, including two high schools (1993, 208).

ACE Eve Nussbaum (Soumerai) in Munich as an allied
civilian employee, 1945–1946. Courtesy of Eve Nussbaum
Soumerai.

In 1948 the birthrate in the DP camps was the highest in the whole world
(Dvorjetski 1963, 219).

THE PROMISED LAND

Denied entrance to most countries, in Europe and abroad, including the
United States, the overwhelming majority of refugees wanted to emigrate
to Palestine. The United States erected so-called paper walls of red tape—
one official measured seventeen yards of paperwork—and managed to
admit fewer than 100,000 Jews from 1945 to 1952. Actually, 50 percent of
the immigrants were Catholic, and some collaborators were also admitted (Berenbaum 1993, 209). Unfortunately, the British, hoping to maintain
their friendship with the Arab nations, refused to admit Jews. After World
War I, they had been given the responsibility for ruling Palestine.

The Jews were nevertheless determined to get to the Promised Land.
They desperately wanted to live in a country where they could feel safe.
Between 1944 and 1948, 200,000 Jews fled to Palestine, illegally crossing

A boxcar used by the Nazis to transport Jews to their deaths in concentration camps is displayed at Yad Vashem in Israel. Courtesy of Dennis Rader.

the Alps and sometimes passing through dozens of countries before arriving at their destination. They were aided by two organizations: the Jewish Brigade and the Hagana (which later became the Jewish Defense Forces). These groups were manned by Jews serving in Europe in the Allied army or civilians, who paved the way by bribing or convincing border guards to admit the Jews. They also were able to buy and refit small ships that were able to cross the Mediterranean Sea (1993, 210–11).

THE *EXODUS*

Sixty-nine thousand Jews made the journey to Palestine on sixty-six boats. Sixty of these vessels were captured by a British blockade, and their passengers were put in camps on the island of Cypress. The most famous of these ships was the *Exodus.*

After being captured by the British and forced to return to Marseilles, France, the 4,500 passengers refused to get off the ship. In order to alert the world of their plight, they staged a hunger strike. Angry, and fearing they would lose control, the British cabinet decided to send the Jews back to Bergen-Belsen concentration camp.

The publicity eventually forced the British mandate to come to an end. In 1948 the newly formed United Nations voted to split Palestine into an Arab state and a Jewish state, and on May 14, 1948, David Ben

Gurion, the new prime minister, announced the establishment of the State of Israel. That night, five Arab countries attacked the newly born nation.

In 1950 Israel passed the Law of the Return. This law provided that any Jew who wanted to become a citizen could do so automatically. By December 17, 1950, all those who wanted to emigrate to Israel had arrived. The Jews finally had a home (212).

WORKS CITED

Berenbaum, Michael. *The World Must Know: The History of the Holocaust as Told in the United States Holocaust Memorial Museum.* Boston: Little, Brown, 1993.

Dvorjetski, Mark. "Adjustment of Detainees to Camp and Ghetto Life: And Their Subsequent Readjustment to Normal Society." *Yad Vashem Studies on the European Jewish Catastrophe and Resistance.* Edited by Nathan Eck and Arieh Leon Kubovy. Jerusalem: Yad Vashem Martyrs' and Heroes' Remembrance Authority, 1963. Vol. 5, 193–220.

Rossel, Seymour. *The Holocaust: The World and the Jews, 1933–1945.* West Orange, N.J.: Behrman House, 1992.

Soumerai, Eve. Unpublished diary, November 1945.

26

DENYING HISTORY

Officials at the Nuremberg Trials carefully documented the Nazis' crimes, filling forty-two volumes, and recorded the testimonies of the twenty-two major Nazi war criminals. None of the defendants denied what happened during the Holocaust, but the perpetrators did refuse to accept responsibility for any crimes against humanity.

For example, during questioning, SS Lieutenant Colonel Rudolf Hoess, commandant of Auschwitz, claimed that he was just following orders from above. Yet, he was responsible for "upgrading" Auschwitz from a "forced labor camp" to an "extermination camp," and he performed his duties so efficiently that his superiors commended him as a "true pioneer" in eliminating those "unworthy of life"(Lipstadt 2005, 293). An incident reported by Marie Vaillant-Courtier, a French resistance fighter who had been imprisoned in Auschwitz in 1942, illustrates Hoess's cold-hearted efficiency and his refusal to accept responsibility for any atrocities. As Vaillant-Courtier recalled:

One night we were awakened by terrifying cries. And we discovered on the following day . . . from the men in the Sonderkommando . . . that on the preceding day, the gas supply having run out, they had thrown the children into the furnaces alive. (Roth 2007, 296)

At his trial, when asked if he felt any remorse, Hoess replied no, since he did not kill anyone personally. He had direct orders from Himmler. He was only the commandant. However, he did complain about the long hours and lamented that he could not play with his own children more often (296).

Today, a small but significant number of individuals wish to convince the public that the Holocaust itself never happened. In her book, *Denying the Holocaust* (1993), Professor Deborah Lipstadt refers to British historian David Irving as a "Holocaust denier." In January of 2000, Irving sued Lipstadt and her publisher, Penguin Books, for libel, claiming that her book "was part of a global conspiracy against him and . . . that the 'enemies of truth' were out to destroy him" (James Libson, as quoted by Lipstadt 2005, 46). According to Irving, there were no gas chambers at Auschwitz, and Adolf Hitler never issued orders to eliminate European Jewry (Lipstadt 2005) and therefore he was not a "denier."

The trial of *Irving v. Lipstadt and Penguin,* took place in courtroom 73 of the Royal High Court in London, with Judge Charles Gray presiding. Since there is no written First Amendment in the United Kingdom, libel laws favor the plaintiff. Therefore, Lipstadt had to prove that her allegations regarding Irving were true.

Professor Deborah Lipstadt and Penguin books chief executive Anthony Forbes Watson arrive at London's High Court on January 11, 2000 for her libel case. AP Photo/Max Nash.

On the first day of the trial, Irving spoke first: "He argued that he should be given credit for drawing attention to the Holocaust by 'selflessly' publicizing historical documents he had uncovered " (Lipstadt 2005, 80), and that Lipstadt's allegations were preventing him from earning enough for his retirement.

Judge Gray clarified the issues at the heart of the trial: The defendants must prove that Irving actually knew that a specific event happened (e.g., the gas chambers were used to kill Jews), and that he then manipulated the facts to show otherwise. They also had to prove that he was motivated by his anti-Semitic feelings and not by a wish to find the truth.

The defendants argued that the facts were readily available in the historical record and that Irving ignored the truth and lied (82), claiming, for example, that the gas chambers shown to the tourists at Auschwitz were built by the Poles after the war (81). The defense also stated that his previous actions had shown that he was anti-Semitic.

Richard Rampton, one of England's leading barristers in the field of defamation and libel, argued, for the defendants, that Irving had distorted the historical record in his book *Hitler's War*, in which he exonerated Hitler from responsibility for atrocities against Jews or any other victims. As early as November 30, 1941, according to Rampton, Irving claimed:

An accordionist leads a sing-a-long for SS officers at their retreat in Solahuette, outside Auschwitz. Historians assume the party was to honor Rudolph Hoess (first row, third from left), who completed his tenure as garrison senior on July 29, 1944. July 22–29, 1944. USHMM/Anonymous Donor, Unknown Photographer.

"Himmler was *summoned* [Lipstadt's italics] to the Wolf's Lair for a secret conference with Hitler, at which the fate of Berlin Jews was clearly raised. At 1:30 P.M.
Himmler was obliged to telephone from Hitler's bunker to Heydrich, with the
explicit order that Jews *were not to be liquidated* [Lipstadt's italics]. "(82)

Rampton termed the whole incident "pure invention," and called
Irving's statements "imaginative assertions" (83). What had actually happened was that Hitler had ordered *one* specific trainload to stop. With very
slight changes, sometimes substituting one word for another, or adding an
s to the singular, Irving had fabricated history (83).

Rampton went on to ask why Irving would resort to these obvious
distortions and concluded that Irving wanted them to be true. Rampton quotes from Irving's 1991 speech to a neo-fascist group in which he
stated that

'more women died in Ted Kennedy's car at Chappaquiddick than in the gas
chambers. . . . There are so many Auschwitz survivors . . . in fact, the number
increases as the years go past, which is biologically very odd, to say the least,
because I am going to form an association of Holocaust survivors, survivors and
other liars . . . A S S H O L S. (Lipstadt 2005, 84)

Rampton told the judge that the defendants "had exposed Irving's
fraud and deliberate manipulations. For that they should "be applauded
for having performed a significant public service not just in this country,
but in all those places in the world where antisemitism is waiting to be
fed" (84–85).

Deborah Lipstadt had been advised by her legal team not to speak to
reporters or give press interviews, as the judge did not approve of litigat-
ing in public during a trial. This was difficult for her, considering Irving
had taken every opportunity to speak publicly. But, one day, outside the
courtroom, an elderly woman with a tattooed number on her forearm
approached Lipstadt and told her, "whatever you do, do not fail us" (86).
Lipstadt felt that this survivor spoke for all those murdered and that winning this case would be a vindication for all of the victims murdered in the
Holocaust and their families.

During the trial, Judge Gray asked Irving to define the Holocaust. Irving
claimed that the word is "very elastic" and has served many purposes:
"*They* (the Jewish community) set it as wide as they want when it is a concern, for example, of taking money from the Swiss banks . . . . and *they* set
it very narrowly when they then try to snare a writer who is dangerous to
them, as they put it" (92).

The next question put to Irving was whether he believed there had been
a systematic program to exterminate the Jews. No, he did not. According to Irving, the mass murders on the eastern front were not systematic
since they "originated at a lower level" (92) (i.e., were conducted by inde-
pendently operating individuals). He claimed that gas chambers were

Jewish women and children from Subcarpathian Rus await selection on the ramp at Auschwitz-Birkenau. May, 1944. USHMM Courtesy of Yad Vashem. Photographer: Bernhardt Walter/Earnst Hofman.

"Hollywood legends," while he did admit that "there was some kind of gassing in Birkenau" (93).

Rampton also showed a video of Irving speaking to a neo-Nazi group in Tampa, Florida. Irving tells the group about an encounter he had had a few days earlier in Louisiana, when a Jew had interrupted his speech, asking him: "Are you trying to say that we are responsible for Auschwitz ourselves?" Irving responded, "Well the short answer is 'Yes!'" (178).

Then there was the verse in Irving's diary, made available to the defense, in which he records singing to his daughter

> I am a Baby Aryan
> Not Jewish or Sectarian
> I have no plans to marry
> Ape or Rastafarian (175)

After a nine-week trial, Judge Gray began his findings by praising Irving as "a military historian . . . able and intelligent" (Gray, as quoted by Lipstadt 1993, 271). But the criticisms of his work were "almost invariably well founded" (271). Judge Gray mentioned the testimony of Auschwitz commandant Hoess as well as many of the Auschwitz survivors as credible. The judge concluded that Irving's willingness to associate with a motley collection of militant neo-Nazis meant that Irving must share their political beliefs, revealing him to be a right-wing Nazi polemicist.

In her statement to the press, following the judge's presentation of his findings, Lipstadt quoted Judge Gray directly: "Falsification of the historical record was deliberate and . . . motivated by a desire to present events in a manner consistent with his own ideological beliefs even if that involved distortion and manipulation of historical evidence" (271). Judge Gray warned Irving that the result, therefore, must be judgment for the defendants.

Deborah Lipstadt did not think the judge's decision was likely to be the last word. "There is no end," she said, "to the fight against racism, anti-semitism, and hatred" (271).

WORKS CITED

Goldensohn, Leon. *Nuremberg Interviews.* New York: Alfred A. Knopf, 2004.

Guttenplan, D. D. *Holocaust On Trial.* New York: W.W. Norton, 2001.

Lipstadt, Deborah E. *Denying the Holocaust: The Growing Assault on Truth and Memory.* New York: Plume (Penguin Books USA), 1993.

———. *History on Trial.* New York: HarperCollins, 2005.

Roth, John K. *The Holocaust Chronicle: A History in Words and Pictures.* Lincolnwood, Illinois: Publications International, Ltd., 2000.

27

GENOCIDE CONTINUES: CAMBODIA, RWANDA, SUDAN

Although it has been nearly sixty-five years since the end of the Holocaust and Nuremburg Trials revealed the extent of the crimes against humanity perpetrated by the Nazi war criminals, the crime of genocide continues to be committed in many regions of the world. Like the irrational pretexts fabricated by Adolf Hitler to justify killing Jews, Gypsies, Poles, Jehovah's Witnesses, the physically disabled, the mentally ill or disabled, homosexuals, and anyone who tried to stop the Nazi war machine, the excuses for the killings of the later twentieth and early twenty-first centuries are unconscionable. In less than four years, Cambodia's Pol Pot destroyed millions of his countrymen and eradicated all signs of modern life: scientific institutions, hospitals, schools, and the entire infrastructure of the country, along with most of the intellectual class that made modern life possible. Pol Pot did not believe in it.

Rwanda's fifty-year civil war between the Tutsis and the Hutus has left villages in ashes and churches filled with people burned to the ground, because long-absent colonial powers favored one tribe over the other. In Sudan, in the nations of the former Yugoslavia and throughout the Middle East, civil wars are being fought in the name of so-called ethnic cleansing.

Though it may seem that humankind has learned the wrong lessons from the Holocaust, there are many people and organizations, including the United Nations (UN), that have begun efforts to end some of these attempts at genocide.

CAMBODIA'S GENOCIDAL LEADER

"Not since Hitler's Holocaust had the world seen such suffering. The Khmer Rouge had slaughtered and starved two million of Cambodia's population of seven million" (*United Nations Chronicles* December 1983, 32). With these words, then ambassador to the UN Jeanne J. Kirkpatrick described the 4.5-year rule of Cambodia's Pol Pot.

In 1970, a Cambodian coup d'etat replaced ruler Prince Norodom Sihanouk with pro–United States premier Lon Nol. At that time, the United States was fighting in Vietnam, and North Vietnam was using Cambodia as a base of operations. Lon Nol demanded that the North Vietnamese remove their troops from Cambodia. The Vietnamese Communists began supporting anti–Lon Nol insurgents, called the Khmer Rouge by Prince Sihanouk. As the Khmer Rouge gradually gained control over the Cambodian countryside, the U.S. Air Force dropped its bombs on Cambodia, three times as many tons of conventional explosives as fell on Japan in all of World War II (Schulz and Soumerai 1998, 65).

On April 17, 1975, the Khmer Rouge entered Phnom Penh and took over Cambodia, turning the beleaguered country into a "nationwide gulag" (65). Within hours the new government began a forced exodus from the city of some 2 million people. Pursuing his vision of a peasant nation modeled on the ancient Kampuchean Empire, Pol Pot forcefully emptied all the cities and towns, driving everyone into the countryside, and methodically executing the educated class. He believed that "cities were useless—empty them! Trade was evil, abolish all markets. Abolish money. Destroy contaminating foreign vestiges—television sets, air conditioners. Destroy contaminated people: former enemy soldiers, teachers, physicians" (White 1982, 598–99). Using slogans like "purification of the people" and "returning the country to the peasant" (599), Pol Pot turned Cambodian society upside down.

Dith Pran, a young Cambodian, worked for *New York Times* reporter Sydney Schanberg as a translator, aide, and later, a stringer for the paper. In 1975, he too was forced to evacuate Phnom Penh. Schanberg tried to find him but failed: "I had watched him disappear into the interior of Cambodia, which would become a death camp for millions" (Schanberg 1985, 44). Four and a half years later, Dith Pran would emerge from Cambodia to tell his story.

What happened to Dith was in many ways typical of life for the Cambodian people, but in one way, it was not: most of the educated Khmer did not survive. Schools were abolished, along with their teachers. Hospitals were destroyed, and ninety percent of the nation's 600 doctors were either executed or fled the country. Two-thirds of the post–Khmer Rouge population was women.

Dith told Schanberg:

They did not kill people in front of us. They took them away at night and murdered them with big sticks and hoes, to save bullets. Life was totally controlled and the Khmer Rouge did not need a good reason to kill someone; the slightest excuse would do—a boy and girl holding hands, and an unauthorized break from work, Anyone they didn't like they would accuse of being a teacher or a student . . . and that was the end. (44)

In order to stay alive, Dith censored his thoughts and watched his vocabulary, keeping it crude and limited to conceal his education.

In the countryside, the people were put to work on collective farms and special construction projects. Families were separated, with husbands, wives, and children all working in different parts of the country, often not seeing each other for seasons at a time. Some children never saw their parents again. Married people needed permission to meet and sleep together. On the collectives, men and women slept in separate, large communal bunk houses. "Imagine sleeping in a 45-foot collective bed," noted one man. "We were expendable, treated worse than prisoners. We were used as machinery" (White 1982, 600).

Mass weddings were arranged by the Khmer Rouge, and waves of suicides resulted. Another Khmer reported that they were forced to work "for 18 hours a day plowing, hoeing or building irrigation works, on pitiful rations of rice gruel, driven by pitiless 'cadre' supervisors with the power of life and death" (600).

Dith estimated that 10 percent of the 7 million Cambodians died of starvation in 1975 alone: "The villagers, desperate, ate snails, snakes, insects, rats, scorpions, tree bark, leaves, flower blossoms, the trunk of banana plants. . . . Some people were digging up the bodies of the newly executed and cooking the flesh" (Schanberg 1985, 44).

Dith Pran also spoke of "killing grounds with bones and skulls everywhere among the trees and wells" (48). In his own village of Siem Reap, he found two execution areas with the bones of 4,000–5,000 people in each. "In the water wells, the bodies were like soup bones in broth, and you could always tell the killing grounds because the grass grew taller and greener where the bodies were buried" (48). Furthermore, Dith feared most the Khmer Rouge soldiers between twelve and fifteen years old:

[They were the] most completely and savagely indoctrinated. . . . they took them very young and taught them nothing but discipline. Just take orders, no need for a reason . . . they do not believe any religion or tradition except Khmer Rouge orders. That's why they killed their own people, even babies, like we kill a mosquito. (48)

Reminiscent of the Hitler Youth, the widespread use of child soldiers would be reported years later, in eighty-five countries around the world, where brutal generals and presidents would fill their militias with boys and girls as young as eight (see chapter 29).

In January of 1979, the Vietnamese army liberated the Kampuchean people from the Khmer Rouge. For the first time in four years, international food assistance was allowed into the famine-stricken country. On

October 3, Dith escaped over the Thai border, and Sydney Schanberg soon flew to Thailand to meet him (Martin 2008, A19).

The "monstrous social experiment that was Pol Pot's reign was over, but the economic infrastructure of Cambodia—the factories, schools, bridges, roads, ports and farms, lay in ruins" (Schanberg 1985, 67). A ten-year-long bloody civil war ensued, until peace accords were finally signed in 1993, providing for free and fair elections and the creation of a constitution. Pol Pot was denounced by his former comrades at a show trial and sentenced to house arrest. He died on August 15, 1998.

On October 27, 2007, the *New York Times* published an article by Seth Myans called "Out from Behind a Camera at a Khmer Torture House" (A3). It was about a photographer, Nhem En, now forty-seven, who was on the staff of the Tuol Sleng prison, "the most notorious torture house of the Khmer Rouge regime" (A3). As this book goes to press, Khmer Rouge leaders are being tried in Cambodia. Defendants include the commandant of the prison, Kain Geuk Eav, known as Duch, who has been charged with crimes against humanity. Nhem En is scheduled to testify at the trial about the man he reported to for three years, when he was forced to photograph many of the 14,000 prisoners tortured to death or sent to the "killing fields" (A3). Though they were unaware of what was going to happen to them, according to Nhem En, as he prepared to take their pictures, they would ask him, "Why was I brought here? What am I accused of? What did I do wrong?" But Nhem En ignored them (A3).

On February 20, 2008, the *Hartford Courant's* Mark Spencer published "Lessons on Genocide" about a lobbying effort to convince members of Connecticut's State Assembly to support antigenocide education. At the rally, Cambodian-American Pholla Craveen told of watching the murder of her father and brother. She recalled the trucks laden with the bodies of men, women, and children and of having walked through minefields at age five, as she fled with her mother and other siblings.

Later during the rally, Craveen cried as she thanked another speaker, a father of three from Oregon, who was the only American aid worker to remain in Rwanda during the civil war. He is credited with risking his own life to save hundreds of Rwandans, including children in orphanages. Craveen told the audience that when people from Western countries aid victims of genocidal wars, hope for the future is restored (Teaching against Genocide rally, Hartford, Connecticut Statehouse, February 19, 2008).

RWANDA'S GENOCIDAL CIVIL WAR

Rwanda, slightly smaller than Maryland, is a landlocked country in central Africa between Zaire on the west and Tanzania on the east, with Uganda to the north and Burundi to the south. Kigali is its capital. Estimates of its population range from 7.5 million to 10 million, since most census reports are estimations, ("Rwanda" 1993–2008).

About 1916, during the colonial period, the Belgians chased the Germans out of the territory inhabited by the Tutsis (10%), an extremely tall, light-skinned people who herded cattle, and by the Hutus (90%), shorter and darker, who farmed vegetables. The Belgians preferred the minority Tutsis, thought them more like Europeans, and elevated them to a position of power over the majority Hutus. Given the enmity already existing between the two groups, this was a mistake, despite the fact that this policy permitted the Belgians to develop and exploit a vast network of coffee and tea plantations without the inconvenience of war or the expense of deploying a large colonial service (Dallaire 2003, 47).

In 1959, a civil war broke out and Tutsi power ended. Many went into exile, and large numbers died of cholera. In 1962, Rwanda, which had become part of the Belgian UN trusteeship of Rwanda-Burundi, achieved independence, but under conditions that guaranteed failure. They faced the impossible task of developing their newly independent country without an educated elite, a functioning economy, or a stable society. Rwandan history "began to split into two" (Kinzer 2008, 32). It had been presumed that the exiled Tutsis would forget their homeland. The opposite happened. They never adjusted to their status as refugees and never forgot the country they had been forced to leave.

Starting in 1960, armed Tutsis reinvaded their homeland to fight the new regime, targeting police stations and government offices. They were met by Rwandan troops, resulting in bloody reprisals. According to Kinzer, "Between one thousand and two thousand Tutsi men, women and children were massacred and burned on the spot. . . . their huts burned and pillaged and their property divided among the Hutu population" (33).

President Gregoire Kayibanda, the leader of the Hutu-dominated government, had decided to kill the country's remaining Tutsi population, including the moderates who had adjusted to the Hutu regime, "so that they would never be tempted to ally themselves with Tutsi" (33). He succeeded in killing as many as 20,000 Tutsis during the early 1960s. The Hutus began to call the Tutsi rebels *inyenzi*, which means "cockroach" (34).

On July 5, 1973, simmering feuds and internal strife between the reigning Hutus led to a bloodless coup in which Hutu General Juvenal Habyarimana became president and dictator. Soldiers surrounded President Kayibanda's home and starved him and his wife to death in captivity. According to Stephen Kinzer, "[t]he deposed president and his first lady spend their last days desperately eating pages from the books in their library" (36). Since he had shed no blood, Gen. Habyarimana, a superstitious man, believed the spirits would not haunt him (36).

Twenty years of continued ethnic strife led to an August 1993 peace accord between the Hutu government and the rebel Tutsi Rwandan Patriotic Front (RPF) led by Paul Kagame. Unfortunately, the resulting "Arusha" peace agreement failed to consider "how former warring factions would share power or resettle refugees, some of whom had left the country

40 years earlier and now had children and grandchildren with a claim on Rwandan citizenship" (Dallaire 2003, 54).

UN Force Commander, Canadian Lt. Gen. Romeo Dallaire, and a small peacekeeping force, were sent to Rwanda to enforce the peace accords from 1993 to 1994. They landed in the Rwandan capita, Kigali, on August 19, 1993. They were met by a group of diplomats, representatives, and Rwandan politicians. The atmosphere was friendly and positive for the most part. They were assured that with the help of the UN neutral peacekeeping force, the peace agreement would mark the beginning of democracy for the country (57).

There were, however, a few voices who understood the legacy of ancient feuds and continuing poverty. One was Tutsi rebel commander Paul Kagame, the military leader of the RPF, nicknamed the "Napoleon of Africa" because of his ability to turn a ragtag group of guerilla fighters into a proud force capable of holding its own (57). Another was Colonel Nsabimana, chief of the Rwandan government forces and a strong supporter of Rwandan dictator Habyarimana. Because of the apparent willingness of the former feuding parties to face each other and discuss enforcement of the Arusha accords, which included safeguarding the demilitarized zone and keeping the feuding parties apart, the discussions ended on a hopeful note (57–58).

But, according to the U.S. Committee for Refugees, Dallaire "was still too innocent to grasp Rwanda's chilling political realities. Radicals were already planning their campaign of extermination . . . when he met them, they assured him they only wanted peace. They could smile and murder while they smiled" (Kinzer 2008, 117).

In 1994, at a packed meeting in Kigali between Dallaire, a peacemaker, Rwanda officials, and ordinary citizens, more and more people tried to squeeze in and voice their concerns on public safety and security. According to Dallaire, "[T]hey complained that the government was no longer governing: a lot of salaries were not being paid, public schools and government sponsored medical care was starved of resources. They were extremely disturbed by the increased banditry and lawlessness. They were very disappointed when we had to explain to them the limit of our mission" (Dallaire 2003, 172).

While visiting a displaced persons camp in the demilitarized zone, Dallaire had been greeted by an awful stench—a reminder of the horror of the long civil war. Here, 60,000 persons were crowded in filthy camps, smelling of feces, urine, vomit, and death. When Dallaire's small group left their vehicle, they were swarmed by a thick cloud of flies, which stuck to their eyes and mouths and crawled into their ears and noses. Deeply disturbed, Dallaire later recalled:

As I stood struggling to regain my composure, I was surrounded by a group of camp children who were either laughing outright or smiling shyly at me . . . They were playing soccer with a ball made of dried twigs and vines and tugged at my pants to have me join their game . . . and I just knew that my primary mission was to do my best to ensure Rwanda's peace for the sake of the children. (Dallaire 2003, 63–64)

On April 6, 1994, an explosion occurred at Kigali airport. A plane had crashed, killing the Hutu presidents of Rwanda-Burundi, Juvenal Habyari-mana and Cyprien Ntaryamira, and the army chief of staff, Deogratias Nsabimana. It is thought that the explosion may have been set off by Hutu extremists who were in the process of targeting the so-called cockroaches.

As had been the case in Cambodia, officials in Rwanda expected that any killings would be "narrowly tailored reprisals rather than harbingers of a broadly ambitious genocide . . . including moderate Hutu as well as Tutsi" (Power 2002, 349–50). They were wrong.

Presidential Guard units spent much of the following day finding and killing moderate Hutu "traitors." Brent Beardsley, Dallaire's executive, received an urgent call for help from UN military observers at a church run by Polish missionaries.

When we arrived I looked at the school across the street and there were children, I don't know how many, forty, sixty, eighty children stacked up outside who had all been chopped up with machetes. . . . Some of their mothers had heard them screaming and had come running, and the militia had killed them too . . . Inside the church . . . we found 150 people dead. . . . [and] some still groaning. The Polish priests said . . . the Rwandan army had cleared out the area. . . . rounded up all the Tutsi and the militia had hacked them to death" (Power 2002, 349).

Tutsi Paul Kagame, leader of the RPF, sent a chilling message, "a straight ulti-matum," (Kinzer 2008, 141–43) to Dallaire. Kagame declared that the Aru-sha peace accords would be dead if the fighting did not stop immediately and argued that he and his force must join with Dallaire's peacemakers to ensure the success of the accords. But Dallaire knew that if he agreed, he would be fired on the spot.

Instead, Dallaire got in touch with Prime Minister Agathe, next in line to the Rwandan president Habyrimana. She was unable to call her cabinet together; many of her ministers were fearful and didn't want to leave their families. The hard-line ministers from the other parties had disappeared. The UN debated (Would the UN peacekeeping mission be able to fulfill its role with fewer than 500 peacekeepers from around the world? Was this a full-blown genocide?), while the perpetrators, the *genocidaires*, as they were called, wasted no time arousing fear. "We were in the middle of a slaughterhouse" (Dallaire 2003, 281). Ten Belgians, wearing the blue helmets of the small UN peacekeeping force, were butchered. Dallaire was blamed. The Belgian government withdrew the rest of its forces, and the UN mission fell apart.

On April 21, 1994, with reports of tens of thousands of Tutsis already mur-dered, the nations comprising the UN Security Council voted to withdraw most of Dallaire's UN forces from Rwanda. Dallaire was permitted 270, but 503 remained. For more than two months, they watched helplessly as the bodies piled up around them. The lack of support by the United Nations was considered shameful (Daillaire 1995). Although, once again, we witness extraordinary bravery by a single individual, Romeo Dallaire, leading his ill-equipped and mentally unprepared United Nations Assistance Mission for Rwanda (UNAMIR) peacekeepers, in outdated blue berets, charged with enforcing the peace but instead witnessing the murder of 800,000 Rwandans, Tutsis, and moderate Hutus in one hundred days (279).

Those able to leave left. Dallaire observed the American ambassador, whom he respected, loading his last belongings into his vehicle. What was even worse, the French elite troops, arriving ten weeks after the genocide had begun, told Dallaire that they had only come to rescue their "old friends" in the genocidal government (286).

Dallaire could also have arranged to leave, but he decided to stay, along with the members of his skeleton force. However, he realized that without a larger contingent of UN peacekeepers, the enforcement of the peace accords was impossible. After the slaughter had begun, member nations agreed with him. But everyone felt that "some other nations should do it" (374). In the Security Council, however, the United States, a highly influential member, believed that African security problems should be solved by African states. They, in turn, were willing, but not able to accomplish the task without the assistance of the First World. The Pentagon judged that the estimated 8,000–10,000 Rwandans killed each day were not worth the cost of the fuel or the violation of Rwandan airways (375). Dallaire was reduced to keeping a tally of the numbers killed (374–75).

On April 22, 1994, the UN Security Council, in Resolution 912, had finally voted for the skeleton force option. Using such phrases as ". . . having considered . . . [Dallaire's ellipses] express regret . . . shocked . . . appalled . . . deeply concerned . . . strongly condemns . . . calls upon . . . decides to remain actively seized, of the matter" (322) in their resolution, the Security Council attempted to demonstrate concern without supplying any significant financial or military support.

The United States, the superpower, continued to aggressively block authorization of UN reinforcements. In *A Problem from Hell*, Power states:

It is shocking to note that during the entire three months of genocide, [President] Clinton never assembled his top policy advisors to discuss the killings . . . When the subject came up it did so along with . . . discussions of Somalia, Haiti and Bosnia. Whereas these crises involved U.S. personnel and stirred some public interest, Rwanda generated no sense of urgency . . . no political cost. (2002, 366)

What happened after the hundred days? The *genocidaires* were driven out of Rwanda by the new president, Paul Kagame, and the RPF. The killers fled into the filthy, disease-infected camps of neighboring Tanzania and Zaire. They were followed by 2 million Hutu civilians who had been warned of great danger if they stayed in Rwanda. In the first month after the exodus, cholera and dysentery epidemics killed 50,000 of the refugees in Zaire, now Congo. In this mix of civilian Hutus, Hutu *genocidaires*, and Tutsis, plans for renewed fighting were once again being hatched. "Unsurprisingly, the same Hutu who had orchestrated the fastest killing spree in recorded history quickly asserted control in their new environment. Extremists were also present among Tutsi" (Power 2008, 192). According to Dalliare, in order to meet with Kagame to discuss a possible cease fire, "we had to inch our way through villages of dead humans . . . to create paths among the dead and half-dead with our hands" (Dallaire 2003, 325).

THE EFFECTS OF WAR ON CHILDREN

Stark statistics compiled by the UN tell the story of the effects of war on Rwandans: 99.9 percent of Rwandan children witnessed violence; 90 percent believed they would die; 87 percent saw dead bodies; 80 percent lost at least one relative; 58 percent saw people being hacked; and 31 percent witnessed rapes.

The present government tries hard to create a health-care system addressing the people's urgent physical needs. There is no access to counselors or therapists even though a quarter of the population suffers from post-traumatic stress syndrome. Because so many people are affected . . . they have coined the word *ihahamuka*. It means "without lungs" or "breathless with fear."

Source: Stephen Kinzer *A Thousand Hills.* (Hoboken: NJ: Wiley and Sons, 2008).

Early in 1995, the world turned its back on both Rwandan refugees and *genocidaires*. The International Rescue Committee and even Doctors without Borders decided to pull out of the camps. In April 2000, Paul Kagame was inaugurated as the fifth president of Rwanda (Dallaire 532). Rwandan leaders including Kagame recommended a "truth and reconciliation process" (Kinzer 2008, 334) similar to that in South Africa, where citizens on both sides of the conflict testified, but were not punished.

Rwanda has no democratic or constitutional tradition. No road map exists to guide their leader, Paul Kagame; however, he told author Stephen Kinzer: "We can reduce the number of people below the poverty line, reduce dependence on donor funds and truly develop our country . . . We want to do it and we will" (2008, 334, 338)

A "SHATTERED SUDAN" LEADS
TO GENOCIDE IN DARFUR

An article featured in the February 2003 edition of *National Geographic* reads, "Shattered Sudan, Drilling for Oil, Hoping for Peace." It is written by Paul Salopec, who describes the war in Sudan as "the oldest civil war in the world, which is being fought by men who wander like demented hospital orderlies across the primordial wastes of Africa" (Salopec 2003, 31).

Salopec describes one hot morning when he followed a group of rebels as they fled a government ambush in the oil fields of southern Sudan:

One has just been shot, his body abandoned on a parched savanna that hides nearly 20 billion dollars' worth of low-sulfur crude . . . they're suffering their bullet wounds in silence, a boy marching in front balances a car battery on his head. He is the radio operator's assistant. Every few hundred yards he puts the battery down and empties blood out of a shoe. (34)

Fifty years earlier, on January 1, 1956, Sudan had voted for complete independence from Egypt and the United Kingdom. In the years that followed, an increasing number of bloodless and bloody coups have occurred. Disputes between so-called arabized northerners and black southerners lead to continual strife. Occasionally, a national emergency would be proclaimed by Khartoum, and hundreds of prominent citizens would be arrested and executed.

George Clooney, actor and UN Messenger of Peace, attends a meeting with delegates from Darfur's civil society. January 2008. AP Photo/UNAMID, Sherren Zorba.

In October of 1990, the U.S. government stopped sending aid to Sudan when it openly supported Iraq during the Persian Gulf War. In 1991, the U.N. suspended its relief efforts to help the estimated 7 million Sudanese threatened by famine.

POVERTY IN SUDAN

Brian Steidle, a former captain in the Marine Corps, was hired by the African Union to document conditions in Darfur. In *The Devil Came on Horseback, Bearing Witness to the Genocide in DARFUR* (2007), which he coauthored with Gretchen Steidle Wallace, he describes a scene that illustrates the conditions in which the Sudanese suffer.

"On my first patrol to the village of Tungoli. . . . We sat down to talk with the chief outside his hut. . . .

'You see,' the chief explained, 'the well that we have been digging has just collapsed again . . . we now have twenty liters of water for our entire village of 450 people . . .' At that moment [a] man who had left returned bringing a single glass of water for me to drink.

'For me?' . . . I looked at the glass and sucked in my breath. Even if they were to give it half an hour to settle, I was certain it would be half-full with dirt. I took the glass with a plastic smile catching a whiff of live-stock. How could they be surviving on this? Despite my . . . dehydration, there was no way I could drink that muddy water.

'I really wish I could but I just cannot accept their gesture,' I gently told our interpreter,

. . . Without translating my remarks, he explained,

'They will be extremely offended if you do not drink that glass imme-diately.'

Forcing a smile, I tipped the greasy vessel, avoiding floating insects, and drank as much as possible without chewing the sediment at the bot-tom. I might as well have licked a goat" (20–21).

Source: Brian Steidle and Gretchen Steidle Wallace. *The Devil Came on Horseback: Bear-ing Witness to the Genocide in Darfur.* (New York: Perseus Book Groups, 2007).

By 2003, a rebellion against unfair treatment in the Darfur region in west-ern Sudan led to a new crisis and another attempted genocide. Maraud-ing Arab militias, known as the *janjaweed,* aided by government troops, retaliated against the rebels, attacking African villagers, looting and burn-ing their homes, and killing the inhabitants. The African Union sent 7,000 peacemakers, but fighting continued. Nothing seemed to work. By mid-2007, at least 200,000 people had been killed. Two million more had fled to overcrowded refugee camps in neighboring Chad.

On July 31, 2007, the UN Security Council voted to begin deploying a joint UN-African Union force of up to 26,000 peacekeepers (UNMIS).

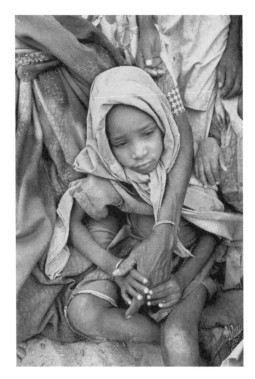

A child waits with his mother in Disa, North Darfur. This photograph by Marcus Bleasdale of Great Britain was chosen as UNICEF'S "Photo of the Year," June 2004. AP Photo UNICEF, Marcus Bleasdale.

Don Cheadle, the actor (*Hotel Rwanda*) and writer, and John Prendergast, a former White House official in the Clinton administration, have written *Not on Our Watch: The Mission to End Genocide and Beyond* (2007). They both believe that the horrors in Darfur can be stopped through raising awareness, fund-raising, and political lobbying.

WHAT DO THESE GENOCIDES HAVE IN COMMON WITH THE HOLOCAUST?

- Strong dictatorial leaders exercising absolute power over any opposition.
- A sense of superiority over those considered inferior, with different cultures or religions.
- Ethnic hatred used by leaders to fuel violence against a perceived enemy.
- Use of modern weapons to murder those considered unworthy of life: gas chambers, bombs, and AK-47s.
- Or the use of ancient weapons, such as machetes, sticks, hoes, whips, fists, and starvation.
- Destroying total villages, towns, and even cities.

In Sudan, the brutal perpetrators are the *janjaweed,* a loose collection of mercenary fighters. In Rwanda, Hutus and Tutsis killed each other. Elsewhere, killings are planned and carried out by all types of people, from well-educated professionals and government officials, to illiterate peasants and untrained child soldiers formed into militias and insurgent rebel gangs, to ordinary criminals released from jails to help the cause.

At the end of their book, Brian Steidle and Gretchen Steidle Wallace write:

Sometimes when I am talking to people, they ask me how they or the United States will benefit from [helping the people in Darfur]. I tell them: You get nothing, except that you did something good, that you did the right thing. You helped people who couldn't help themselves. Every human being should have the chance to grow up without violence . . . to drink a glass of clean water, to be free of fear—the fear of rape or a bullet in the back during the simple act of collecting firewood for daily meals. (229)

Then they ask: "When the genocide in Darfur has ended, what will you say you did to stop it?" (230).

WORKS CITED

Cheadle, Don, and John Prendergast. *Not on Our Watch: The Mission to End Genocide and Beyond.* New York: Hyperion, 2007.

Dallaire, Romeo. *Shake Hands with the Devil.* New York: Carroll and Graf Publishers, 2003.

Daillaire, R. A. and B. Poulin. "UNAMIR Mission to Rwanda." JFQ, Spring 1995. http://www.dtic.mil/doctrine/jel/jfg_pubs/0534.pdf.

Kinzer, Stephen. *A Thousand Hills.* Hoboken: NJ: Wiley and Sons, 2008.

Martin, Douglas. "Dith Pran, Photojournalist and Survivor of the Killing Fields, Dies at 65." *New York Times,* March 31, 2008.

"Memo from Africa: The Pursuit of Justice vs. the Pursuit of Peace." *New York Times,* July 11, 2008.

Myans, Seth. "Out from Behind a Camera at a Khmer Torture House." *New York Times,* October 27, 2007.

Power, Samantha. *A Problem from Hell.* New York: HarperCollins, 2002.

———. *Chasing the Flame.* New York: Penguin Group, 2008.

"Rwanda." MSN Encarta. *Microsoft Corporation,* 1993–2008. Available at http://encarta.msn.com/encyclopedia_761560996_2/rwanda.html

Salopec, Paul. "Shattered Sudan, Drilling for Oil, Hoping for Peace." *National Geographic,* February 2003.

Schanberg, Sydney. *The Death and Life of Dith Pran.* New York: Penguin Books, 1985.

Schulz, Carol, and Eve Soumerai. *Human Rights: The Struggle for Freedom, Dignity and Equality.* Hartford, CT Board of Education, 1998.

Spencer, Mark. "Lessons on Genocide." *Hartford Courant,* Section B, February 20, 2008.

Steidle, Brian, and Gretchen Steidle Wallace. *The Devil Came on Horseback: Bearing Witness to the Genocide in Darfur.* New York: Perseus Book Groups, 2007.

United Nations Chronicles. December, 1983.

White, Peter T. "Kampuchea Wakens from a Nightmare." *National Geographic Magazine,* May. 1982.

28

THE TWENTY-FIRST CENTURY: MODERN SLAVERY IN A GLOBAL ECONOMY

Above the gates of Auschwitz are the words *Arbeit macht frei* (work makes freedom). The irony of the slogan, in a place in which *work* equaled *slavery* and slavery most often resulted in death was not lost on anyone. Today, no civilized human being believes that slavery is moral or legitimate. Yet thousands of people all over the planet are working for little more than food and shelter, as part of the most technologically advanced global economy in history.

In Haiti, they are called "stay withs" (*restaveks*). Mostly children, they are "placed" in homes by "brokers" (with professional business cards) and are expected to serve as a "be-there-for-that" when not performing their other duties (Skinner 2008, 7). In Europe they are considered "social orphans"—left behind by parents searching for jobs (Finnegan 2008, 50). They are easy prey for pimps, kidnappers, and investors in businesses short on labor. UNICEF calls them "children in domesticity" (Skinner 2008, 24), presumably because they are trapped in homes by wealthy families. In India they are called "backward poor people" (209). Though many are children, even more are adults, some quite old (or prematurely aged).

Some have been abducted; others have been lured by promises of employment or even adoption and then physically imprisoned. The youngest have been sold by parents who are desperate to give their children food, education, and a better life. British officials have reported people being kidnapped from Eastern Europe, flown to London, and sold at auction in the airport ("Black Market" 2006, 11). And still others remain in their own countries, born into slavery because of generations-old debts, often as small a sum as one dollar.

These men, women, and children are part of a growing system of "human trafficking"; though few are called "slaves" by world leaders who have signed three hundred international treaties banning slavery (Skinner 2008, xiii). They are hidden behind a veil of euphemisms: "social orphans," "children in domesticity," and children who are "placed" in homes by "brokers," as if they were being adopted by loving families (23).

By definition, a slave is a "human being forced to work under threat of violence, for no pay" (from Kevin Bales' *Disposable People,* quoted in Skinner 2008, xv). According to Skinner, today "there are more slaves than at any point in human history" (xv). Although it is impossible to take a precise census, humanitarian organizations have determined that between 500,000 and 800,000 people are trafficked across borders annually, including 14,500–17,000 into the United States ("Forced Labor" 2005).

Approximately 27 million people worldwide are currently enslaved ("Black Market" 2006, 11), some as young as three years old (Skinner 2008, xvi, 5). They are taken from the poorest states and regions in the world—for example, Asia (especially China and Laos), India, Africa, Eastern Europe (notably Moldova and Romania), Central America, and Haiti—and sold to buyers in the wealthiest (or even only moderately wealthy) regions in the Middle East (Dubai is a favorite of traffickers), Western Europe, Turkey, Israel, Saudi Arabia, Greece, Canada, and the United States (Finnegan 2008, 47).

Ranked third, after weapons and drugs, human beings comprise the most lucrative illegal trade in the world. The sale and purchase of slaves brings in $31 billion a year ("Black Market" 2006, 11). Legitimate businesses profit as well: travel agencies that arrange for flights from one country to the next and enterprises active in the tourist world, such as hotels, tour bus companies, and night clubs that provide prostitutes and other services for a fee.

Professionals and law enforcement officials also profit: accountants, lawyers, doctors, landlords, forgers, police, border guards, and embassy personnel. Some do so unknowingly, and others are willing partners in the general corruption and exploitation. Fraudulent contracts are drawn up, passports forged, injured or diseased young girls treated or drugged, and officials bribed to let all this go on without interference. A 2003 study in the Netherlands found that "on average, a single sex slave earned her pimp $250,000 per year" (Skinner 2008, 144). Finnegan notes that "[e]veryone seems to be making money except the trafficked women and girls" (2008, 46, 47).

THE GLOBALIZATION OF HUMAN TRAFFICKING

The primary push factor in all of this is poverty. Pervasive, desperate poverty around the globe. In 1989, there were 14 million poor in Eastern

Europe; in 1999, following the fall of Communism, there were 147 million (Skinner 2008, 134).

The machinery that connects the slaves to the buyers varies. In some countries, such as Russia, Italy, Turkey, and most of Eastern Europe, the mafia, or other organized crime network, is the engine that drives the trafficking, just as it does with arms and narcotics. Says Finnegan, "[T]hey [run] women alongside traditional contraband, like drugs and guns" (2008, 46). In states like Moldova, the system is primarily "horizontal" (49): recruiters, front companies, forgers, and corrupt officials are all homegrown. Then the slave is sent abroad.

Here is how the cross-border system operates in one typical Eastern European country, the tiniest of the former Soviet republics, Moldova (population 4 million). Moldova is now the poorest country in Europe; its per capita income is the size of Sudan's. Since the break up of the U.S.S.R., 600,000 workers have left the country for employment. Moreover, many of the remaining children have suffered from neglect, starvation, or abuse. Everyone needs work, and everyone wants to leave.

Not surprisingly, Moldova is also the largest source of sex slaves in Europe (Skinner 2008, 153). The traffickers advertise job openings for waitresses, nurses' aids, au pairs, maids, even "good looking women for saleswomen" (Finnegan 2008, 57). One business advertised for "surrogate mothers" in order to use the stem-cell spinal fluid from aborted fetuses (57). Since only 1%–2% of those who answer the ads become "Victims of Trafficking" (VOT) (52), most of the young people are fooled by the phony offers. This occurs despite the government's efforts to warn them to be careful, through films in schools, ubiquitous posters on public walls, and anti-trafficking concerts (7). Some are lured by former slaves who have been promised freedom in return for a replacement; others get taken in by a new boyfriend—part of the bait—who earns a commission.

"MARIA" FROM MOLDOVA

In some countries, prostitutes are blamed rather than treated as victims and can't even go home. "Victim blaming is the Moldovan national sport," says one writer (Finnegan 2008, 50). Maria, originally captured by a boy, raped, and then forced by her mother to marry him, was beaten by her new husband. She had a baby at eighteen. Trying to get away, she was tricked into becoming a prostitute. She tried suicide, jumping out of a window and breaking all four limbs. Eventually, she was rescued and treated for her injuries. Now she lives with her mother and her daughter (51).

Source: William Finnegan. "The Countertraffickers." *New Yorker,* May 5, 2008.

Convinced that a new job awaits them, they are taken to the airport; abandoned by their friend; flown to Dubai or Russia or Turkey by a front company; and sold to a pimp or other type of employer, who then takes their passport (Porteous 2006,)

They are then terrorized. Prostitutes are forced to "service" (be raped by) as many as 15–20 johns a day. They are often beaten as well, as a warning not to try to escape (Skinner 2008, 131). Factory workers must labor for long hours, seven days a week. They too are locked up, beaten, and often starved. They are told that they owe their bosses travel fees and can't go home until their debt is paid. Lost in a foreign country, with no money, no connections, and no skills, they are trapped. Should they escape and run to the police, they are almost certainly returned to their pimp or boss (Finnegan 2008, 51)

"LENA" FROM MOLDOVA

Lena was told by her boyfriend to take a job in Portugal as a waitress. She was tricked into changing her plans and ended up in Dubai, where she was sold to, in her words, a "she-pimp" (Finnegan 2008, 47). After two years, she escaped and went to the police station. Despite daily beatings and rapes by her owner, she was arrested because she had no passport. Her pimp was left to carry on her trade. Although Lena was released, she had no money, could not find a job, and ended up back in prostitution. Eventually, she fell in love and quit working but was later arrested for having no documentation. After several years, she was deported and moved in with her grandmother. She eventually got help from an American-funded women's center (48).

Source: William Finnegan. "The Countertraffickers." *New Yorker,* May 5, 2008.

SLAVERY IN THE UNITED STATES

Nearly 150 years after the end of the Civil War, there are approximately 50,000 slaves living in the United States (Skinner 2008, 265). Most are from Asia or Mexico, though they come from elsewhere as well. Most are illegal immigrants and do not know that there might be legal assistance for them if they are being held as prisoners. Currently, there are 200 million migrants in the world, living outside their own borders as a result of war, extreme poverty, fear of imprisonment or violence, or a desire to live in a democratic country (Finnegan 2008, 46). There is no lack of vulnerable people, and protecting them, even keeping track of them, is difficult.

Some of America's slaves have simply been kidnapped or purchased elsewhere and brought into the country as "family." These include nine-year-old Haitian "stay withs" living in Florida, teenaged Asian prostitutes living in New York City, Central American farm workers in Texas, and Mexican factory workers in California. According to Benjamin Skinner, the author of *A Crime So Monstrous,* only five hours from the United Nations building in Manhattan, one can purchase a ten-year-old girl for fifty dollars (2008, 1). In the past, children were bought by wealthy families who lived in decent circumstances and were at least willing to feed, clothe, and shelter their domestic slaves. Now that lower middle class families can afford a slave, owners lack the resources, or the desire, to provide sufficient food, clothing, shelter, medical care, or education to these children. In addition, many are just plain cruel.

Skinner tells the story of Williathe Narcisse, owned by a wealthy Haitian-American family. When her mother, Immacula, died, Williathe was purchased by her Haitian employer's sister, Marie Pompee, and taken to Miami. For three years, "Little Hope," as she was later called by the Haitian-American community, was forced to clean house, wait on the family, care for a baby and a preschooler, and work in the family's clothing business. She was frequently beaten by Marie for not working hard enough. When other children came to visit the household, she was not allowed to talk but had to behave like a servant. One night, Marie's son Willy Jr., eight years Williathe's senior, violently raped her, and then continued to do so daily, threatening to kill her if she told anyone.

Four years after kidnapping Williathe, Marie enrolled her in a newly built, free private school. Eventually, a teacher, and a woman Williathe found by dialing a number she saw in an advertisement for the "John Casablancas Modeling and Career Center" (Skinner 270) became suspicious and tried to get the Department of Children and Families (DCF) involved. But the DCF did not believe what the child told them. When her teacher threatened to call a news station, the DCF finally called the police.

In the end, Williathe was rescued and treated for undernourishment, infections, rotting teeth, and physical and psychological abuse. The son and his father escaped the country, and the mother pled guilty to a charge of harboring an illegal alien—the only crime that could be proved without putting Williathe, still a teenager, on the stand (263–85).

During her trial, Marie Pompee "begged the forgiveness of the court judge, but not of Williathe, who was not there" (279). Her claim was as follows: "I was just helping a kid and I didn't realize that helping someone would bring me so many problems!" (279).

In Haiti, though drug trafficking is against the law, human trafficking is not, as long as children are not "mistreated" (25). There does exist a twenty-three man Brigade for the Protection of Minors (BPM). Its head is Renel Costume. When Skinner visited Costume, he found that the agency's office was tiny, the landline was out of order, the cell phone was out of minutes, and the computer was "nonfunctional" (24). When Skinner reported a child-selling business, Costume seemed to be disinterested. When pushed to respond, "[H]e even acknowledged that he had *restavek* children living with him. 'But I don't rape them'" (25).

"DALYN" FROM CAMBODIA

Dalyn was twelve when a woman asked if she'd like to work in a factory. When they got to Phnom Penh, Cambodia, she was sold to the owner of a brothel. In a 2007 interview with BBC News, she told how she was forced to become a prostitute:

> "A group of men came into my room and told me to receive a client. I asked what I was supposed to do. They told me: 'Don't worry, you'll know what to do. And if you don't, you'll do it until you do.' I refused but they told me to shut up and said that 'one way or the other' I was going to have to do as they say. They dragged me out of the room and I screamed and called out for help. They put a gun to my head. I pleaded for my life, telling them this wasn't the work I had been led to believe I was doing. . . . But then he [the brothel owner] said I would be shot if I refused."

Dalyn was tortured and locked in a cage, only let out for clients. Although she was eventually rescued, she continued to feel a sense of shame and self-hatred. Coming from a society in which sex outside of marriage is still considered a sin, most of these girls suffer severe psychological trauma. Dalyn told her interviewer, "I felt a sense of utter disgust. I had become the very thing I most despised. It is slavery of the worst kind. They have total power over you—they get you to do anything they want."

Source: "My Life as a Prostitute" *This World*. BBC News, March 27, 2007.

INDIA'S CYCLE OF BONDED LABOR

Not all of the slave trade involves crossing borders or kidnapping people. In India a system of so-called bonded labor traps more than 10 million people in a generational cycle. Most are from the lowest level of a caste system that has been officially banned. Slavery itself is outlawed. However, much like the sharecroppers in the hundred years following the Civil War, they are still enslaved.

Eight percent of the world's poor live in the hamlet of Lohagara Dhal, in the state of Uttar Pradesh, in North India. In 2005, "[e]very single man, woman and child in Lohagara Dhal was a slave" (Skinner 2008, 205). Gonoo Lal Kol was one of them. His job was to smash rock into sand with a hammer, for fourteen hours a day, periodically setting off deadly chemical explosions to detach large chunks. This sometimes resulted in killing slaves as well.

Gonoo's boss was a very wealthy landowner. He was also known to have killed a number of his employees and gotten away with it. Though officially slavery is illegal in India, he was allowed to carry on his business, paying his workers in alcohol, grain, and subsistence wages, because they owed him money. Some originally owed less than a dollar, which, with one hundred percent interested compounded over generations, amounts to many times that (206). Given their wages, they of course had no way to pay off their debts—even though the debts are fictitious, since the amount they earned in their first two years should have retired the debt long ago. Gonoo was paying off his grandfather's loan of sixty-two cents—his mother's bride price—which has now grown to about five hundred dollars (206).

According to Skinner, there are between 10 and 20 million slaves currently working in India (207). They work in tea stalls, sari factories, and at carpet looms. They harvest fish and roll cigarettes. They make glass bracelets, and they plant and harvest crops. But the government of India does not call them slaves. They are referred to as " 'bonded laborers,' 'exploited workers' or simply 'backward people' " (209).

EFFORTS TO ABOLISH SLAVERY

In October of 2000, the United States passed the Trafficking Victims Protection Act. Its provisions require the State Department to call for programs to eradicate slavery. They must rank countries according to a three-tier system: Tier 1 countries are doing their part to end slavery; Tier 2 countries need to do more; Tier 3 countries are doing little or nothing and may have sanctions issued against them. In 2003, a Tier 2 Watch List was created to scare countries without alienating them. According to Finnegan, the rankings are often based on political considerations (2008, 54). The United States has also set aside five thousand visas for immigrants who have been used as slaves to attain legal status.

SUDAN'S FORGOTTEN SLAVES

As a result of the continuing civil war in Sudan, thousands of people are believed to be living in slavery, having been captured years ago and never returned to their tribes. In 2007, the BBC's Joseph Winter reported on the capture of Arek Anyiel Deng in 1988, when she was ten years old.

> Arab militias rode into her village on horseback, firing their guns. When the adults fled, the children and cattle were rounded up and made to walk north for five days before they were divided between members of the raiding party. . . . "My abductor told me that I was his slave and I had to do all the work he told me to—fetching water and firewood looking after animals and farming. . . . When I was 12, he said he wanted to sleep with me. I could not refuse because I was a slave, I had to do everything he wanted, or he could have killed me" (1).

According to one study, reported by the BBC, about 11,000 young boys and girls were captured during the twenty-one years of warfare by Arab militias. The boys watched over cattle, and the girls did domestic chores until they were married off at twelve (2). In 1999, the government of Sudan agreed to return these now grown children, as long as they were referred to as *abductees*, not slaves. About 3,000 were returned home by 2005 when the program ran out of funds (2).

Source: Joseph Winter. "No Return for Sudan's Forgotten Slaves." *This World*. BBC News, March 16, 2007.

Unfortunately, few countries have been sanctioned for doing nothing to stop the slave trade, and only a handful of people have applied for U.S. visas, out of the thousands already in the United States. Most likely, they are unaware of this offer or afraid of deportation (54).

An antitrafficking task force consisting of twelve federal agencies has sent FBI agents to dozens of countries to help local authorities. These measures are admirable but still largely ineffective. One of the problems in ending this deplorable situation is that there are too many conflicting agendas involved in an abolition effort.

The issue of prostitution is one complicating factor. A major antislavery effort has come from the Evangelical Christian movement in the United States. Their focus is on ending prostitution, which they see as, by its nature, coercive. Women's rights groups agree. In fact, the religious right has been called a "rescue industry." However, some unionized sex workers and independent prostitutes—who are better able to protect themselves from abusive pimps—may resist being rescued, especially when they have no other means of survival. Under pressure from the right, the United States has passed a law that cuts off funds from nongovernmental organizations (NGOs) and countries with legalized prostitution, which forces prostitution to go underground, making it even harder to stop the trade in sex slaves. As a Bush appointee, John Miller, America's antislavery czar, does not object to legalizing prostitution but needs the support of those who do to convince the administration to support his fight against trafficking.

RESCUER, STELLA ROTARU (MOLDOVA)

At the UN's International Organization for Migration, twenty-six-year-old social worker Stella Rotaru works out of a tiny office in Chisinau, Moldova. Her job is to help captive victims come home. Rotaru has helpers around the globe: a "Dubai prison officer. . . . Russian policemen, an Israeli lawyer, a Ukrainian psychologist, an Irish social worker, a Turkish women's shelter, Interpol . . . consulates and embassies . . .travel agents, priests, and partner organizations" who share resources (Finnegan 2008, 44).

When Rotaru gets a plea for rescue, it is not always easy to find the victims:

> The women don't always have the information themselves; in extreme cases, they may not be sure what country they're in. Look out the window . . . Any sign you can see? . . . Look for an address on matchbooks, or McDonald's bags. What languages do the johns speak? If [I] can capture a number on caller I.D., it can be useful, although simply calling back without an all-clear is generally too dangerous (44).

> Rotura's hours are long and sometimes emotionally draining. "You can't let these stories go through you," she told a journalist for the *New Yorker*. "You have to be practical, and do what you can" (46).

Source: William Finnegan. "The Countertraffickers." *New Yorker*, May 5, 2008.

In Sweden the government does not prosecute prostitutes but considers them victims. It has outlawed pimping, trafficking, and buying sex and provides help for women who wish to escape prostitution. The U.S. Justice Department disagrees with this policy, but Miller does not. He would like to see the United States adopt Sweden's law and continue providing aid to other countries that do the same (Skinner 2008, 190–191).

Since most of the world's slaves are not sex workers, Miller and others would like to broaden their fight for abolition to include other types of victims. However, another obstacle is the unwillingness of the government to penalize allies by ranking them as Tier 3 countries (195).

The United States has been criticized for focusing on prosecuting traffickers instead of the far more effective, but more costly, approach of alleviating the main push factor—poverty. Prosecution is extremely difficult for a whole raft of reasons: victims are terrified or ashamed to testify against their kidnappers, bosses, or pimps; victims are traumatized from months or years of physical, emotional, and psychological abuse; the law enforcement system in some cities is too corrupt (e.g., "the most powerful pimps in Moldova are all former cops" [Finnegan 2008, 53]); no laws exist against racketeering in some countries; and fighting poverty and injustice is expensive, though not impossible.

WORKS CITED

"The Ongoing Tragedy of International Slavery and Human Trafficking: An Overview" "Black Market in Human Beings." *This Week*, December 15, 2006.

Finnegan, William. "The Countertraffickers." *New Yorker*, May 5, 2008.

Forced Labor. BBC World Service. 2005. http://news.bbc.co.uk/1/shared/ spl/hi/world/05/slavery.

"My Life as a Prostitute." *This World*. BBC News, March 27, 2007. Available at http://news.bbc.co.uk/2/hi/programmes/this_world/64 22729.stm.

Porteous, Tom. "Women's Human Rights." Human Rights Watch. 2006. Available at http://hrw.org.

Skinner, Benjamin E. A *Crime So Monstrous: Face-to-Face with Modern-Day Slavery*. New York: Free Press (Division of Simon and Schuster), 2008.

Winter, Joseph. "No Return for Sudan's Forgotten Slaves." *This World*. BBC News, March 16, 2007. Available at http://news.bbc.co.uk/2/hi/programmes/this_world/6422729.stm.

29

CHILD SOLDIERS IN THE MODERN ARMY

Perhaps the most frightening form of slavery is the employment of young boys and girls in armies, militias, and armed gangs of rebels. As with other types of slavery, determining exactly how many children have become victims is not possible. According to Amnesty International (2007), some research suggests that 500,000 children are members of armed groups in eighty-five countries, and more that 300,000 of them are at present actively involved in thirty conflicts around the world. And the number of child soldiers is increasing. They can be found in Sierra Leone, Liberia, Sudan, Afghanistan, Iraq, India, Indonesia, and dozens more countries. Several, including the Tamil Tigers in Sri Lanka, the FARC and ELN in Colombia, the Lord's Resistance Army in Uganda, and the government forces of the Democratic Republic of Congo, and Myanmar have been "named in five consecutive reports from the secretary-general of the UN since 2002" (Human Rights Watch 2008, 1).

Although the tradition of using children in war goes back thousands of years, to the earliest Mediterranean cultures, ancient Greece and Rome, the Ottoman Empire, medieval Europe, nineteenth-century Russia, and the American colonies during the Revolution, even the ancient Romans knew that it was cruel to use children in this way. As with other human rights abuses, the use of child soldiers around the world has at least come to the attention of some caring institutions that monitor and attempt to put a stop to such practices. The Coalition to Stop the Use of Child Soldiers reports that, in addition to combat, children are employed "laying mines

Congolese child soldiers, previously captured by Uganda for "political re-education," wait to board a UNICEF bus home. February 22, 2001. AP Photo/ Muweneri John.

and explosives, scouting, spying, acting as decoys, couriers or guards; training, drilling or other preparations; logistics and support functions, portering, cooking and domestic labor, and sexual slavery" (Amnesty International 2007, 1). They also have been used as minesweepers, running or bicycling through fields (1).

TWO CHILDREN TELL THEIR STORIES

The usual pattern of recruitment is for an army or militia to attack a village, abduct the children, slaughter their parents in front of them, and put them in camps to train them. "Charles," aged twelve, told one reporter, "I was so afraid of dying. But my friends warned me if the rebel commanders detected any fear in me they would kill me. So I had to pretend to be brave" (Msoka 2007).

Descriptions of their experiences are both horrifying and sad. Two former soldiers, China Keitetsi and Ishmael Beah, have published remarkable memoirs documenting their childhoods. It is a wonder that they have survived.

ANGELA, JOINED FARC-EP IN COLOMBIA AT AGE TWELVE

"I had a friend, Juanita, who got into trouble for sleeping around. We had been friends in civilian life. The commander said that it didn't matter that she was my friend. She had committed an error and had to be killed. I closed my eyes and fired the gun, but I didn't hit her. So I shot again. The grave was right nearby. I had to bury her and put dirt on top of her. The commander said, 'You did very well. Even though you started to cry, you did well. You'll have to do this again many more times, and you'll have to learn not to cry'" (2).

Source: "Facts about Child Soldiers." Human Rights Watch. 2006. Available at http://hrw.org/english/docs/2008/02/12/global1803d.htm.

In October 2007, China Keitetsi of Uganda, a former child soldier, told her story to a group of students at a conference at the University Connecticut's West Hartford Branch. When she approached the podium, the students in the auditorium were mesmerized. No one made a sound. At twenty-nine, her slight figure and delicate, smiling face made her look almost like the porcelain doll her name suggests. She hardly seemed like someone who had spent nearly all of her childhood as a soldier in a savage war. But as China's story unfolded, the students learned about what she had seen and how she had suffered.

Former child soldier, China Keitetsi, February 9, 2006. AP Photo/Fraka Bruns.

Almost nine when she ran away from her abusive father and grand-mother, she landed right in a National Resistance Army rebel camp. General Yoweri K. Museveni's army was in the process of overthrowing President Milton Obote. Like thousands of child soldiers in Africa, China had found that the only people that were willing to feed and protect her were the com-manders that needed more soldiers (Human Rights Watch 2006, 1). From 1985 until 1997, when she was eighteen years old, China lived as a soldier in Uganda (Keitetsi 2004, 114).

Her life consisted of bloody combat in a constant stream of gruesome battles, during which her young friends were slaughtered. In her mem-oir, *Child Soldier,* she remembers a friend who was killed: "He was this little wise kid who always comfort [*sic*] us with words, telling us to be strong without worrying" (2004, 122). Later, she wrote, "I was confused and afraid, because now I had finally realized that the terror I had seen also could happen to me" (122).

Discipline in the NRA was just like one would expect in the army, but these soldiers were elementary school age. When they were hungry they were afraid to eat without permission, because "those who stole food from the civilians were tied on the trees and shot" (121). After each battle, they had to strip the bodies of dead soldiers, taking clothing and weapons. Between battles, or when they were outnumbered or unprepared to fight, they were commanded to carry weapons and supplies while running from village to village to escape the government army.

Sometimes we had to walk for a whole day without camping any place, because of gunships [military helicopters] who would pass over our head with loudspeakers telling us to give up or face what they called "wipe-out." But we could not give up because we had already crossed our hearts to finish what we had started. (121)

China's first assignment was to act as bait in an ambush. She and the other youngsters were forced to pretend to play a game in the road, as enemy soldiers approached, lulled into thinking they were safe. Then a gunfight broke out around them, and they dashed into the jungle dodging bullets (116). She was issued an AK-47, but she was too little to carry it, despite its being light enough to be standard issue for children. In the beginning, China recalls, their boots and uniforms "almost swallowed us" (118).

The NRA was filled with orphans and abandoned children (118). Human Rights Watch reports that "[c]hildren are uniquely vulnerable to military recruitment because of their emotional and physical immaturity. They are easily manipulated and can be drawn into violence that they are too young to resist or understand" (Human Rights Watch 2006, 1)

According to China, "killing and torturing was the most exciting job for many of the children" (Keitetsi 2004, 124). They wanted to "please their bosses" (124) in order to gain a promotion. For their cruel behav-ior, she blames the indoctrination and the fear instilled by the officers, former Idi Amin soldiers. "The stranger forced us to find love from the gun. We were told that the gun was our mother, our friend, and our everything . . ." (135). "But we were too young to realize that our actions against any captured enemy would haunt our dreams and thoughts forever . . . ." (124).

China recalls the sentiments of a speech by Museveni that instilled enthusiasm for the war:

> He told us that we were fighting for freedom and against [tribalism]. As most of us didn't know what happened to our parents, he told us that they were killed by government troops and those who were still alive were in jails and their hope was us [*sic*] to liberate them. (123)

The children were praised as heroes and believed the promises and the lies they were told; then they were deliberately put in harm's way as bodyguards for the officers. The girls were also forced to "serve" the men at night (155). At fourteen, China gave birth to her first child (210). Fortunately for her, she had positive feelings for his father because he "did not discard us as a freak accident" (210). This was unusual for a commanding officer. "The NRA gave us weapons, made us fight their war, made us hate, kill, torture and made us their girlfriends. We had no choice . . . Most

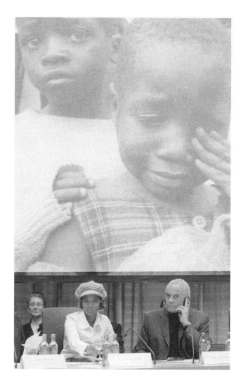

China Keitetsi, from Uganda, and United States singer and UNICEF ambassador, Harry Belafonte, chair a meeting of the UN in Berlin, December 1, 2004. AP Photo/ Jockel Finck.

of the high-ranking officers behaved like mad people" (156). China soon realized that "we kids never existed in our leaders' hearts" (125). "All they wanted was power, cars, and women" (131).

CHILD SOLDIERS SPEAK OUT

In a Human Rights Watch report on the plight of child soldiers, "The Voices of Child Soldiers," (2006, 1) children recount their experiences being recruited and serving in armies.

KHIN MAUNG THAN, RECRUITED BY BURMA'S NATIONAL ARMY AT AGE ELEVEN:

"The section leader ordered us to take cover and open fire. There were seven of us, and seven or ten of the enemy. I was too afraid to look, so I put my face in the ground and shot my gun up at the sky. I fired two magazines, about forty round. I was afraid that if I didn't fire, the section leader would punish me" (1).

UNNAMED GIRL RECRUITED BY THE TAMIL TIGERS IN SRI LANKA AT AGE SIXTEEN:

"My parents refused to give me to the LTTE so about fifteen of them came to my house—in uniforms, with rifles, and guns in holsters. . . . I was fast asleep when they came to get me at one in the morning . . . These people dragged me out of the house. My father shouted at them, saying, 'what is going on?' but some of the LLTE soldiers took my father away towards the woods and beat him" (1).

Source: "Facts about Child Soldiers." Human Rights Watch. 2006. Available at http://hrw.org/english/docs/2008/02/12/global1803d.htm.

In *A Long Way Gone: Memoirs of a Child Soldier,* Ishmael Beah describes his life as a soldier during Sierra Leone's civil war. At twelve, he learned that his parents and two brothers had been killed by the rebel army while he had been visiting his grandmother. He and some friends spent nearly a year running and hiding until they finally sought refuge in an army camp. Like China, they thought they were now safe (Beah, "The Making and Unmaking of a Child Soldier" 38).

Ishmael was terrified by what he soon witnessed. He and a friend watched soldiers burn down one village:

As we were watching a flaming tin roof in flight, we heard screams and loud banging a few houses away. We ran behind the houses at the edge of the coffee trees and came upon the house where the cries were coming from. There were people locked in it. The fire was already too much inside. It showed its face through the windows and the roof. We picked up a mortar and banged the door open, but it was too late. Only two people came out, a woman and a young child. They were on fire . . . The child's yelp was still echoing in my head, as if it had taken on a life of its own inside me. (Beah *A Long way Gone,* 94)

Later, he writes, "[m]y entire body went into shock" (95).

To assure that children like Ishmael and China continued to fight despite being terrified, commanders would give them cocaine and "white capsules" (Beah, *A Long way Gone,* 121). Ishmael describes the effect of the drugs: "The combination of these drugs gave us a lot of energy and made us fierce. The idea of death didn't cross my mind at all and killing had become as easy as drinking water. My mind only snapped during the first killing, it had also stopped making remorseful records, or so it seemed" (122).

All of these children are weakened by hunger, thirst, and extremes of heat and cold, and they were often wounded, bleeding, and in pain. Even so, notes China, "if we were 'out of order' we would be sent to the front line to die . . . many disappeared just like that" (Keitetsi 2004, 125).

When the Ugandan government was overthrown, China expected to be relieved from duty and sent home, but that never happened. Instead, she was given a new job. She escaped and went home to her mother. But "being a small girl with a vast military experience" (155), she felt she no longer belonged. Instead, she pretended to be a new recruit and joined a new regiment. She was quickly promoted. "Our instructors had been given our souls, and if we wanted them back, we would have to pay a heavy price" (155).

Eventually, pregnant with another child, China ran away. She made her way to Kampala, and after months of working and begging former friends and relatives for money for a passport (forged) and transportation, she snuck across the border into Kenya. She bought a ticket to the United States, but despite having obtained a visa to visit the United States with a Special Olympics team, it was cancelled. At this point, she was so despondent that she wanted to commit suicide (247), but when she returned to her hotel, she was discovered by friend. Together they took a series of busses from Kenya all the way to South Africa.

For four years she lived precariously in Johannesburg. Then she was kidnapped and tortured by people who were trying to take down Museveni's government and wanted her to testify. She escaped and was eventually aided by a kind official at the UN High Commissioner for Refugees (264). Now a grown young woman, Keitetsi lives in Denmark. She has been reunited with her son, whom she had been forced to leave in the care of others. Keitetsi has told her story to UN officials and government officials and continues to speak around the world. She has published two books about her life and has established a foundation to help free other child soldiers as well as a Web site: http://www.chinakeitetsi.onfo/index.

Ishmael Beah was eventually rescued by UNICEF, though at first, knowing no other life, he was suspicious and afraid to accept help from anyone. After many months of medical treatment for his multiple bullet wounds, and psychological therapy, he moved to the United States, completed high school, and graduated from Oberlin College in 2004. He, too, continues to speak out, as a member of Human Rights Watch Children's Rights Division Advisory Committee, to national and international councils and governments on the effects of war on children.

EVELYN, RECRUITED IN LIBERIA BY GOVERNMENT FORCES AT AGE FOURTEEN:

"I was captured in Lofa County by government forces. The forces beat me, they held me and kept me in the bush. I was tied with my arms kept still and was raped there. I was fourteen years old . . . .I was used in the fighting to carry medicine on my head and was not allowed to talk. I had to do a lot of work for the soldiers, sweeping, washing, cleaning. During this time . . . I was afraid. I wanted to go home, but was made to stay with the soldiers" (1).

Source: "Facts about Child Soldiers." Human Rights Watch. 2006. Available at http://hrw.org/english/docs/2008/02/12/global1803d.htm.

WHAT CAN BE DONE TO STOP THE USE OF CHILDREN AS SOLDIERS?

There are a few organizations that participate in a global campaign to end the recruitment and use of child soldiers, but as with attempts to abolish slavery, they have not proved very effective yet. Making the public aware of the existence of child soldiers and their abysmal treatment is a first step. Human Rights Watch, the Foundation for Human Rights Initiative, the UN Special Representative for Children and Armed Conflict, Amnesty International, and the Coalition to Stop the Use of Child Soldiers have Web sites on which they publish articles on current events and historical information that is easy to access. These resources are also used by the U.S. Department of State to prepare yearly Country Reports to Congress on the status of human rights, including human trafficking and the use of child soldiers in every country in the world (*Country Reports* 2007). For example, in the most recent report, Uganda was cited for human rights abuses that included the use of eleven- to sixteen-year-olds in the Lord's Resistance Army, noting specifically that children were being forced to kill other children (*Country Reports, Uganda* 2007). Positive moves by various countries are also reported, such

Lucy Aol, now a medical student at Mulago Medical College in Kampala, Uganda, was snatched by rebels of Uganda's Lord's Resistance Army, along with an estimated 25,000 children, during the course of the 20-year insurgency. May 25, 2007. AP Photo/Vanessa Vick.

as Rwanda's recent support of demobilization of children and their subsequent reintegration into society (*Country Reports, Rwanda* 2007).

One promising initiative in the effort to save these children was the February 12, 2002, passage of the Optional Protocol to the Convention of the Rights of the Child. It raises the minimum age for direct participation in war to eighteen years, up from fifteen, which is now the age for volunteering. For nonstate armed groups, recruitment is prohibited under age eighteen (Amnesty International 2007). Since enforcement of this treaty has been minimal, an addition to the treaty was proposed in 2008 and is being debated by the United Nations Security Council. This proposed addition to the protocol "would consider targeted measures, including arms embargoes, against parties to armed conflict that refused to end their use of child soldiers" (Human Rights Watch2008, 1). Unfortunately, the UN has actually only used this measure once, against one former commander from Cote d'Ivoire (1). It is hoped that this measure would improve that record.

WORKS CITED

Beah, Ishmael. "The Making and Unmaking of a Child Soldier." *New York Times Magazine.* January 14, 2007.

———. *A Long Way Gone: Memoirs of a Boy Soldier.* New York: Farrar, Straus and Giroux, 2007.

"Child Soldiers." Amnesty International. October 8, 2007. http://web.
    amnesty.org/pages/childsoldiers.
Country Reports of Human Rights Practices—Cambodia. United States Depart-
    ment of State, Bureau of Democracy, Human Rights and Labor, 2007.
    http://www.state.gov/g/drl/rls/hrrpt.
Country Reports of Human Rights Practices—Rwanda. United States Depart-
    ment of State, Bureau of Democracy, Human Rights and Labor, 2007.
    http://www.state.gov/g/drl/rls/hrrpt.
Country Reports of Human Rights Practices—Sudan. United States Depart-
    ment of State, Bureau of Democracy, Human Rights and Labor, 2007.
    http://www.state.gov/g/drl/rls/hrrpt.
 "Facts about Child Soldiers." Human Rights Watch. 2006. http://hrw.
    org/english/docs/2008/02/12/global1803d.htm.
Keitetsi, China. *Child Soldier.* London: Souvenir Press, 2004.
Msoka, Valerie. "Child Soldiers." London: BBC World Service.
"UN Security Council Should Act against Child Recruiters." Human rights
    Watch, December 2, 2008. Available at http://www.hrw.org/en/
    search/apachesolr_search/UN+Security+Council+Should+Act+
    against+Child+Recruiters.

EPILOGUE

On July 1, 1939, I became a refugee in England. Loneliness became my daily companion. Thank God for the stars and the moon and my mother's poem. I recited "her" words over and over while I looked at the night sky from my window. I loved the full moon. "He" (in German *der Mond*) became my friend. I looked forward to his presence. It was something to rely on—a connection to my family.

I continued writing, reporting important events on scraps of paper to one day tell my parents or anyone else interested. These events became the seeds of my memoir, which I spent many years writing and rewriting. I became a teacher, and my students helped in my search for answers. I was no longer alone. Together we found that expressions of human kindness made those terrible answers bearable, and survival possible even amongst the horrors of Auschwitz. We read Primo Levi's book *Survival in Auschwitz*, in which he wrote how Lorenzo, a gentile and civilian worker, brought him a piece of bread and some of his own rations every day. How he gave Primo his patched coat and sent a postcard to Primo's family and even brought him a response—something unexpected and infinitely precious. This is how Primo described his feelings:

I believe that it was really due to Lorenzo that I am alive today; and not so much for his material aid as for his having constantly reminded me by his presence, by his natural and plain manner of being good, that there still existed a just world outside our own, something and someone still pure and whole . . . for which it was worth surviving. . . . His humanity was pure . . . he was outside this world of negation. Thanks to Lorenzo, I managed not to forget that I myself was a man. (Levi 1971, 111)

Ursula Hegi, the award-winning and bestselling German-born author of *Stones from the River,* explores the legacy of shame and grief that shadows German-born Americans who were small children during or just after World War II in her book, *Tearing the Silence.* She writes, "What we must do is try to understand how it began, why it happened and mourn every single person who was murdered" (15–16). "Every single person" includes my mother, my father, and my brother. Remembering is part of healing. In Hebrew it is called *Tikkun Olam.*

Eve Nussbaum Soumerai

WORKS CITED

Hegi, Ursula. *Tearing the Silence: Being German in America.* New York: Simon and Schuster, 1997.

Levi, Primo. *Survival in Auschwitz: The Nazi Assault on Humanity.* Translated by Stuart Woolf. New York: Collier-Macmillan, 1971.

APPENDIX: SEARCHING FOR ANSWERS THROUGH TRIBUTE CELEBRATIONS

The twentieth century, which brought with it tremendous progress in industrial, electronic, and scientific technology, was also an age of war, genocide, torture, and slavery, all of which have continued into our new century. The result has been the suffering and death of millions of innocent people. In order to strive to create a world in which crimes against humanity cease to exist, we must give people, especially children, role models to emulate. Gandhi, who brought down the British Empire with his nonviolent protest, concluded that in order to end violence we must start with children.

Since the 1970s, Eve Nussbaum Soumerai created a series of tribute celebrations using original sources with the help of her students. They conducted research, discussed ideas, and wrote the scripts, which included music, art, and poetry. Together, she and her students and community volunteers then produced these theatrical celebrations for public and private audiences.

These tributes are not difficult to create. They don't require that students memorize parts or build elaborate sets, but, instead, focus on sharing with participants of many ages, abilities, and ethnic backgrounds a readers' theater experience. In the process of working toward a common goal, they gain respect, and a sense of responsibility, for one another, and a strong sense of self-worth. By studying the accomplishments of historical figures such as Thurgood Marshall, Anne Frank, and Nelson Mandela, students also develop a moral compass. Martin Luther King Jr. called such a process Creating the "Beloved Community" (Smith and Zepp 1997).

THE ORIGIN OF TRIBUTES

A "beloved community" was what Eve Nussbaum Soumerai longed for when as a 15-year-old, lonely, frightened refugee from Nazi Germany she became a helper in a London County Council residential nursery school for children affected by World War II. She was given charge of five children, three- to five-year-olds. Having never faced such a task, she improvised, reading to them, playing with them, singing and dancing, as her parents had done with her. When she read Hans Christian Anderson's "Ugly Duckling," which had a special meaning to her since her father had read it to her, she had her tiny class sing, waddle around the room, clap their hands, and draw pictures. She found that they loved being with her, and that celebrating the life and works of others lifted their spirits and inspired hope.

In 1972, as a teacher at Conard High School in West Hartford, Connecticut, Soumerai decided to work with older students in the same way she had with nursery school children. She called her lessons "Tribute Celebrations." Her first subject was Albert Camus, a man none of her students had heard of. The cooperation of the characters in Camus's *The Plague* inspired the original idea to have students of all abilities, along with their teachers, work together to write and perform tribute celebrations. Using special adaptations, such as slide shows, enables her to present tributes at the American School for the Deaf, the Cerebral Palsy Center, and in dozens of other venues. The first tribute to Albert Camus involved 187 students. The 1974 tribute to Mark Twain involved 250 students.

Later, as an instructor at St. Joseph's College in West Harford, Soumerai and her college students wrote scripts for inner-city students, resulting in many interdistrict celebrations.

A Web site (http://www.tribute-story.com) describes the tributes and offers sample scripts that can be used by anyone free of charge. The tribute to Franklin Delano Roosevelt, entitled "A Tribute to Franklin Delano Roosevelt: Challenge and Response," includes passages such as the one below from his speeches:

A nation must believe in three things.
It must believe in the past.
It must believe in the future.
It must, above all, believe in the capacity of its own people so to
Learn from the past that they gain
In judgment in creating their own future.

—Franklin Delano Roosevelt

The script also includes narrations that put these quotes into a meaningful context:

Both FDR and Adolf Hitler came to power in 1933 in the midst of a great depression, and both died in April of 1945. Hitler was determined to create a master race that would rule the world for a thousand years. FDR fought much opposition to help those in need. He brought about the New Deal from which we still benefit. Hitler carefully planned to humiliate, torture, and murder every Jew on earth. Fifty million died as a result of the war Hitler initiated, including millions of Germans.

EXCERPT FROM "A TRIBUTE TO A GATHERING OF PEACE PIONEERS"

Another script includes lines from the writings of historical figures who have contributed to the establishment of peace and freedom during their lifetimes.

Gandhi: All of us, Badshah, the Muslim; I, the Hindu; Martin, the Baptist minister; Isaiah, the Hebrew prophet; John, the believer in peace and love; Anne Frank, the diary writer; Dona Felisa, the first woman mayor of San Juan, Puerto Rico; Winston Churchill, the British prime minister; Harriet Tubman, the slave rescuer; and all the children of the world, especially those who have suffered and are suffering,
We are all brothers and sisters, Hallelujah!

Additional scripts pay tribute to men and women whose courageous acts have inspired others.

WORK CITED

Smith Kenneth and Ira G. Zepp, Jr. "Martin Luther King's 'Beloved Community.'" *Christian Century*, April 3, 1974.

GLOSSARY

Aktion (Action)—Rounding up of Jews for deportation to death camps or labor camps.

Allies—Twenty-six nations, led by Britain, the United States, and the Soviet Union, who fought against Germany, Italy, Japan, and their allies, known as the Axis powers.

Anschluss—GERMAN takeover of Austria in March 1938, incorporating 200,000 more Jews into the Nazi net.

Appel—Roll call in the camps.

Aryan—Term used by Nazis to describe those whom they believed to be superior: white, Nordic supermen and women.

Auschwitz II-Birkenau—AUSCHWITZ, a city in southwestern Poland, became the site of the largest, most famous death complex. Birkenau, the site of the four gas chambers, became its extermination center.

Axis—Political, military, and ideological alliance of Nazi Germany and Fascist Italy, later joined by Japan.

Beizec—One of six extermination camps in Poland; the others were Auschwitz, Treblinka, Sobibor, Majdanek, and Chelmno.

Chelmno—Established in December 1941, Chelmno was the first killing center in Western Poland; here Jews were gassed in specially equipped vans and buried in mass graves.

Concentration camps—There were three types of camps: (1) concentration camps, created to destroy large numbers of enemies of the state, especially Jews, but also Jehovah's Witnesses, Communists, Unionists, and others; (2) labor camps where inmates, non-Germans living in occupied countries, worked as slave laborers for the Third Reich and most died of abuse, starvation, and disease; and 3) death camps or killing centers, where victims were sent to die immediately, if possible, otherwise, soon after arrival. Although not all of those who died in the camps were Jews, the National Socialists' plan was to exterminate all Jews.

Crematoria—Ovens in which the bodies of the gassed victims were turned to ashes.

Dachau—First concentration camp, it was opened by the Nazis in 1933 near Munich, Germany. Originally intended for political opponents of the Third Reich.

Deportation—Forced removal of Jews from their homes for "resettlement" in ghettos or death camps.

Eichmann, Adolf (1906–1962)—Lieutenant-colonel in charge of the Jewish Section of the Gestapo; organized and supervised the transports of Jews from all over Europe to the killing centers.

Einsatzgruppen—SS mobile killing units that accompanied the German army as it moved through Poland and the Soviet Union; their task was to seek out and murder Jews in eastern Poland and the Soviet Union.

Euthanasia (mercy killing)—The Nazi government used this term to describe their policy of ridding the German *Volk* (people) of the mentally retarded, those who were handicapped, and others they deemed useless.

Final Solution—Term used for the deliberate annihilation of the Jewish people.

Frank, Anne (1929–1945)—German Jewish girl who hid with her family and others in an attic in Amsterdam during the German occupation of Holland. She and the others were arrested by the Gestapo on August 4, 1944, and held at the Westerbork transit camp until September 3, 1945, when they were deported to Auschwitz. She and her sister, Margot, died of typhus at Bergen-Belsen in March 1945.

Freikorps—Groups of violent, armed street fighters in the 1920s who defended right-wing political ideas and parties. The Nazi SA (*Sturmabteilung*—also known as "Brownshirts") originated in one of those groups.

Fuehrer—German word for "leader."

Geheime Staatspolizei (Gestapo)—Secret state police established in 1933 by Hermann Goering under the auspices of Adolf Hitler. It became the Nazi's main tool for oppression and destruction of the Reich's enemies, who included Communists, Jews, liberals, and others perceived as political opponents. The Gestapo ruled outside of the law, enforcing conformity and total obedience at every level of society.

Genocide—Killing of an entire race, ethnic group, or nationality.

Ghetto—During the Middle Ages, *ghetto* referred to the section of a European city to which the Jews were restricted at night, although they were allowed to come and go during the daytime. The term was used during the Holocaust to describe that part of the city in which all the Jews were forced to live in wretched conditions, until they died or were deported to the camps.

Goebbels, Paul Joseph (1897–1945)—Nazi propaganda minister. His speech, delivered on November 9, 1939, incited the *Kristallnacht* attack on the Jews. The most loyal of Hitler's associates, he killed himself and his family in the last days of the war when hiding out along with Hitler and Eva Braun in the bunker below the chancellery.

Goethe, Johann Wolfgang von (1749–1832)—Most famous eighteenth-century German poet and philosopher who wrote about tolerance, reason, and human values. The Buchenwald concentration camp, located near Weimar, the German cultural capital, was built around the "Goethe Oak," the tree under which the poet reflected and wrote poetry.

Goering, Hermann (1893–1946)—Second in command of the Third Reich. He was head of the German economy; also in charge of the air force and the *Blitzkrieg* (lightning air war), he gave the order to Reinhard Heydrich to begin the Final Solution. He was sentenced to die during the Nuremberg trials but escaped that fate by committing suicide.

Gypsies (Rom)—Considered "unworthy" people, and criminals, by the Nazis. Approximately 250,000 Gypsies were murdered, most of them in Auschwitz. The Gypsies were also the victims of horrible medical experiments.

Heydrich, Reinhard (1904–1942)—Rabid anti-Semite. He served under Heinrich Himmler as implementer of the Final Solution. He was shot by Czech resistance fighters in 1942. To honor him, the Nazis gave the codename Operation Reinhard to the murdering of the Jews at the Belzec, Sobibor, and Treblinka death camps.

Himmler, Heinrich (1900–1945)—Reichsführer-SS and chief of the German police. The former chicken farmer rose to become the leader of the SS. He coordinated every aspect of its operations and was the absolute authority on the concentration and labor camps. At the end of the war, Himmler committed suicide.

Hitler, Adolf (1889–1945)—Founder and leader of the Nazi Party, chancellor of the Third Reich from 1933 to 1945, and head of state and supreme commander of the German armed forces. He was born in Braunau-am-Inn, Austria, on April 30, 1889, the son of a fifty-two-year-old customs official named Alois Schickelgruber and his third wife, Klara Poelzl, a young peasant girl. In 1907 Hitler was rejected by the Viennese Academy of Fine Arts and had plenty of time to brood and develop his racial theories, which he later extolled in great length in his book *Mein Kampf,* written in prison while serving time for trying to overthrow the state government of Bavaria in November 1923.

Holocaust—Greek word meaning "total burning." It refers to the murder of approximately 6 million Jews between 1933 and 1945.

I. G. Farben—Germany's largest chemical conglomerate, this company used slave labor in, among other places, Auschwitz III-Buna (also called Monowitz) to build the largest synthetic rubber factory in the world. They also financed the medical experiments conducted in the camps.

Jehovah's Witnesses—Religious sect, known as *Bibelforscher,* who numbered about 20,000 in Germany in 1933. Their beliefs did not permit them to salute the flag or swear allegiance to the fuehrer. About half of them were imprisoned in the camps, and some 2,500 died there.

Kapo (*Kameraden Polizei*)—Prisoners in charge of inmates in the camps.

Karski, Jan (1914–)—Liaison officer between the Polish government in exile and the underground in Poland. He brought information about the fate of the Jews to the highest ranks of the Allied governments.

Kristallnacht (Crystal Night, or "Night of the Broken Glass")—On November 9/10, 1938, synagogues were torched, Jewish businesses trashed, and thousands arrested in a Nazi program in various German cities.

Mauthausen—Concentration camp, located near Linz in Austria, which opened in 1938. It was considered one of the harshest. Many prisoners there were killed by being pushed from 300-foot cliffs into stone quarries.

Mein Kampf (*My Struggle*)—Book written by Hitler while he was a prisoner in Landsberg prison, in which he delineated his goals, including his belief in the need for *Lebensraum* (living space), which referred to his desire to expand Germany into Central and Eastern Europe. *Mein Kampf* became the Nazi bible, and by 1939 there were 5 million copies in circulation, and the text had been translated into 11 languages.

Mengele, Joseph (1911–1979)—senior SS physician during 1943 and 1944 at Auschwitz-Birkenau, where he carried out *selections* of prisoners upon their arrival in the camp and performed inhumane medical experiments on camp inmates.

National Socialist German Workers' Party (NSDAP or Nazi)—On September 16, 1919, Hitler joined the German Workers' Party, a small right-wing party with only forty members. He soon changed the name to the NSDAP and became its chairman in July 1921. By November 1921, the party membership had increased to 3,000 and was formulating the SA (Storm troopers), headed by Captain Ernst Roehm. Their philosophy included the concept of Aryan supremacy and the total exclusion of the Jews from the community of the German *Volk* (people).

Nuremberg Laws—In 1935, anti-Semitism officially became incorporated into the German legal code. The new set of laws defined Jews, excluded them from society, and stripped them of legal, political, and civil rights.

Nuremberg Trials—Trials conducted after World War II by an International Military Tribunal established by the Allies.

Partisans—Resistance fighters who operated secretly, often hiding in the forests, and used guerrilla tactics.

Propaganda—Information used to advance a particular cause.

Reich (see Third Reich)

Reichstag—German parliament. The building housing this body was constructed in 1894 while Germany was still a monarchy. It was from a second-floor window of the Reichstag that the German republic was proclaimed in 1918. In 1933 the building was gutted by a mysterious fire, which enabled Hitler to impose emergency legislation and put an end to Germany's fledging democracy.

Right wing—Term derived from the French parliament during the French Revolution, which refers to conservative politicians and their supporters. Right-wing extremists, such as the Nazis, are usually rabidly nationalistic, sometimes anti-Semitic or racist, and generally wish to return conditions to those of an imagined time in history when, they believe, their nation was supreme. (Left-wingers are more liberal, believe that the present is preferable to the past, and view change as progress. In Germany, the liberals supported the newly created democracy. The extreme left-wingers were the Communists, who advocated not only sharing the governing, but also sharing the wealth.)

SA (see *Sturmabteilung*).

Schutzstaffel (SS, or protection squads)—elite members of the Nazi Party. Led by Heinrich Himmler, they were models of efficiency. They ran the Gestapo and controlled all operations of the Final Solution. By 1940 their membership had risen to 4 million and included the Waffen SS, a part of the armed forces. The SS, chosen from volunteers, received special instruction in the art of hating the so-called enemies of the Reich.

SS (see *Schutzstaffel*).

Selections—Process of selecting who would die immediately and who would work for a limited period before being killed, from among Jewish deportees arriving at Nazi camps.

Sturmabteilung (SA or storm troopers)—Also called "Brownshirts," these street fighters originally organized to protect the early Nazi meetings and to terror-ize those who opposed them. The SA was a home for the malcontent and the angry. Their membership, small at first, had grown to almost 400,000 by 1930. They were known for their rowdiness. When they became an embarrassment to Hitler, he had their leadership murdered in June 1934.

Sudetenland—To appease Hitler, this section of Czechoslovakia was given to Ger-many in 1938 in a negotiated agreement among Germany, England, and France. The Czech government was not consulted. Within months, without any warn-ing, Hitler moved his forces into the rest of Czechoslovakia.

Swastika—Ancient symbol originating in South Asia and frequently used by members of Eastern religions as a symbol of life. The Nazi version became a symbol of death.

Third Reich—Nazi designation of Germany and the Nazi regime during the period of 1933–1945. The First Reich was the Medieval Holy Roman Empire of the German People, which lasted until 1806; the Second Reich was the German Empire, which extended from 1871 to 1918. The Third Reich was supposed to last a thousand years.

Wehrmacht—Regular German army.

Weimar Republic (1918–1933)—In 1918, the Imperial Germany collapsed and was replaced by this democratic regime.

Yom Kippur—Day of Atonement, the holiest day of the year for Jews.

Zionism—Movement to establish the land of Israel as an autonomous Jewish national home or state.

Zyklon B—Substance used in the gas chambers of Auschwitz and Majdanek death camps. Other death camps used carbon monoxide. Zyklon B was manufactured by a company called DEGESC, owned partly by I. G. Farben.

SELECTED BIBLIOGRAPHY AND RESOURCE CENTER

Suggested Web sites, organizations, videos, and books that provide information on the Holocaust, recent incidents of genocide, modern-day slavery, child soldiers, and related human rights topics

BOOKS

Bales, Kevin. *Disposable People: New Slavery in the Global Economy*. Berkeley: University of California, 2004.

Benanav, Michael. *Joshua and Isadora: A True Tale of Loss and Love in the Holocaust*. Guilford, CT: Lyons Press, 2008.

Borowski, Tadeusz. *This Way for the Gas, Ladies and Gentlemen*. New York: Viking Penguin, 1992.

Friedlander, Saul. *The Years of Extermination: Nazi German and the Jews 1939–1945*. New York: HarperCollins, 2007.

Guttenplan, D. D. *Holocaust on Trial*. New York: W.W. Norton, 2001.

Hallie, Philip P. *Lest Innocent Blood Be Shed: The Story of the Village of Le Chambon and How Goodness Happened There*. New York: HarperCollins, 1994.

Holliday, Kayrek. *Children in the Holocaust and World War II: The Secret Diaries*. New York: Pocket Books, 1995.

Keneally, Thomas. *Schindler's List*. New York: Simon and Schuster, 1993.

Klein, Gerda Weissmann. *A Memoir: All but My Life*. New York: Hill and Want, 1995.

Levi, Primo. *Survival in Auschwitz*. New York: Collier, 1971.

McCormick, Patricia. *Sold*. New York: Hyperion Books for Children, 2006.

Mendelsohn, Daniel. *The Lost: A Search for Six of Six Million*. New York: HarperCollins, 2007.

Morris, Douglas G. *Justice Imperiled: The Anti-Nazi Lawyer Max Hirschberg in Wiemar Germany.* Ann Arbor: University of Michigan Press, 2005.
Nemirovsky, Irene. *Suite Francoise.* New York: Knopf Publishing Group, 2007.
Spiegelman, Art. *Maus: A Survivor's Tale I.* New York: Pantheon, 1986.
———. *Maus II.* New York: Pantheon, 1991.
Vinke, Hermann. *The Short Life of Sophie Scholl.* New York: Harper and Row, 1984.
Volarkova, Hana. *I Never Saw Another Butterfly.* New York: Schocken Books, 1994.
Wiesel, Eli. *Dawn.* New York: Avon, 1960
———. *Night.* New York: Bantam, 1982.

ORGANIZATIONS THAT PROVIDE INFORMATION ON THE HOLOCAUST AND HUMAN RIGHTS CONCERNS

The American Anti-slavery Group (http://www.iabolish.org): works with former victims to abolish human trafficking.

Amnesty International (http://www.amnesty.org): campaigns and reports on human rights abuses worldwide.

Association of Holocaust Organizations (http://www.ahoinfo.org): lists by state organizations (museums, institutes, and learning centers) and includes Web addresses.

British Red Cross (http://www.redcross.org/uk): provides briefings and lesson plans for teachers.

Equality and Human Rights Commission (http://www.equalityandhumanrights.com).

Freedom House (www.freedomhouse.org): a nongovernmental, nonpartisan organization, founded in 1941, that advances political and economic freedom worldwide.

Human Rights Watch (http://www.hrw.org): provides the best human rights reports in the field for researchers, and information about careers.

The International Anti-Slavery Society (London) (http://www.anti-slavery.org): provides educational resources, greeting cards, and historical information; its roots go back to 1787.

SOS Children's Villages (http://www.soschildrensvllages.org): provides information on the status of children worldwide.

The United States Holocaust Memorial Museum Genocide Prevention Mapping Initiative (http://www.ushmm.org/worldiswitness): works with Google Earth to document and map regions in which genocide is happening.

ADDITIONAL INFORMATIVE WEB SITES

There are more than 4,500 Web sites relating to human rights issues. These are a few that we believe provide worthwhile information and connections to others interested in human rights issues.

www.children.foreignpolicyblog.com, run by the Foreign Policy Association.
www.chinakeitetsi.info/index, China Keitetsi's interactive site connects to people advocating for child soldiers run by the Equality and Human Rights Commission.

www.enoughproject.org, ENOUGH is a project to abolish genocide and other crimes against humanity.

www.freetheslaves.net, works to eliminate slavery around the world.

www.globalyouthconnect.org, supports a community of youths who promote and protect human rights.

www.hrweb.org, answers questions about human rights and provides historical information, documents, ways to promote human rights, and lists of human rights organizations.

www.idealist.org, provides a human rights directory of resources.

www.irinnews.org, Integrated Regional Information Network (iRIN) is the United Nations Office for the Coordination of Humanitarian Affairs. It provides weekly and in-depth reports.

www.studentsworldassembly.org, nongovernmental and nonpartisan; represents students globally; offers online discussion.

www.tfht.org, Web site of the Taskforce on Human Trafficking.

www.tribute-thestory.com, provides scripts of tributes to inspirational people.

www.youthforhumanrights.org, independent, nongovernmental, international corporation based in Los Angeles; works to promote understanding of the UN Declaration of Human Rights.

HOLOCAUST FILMS

Anne Frank—The Whole Story. American Broadcasting Company, 2005.

Au Revoir Les Enfants. Nouvelles Editions de Films/Orion Classics, 1987.

Avenue of the Just. Anti-Defamation League, 1983.

Escape from Sobibor. Blum Group Productions, 1987.

Judgement at Nuremberg. United Artists, 1961.

My Knees Were Jumping. National Center for Jewish Film, 1996.

Night and Fog. Argos Films, 1946.

The Pianist. Universal Studios Home Video, 2003.

Schindler's List. Amblin Entertainment, 1993.

Testimony of the Human Spirit: Six Survivors of the Holocaust Tell Their Stories. Westchester Holocaust Education Center, 2004.

The Wave. Virginia Carter, 1982.

Weapons of the Spirit. National Center for Jewish Film (Distributor), 1986.

The White Rose. TeleCulture Films, 1983.

FILMS AND VIDEOS RELATING TO GENOCIDE, CHILD SOLDIERS, AND OTHER HUMAN RIGHTS ISSUES

Blood Diamond. Lyons Press, 2003.

The Constant Gardener. Universal Studios Home Entertainment, 2005.

Darfur Diaries: Message from Home. Cinema Libre Studio, 2006.

The Devil Came on Horseback: Bearing Witness to the Genocide. International Film Circuit, 2007.

Holly (Cambodia). Priority Films, 2007.

Hotel Rwanda. United Artists, 2004.

Lilya 4-ever (Sweden). Newmarket Films, 2003.
Out of the Ashes. Showtime Networks, 2003.
POV: Lost Boys of Sudan. Shadow Distributors, 2003.
Price of Sugar (Haiti). Mitropoulos Films, 2007.
Sand and Sorrow. HBO, 2007.

INDEX

About the Authors

EVE NUSSBAUM SOUMERAI is an author, lecturer, teacher, and Holocaust survivor. She is the author of many publications, including *Human Rights: The Struggle for Freedom, Dignity and Equality* (1998), which she coauthored with Carol Schulz.

CAROL D. SCHULZ has been a teacher of history and English for thirty-four years. She is also the editor of Greenwood Press's Voices of Twentieth-Century Conflict series. She currently chairs the English department and teaches high school English in a school district in Connecticut.